THEY CALLED US ENEMY

THEY CALLED US ENEMY © 2019 GEORGE TAKEI.

ISBN: 978-1-60309-450-4   26 25 24 23   14 13 12 11

Published by Top Shelf Productions, an imprint of IDW Publishing, a division of Idea and Design Works, LLC. Offices: Top Shelf Productions, c/o Idea & Design Works, LLC, 2355 Northside Drive, Suite 140, San Diego, CA 92108. Top Shelf Productions*, the Top Shelf logo, Idea and Design Works*, and the IDW logo are registered trademarks of Idea and Design Works, LLC. All Rights Reserved. With the exception of small excerpts of artwork used for review purposes, none of the contents of this publication may be reprinted without the permission of IDW Publishing. IDW Publishing does not read or accept unsolicited submissions of ideas, stories or artwork.

Printed in Canada.

Editor-in-Chief: Chris Staros.
Edited by Leigh Walton.
Designed and lettered by Gilberto Lazcano.

Visit our online catalog at topshelfcomix.com.

THEY CALLED US ENEMY

WRITTEN BY

GEORGE TAKEI
JUSTIN EISINGER
STEVEN SCOTT

ART BY

HARMONY BECKER

Top Shelf PRODUCTIONS

In memory of Daddy and Mama,
for their undying love and life guidance.

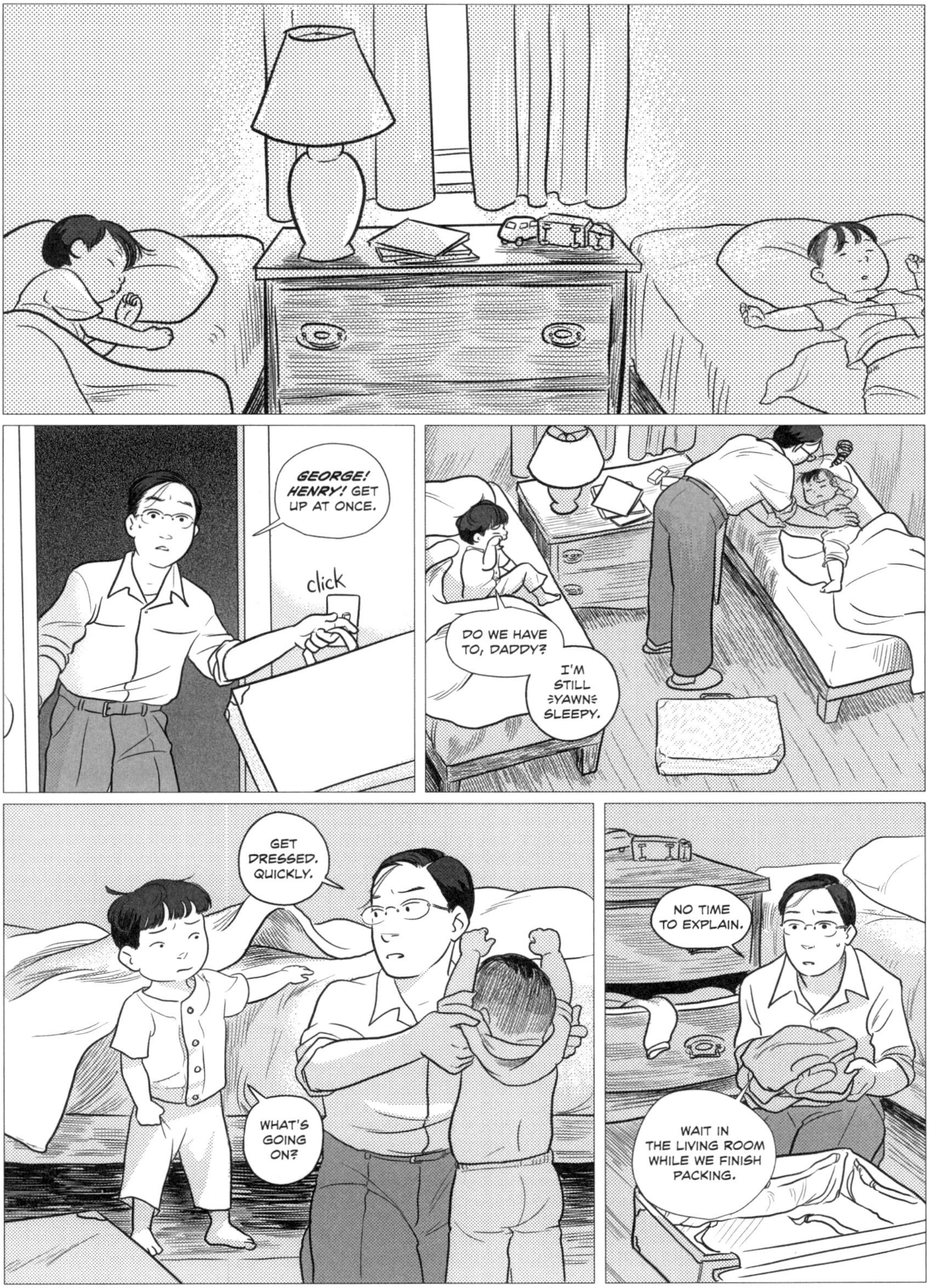
GEORGE! HENRY! GET UP AT ONCE.
click
DO WE HAVE TO, DADDY?
I'M STILL =YAWN= SLEEPY.
GET DRESSED. QUICKLY.
WHAT'S GOING ON?
NO TIME TO EXPLAIN.
WAIT IN THE LIVING ROOM WHILE WE FINISH PACKING.

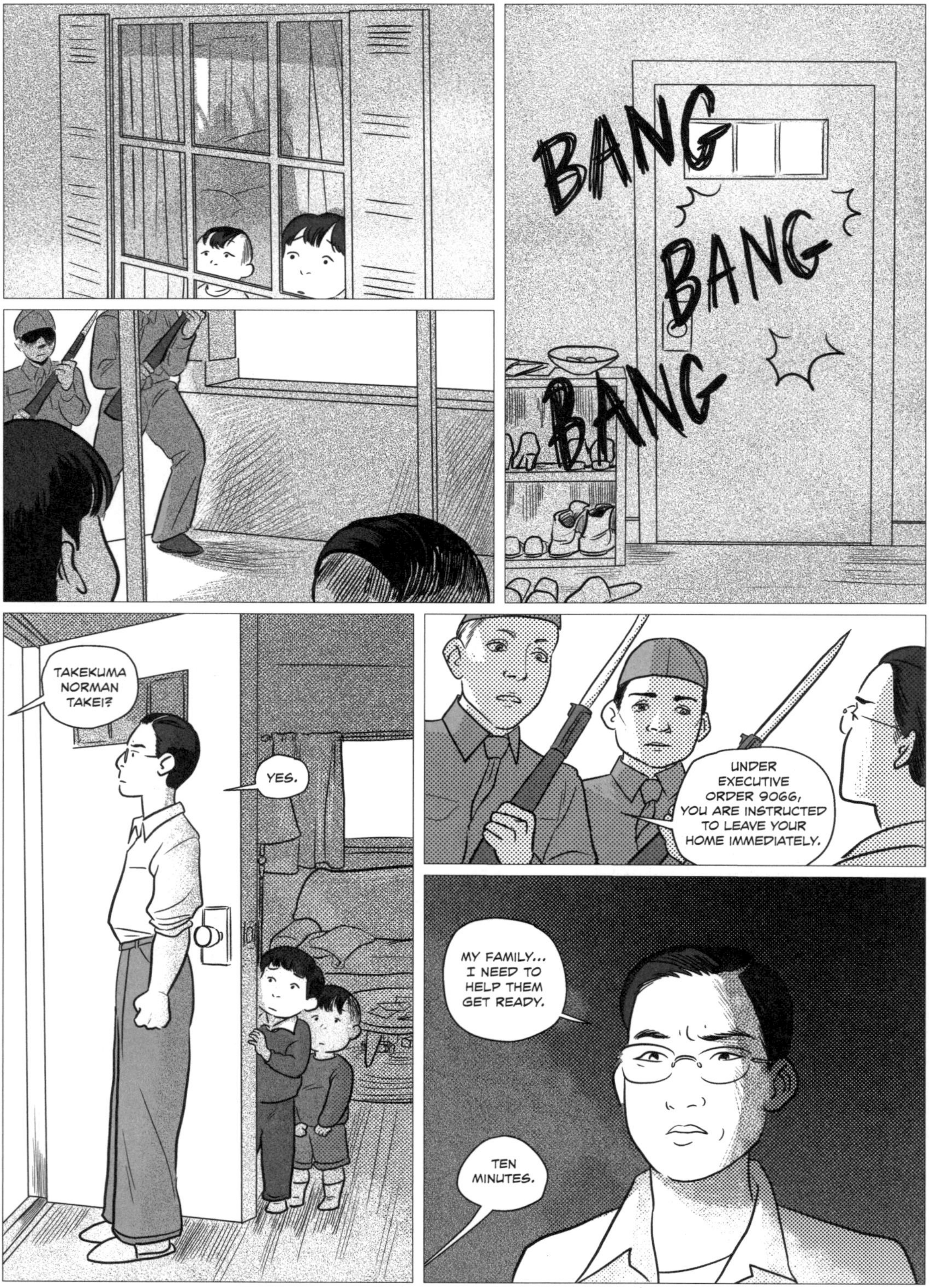
BANG
BANG
BANG
TAKEKUMA NORMAN TAKEI?
YES.
UNDER EXECUTIVE ORDER 9066, YOU ARE INSTRUCTED TO LEAVE YOUR HOME IMMEDIATELY.
MY FAMILY... I NEED TO HELP THEM GET READY.
TEN MINUTES.

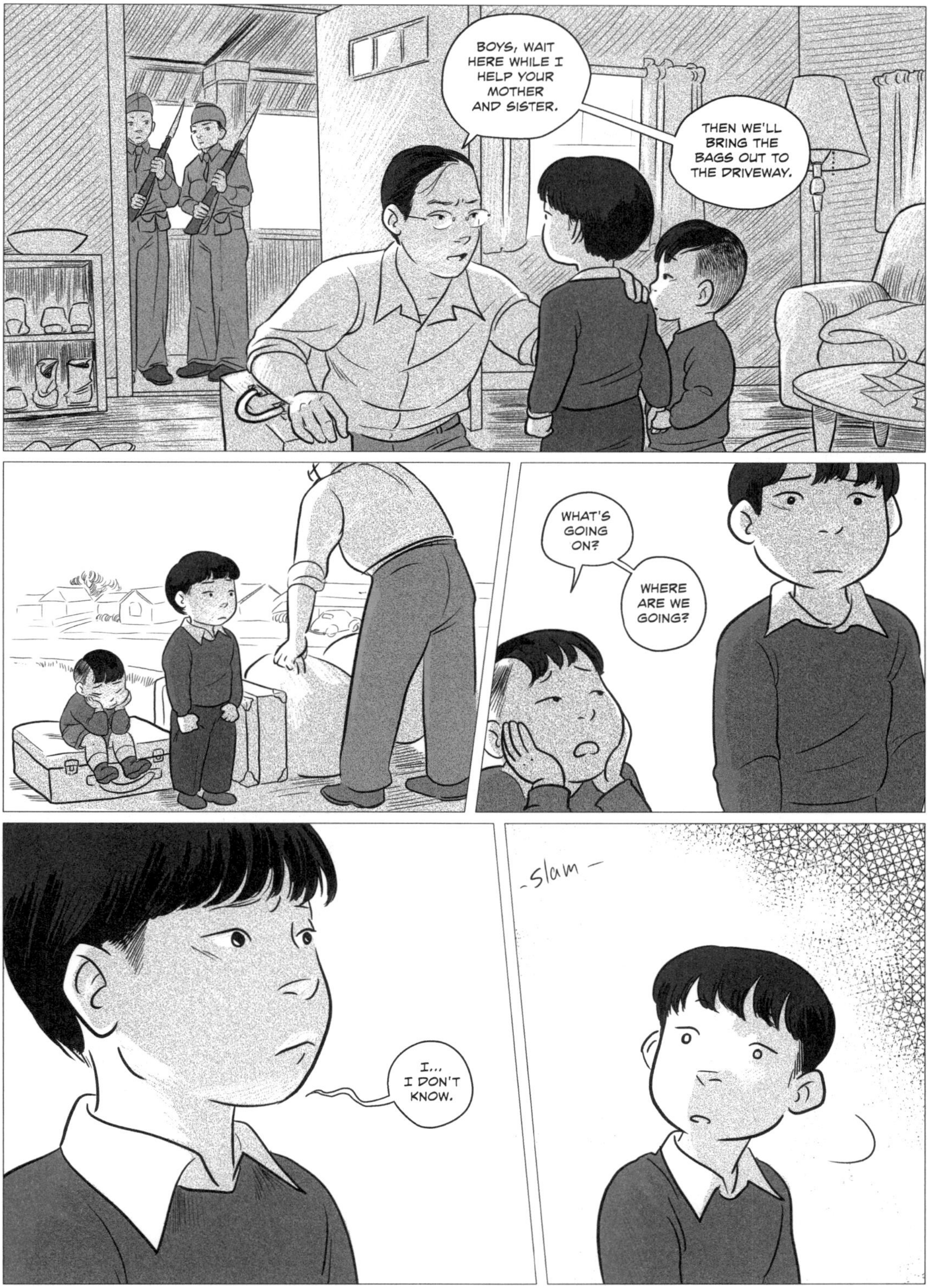
BOYS, WAIT HERE WHILE I HELP YOUR MOTHER AND SISTER.
THEN WE'LL BRING THE BAGS OUT TO THE DRIVEWAY.
WHAT'S GOING ON?
WHERE ARE WE GOING?
I... I DON'T KNOW.
-slam-

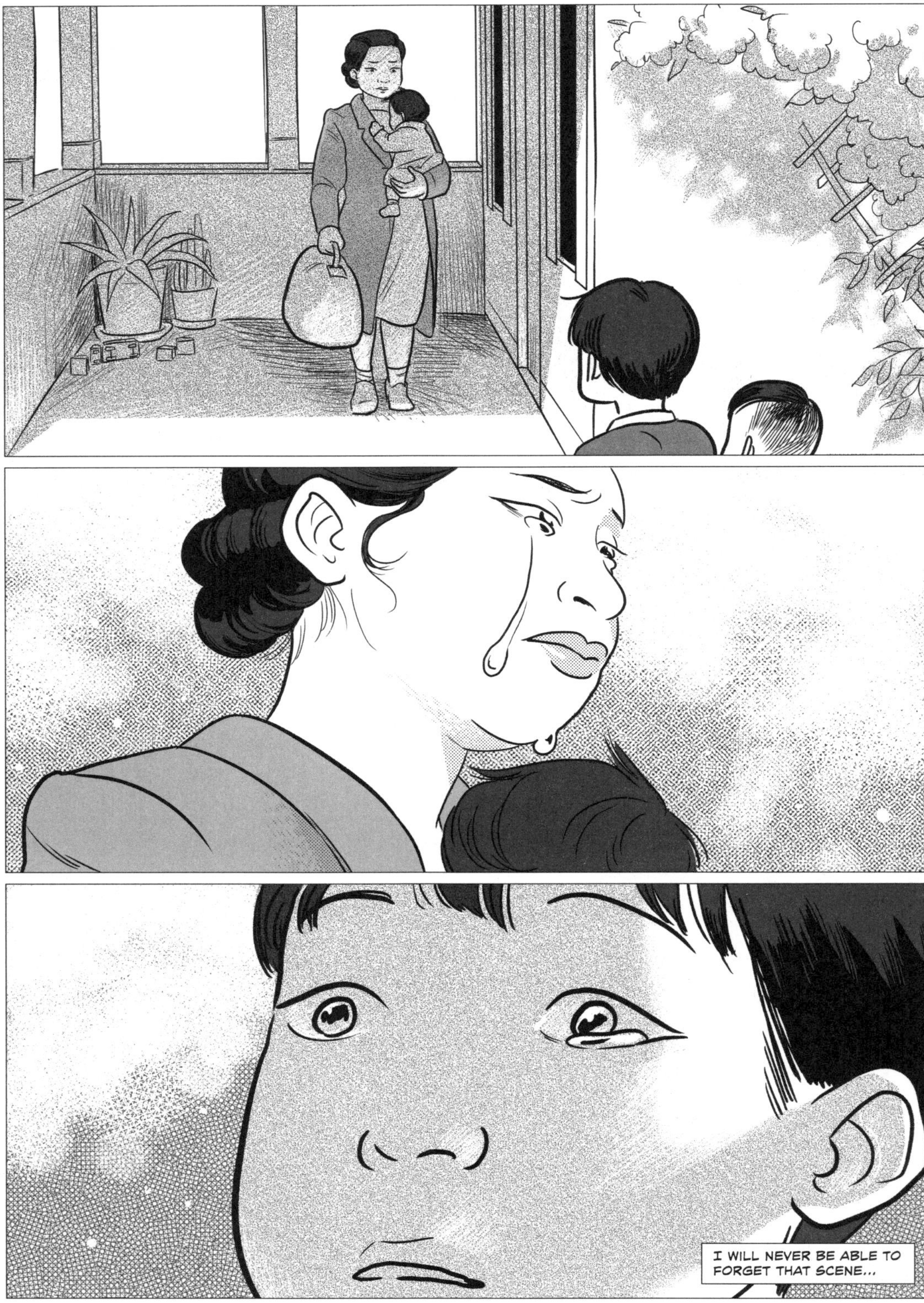
I WILL NEVER BE ABLE TO
FORGET THAT SCENE...

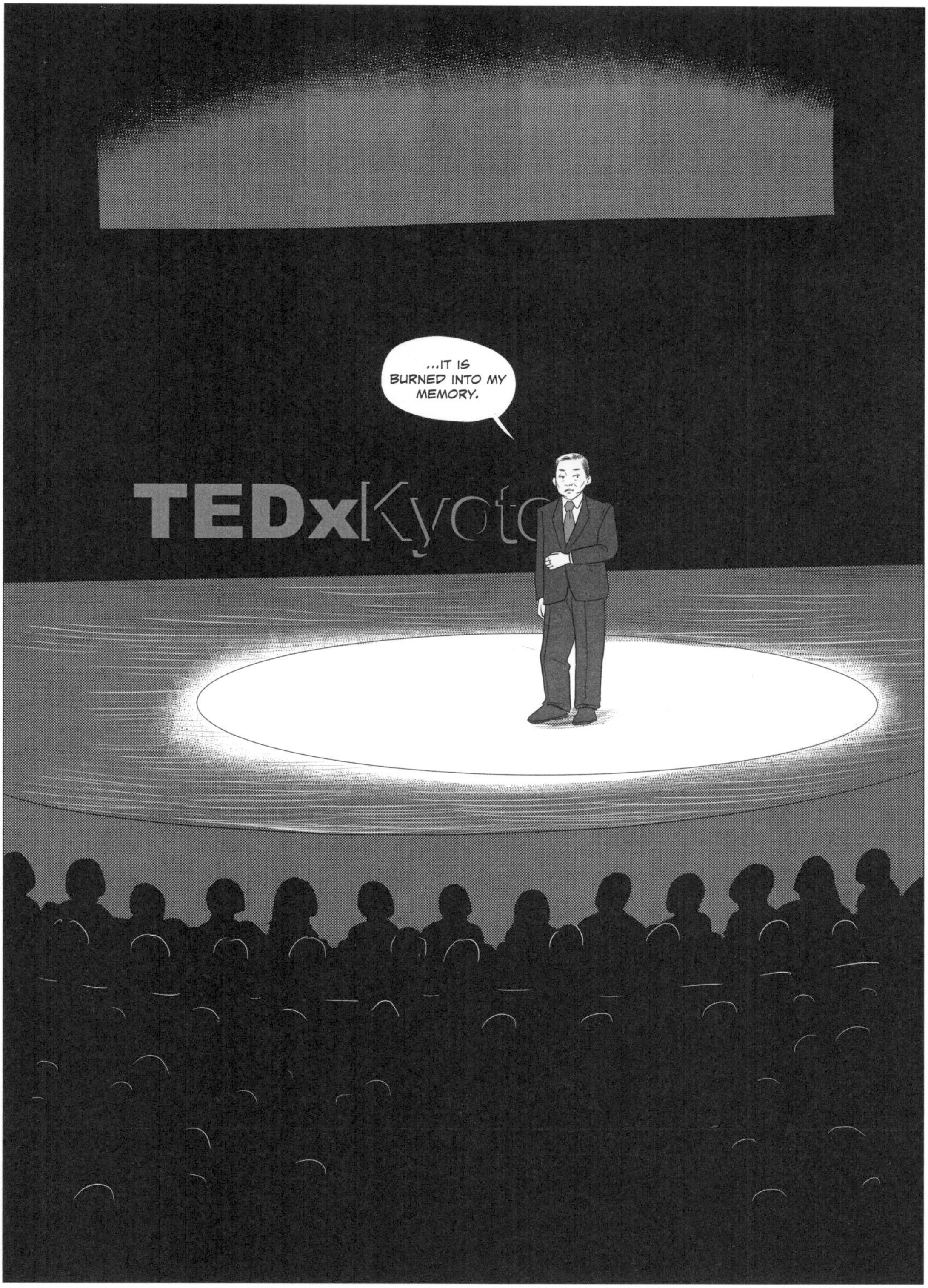
...IT IS BURNED INTO MY MEMORY.
TEDxKyoto

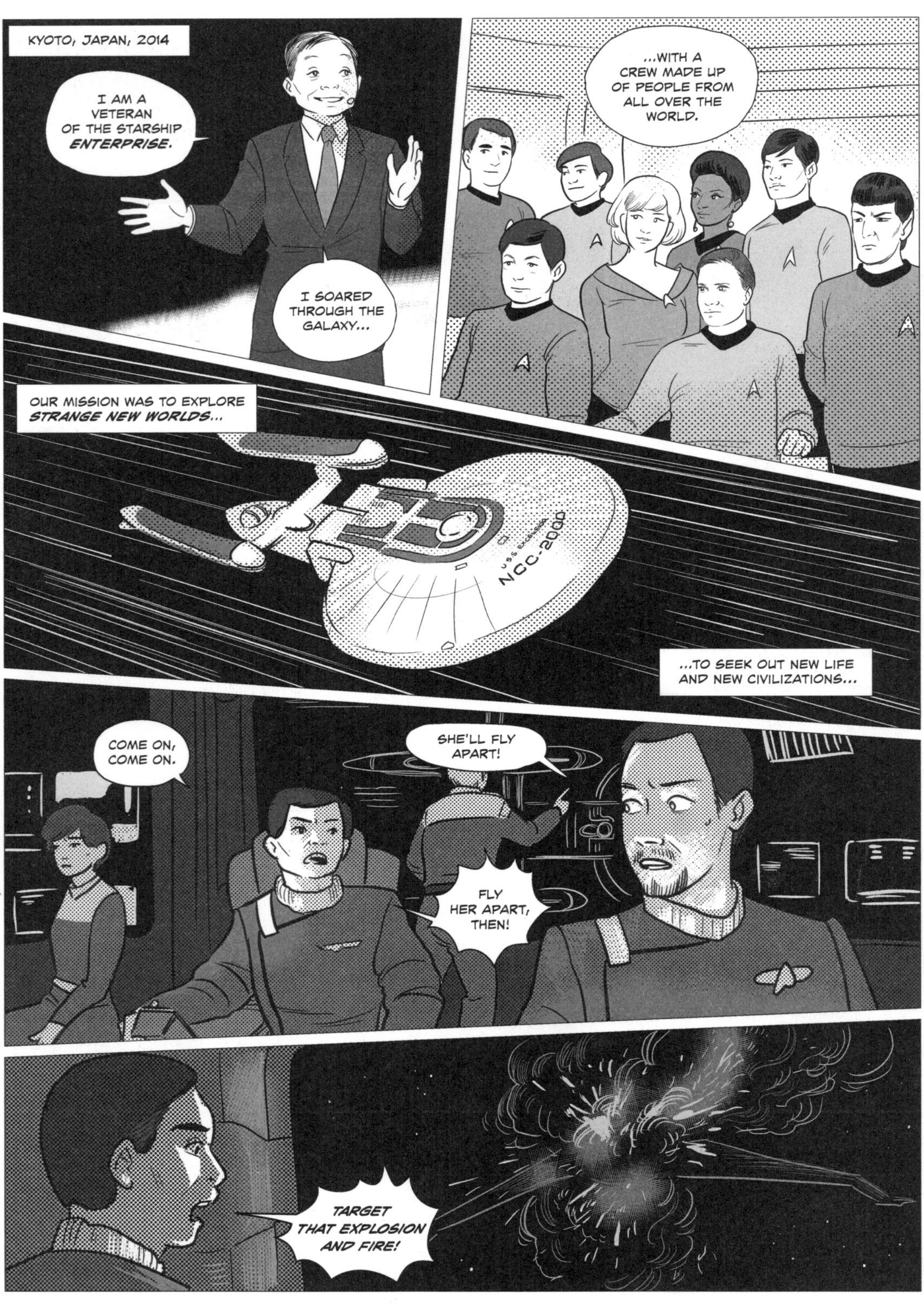
KYOTO, JAPAN, 2014
I AM A VETERAN OF THE STARSHIP *ENTERPRISE.*
I SOARED THROUGH THE GALAXY...
...WITH A CREW MADE UP OF PEOPLE FROM ALL OVER THE WORLD.
OUR MISSION WAS TO EXPLORE *STRANGE NEW WORLDS...*
U.S.S. EXCELSIOR
NCC-2000
...TO SEEK OUT NEW LIFE AND NEW CIVILIZATIONS...
COME ON, COME ON.
SHE'LL FLY APART!
FLY HER APART, THEN!
TARGET THAT EXPLOSION AND FIRE!

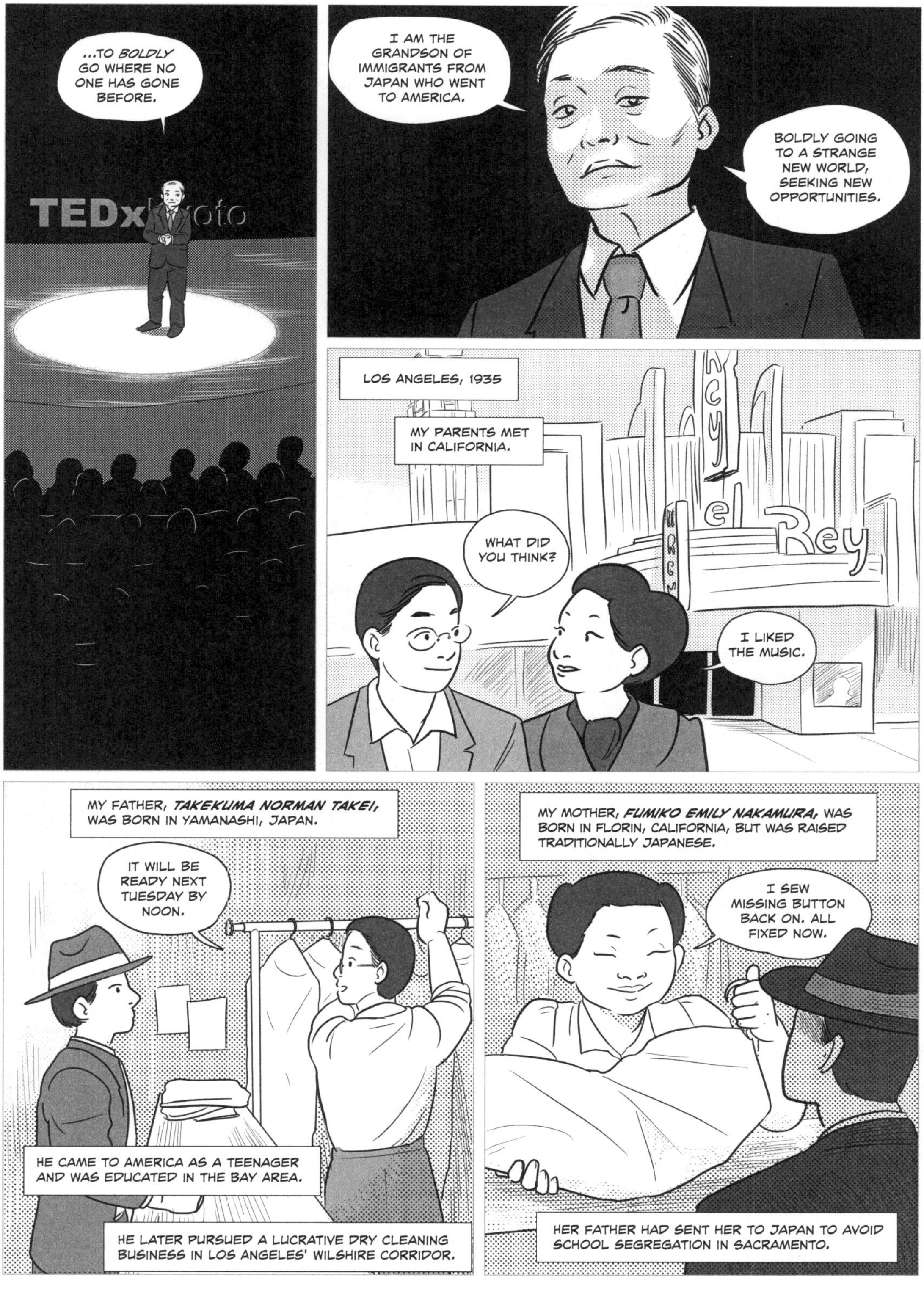

...TO BOLDLY GO WHERE NO ONE HAS GONE BEFORE.
TEDxKyoto
I AM THE GRANDSON OF IMMIGRANTS FROM JAPAN WHO WENT TO AMERICA.
BOLDLY GOING TO A STRANGE NEW WORLD, SEEKING NEW OPPORTUNITIES.
LOS ANGELES, 1935
MY PARENTS MET IN CALIFORNIA.
el Rey
WHAT DID YOU THINK?
I LIKED THE MUSIC.
MY FATHER, TAKEKUMA NORMAN TAKEI, WAS BORN IN YAMANASHI, JAPAN.
IT WILL BE READY NEXT TUESDAY BY NOON.
HE CAME TO AMERICA AS A TEENAGER AND WAS EDUCATED IN THE BAY AREA.
HE LATER PURSUED A LUCRATIVE DRY CLEANING BUSINESS IN LOS ANGELES' WILSHIRE CORRIDOR.
MY MOTHER, FUMIKO EMILY NAKAMURA, WAS BORN IN FLORIN, CALIFORNIA, BUT WAS RAISED TRADITIONALLY JAPANESE.
I SEW MISSING BUTTON BACK ON. ALL FIXED NOW.
HER FATHER HAD SENT HER TO JAPAN TO AVOID SCHOOL SEGREGATION IN SACRAMENTO.

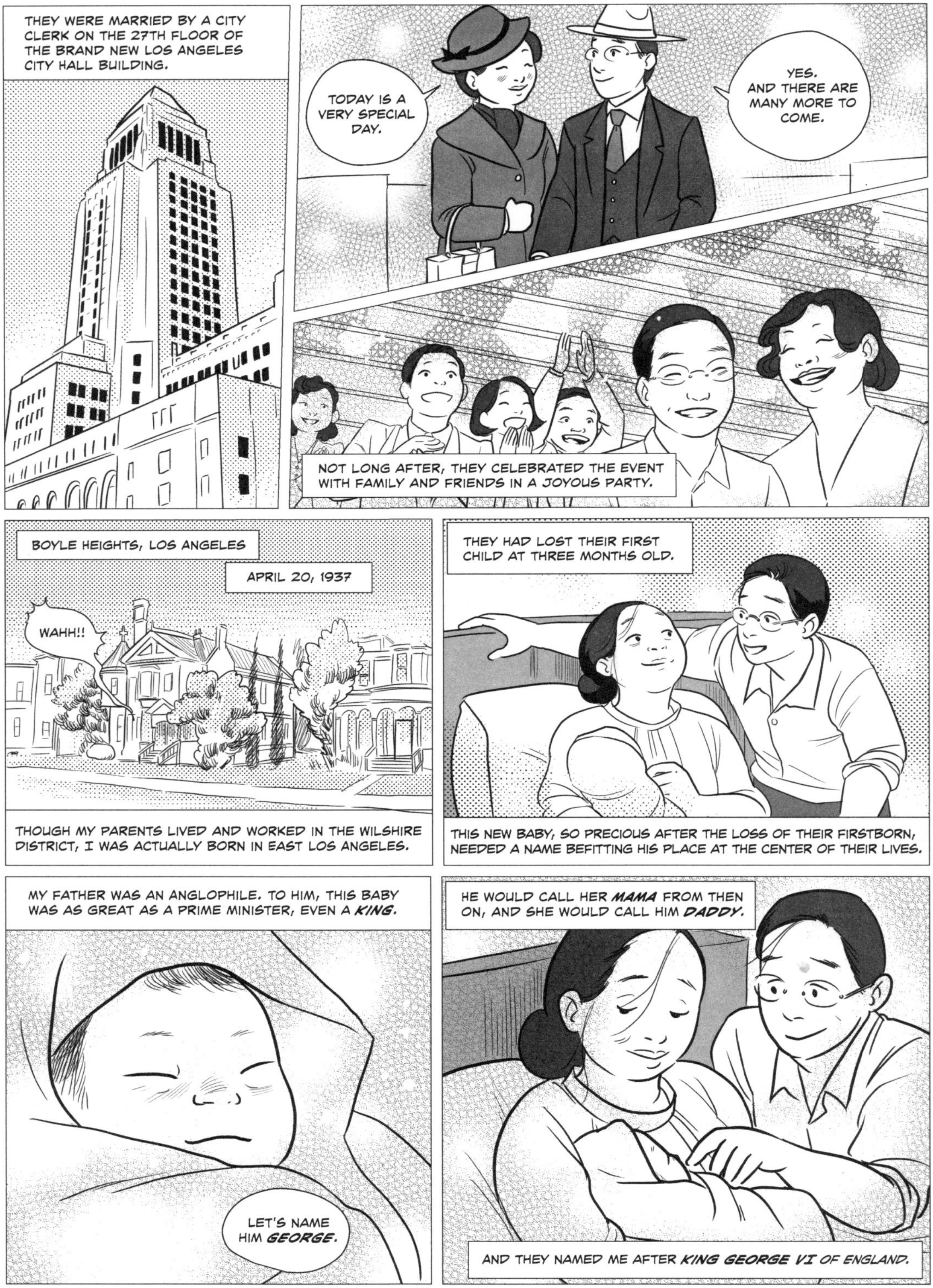
THEY WERE MARRIED BY A CITY CLERK ON THE 27TH FLOOR OF THE BRAND NEW LOS ANGELES CITY HALL BUILDING.
TODAY IS A VERY SPECIAL DAY.
YES. AND THERE ARE MANY MORE TO COME.
NOT LONG AFTER, THEY CELEBRATED THE EVENT WITH FAMILY AND FRIENDS IN A JOYOUS PARTY.
BOYLE HEIGHTS, LOS ANGELES
APRIL 20, 1937
WAHH!!
THOUGH MY PARENTS LIVED AND WORKED IN THE WILSHIRE DISTRICT, I WAS ACTUALLY BORN IN EAST LOS ANGELES.
THEY HAD LOST THEIR FIRST CHILD AT THREE MONTHS OLD.
THIS NEW BABY, SO PRECIOUS AFTER THE LOSS OF THEIR FIRSTBORN, NEEDED A NAME BEFITTING HIS PLACE AT THE CENTER OF THEIR LIVES.
MY FATHER WAS AN ANGLOPHILE. TO HIM, THIS BABY WAS AS GREAT AS A PRIME MINISTER, EVEN A ***KING.***
LET'S NAME HIM ***GEORGE.***
HE WOULD CALL HER ***MAMA*** FROM THEN ON, AND SHE WOULD CALL HIM ***DADDY.***
AND THEY NAMED ME AFTER ***KING GEORGE VI*** OF ENGLAND.

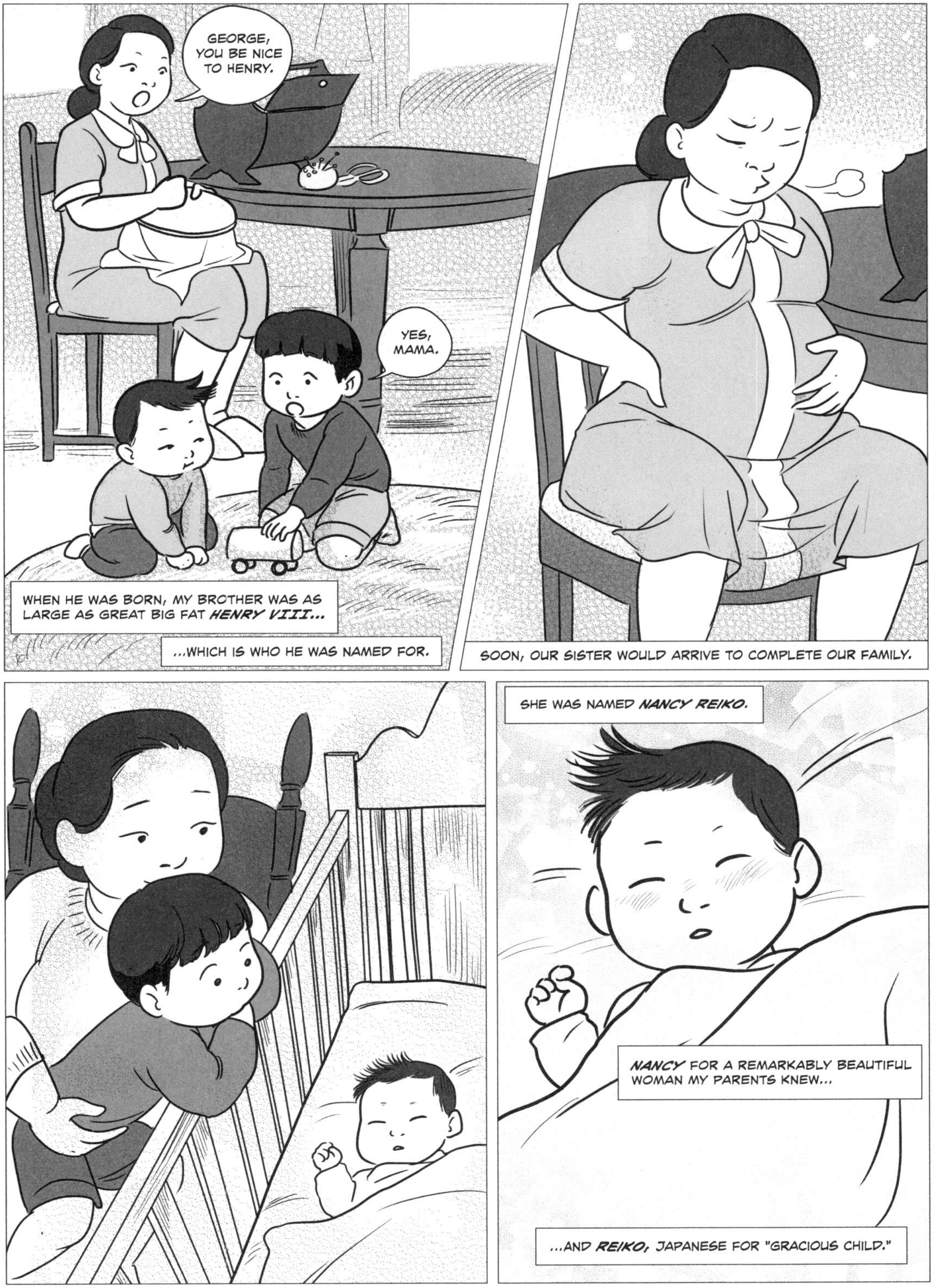
GEORGE, YOU BE NICE TO HENRY.
YES, MAMA.
WHEN HE WAS BORN, MY BROTHER WAS AS LARGE AS GREAT BIG FAT HENRY VIII...
...WHICH IS WHO HE WAS NAMED FOR.
SOON, OUR SISTER WOULD ARRIVE TO COMPLETE OUR FAMILY.
SHE WAS NAMED NANCY REIKO.
NANCY FOR A REMARKABLY BEAUTIFUL WOMAN MY PARENTS KNEW...
...AND REIKO, JAPANESE FOR "GRACIOUS CHILD."

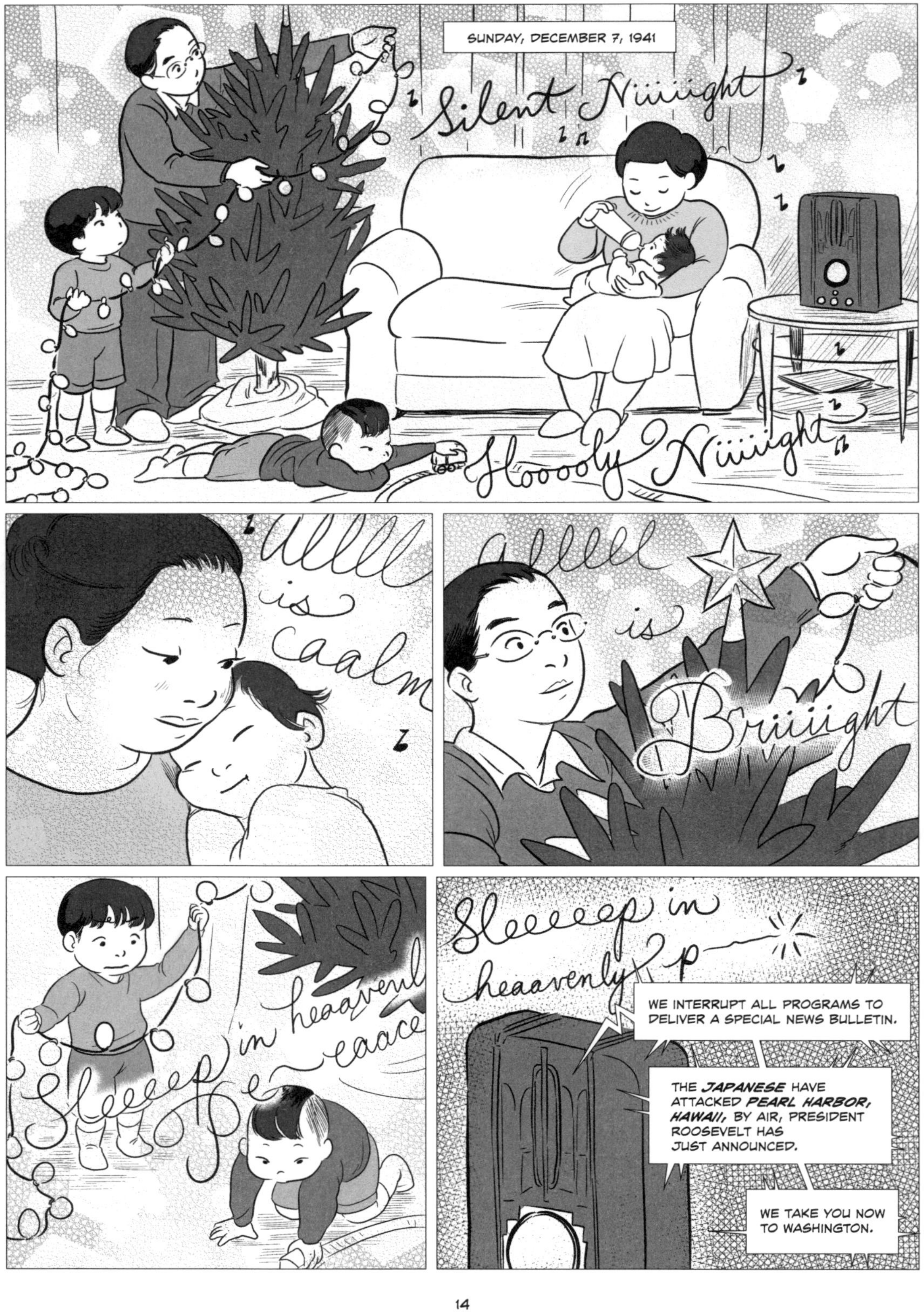
SUNDAY, DECEMBER 7, 1941
Silent Niiiiight
Hoooly Niiiight
Allll is caalm
Allll is Briiiight
Sleeeep in heaavenl peeaace
Sleeeep in heaavenly p—
WE INTERRUPT ALL PROGRAMS TO DELIVER A SPECIAL NEWS BULLETIN.
THE JAPANESE HAVE ATTACKED PEARL HARBOR, HAWAII, BY AIR, PRESIDENT ROOSEVELT HAS JUST ANNOUNCED.
WE TAKE YOU NOW TO WASHINGTON.

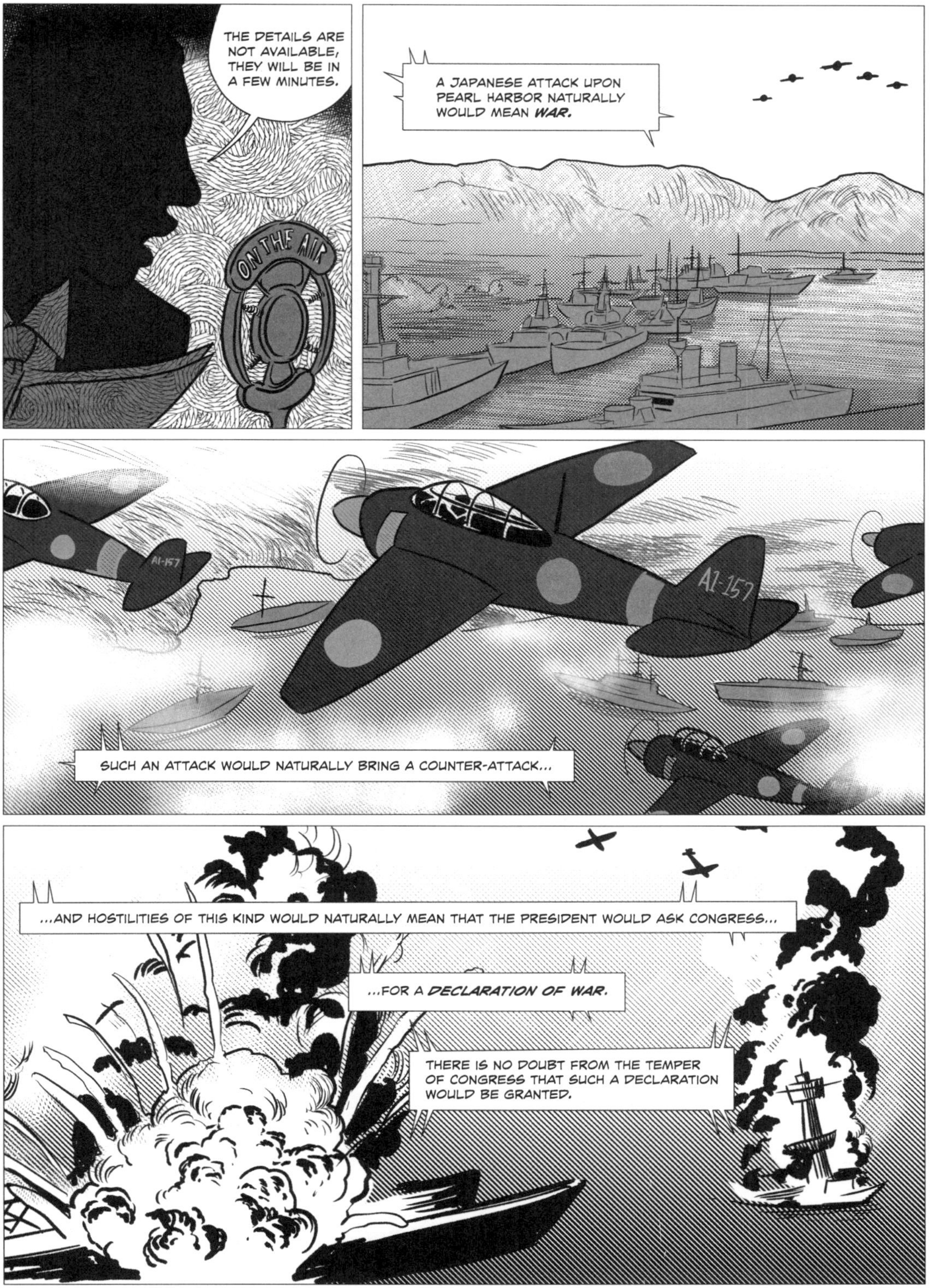
THE DETAILS ARE NOT AVAILABLE, THEY WILL BE IN A FEW MINUTES.
ON THE AIR
A JAPANESE ATTACK UPON PEARL HARBOR NATURALLY WOULD MEAN **WAR.**
A1-157
A1-157
SUCH AN ATTACK WOULD NATURALLY BRING A COUNTER-ATTACK...
...AND HOSTILITIES OF THIS KIND WOULD NATURALLY MEAN THAT THE PRESIDENT WOULD ASK CONGRESS...
...FOR A ***DECLARATION OF WAR.***
THERE IS NO DOUBT FROM THE TEMPER OF CONGRESS THAT SUCH A DECLARATION WOULD BE GRANTED.

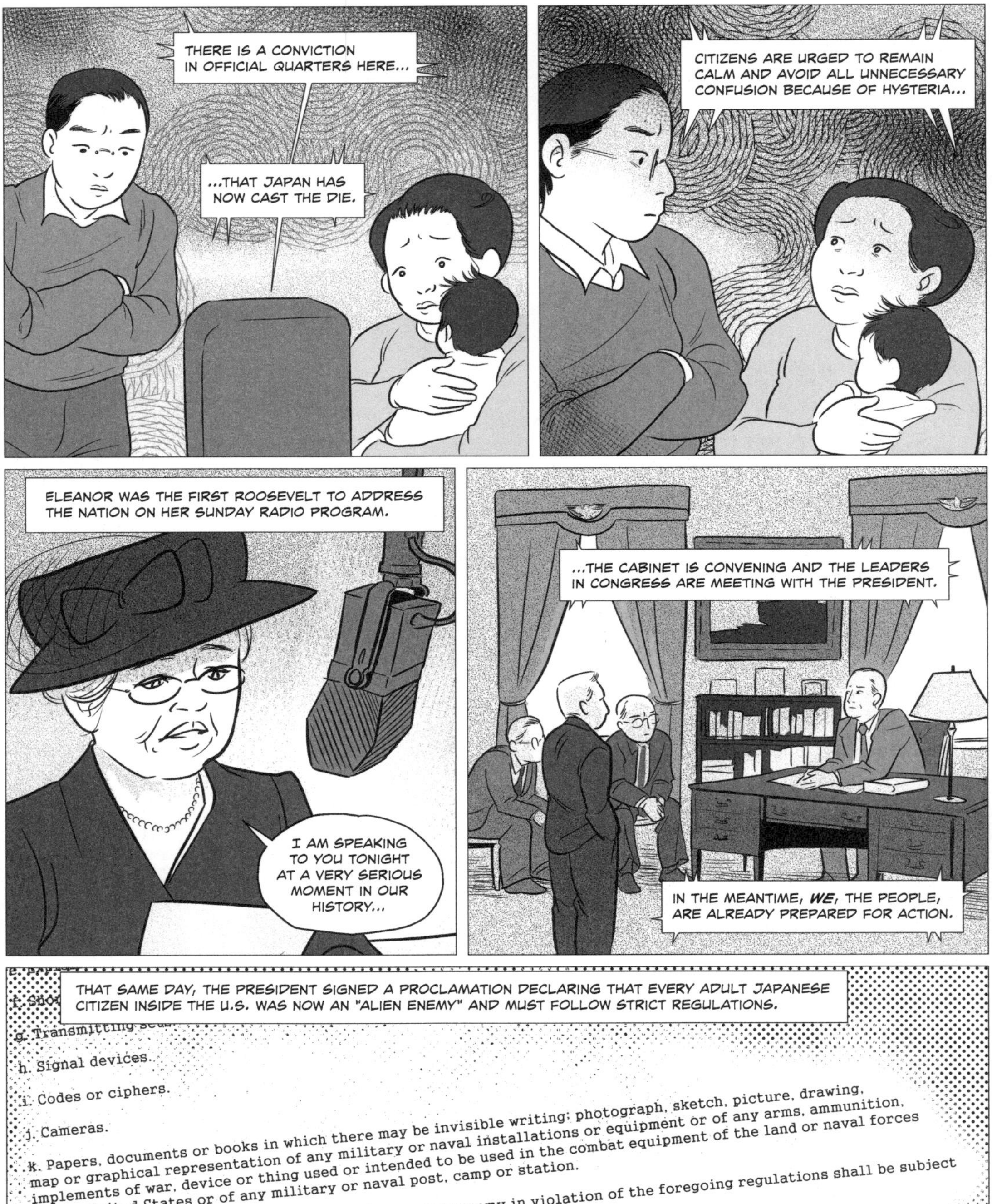
THERE IS A CONVICTION IN OFFICIAL QUARTERS HERE...
...THAT JAPAN HAS NOW CAST THE DIE.
CITIZENS ARE URGED TO REMAIN CALM AND AVOID ALL UNNECESSARY CONFUSION BECAUSE OF HYSTERIA...
ELEANOR WAS THE FIRST ROOSEVELT TO ADDRESS THE NATION ON HER SUNDAY RADIO PROGRAM.
I AM SPEAKING TO YOU TONIGHT AT A VERY SERIOUS MOMENT IN OUR HISTORY...
...THE CABINET IS CONVENING AND THE LEADERS IN CONGRESS ARE MEETING WITH THE PRESIDENT.
IN THE MEANTIME, *WE*, THE PEOPLE, ARE ALREADY PREPARED FOR ACTION.
THAT SAME DAY, THE PRESIDENT SIGNED A PROCLAMATION DECLARING THAT EVERY ADULT JAPANESE CITIZEN INSIDE THE U.S. WAS NOW AN "ALIEN ENEMY" AND MUST FOLLOW STRICT REGULATIONS.
h. Signal devices.
i. Codes or ciphers.
j. Cameras.
k. Papers, documents or books in which there may be invisible writing; photograph, sketch, picture, drawing, map or graphical representation of any military or naval installations or equipment or of any arms, ammunition, implements of war, device or thing used or intended to be used in the combat equipment of the land or naval forces of the United States or of any military or naval post, camp or station.
All such property found in the possession of any alien enemy in violation of the foregoing regulations shall be subject to seizure and forfeiture.
(6) No alien enemy shall undertake any air flight or ascend into the air in any airplane, aircraft or balloon of any sort whether owned governmentally, commercially or privately, except that travel by an alien enemy in an airplane or aircraft
General, or his representative, or the Secretary of War, or his representative, in their
as they shall prescribe.
MY FATHER LOVED THIS COUNTRY AND HAD LIVED HERE FOR TWENTY-FIVE YEARS, BUT THE U.S. HAD NEVER ALLOWED HIM TO APPLY FOR CITIZENSHIP. NOW HE WAS CONSIDERED AN ENEMY IN A WAR THAT HADN'T EVEN BEEN DECLARED YET.

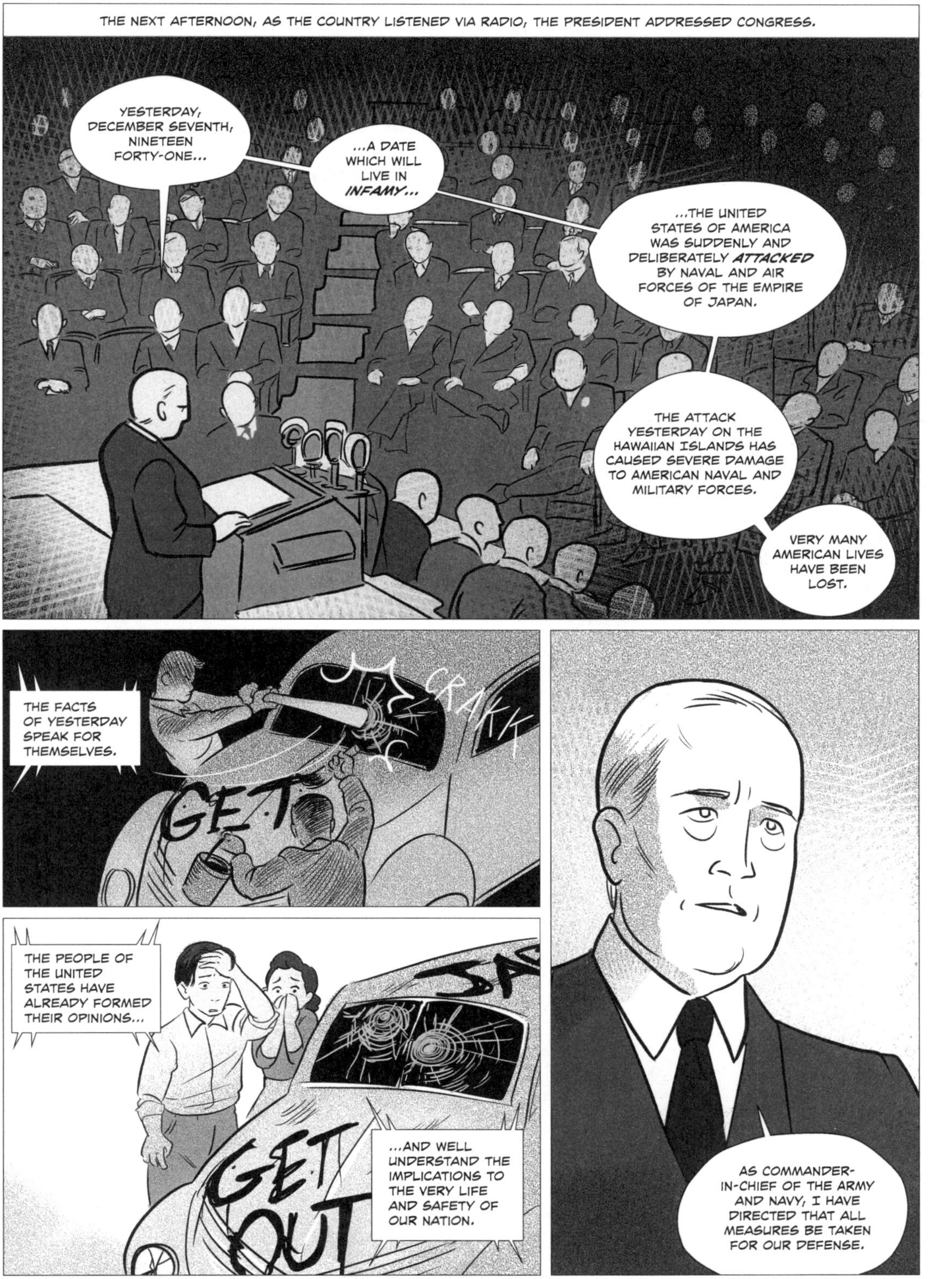
THE NEXT AFTERNOON, AS THE COUNTRY LISTENED VIA RADIO, THE PRESIDENT ADDRESSED CONGRESS.
YESTERDAY, DECEMBER SEVENTH, NINETEEN FORTY-ONE...
...A DATE WHICH WILL LIVE IN *INFAMY*...
...THE UNITED STATES OF AMERICA WAS SUDDENLY AND DELIBERATELY *ATTACKED* BY NAVAL AND AIR FORCES OF THE EMPIRE OF JAPAN.
THE ATTACK YESTERDAY ON THE HAWAIIAN ISLANDS HAS CAUSED SEVERE DAMAGE TO AMERICAN NAVAL AND MILITARY FORCES.
VERY MANY AMERICAN LIVES HAVE BEEN LOST.
THE FACTS OF YESTERDAY SPEAK FOR THEMSELVES.
CRAKKT
GET
THE PEOPLE OF THE UNITED STATES HAVE ALREADY FORMED THEIR OPINIONS...
GET OUT
...AND WELL UNDERSTAND THE IMPLICATIONS TO THE VERY LIFE AND SAFETY OF OUR NATION.
AS COMMANDER-IN-CHIEF OF THE ARMY AND NAVY, I HAVE DIRECTED THAT ALL MEASURES BE TAKEN FOR OUR DEFENSE.

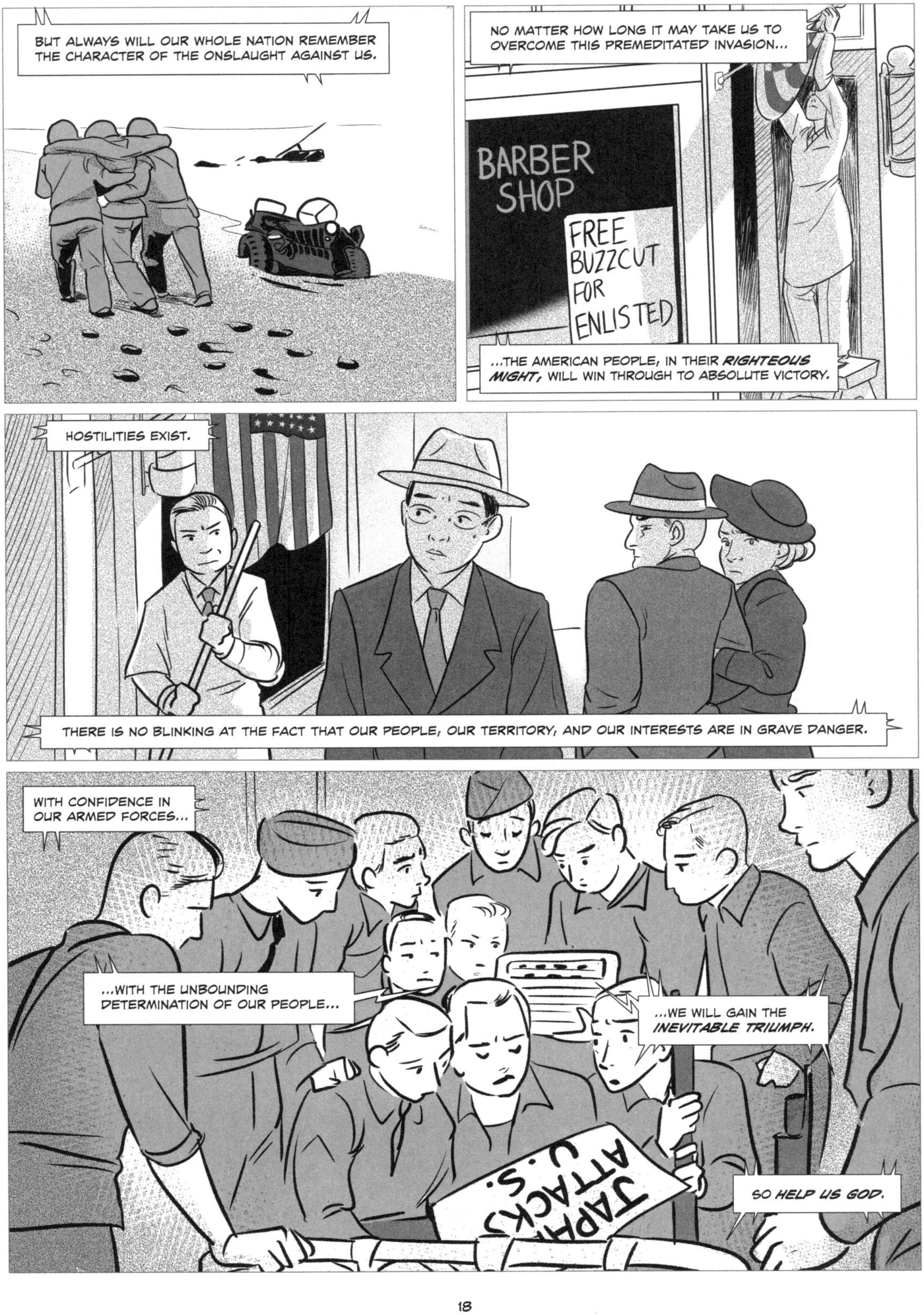

BUT ALWAYS WILL OUR WHOLE NATION REMEMBER THE CHARACTER OF THE ONSLAUGHT AGAINST US.
NO MATTER HOW LONG IT MAY TAKE US TO OVERCOME THIS PREMEDITATED INVASION...
BARBER SHOP
FREE BUZZCUT FOR ENLISTED
...THE AMERICAN PEOPLE, IN THEIR *RIGHTEOUS MIGHT,* WILL WIN THROUGH TO ABSOLUTE VICTORY.
HOSTILITIES EXIST.
THERE IS NO BLINKING AT THE FACT THAT OUR PEOPLE, OUR TERRITORY, AND OUR INTERESTS ARE IN GRAVE DANGER.
WITH CONFIDENCE IN OUR ARMED FORCES...
...WITH THE UNBOUNDING DETERMINATION OF OUR PEOPLE...
...WE WILL GAIN THE *INEVITABLE TRIUMPH.*
JAPAN ATTACKS U.S.
SO *HELP US GOD.*

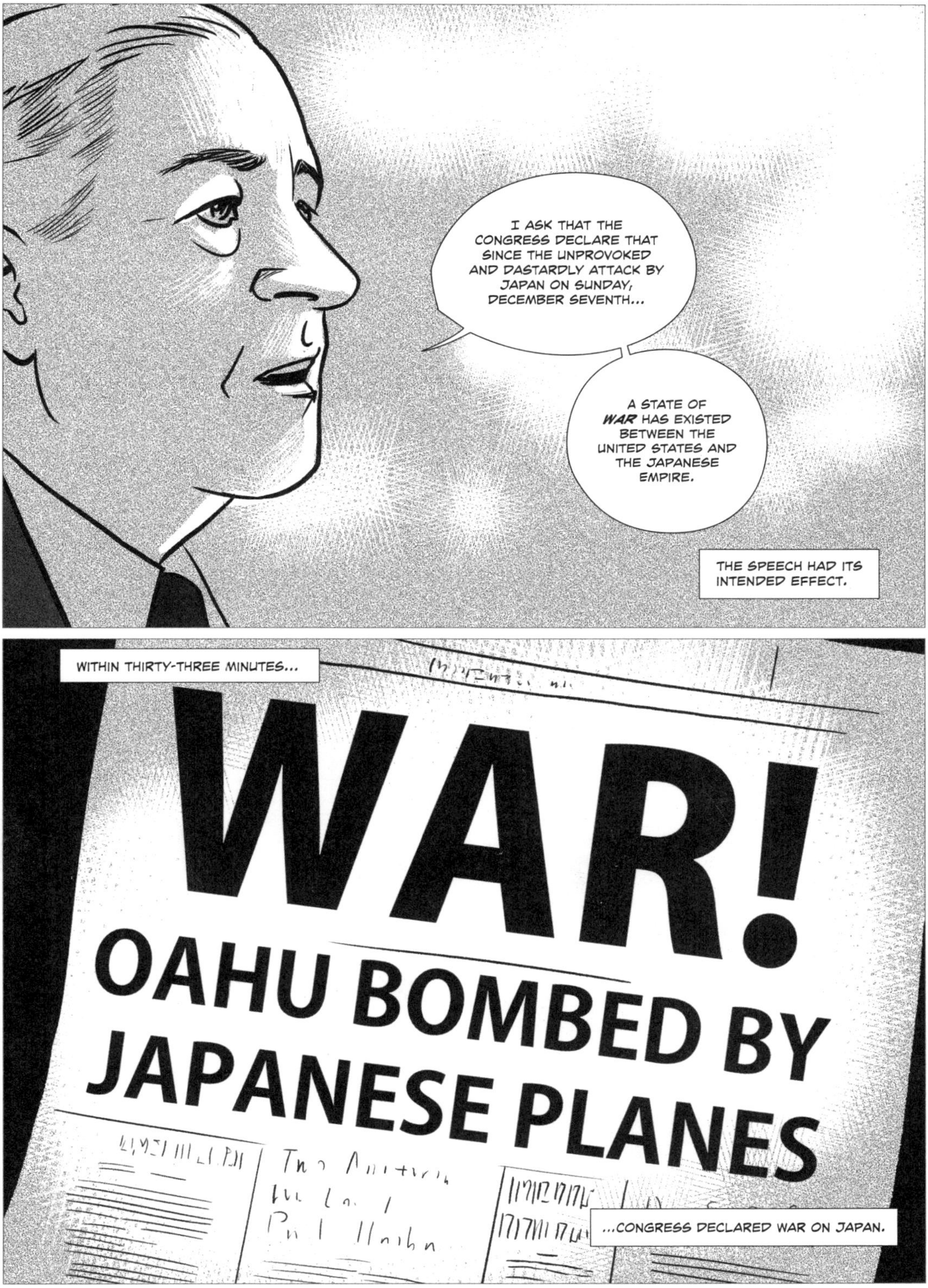
I ASK THAT THE CONGRESS DECLARE THAT SINCE THE UNPROVOKED AND DASTARDLY ATTACK BY JAPAN ON SUNDAY, DECEMBER SEVENTH...
A STATE OF ***WAR*** HAS EXISTED BETWEEN THE UNITED STATES AND THE JAPANESE EMPIRE.
THE SPEECH HAD ITS INTENDED EFFECT.
WITHIN THIRTY-THREE MINUTES...
WAR!
OAHU BOMBED BY JAPANESE PLANES
...CONGRESS DECLARED WAR ON JAPAN.

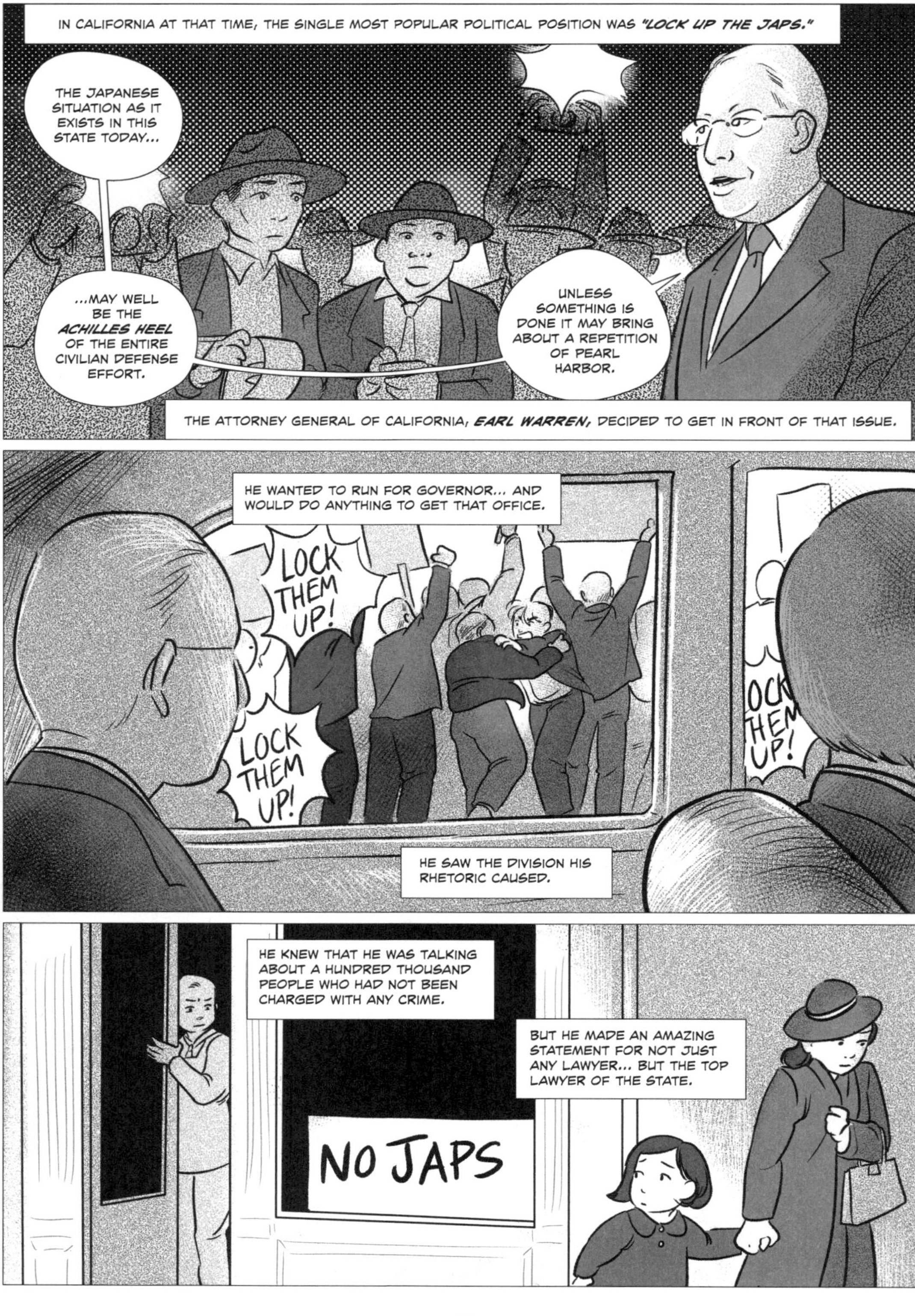
IN CALIFORNIA AT THAT TIME, THE SINGLE MOST POPULAR POLITICAL POSITION WAS *"LOCK UP THE JAPS."*
THE JAPANESE SITUATION AS IT EXISTS IN THIS STATE TODAY...
...MAY WELL BE THE *ACHILLES HEEL* OF THE ENTIRE CIVILIAN DEFENSE EFFORT.
UNLESS SOMETHING IS DONE IT MAY BRING ABOUT A REPETITION OF PEARL HARBOR.
THE ATTORNEY GENERAL OF CALIFORNIA, *EARL WARREN,* DECIDED TO GET IN FRONT OF THAT ISSUE.
HE WANTED TO RUN FOR GOVERNOR... AND WOULD DO ANYTHING TO GET THAT OFFICE.
LOCK THEM UP!
LOCK THEM UP!
LOCK THEM UP!
HE SAW THE DIVISION HIS RHETORIC CAUSED.
HE KNEW THAT HE WAS TALKING ABOUT A HUNDRED THOUSAND PEOPLE WHO HAD NOT BEEN CHARGED WITH ANY CRIME.
BUT HE MADE AN AMAZING STATEMENT FOR NOT JUST ANY LAWYER... BUT THE TOP LAWYER OF THE STATE.
NO JAPS

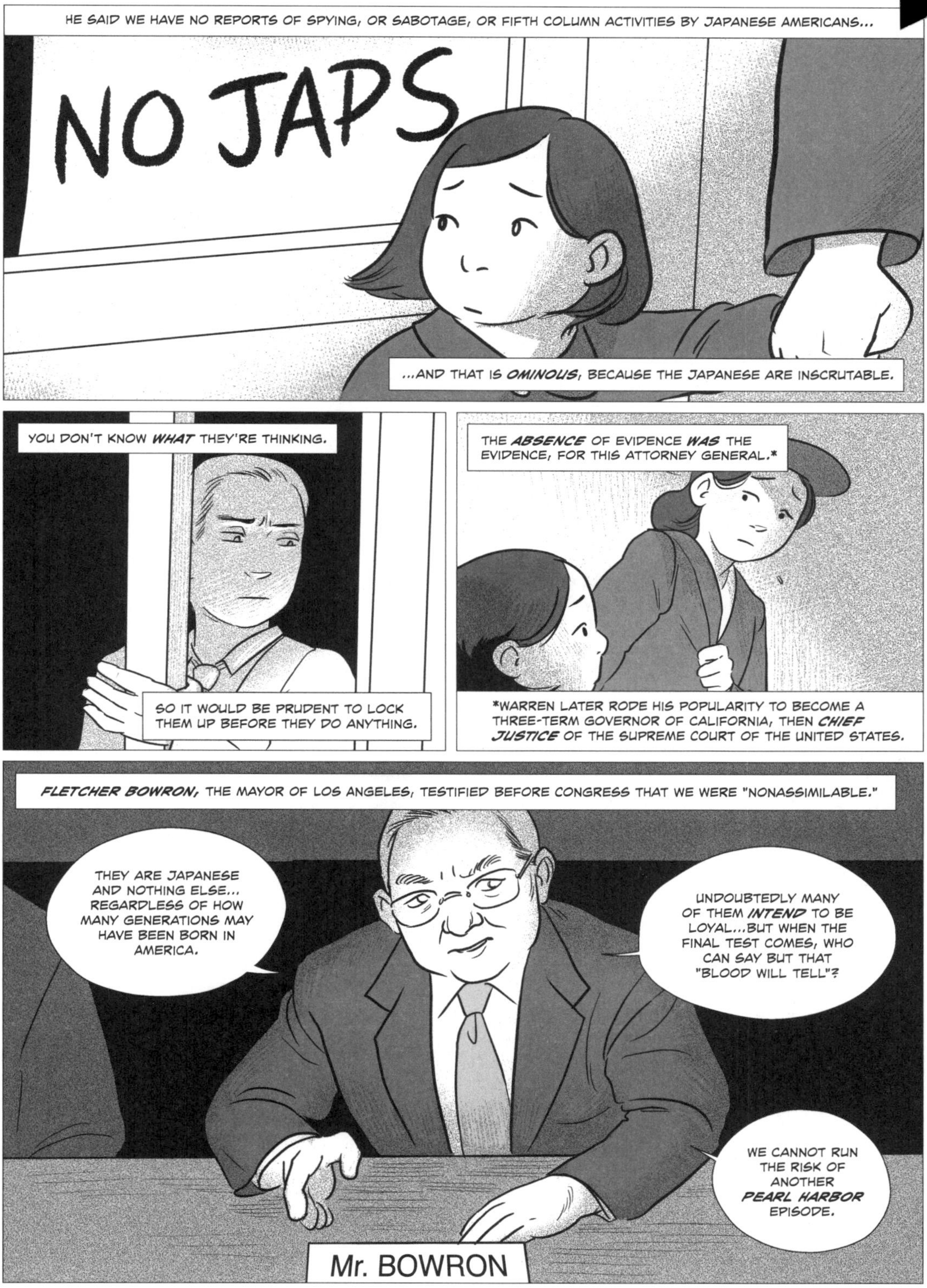
HE SAID WE HAVE NO REPORTS OF SPYING, OR SABOTAGE, OR FIFTH COLUMN ACTIVITIES BY JAPANESE AMERICANS...
NO JAPS
...AND THAT IS *OMINOUS*, BECAUSE THE JAPANESE ARE INSCRUTABLE.
YOU DON'T KNOW *WHAT* THEY'RE THINKING.
SO IT WOULD BE PRUDENT TO LOCK THEM UP BEFORE THEY DO ANYTHING.
THE *ABSENCE* OF EVIDENCE *WAS* THE EVIDENCE, FOR THIS ATTORNEY GENERAL.*
*WARREN LATER RODE HIS POPULARITY TO BECOME A THREE-TERM GOVERNOR OF CALIFORNIA, THEN *CHIEF JUSTICE* OF THE SUPREME COURT OF THE UNITED STATES.
FLETCHER BOWRON, THE MAYOR OF LOS ANGELES, TESTIFIED BEFORE CONGRESS THAT WE WERE "NONASSIMILABLE."
THEY ARE JAPANESE AND NOTHING ELSE... REGARDLESS OF HOW MANY GENERATIONS MAY HAVE BEEN BORN IN AMERICA.
UNDOUBTEDLY MANY OF THEM *INTEND* TO BE LOYAL...BUT WHEN THE FINAL TEST COMES, WHO CAN SAY BUT THAT "BLOOD WILL TELL"?
WE CANNOT RUN THE RISK OF ANOTHER *PEARL HARBOR* EPISODE.
Mr. BOWRON

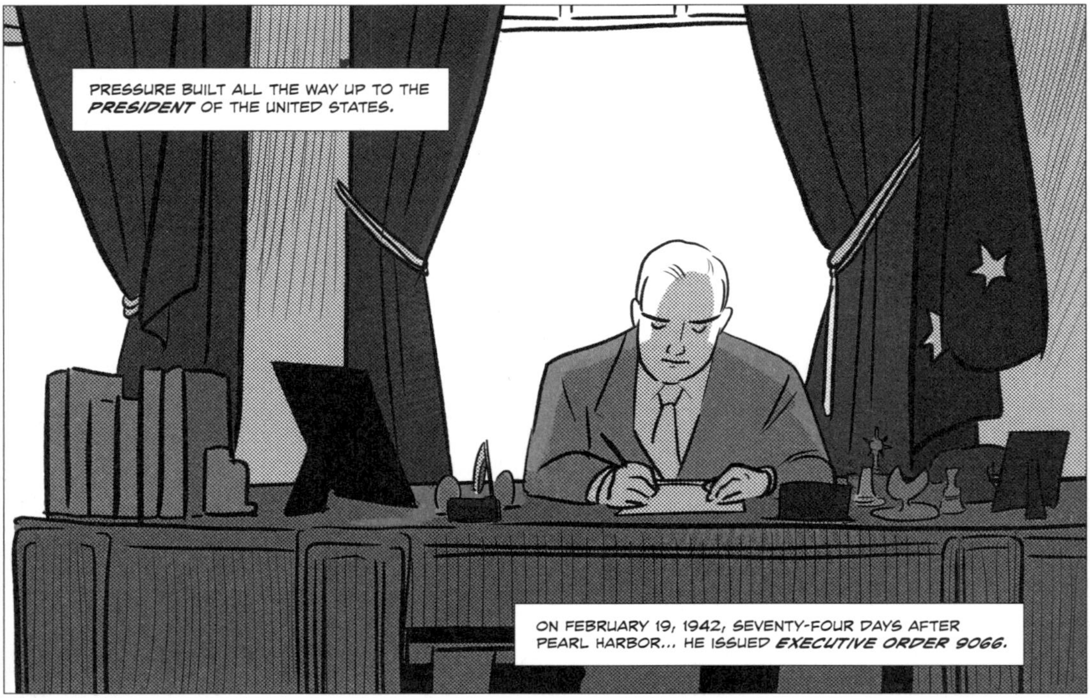
PRESSURE BUILT ALL THE WAY UP TO THE *PRESIDENT* OF THE UNITED STATES.
ON FEBRUARY 19, 1942, SEVENTY-FOUR DAYS AFTER PEARL HARBOR... HE ISSUED *EXECUTIVE ORDER 9066.*

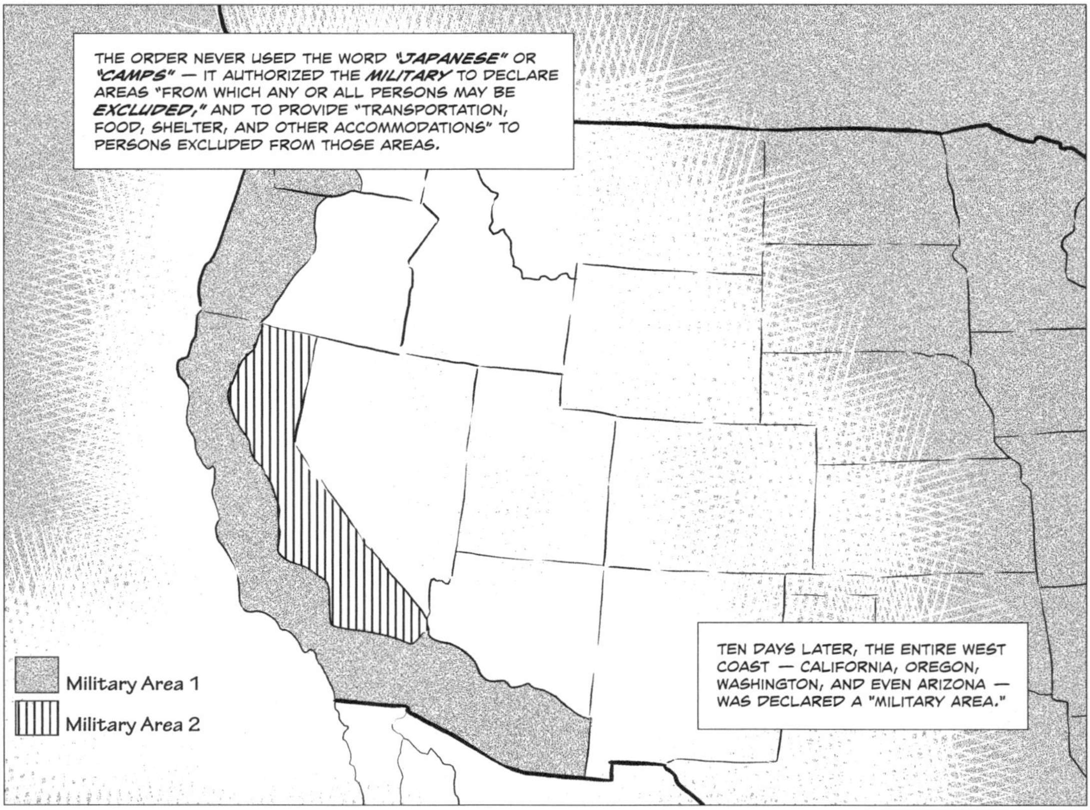
THE ORDER NEVER USED THE WORD *"JAPANESE"* OR *"CAMPS"* — IT AUTHORIZED THE *MILITARY* TO DECLARE AREAS "FROM WHICH ANY OR ALL PERSONS MAY BE *EXCLUDED,"* AND TO PROVIDE "TRANSPORTATION, FOOD, SHELTER, AND OTHER ACCOMMODATIONS" TO PERSONS EXCLUDED FROM THOSE AREAS.
Military Area 1
Military Area 2
TEN DAYS LATER, THE ENTIRE WEST COAST — CALIFORNIA, OREGON, WASHINGTON, AND EVEN ARIZONA — WAS DECLARED A "MILITARY AREA."

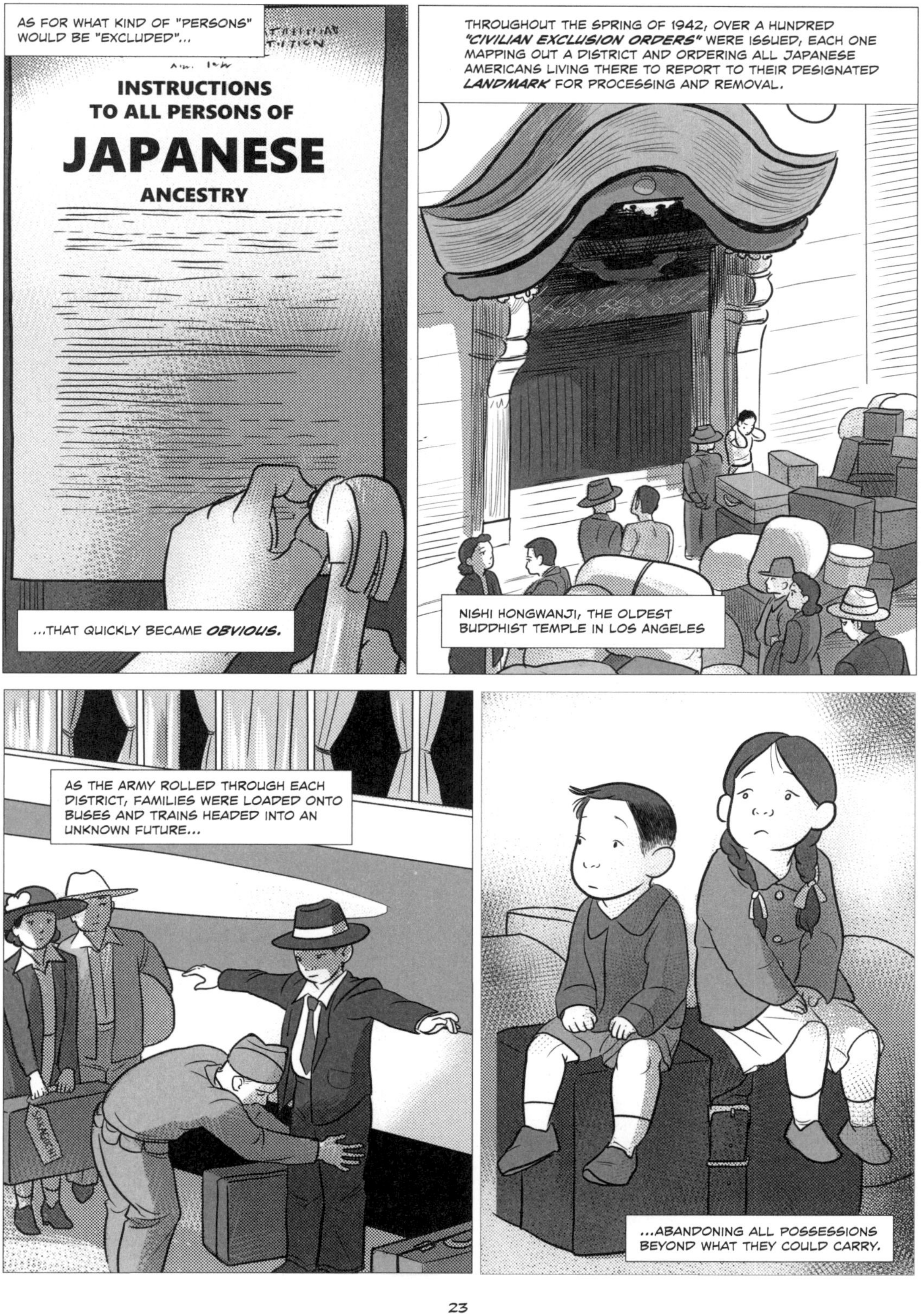
AS FOR WHAT KIND OF "PERSONS" WOULD BE "EXCLUDED"...
INSTRUCTIONS TO ALL PERSONS OF JAPANESE ANCESTRY
...THAT QUICKLY BECAME OBVIOUS.
THROUGHOUT THE SPRING OF 1942, OVER A HUNDRED "CIVILIAN EXCLUSION ORDERS" WERE ISSUED, EACH ONE MAPPING OUT A DISTRICT AND ORDERING ALL JAPANESE AMERICANS LIVING THERE TO REPORT TO THEIR DESIGNATED LANDMARK FOR PROCESSING AND REMOVAL.
NISHI HONGWANJI, THE OLDEST BUDDHIST TEMPLE IN LOS ANGELES
AS THE ARMY ROLLED THROUGH EACH DISTRICT, FAMILIES WERE LOADED ONTO BUSES AND TRAINS HEADED INTO AN UNKNOWN FUTURE...
...ABANDONING ALL POSSESSIONS BEYOND WHAT THEY COULD CARRY.

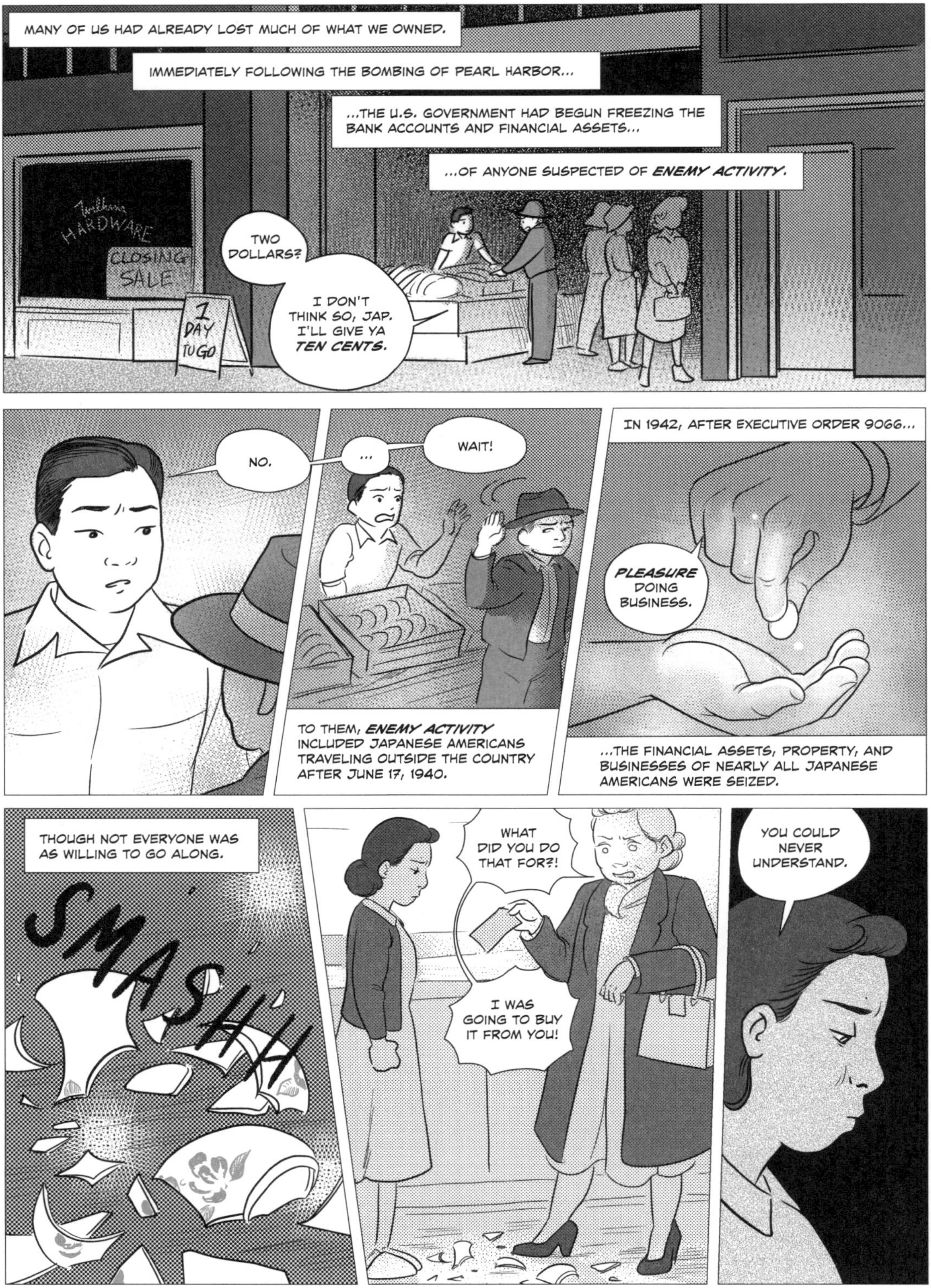
MANY OF US HAD ALREADY LOST MUCH OF WHAT WE OWNED.
IMMEDIATELY FOLLOWING THE BOMBING OF PEARL HARBOR...
...THE U.S. GOVERNMENT HAD BEGUN FREEZING THE BANK ACCOUNTS AND FINANCIAL ASSETS...
...OF ANYONE SUSPECTED OF ENEMY ACTIVITY.
HARDWARE
CLOSING SALE
1 DAY TO GO
TWO DOLLARS?
I DON'T THINK SO, JAP. I'LL GIVE YA TEN CENTS.
NO.
...
WAIT!
TO THEM, ENEMY ACTIVITY INCLUDED JAPANESE AMERICANS TRAVELING OUTSIDE THE COUNTRY AFTER JUNE 17, 1940.
IN 1942, AFTER EXECUTIVE ORDER 9066...
PLEASURE DOING BUSINESS.
...THE FINANCIAL ASSETS, PROPERTY, AND BUSINESSES OF NEARLY ALL JAPANESE AMERICANS WERE SEIZED.
THOUGH NOT EVERYONE WAS AS WILLING TO GO ALONG.
SMASHH
WHAT DID YOU DO THAT FOR?!
I WAS GOING TO BUY IT FROM YOU!
YOU COULD NEVER UNDERSTAND.

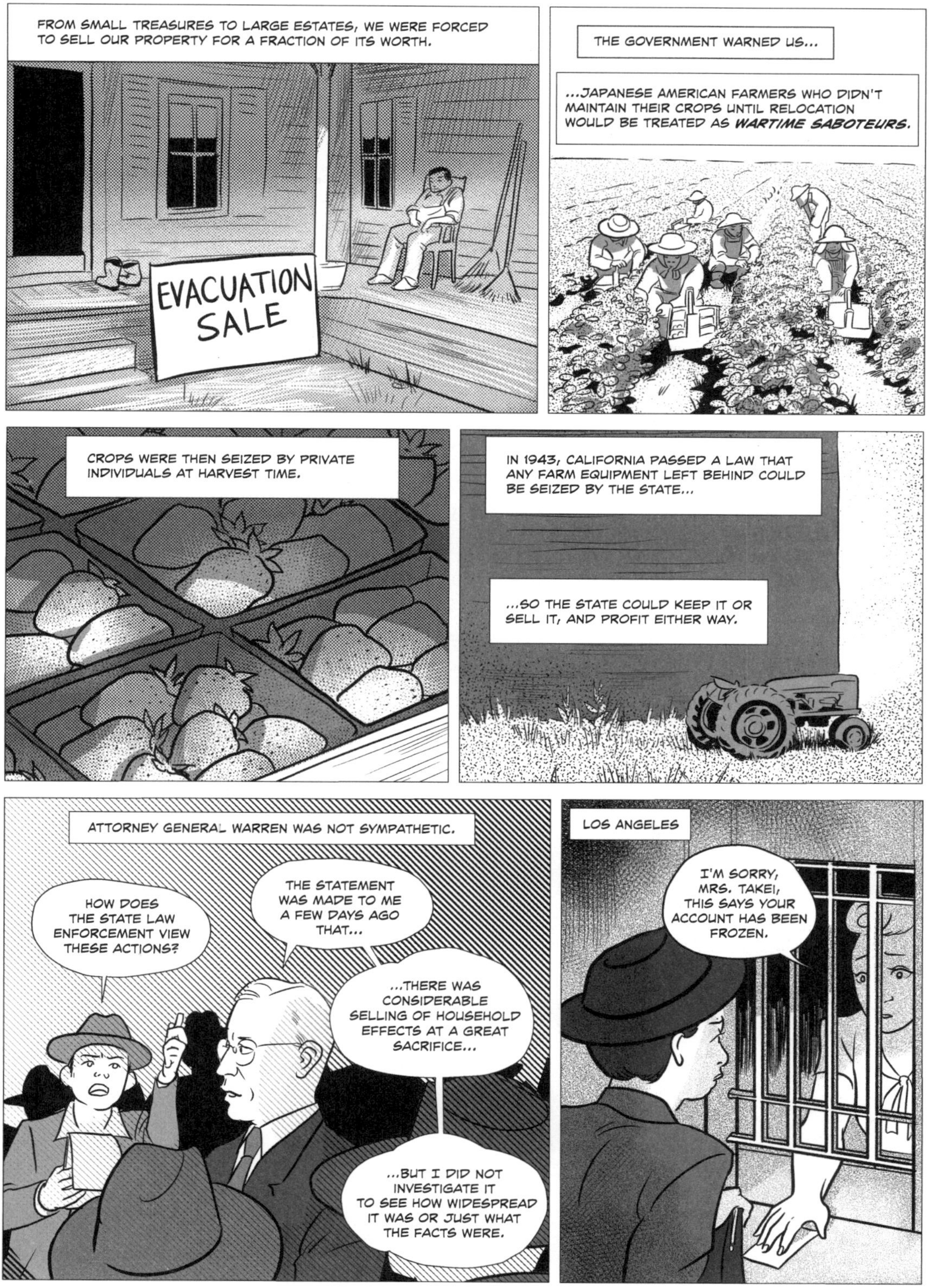
FROM SMALL TREASURES TO LARGE ESTATES, WE WERE FORCED TO SELL OUR PROPERTY FOR A FRACTION OF ITS WORTH.
EVACUATION SALE
THE GOVERNMENT WARNED US...
...JAPANESE AMERICAN FARMERS WHO DIDN'T MAINTAIN THEIR CROPS UNTIL RELOCATION WOULD BE TREATED AS ***WARTIME SABOTEURS.***
CROPS WERE THEN SEIZED BY PRIVATE INDIVIDUALS AT HARVEST TIME.
IN 1943, CALIFORNIA PASSED A LAW THAT ANY FARM EQUIPMENT LEFT BEHIND COULD BE SEIZED BY THE STATE...
...SO THE STATE COULD KEEP IT OR SELL IT, AND PROFIT EITHER WAY.
ATTORNEY GENERAL WARREN WAS NOT SYMPATHETIC.
HOW DOES THE STATE LAW ENFORCEMENT VIEW THESE ACTIONS?
THE STATEMENT WAS MADE TO ME A FEW DAYS AGO THAT...
...THERE WAS CONSIDERABLE SELLING OF HOUSEHOLD EFFECTS AT A GREAT SACRIFICE...
...BUT I DID NOT INVESTIGATE IT TO SEE HOW WIDESPREAD IT WAS OR JUST WHAT THE FACTS WERE.
LOS ANGELES
I'M SORRY, MRS. TAKEI, THIS SAYS YOUR ACCOUNT HAS BEEN FROZEN.

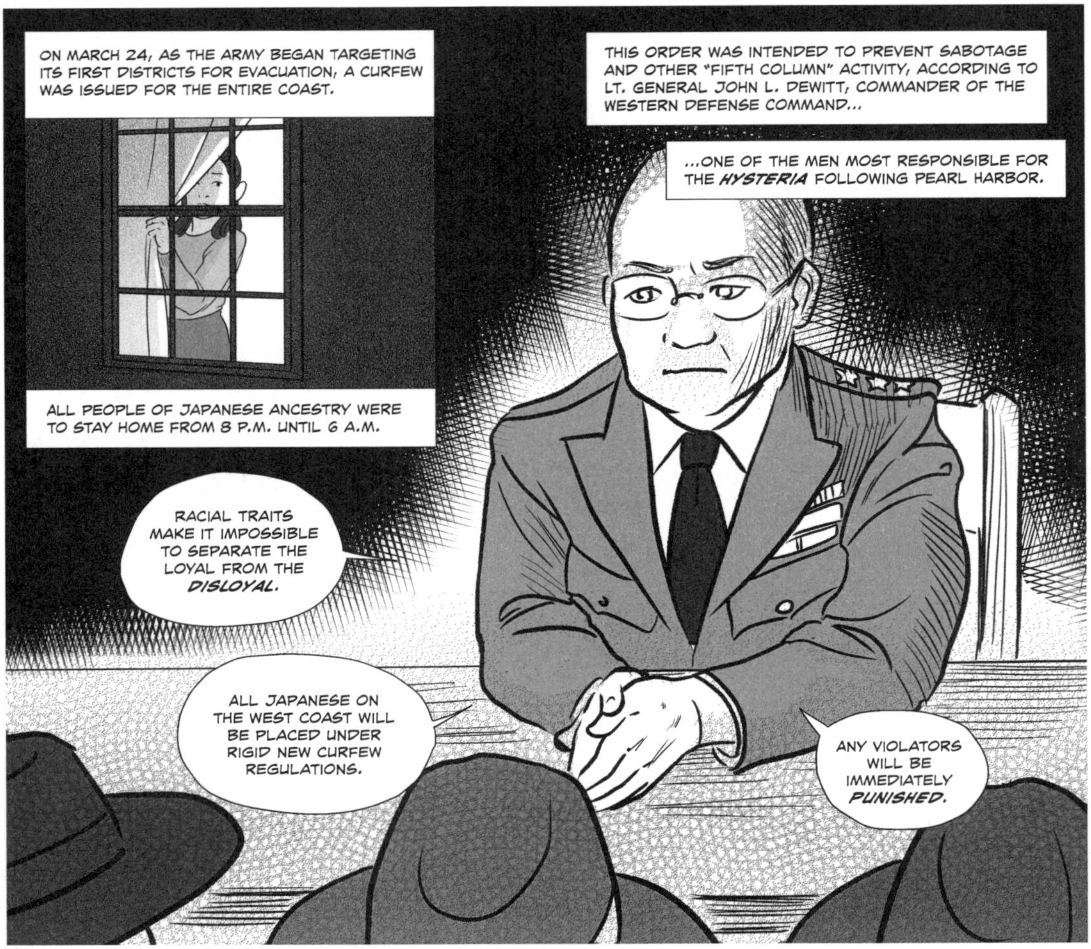
ON MARCH 24, AS THE ARMY BEGAN TARGETING ITS FIRST DISTRICTS FOR EVACUATION, A CURFEW WAS ISSUED FOR THE ENTIRE COAST.
ALL PEOPLE OF JAPANESE ANCESTRY WERE TO STAY HOME FROM 8 P.M. UNTIL 6 A.M.
THIS ORDER WAS INTENDED TO PREVENT SABOTAGE AND OTHER "FIFTH COLUMN" ACTIVITY, ACCORDING TO LT. GENERAL JOHN L. DEWITT, COMMANDER OF THE WESTERN DEFENSE COMMAND...
...ONE OF THE MEN MOST RESPONSIBLE FOR THE *HYSTERIA* FOLLOWING PEARL HARBOR.
RACIAL TRAITS MAKE IT IMPOSSIBLE TO SEPARATE THE LOYAL FROM THE *DISLOYAL.*
ALL JAPANESE ON THE WEST COAST WILL BE PLACED UNDER RIGID NEW CURFEW REGULATIONS.
ANY VIOLATORS WILL BE IMMEDIATELY *PUNISHED.*

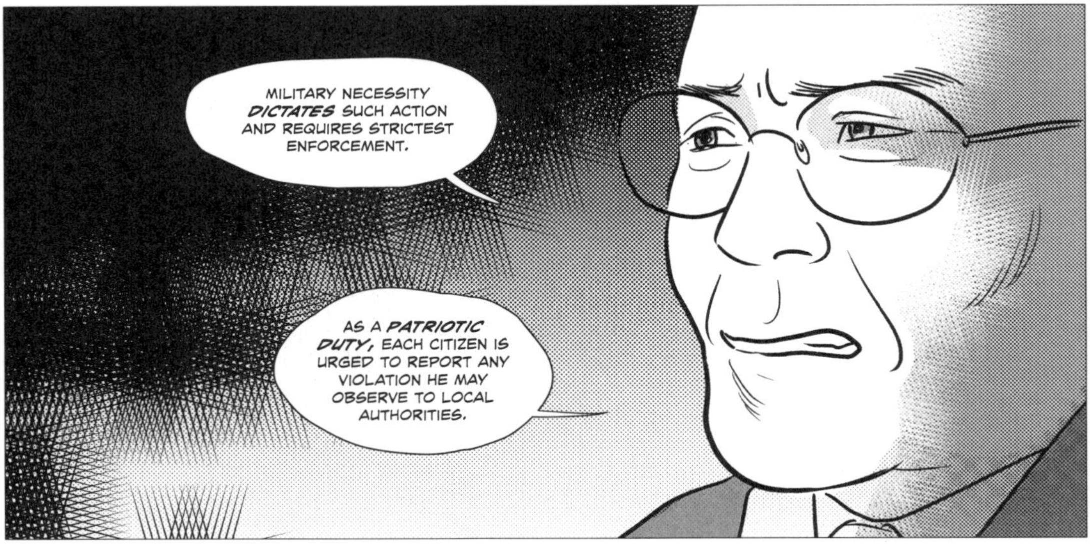
MILITARY NECESSITY *DICTATES* SUCH ACTION AND REQUIRES STRICTEST ENFORCEMENT.
AS A *PATRIOTIC DUTY,* EACH CITIZEN IS URGED TO REPORT ANY VIOLATION HE MAY OBSERVE TO LOCAL AUTHORITIES.

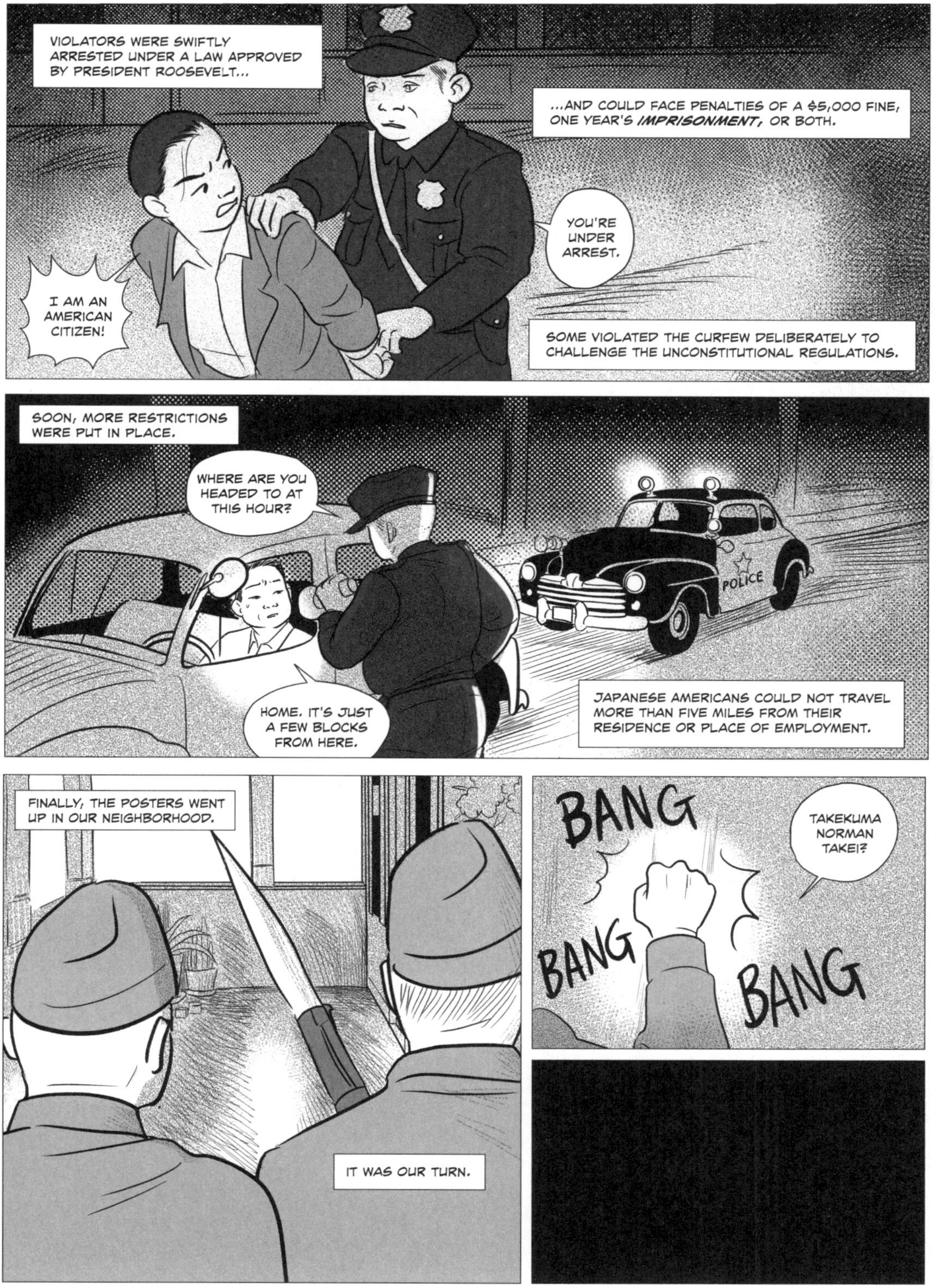
VIOLATORS WERE SWIFTLY ARRESTED UNDER A LAW APPROVED BY PRESIDENT ROOSEVELT...
...AND COULD FACE PENALTIES OF A $5,000 FINE, ONE YEAR'S *IMPRISONMENT*, OR BOTH.
YOU'RE UNDER ARREST.
I AM AN AMERICAN CITIZEN!
SOME VIOLATED THE CURFEW DELIBERATELY TO CHALLENGE THE UNCONSTITUTIONAL REGULATIONS.
SOON, MORE RESTRICTIONS WERE PUT IN PLACE.
WHERE ARE YOU HEADED TO AT THIS HOUR?
POLICE
HOME. IT'S JUST A FEW BLOCKS FROM HERE.
JAPANESE AMERICANS COULD NOT TRAVEL MORE THAN FIVE MILES FROM THEIR RESIDENCE OR PLACE OF EMPLOYMENT.
FINALLY, THE POSTERS WENT UP IN OUR NEIGHBORHOOD.
IT WAS OUR TURN.
BANG
TAKEKUMA NORMAN TAKEI?
BANG
BANG

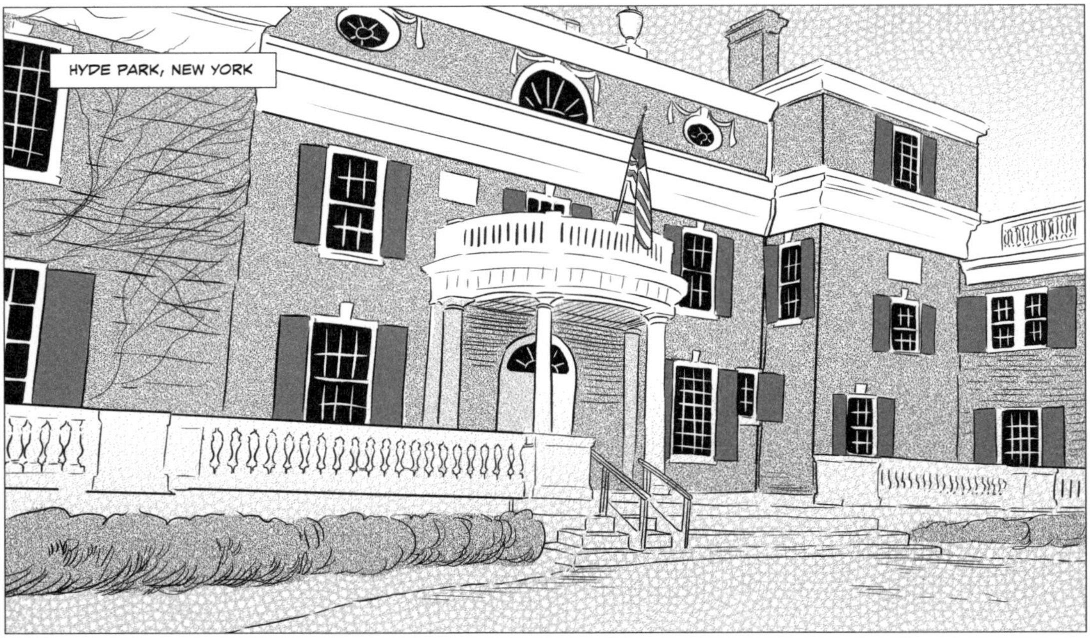
HYDE PARK, NEW YORK

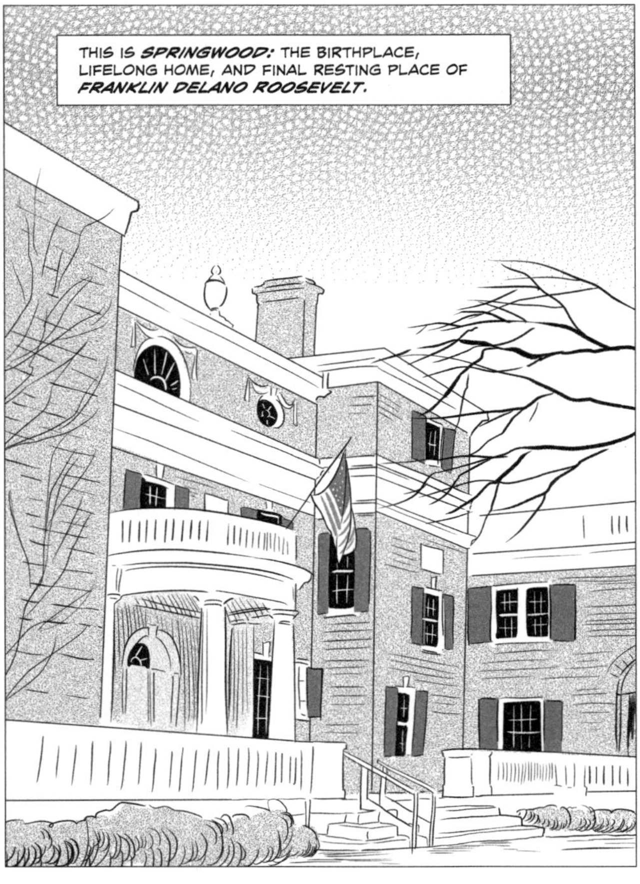
THIS IS SPRINGWOOD: THE BIRTHPLACE, LIFELONG HOME, AND FINAL RESTING PLACE OF FRANKLIN DELANO ROOSEVELT.

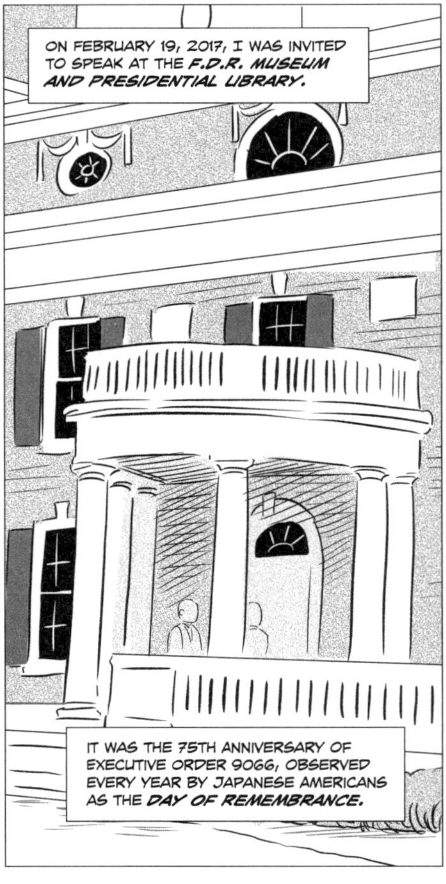
ON FEBRUARY 19, 2017, I WAS INVITED TO SPEAK AT THE F.D.R. MUSEUM AND PRESIDENTIAL LIBRARY.
IT WAS THE 75TH ANNIVERSARY OF EXECUTIVE ORDER 9066, OBSERVED EVERY YEAR BY JAPANESE AMERICANS AS THE DAY OF REMEMBRANCE.

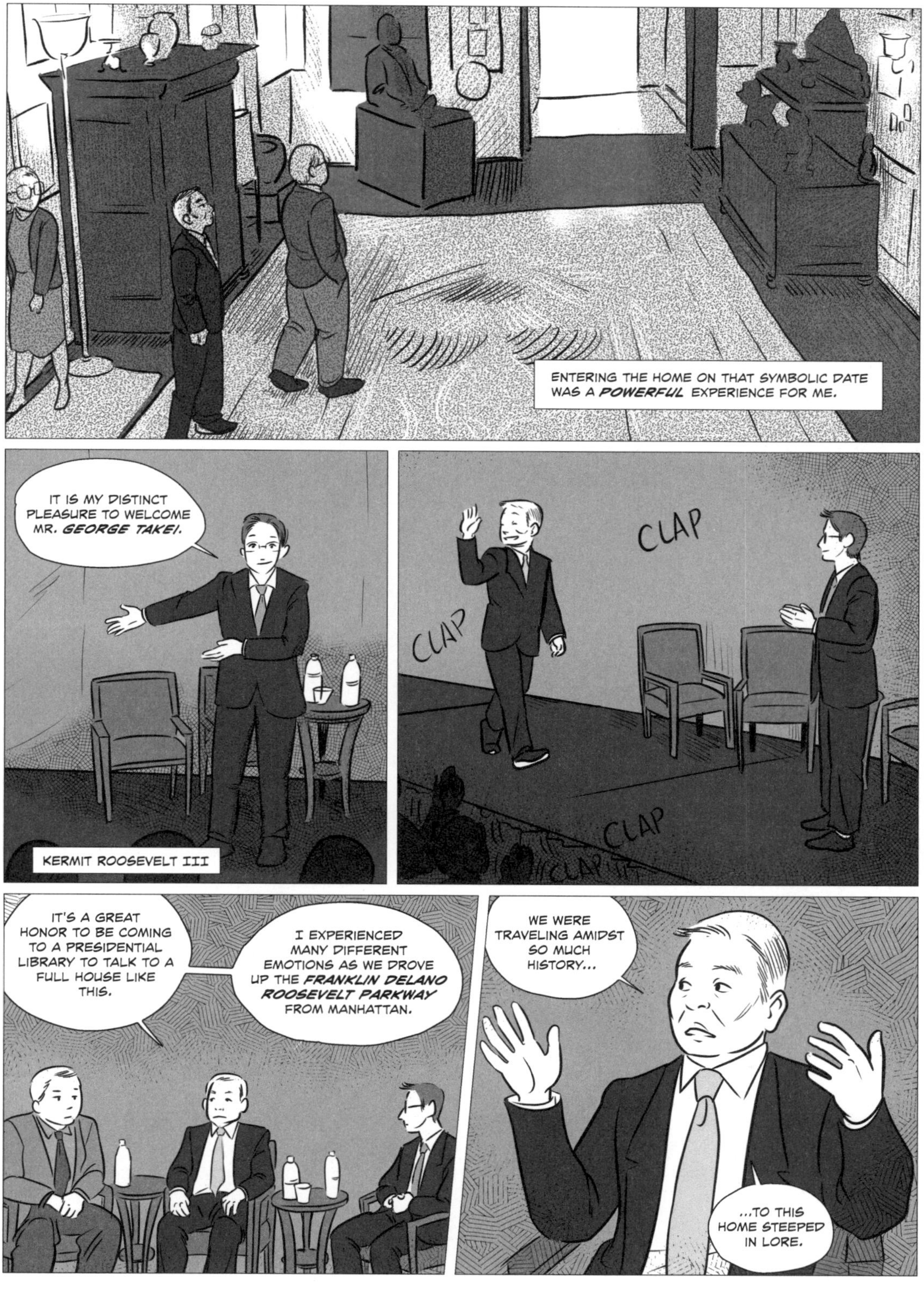
ENTERING THE HOME ON THAT SYMBOLIC DATE WAS A POWERFUL EXPERIENCE FOR ME.
IT IS MY DISTINCT PLEASURE TO WELCOME MR. GEORGE TAKEI.
KERMIT ROOSEVELT III
CLAP
CLAP
CLAP
CLAP
IT'S A GREAT HONOR TO BE COMING TO A PRESIDENTIAL LIBRARY TO TALK TO A FULL HOUSE LIKE THIS.
I EXPERIENCED MANY DIFFERENT EMOTIONS AS WE DROVE UP THE FRANKLIN DELANO ROOSEVELT PARKWAY FROM MANHATTAN.
WE WERE TRAVELING AMIDST SO MUCH HISTORY...
...TO THIS HOME STEEPED IN LORE.

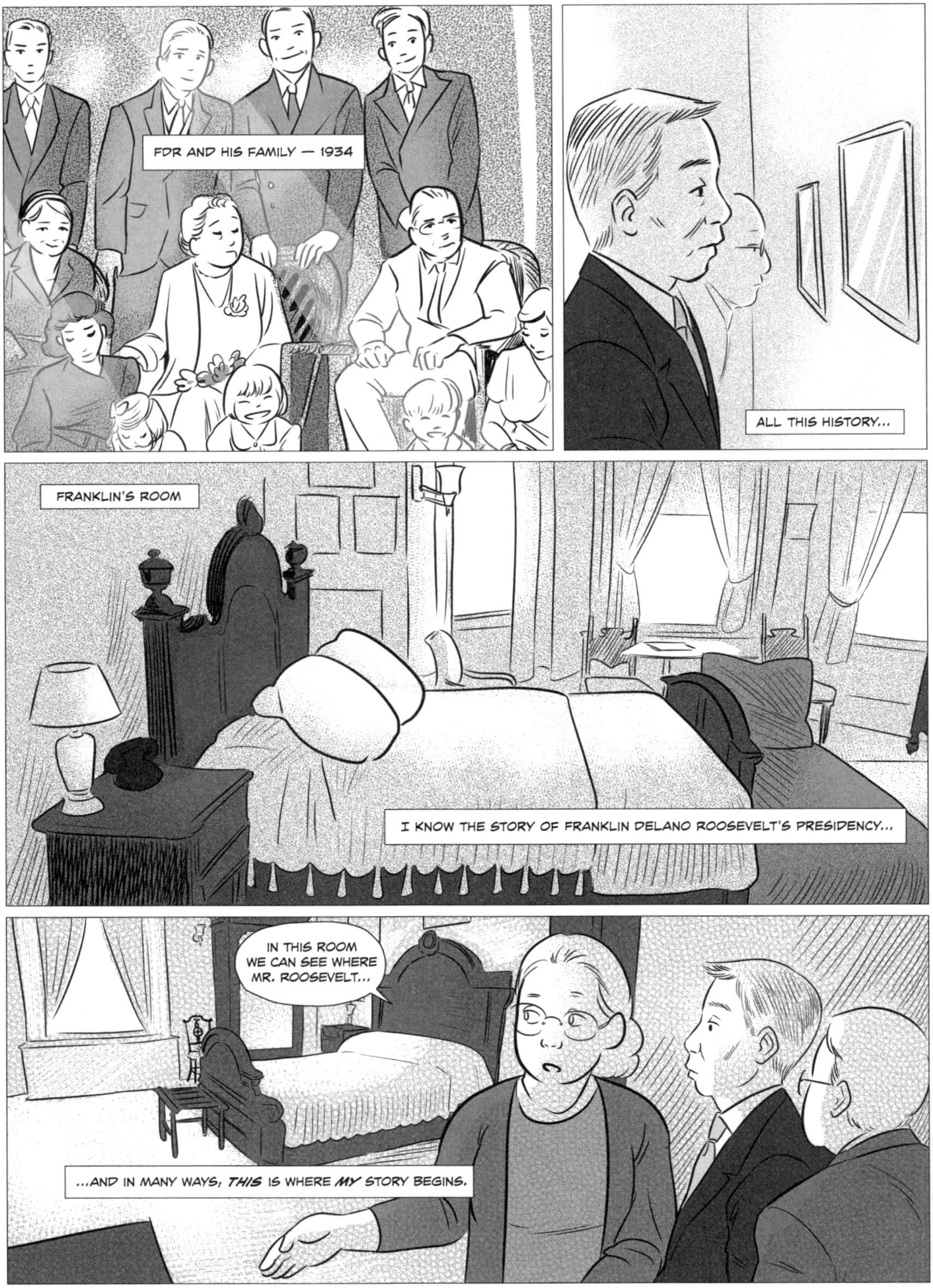
FDR AND HIS FAMILY — 1934
ALL THIS HISTORY...
FRANKLIN'S ROOM
I KNOW THE STORY OF FRANKLIN DELANO ROOSEVELT'S PRESIDENCY...
IN THIS ROOM WE CAN SEE WHERE MR. ROOSEVELT...
...AND IN MANY WAYS, *THIS* IS WHERE *MY* STORY BEGINS.

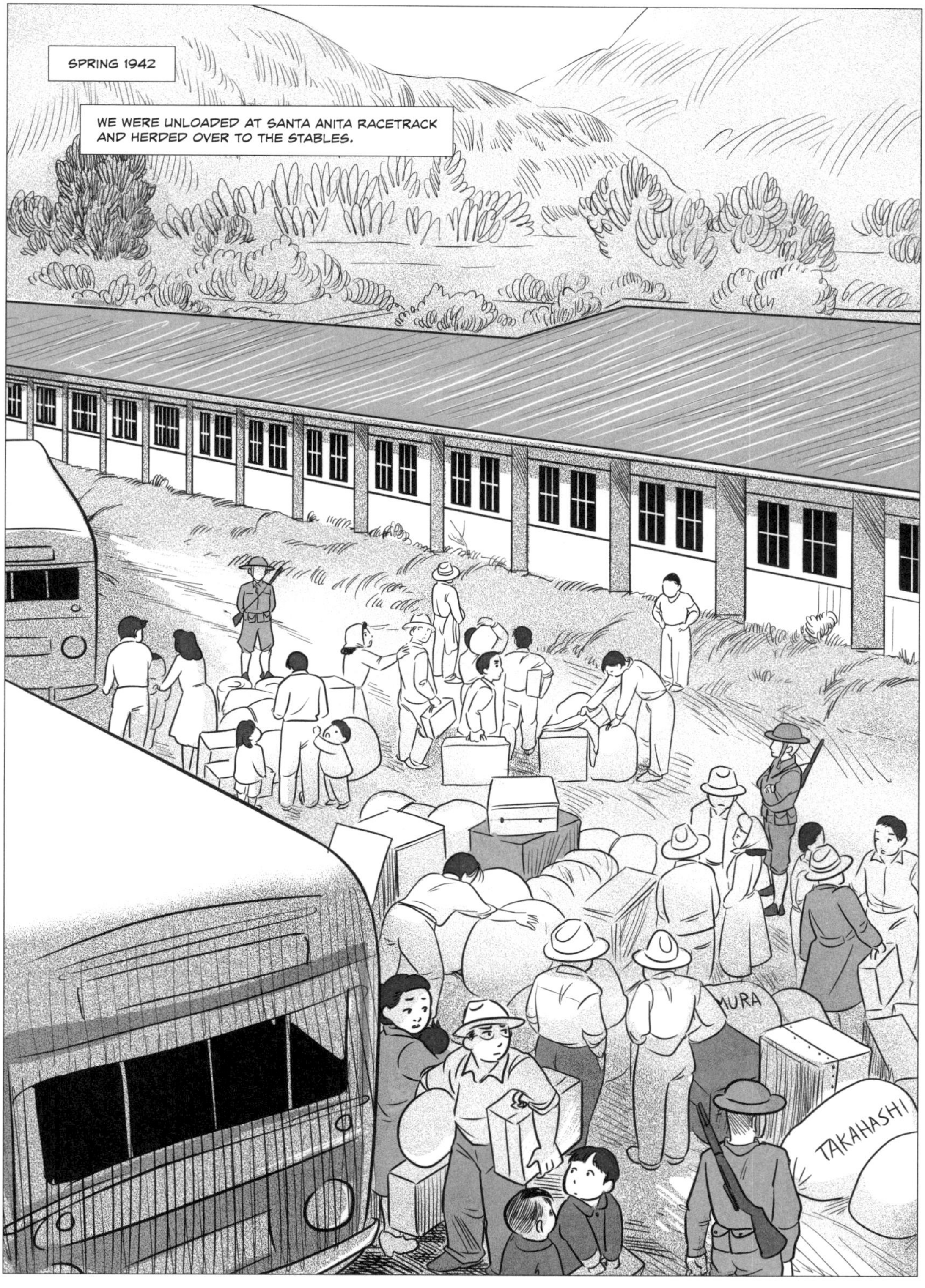
SPRING 1942
WE WERE UNLOADED AT SANTA ANITA RACETRACK AND HERDED OVER TO THE STABLES.
MURA
TAKAHASHI

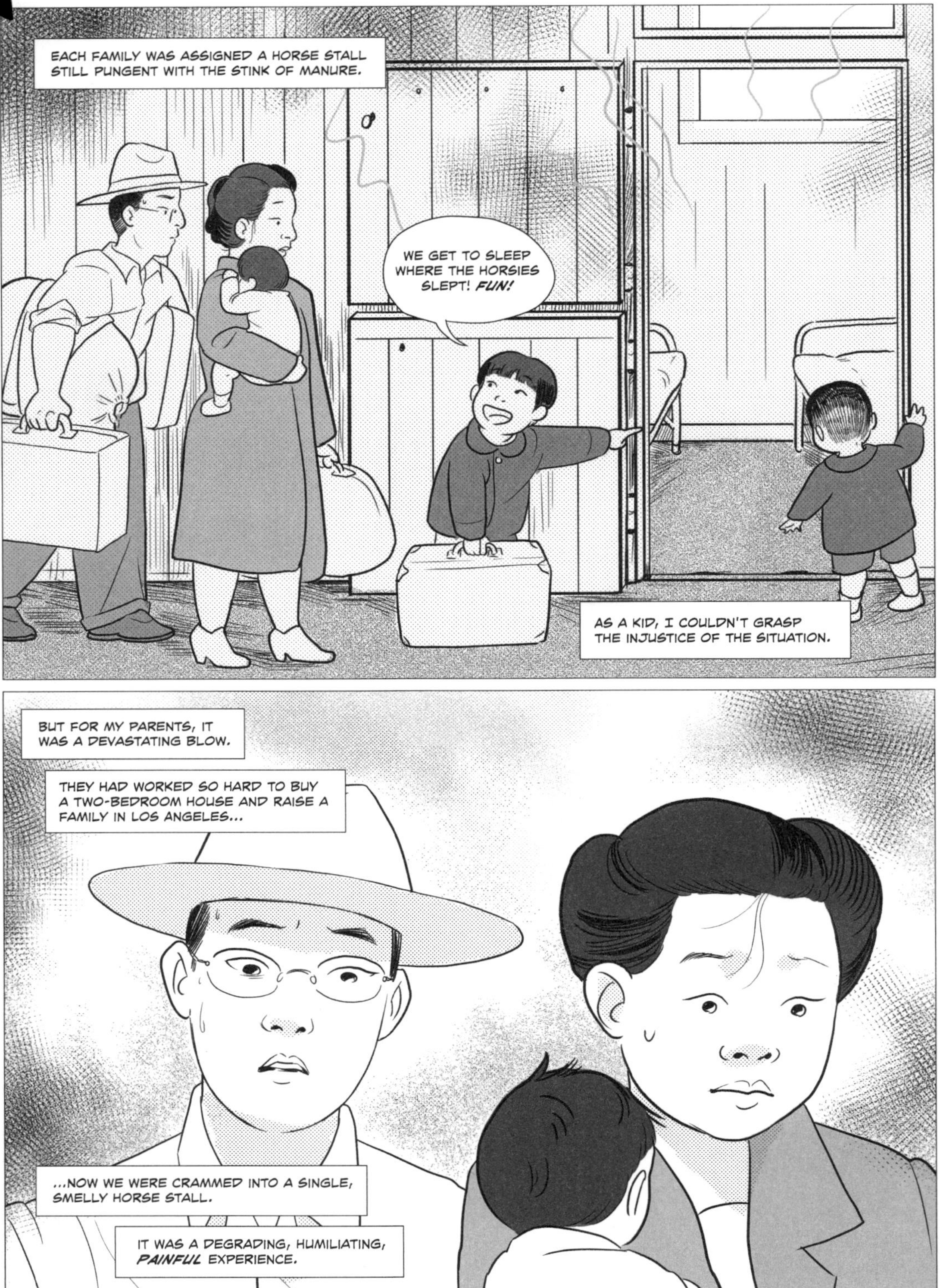
EACH FAMILY WAS ASSIGNED A HORSE STALL STILL PUNGENT WITH THE STINK OF MANURE.
WE GET TO SLEEP WHERE THE HORSIES SLEPT! *FUN!*
AS A KID, I COULDN'T GRASP THE INJUSTICE OF THE SITUATION.
BUT FOR MY PARENTS, IT WAS A DEVASTATING BLOW.
THEY HAD WORKED SO HARD TO BUY A TWO-BEDROOM HOUSE AND RAISE A FAMILY IN LOS ANGELES...
...NOW WE WERE CRAMMED INTO A SINGLE, SMELLY HORSE STALL.
IT WAS A DEGRADING, HUMILIATING, *PAINFUL* EXPERIENCE.

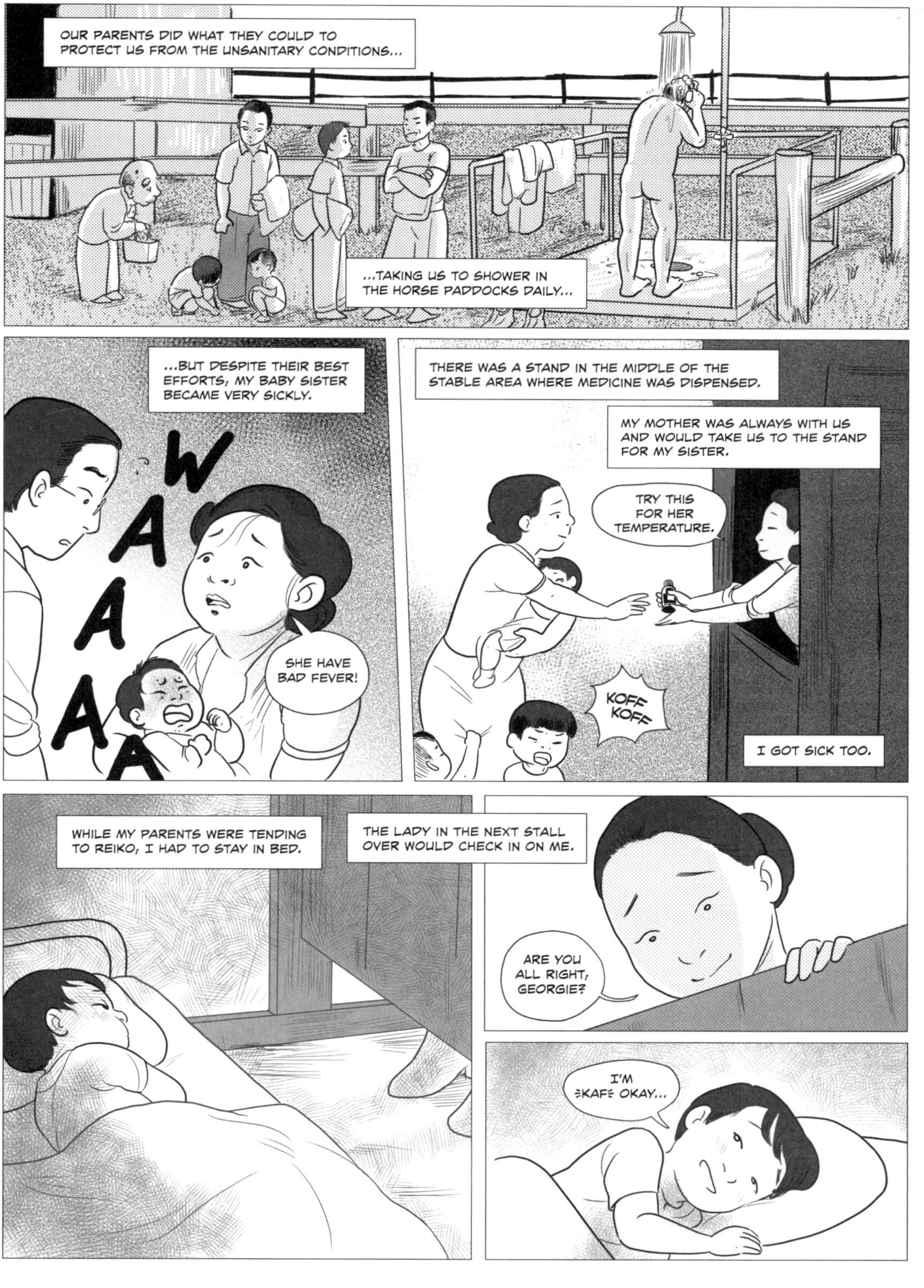
OUR PARENTS DID WHAT THEY COULD TO PROTECT US FROM THE UNSANITARY CONDITIONS...
...TAKING US TO SHOWER IN THE HORSE PADDOCKS DAILY...
...BUT DESPITE THEIR BEST EFFORTS, MY BABY SISTER BECAME VERY SICKLY.
WAAAAA
SHE HAVE BAD FEVER!
THERE WAS A STAND IN THE MIDDLE OF THE STABLE AREA WHERE MEDICINE WAS DISPENSED.
MY MOTHER WAS ALWAYS WITH US AND WOULD TAKE US TO THE STAND FOR MY SISTER.
TRY THIS FOR HER TEMPERATURE.
KOFF KOFF
I GOT SICK TOO.
WHILE MY PARENTS WERE TENDING TO REIKO, I HAD TO STAY IN BED.
THE LADY IN THE NEXT STALL OVER WOULD CHECK IN ON ME.
ARE YOU ALL RIGHT, GEORGIE?
I'M *KAF* OKAY...

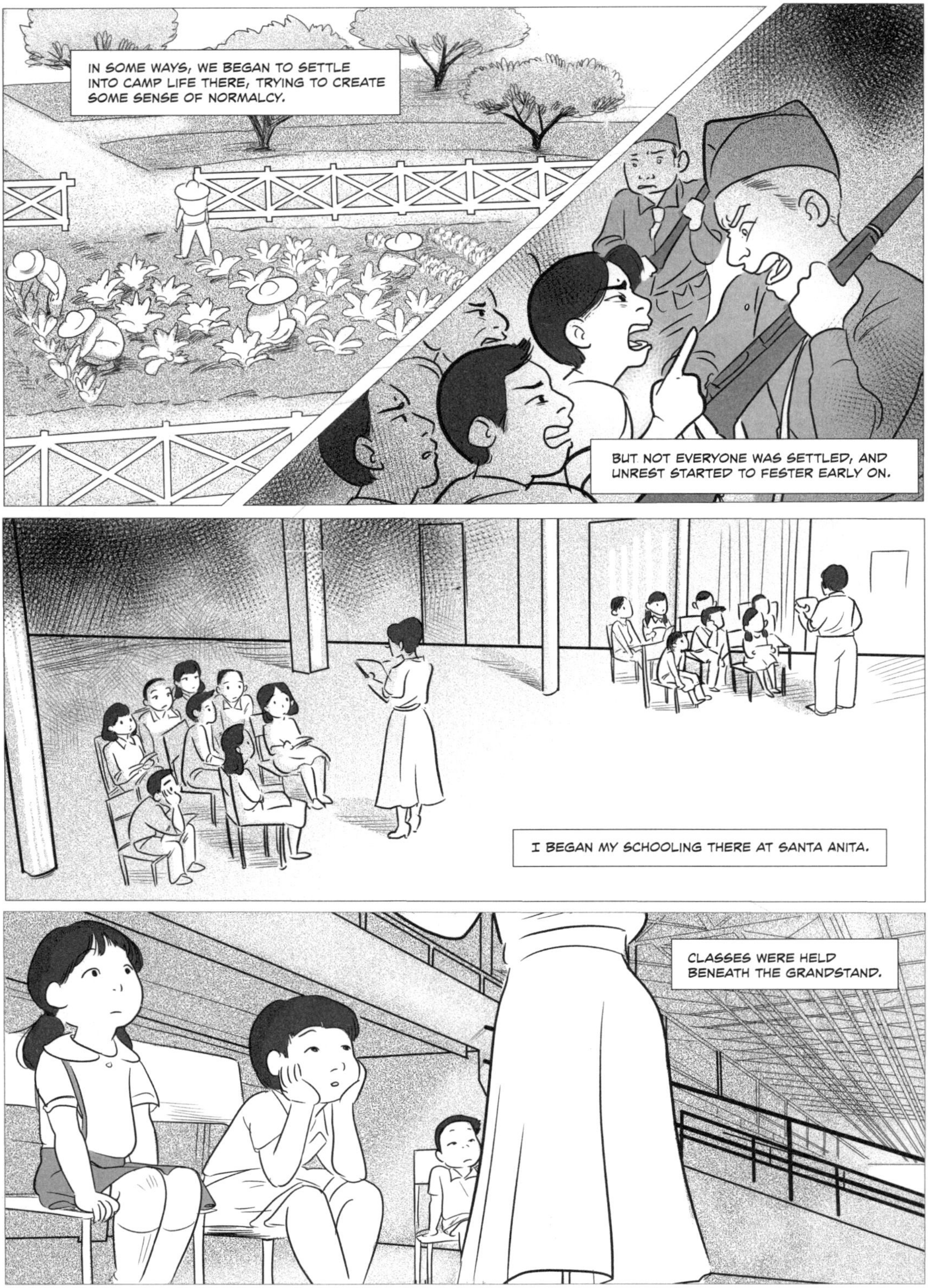
IN SOME WAYS, WE BEGAN TO SETTLE INTO CAMP LIFE THERE, TRYING TO CREATE SOME SENSE OF NORMALCY.
BUT NOT EVERYONE WAS SETTLED, AND UNREST STARTED TO FESTER EARLY ON.
I BEGAN MY SCHOOLING THERE AT SANTA ANITA.
CLASSES WERE HELD BENEATH THE GRANDSTAND.

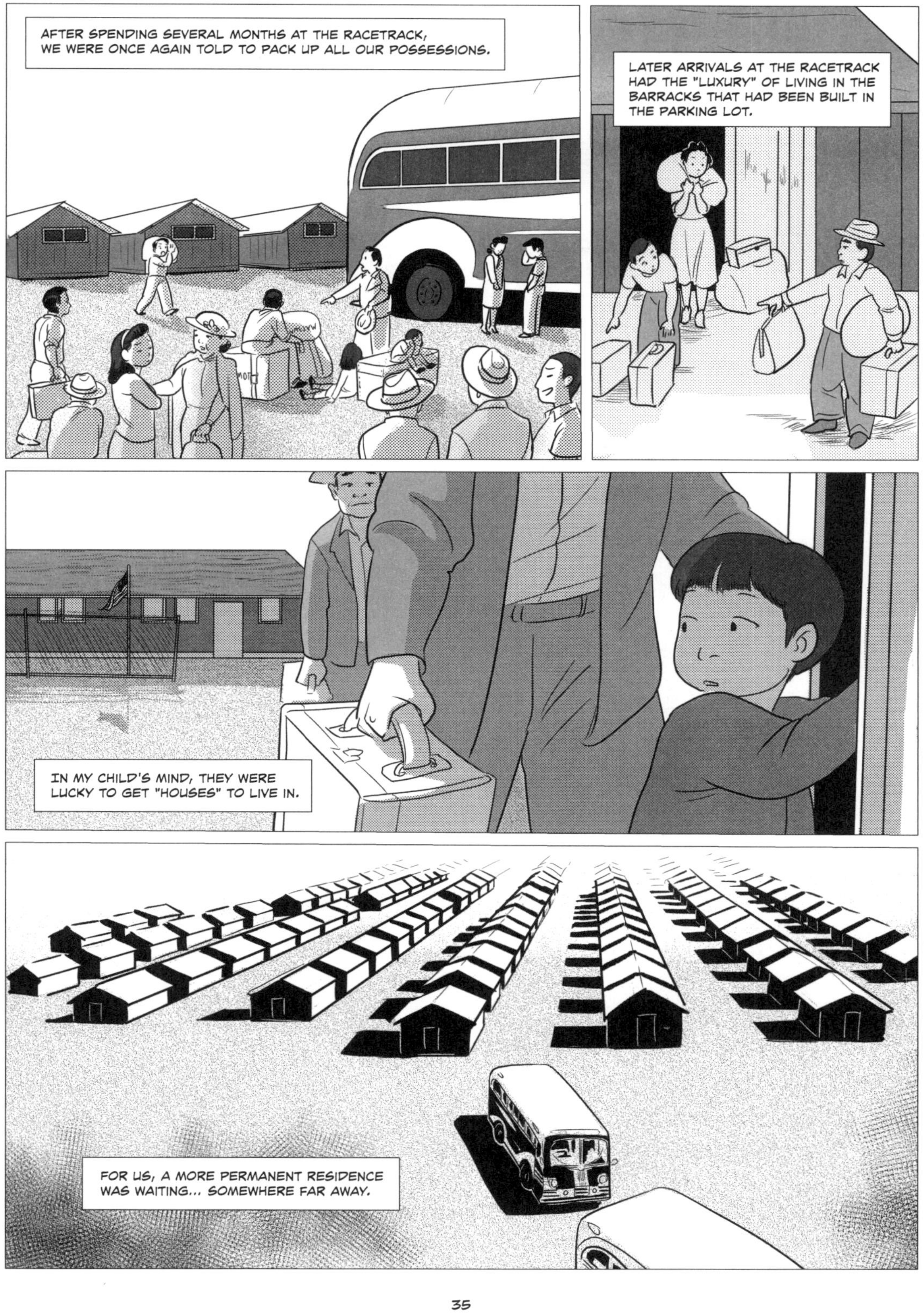
AFTER SPENDING SEVERAL MONTHS AT THE RACETRACK, WE WERE ONCE AGAIN TOLD TO PACK UP ALL OUR POSSESSIONS.
LATER ARRIVALS AT THE RACETRACK HAD THE "LUXURY" OF LIVING IN THE BARRACKS THAT HAD BEEN BUILT IN THE PARKING LOT.
IN MY CHILD'S MIND, THEY WERE LUCKY TO GET "HOUSES" TO LIVE IN.
FOR US, A MORE PERMANENT RESIDENCE WAS WAITING... SOMEWHERE FAR AWAY.

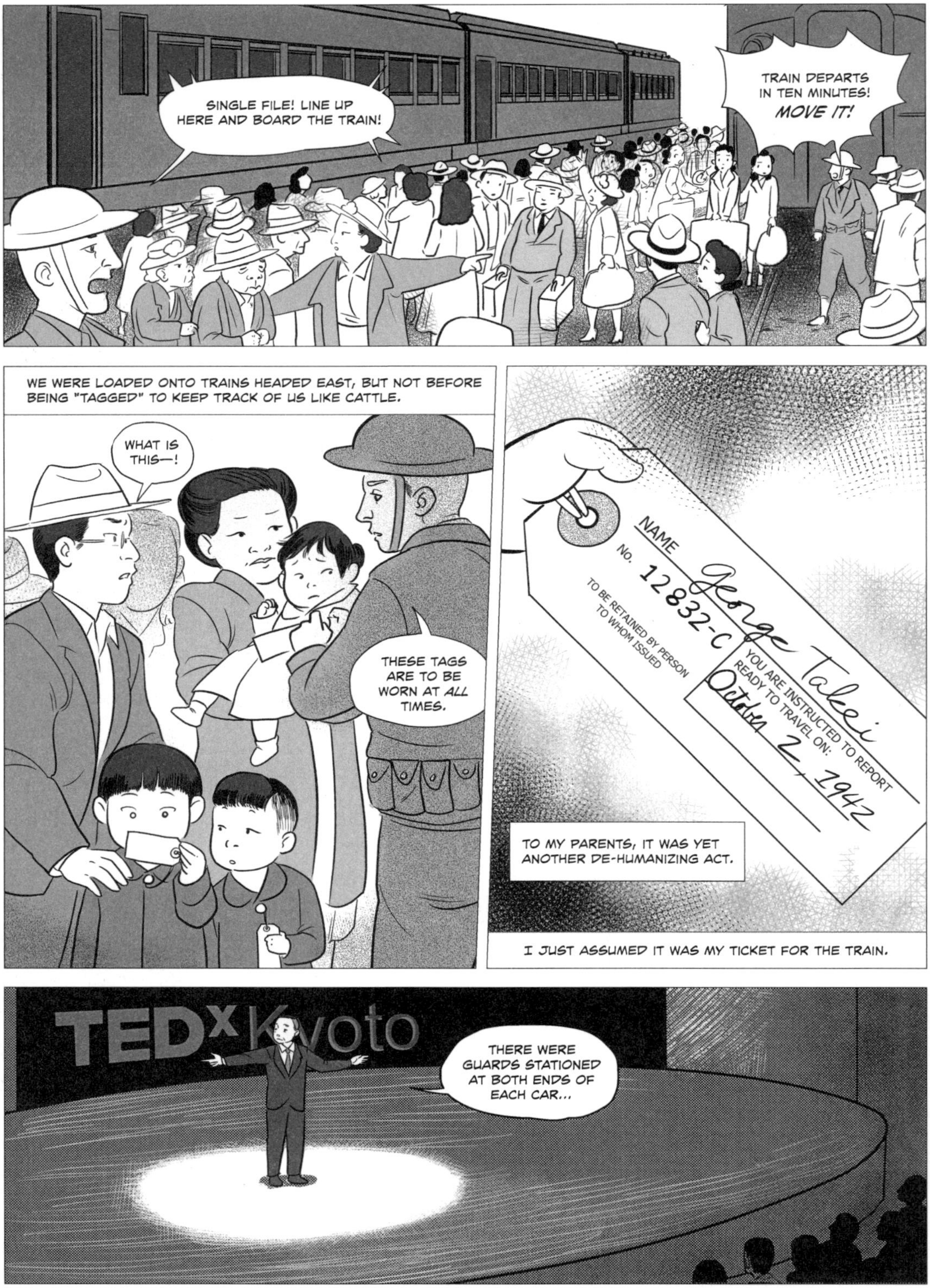

SINGLE FILE! LINE UP HERE AND BOARD THE TRAIN!
TRAIN DEPARTS IN TEN MINUTES! *MOVE IT!*
WE WERE LOADED ONTO TRAINS HEADED EAST, BUT NOT BEFORE BEING "TAGGED" TO KEEP TRACK OF US LIKE CATTLE.
WHAT IS THIS—!
THESE TAGS ARE TO BE WORN AT *ALL* TIMES.
NAME George Takei
No. 12832-C
TO BE RETAINED BY PERSON TO WHOM ISSUED
YOU ARE INSTRUCTED TO REPORT READY TO TRAVEL ON: October 2, 1942
TO MY PARENTS, IT WAS YET ANOTHER DE-HUMANIZING ACT.
I JUST ASSUMED IT WAS MY TICKET FOR THE TRAIN.
TEDx Kyoto
THERE WERE GUARDS STATIONED AT BOTH ENDS OF EACH CAR...

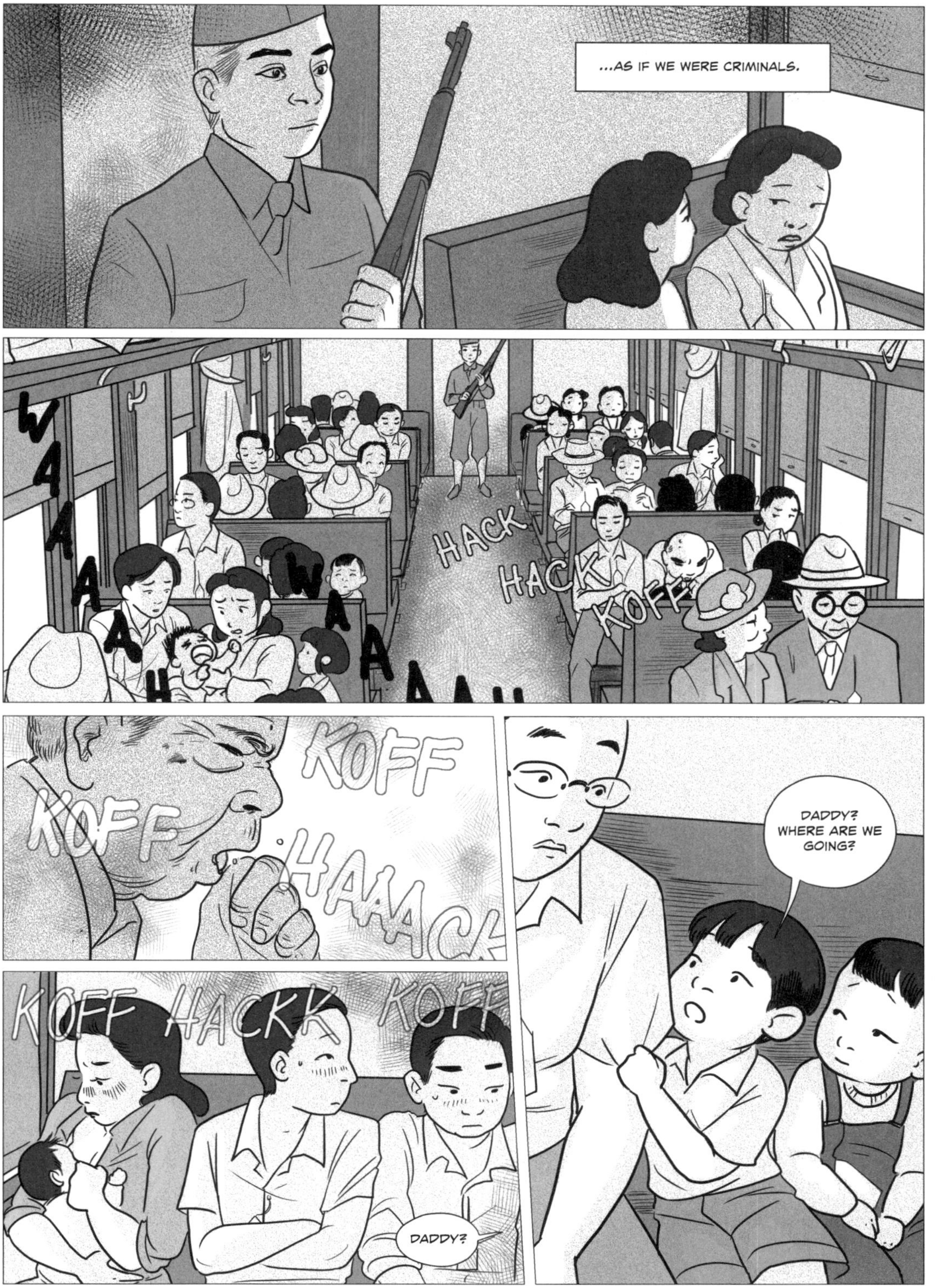

...AS IF WE WERE CRIMINALS.
WAAAAAAH
WAAAAAAH
HACK
HACK
KOFF
KOFF
KOFF
HAAACK
DADDY? WHERE ARE WE GOING?
KOFF HACKK KOFF
DADDY?

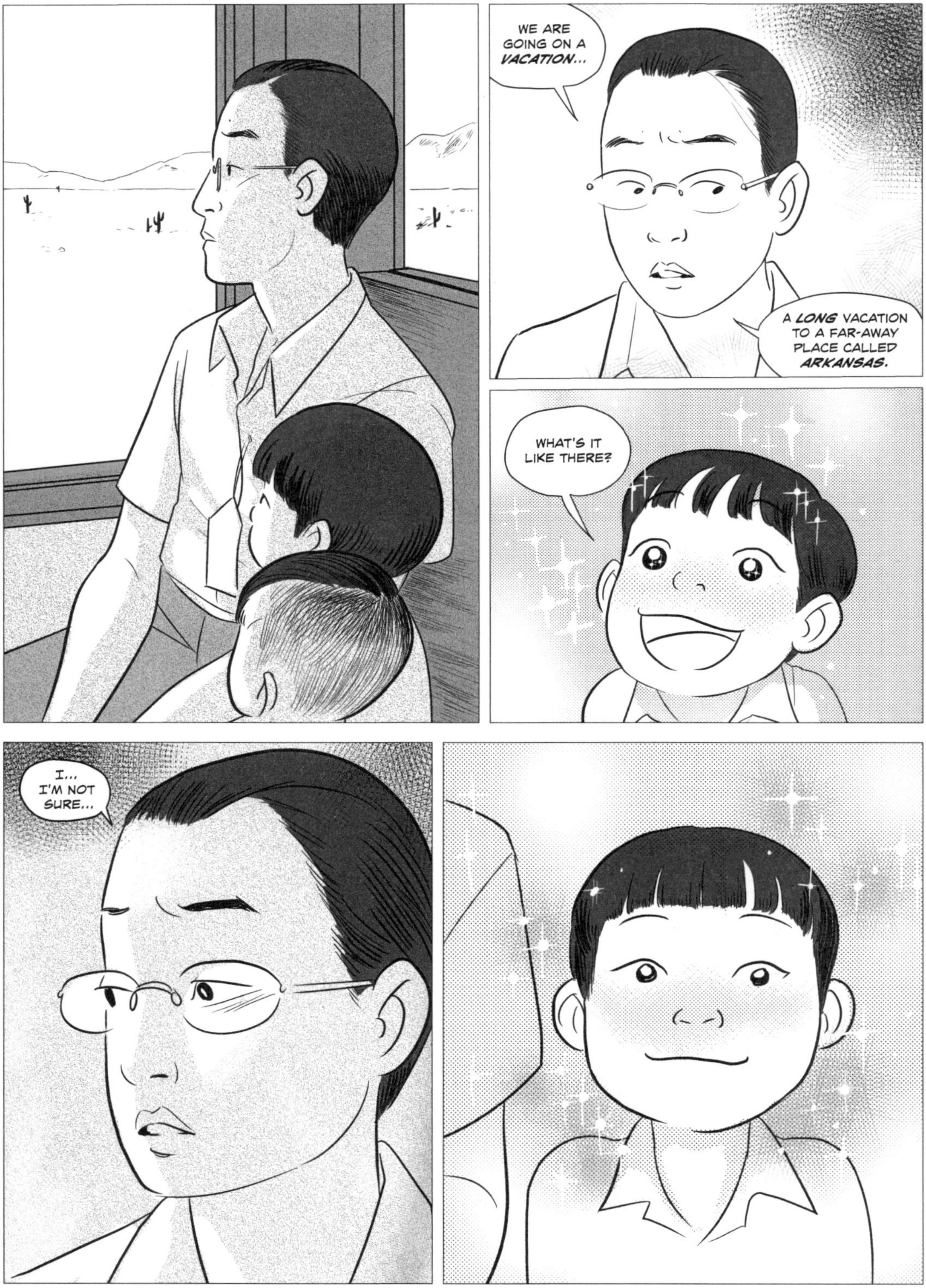
WE ARE GOING ON A *VACATION*...
A *LONG* VACATION TO A FAR-AWAY PLACE CALLED *ARKANSAS.*
WHAT'S IT LIKE THERE?
I... I'M NOT SURE...

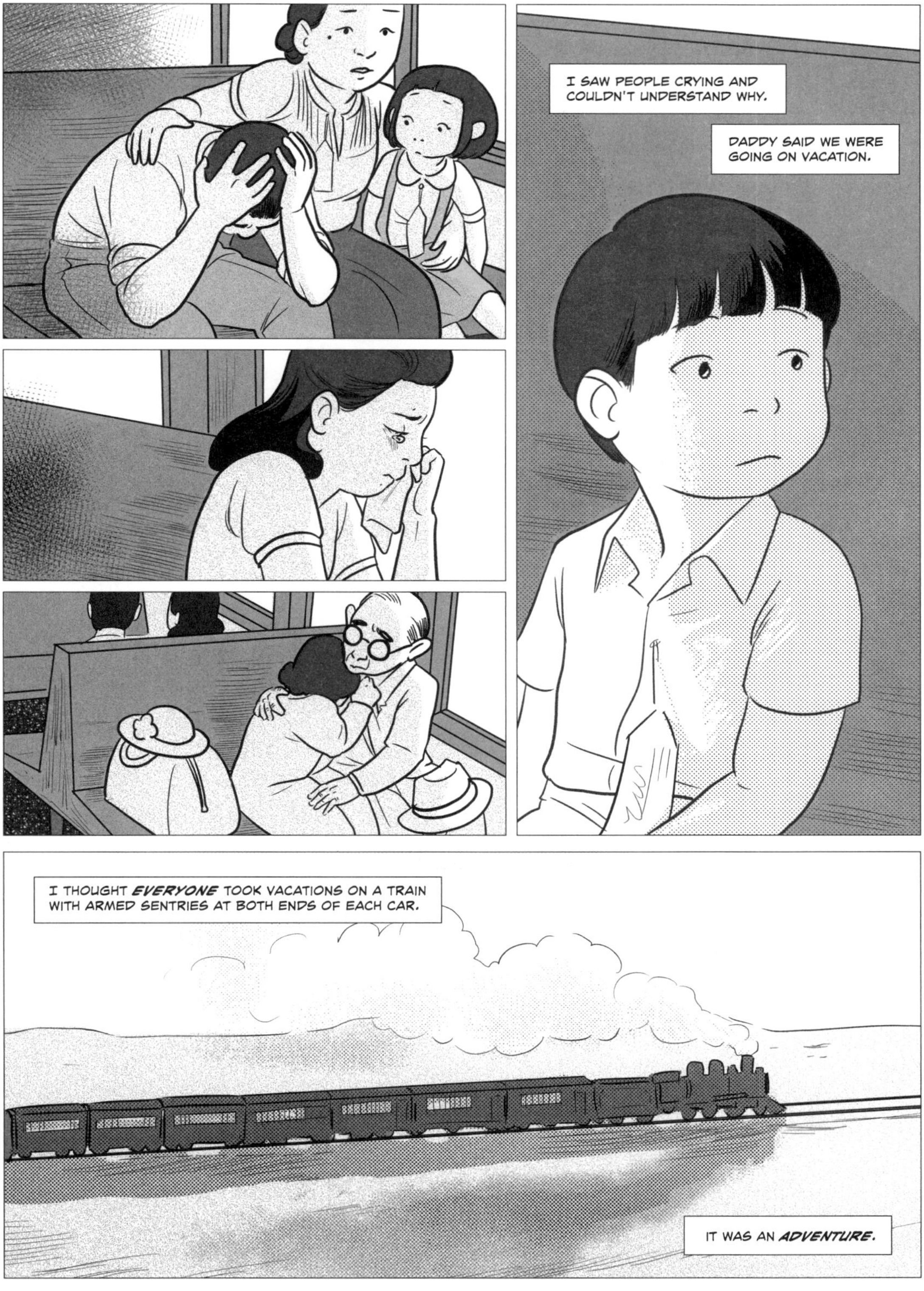
I SAW PEOPLE CRYING AND COULDN'T UNDERSTAND WHY.
DADDY SAID WE WERE GOING ON VACATION.
I THOUGHT *EVERYONE* TOOK VACATIONS ON A TRAIN WITH ARMED SENTRIES AT BOTH ENDS OF EACH CAR.
IT WAS AN *ADVENTURE*.

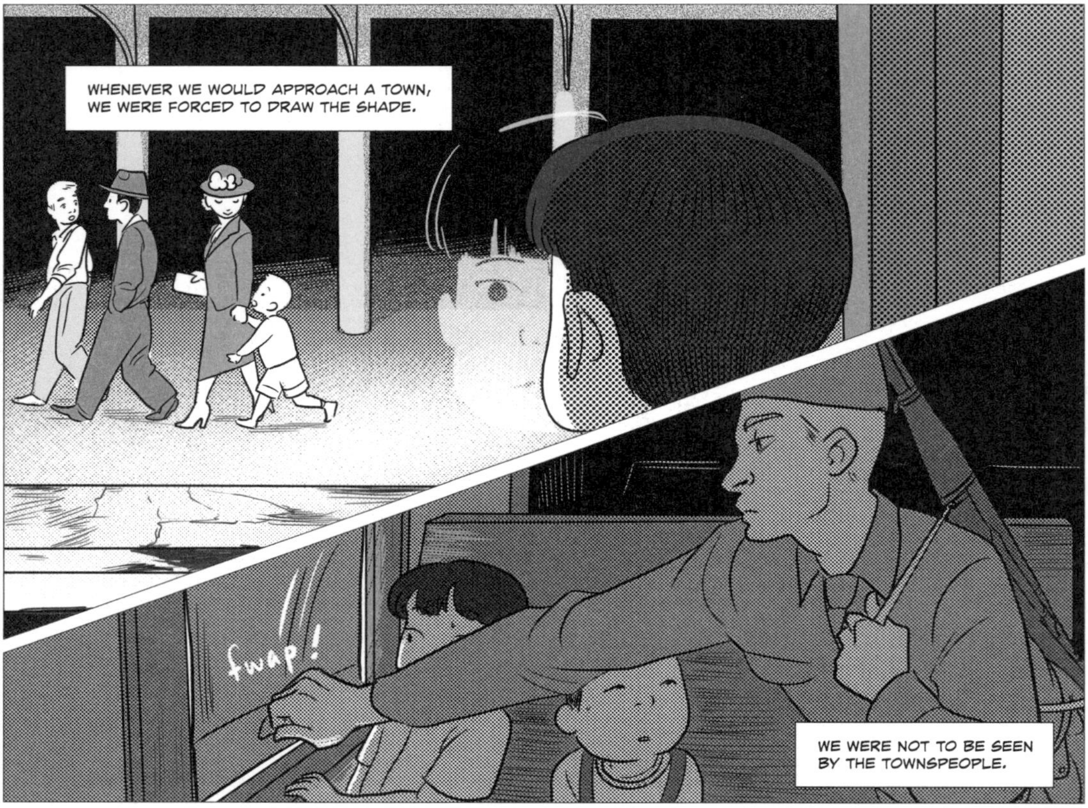
WHENEVER WE WOULD APPROACH A TOWN, WE WERE FORCED TO DRAW THE SHADE.
fwap!
WE WERE NOT TO BE SEEN BY THE TOWNSPEOPLE.

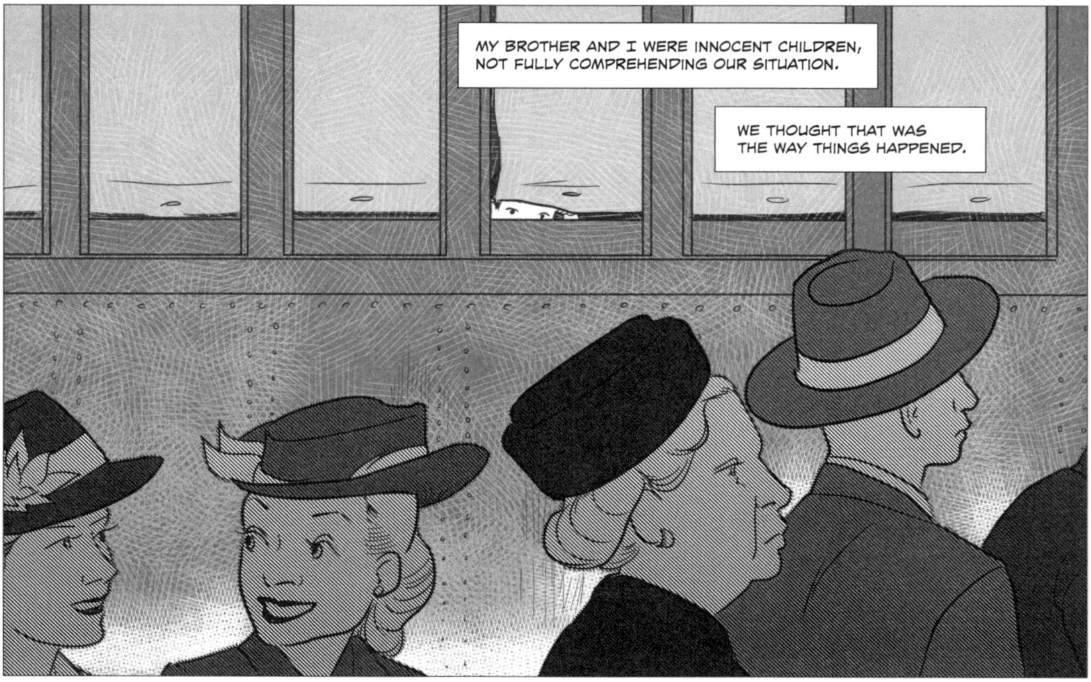
MY BROTHER AND I WERE INNOCENT CHILDREN, NOT FULLY COMPREHENDING OUR SITUATION.
WE THOUGHT THAT WAS THE WAY THINGS HAPPENED.

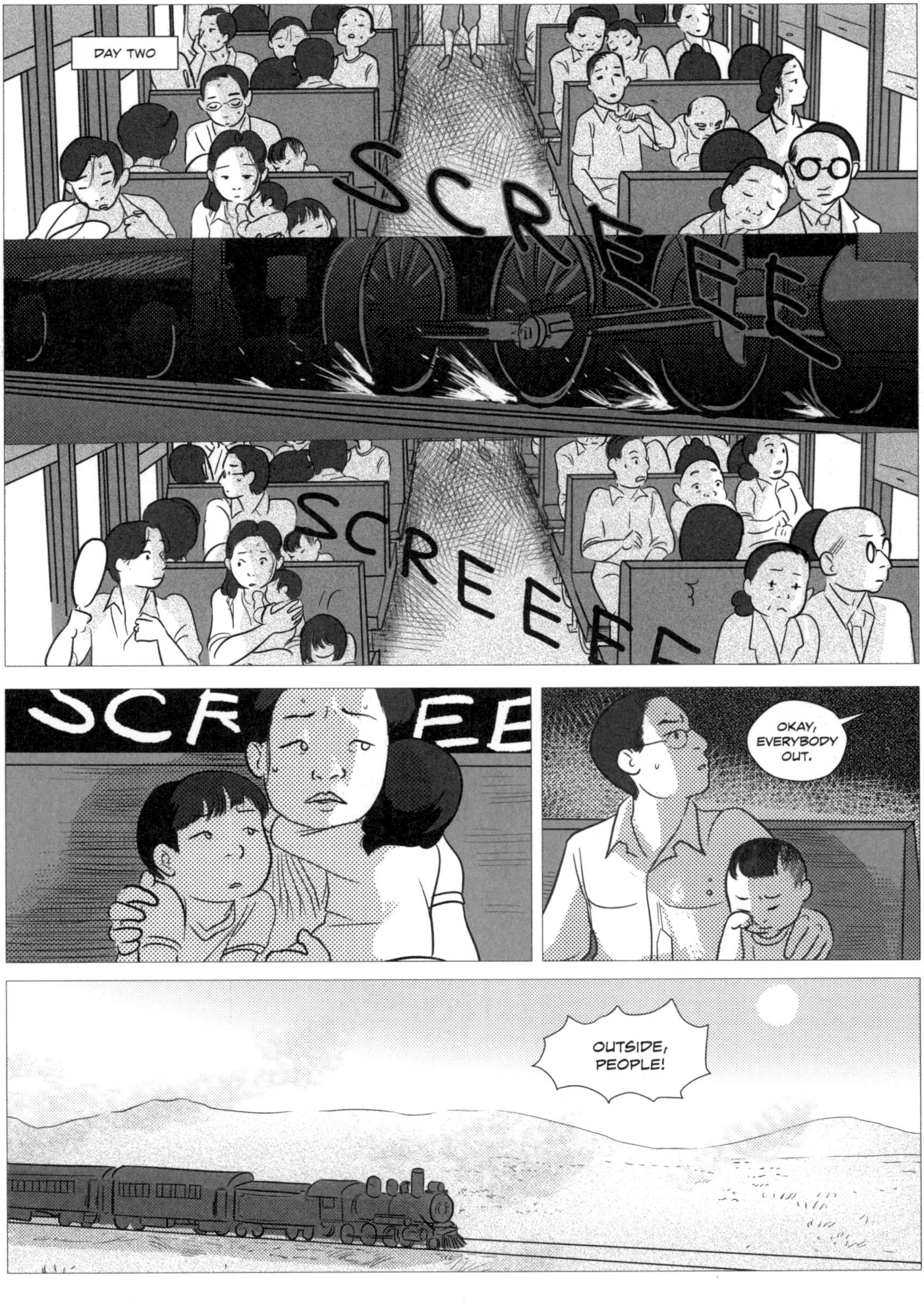
DAY TWO
SCREEEE
SCREEEE
SCREE
OKAY, EVERYBODY OUT.
OUTSIDE, PEOPLE!

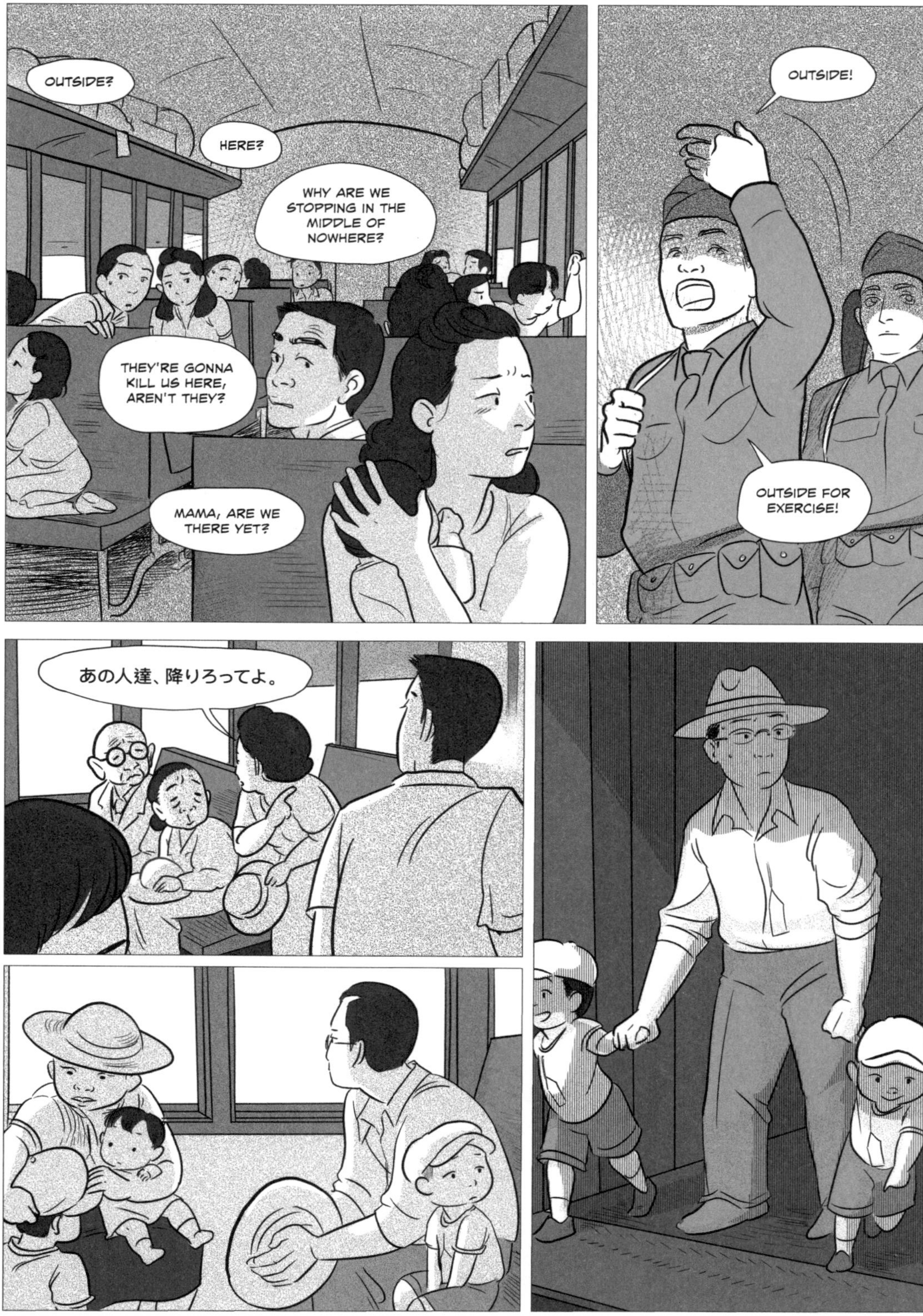
OUTSIDE?
HERE?
WHY ARE WE STOPPING IN THE MIDDLE OF NOWHERE?
THEY'RE GONNA KILL US HERE, AREN'T THEY?
MAMA, ARE WE THERE YET?
OUTSIDE!
OUTSIDE FOR EXERCISE!
あの人達、降りろってよ。

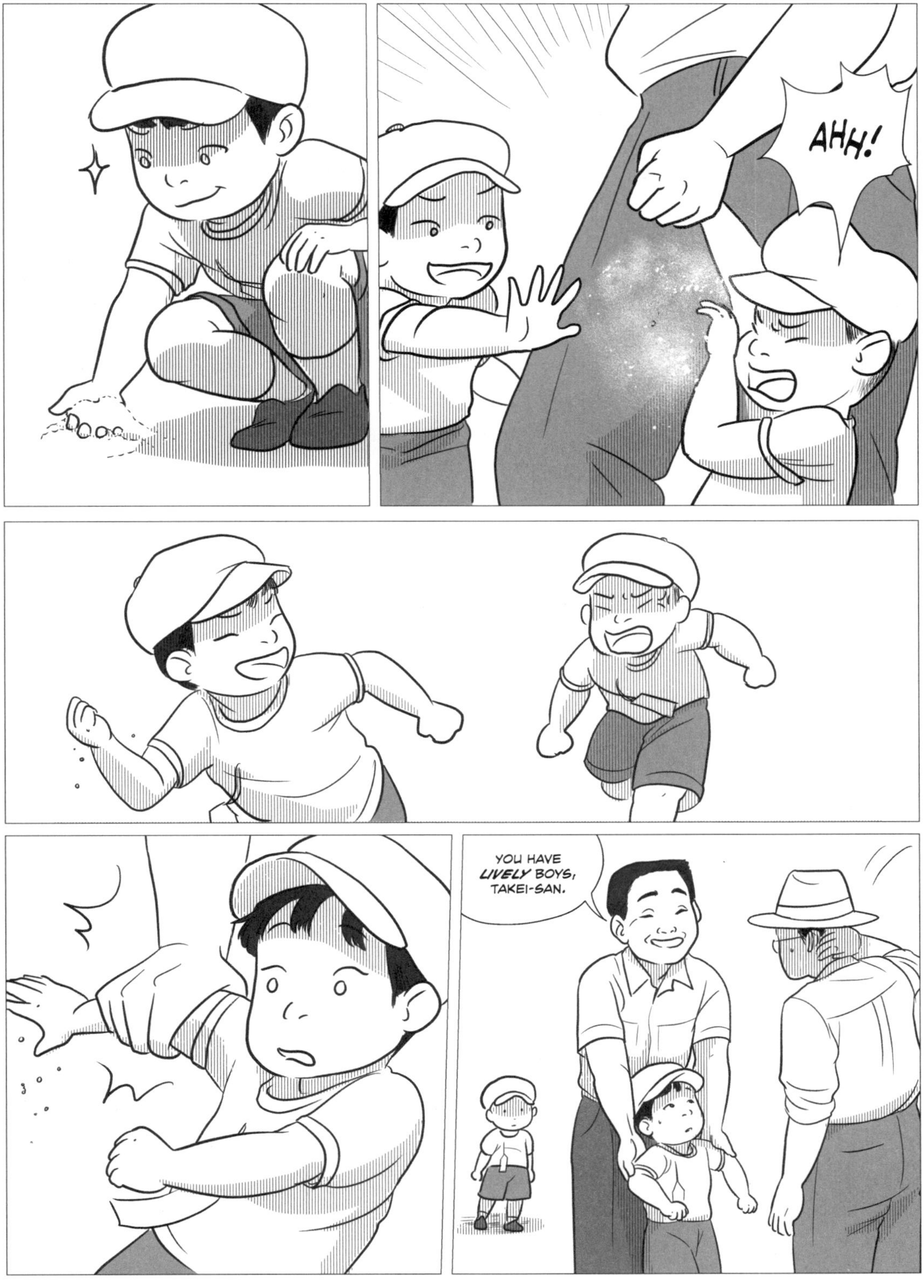
AHH!
YOU HAVE *LIVELY* BOYS, TAKEI-SAN.

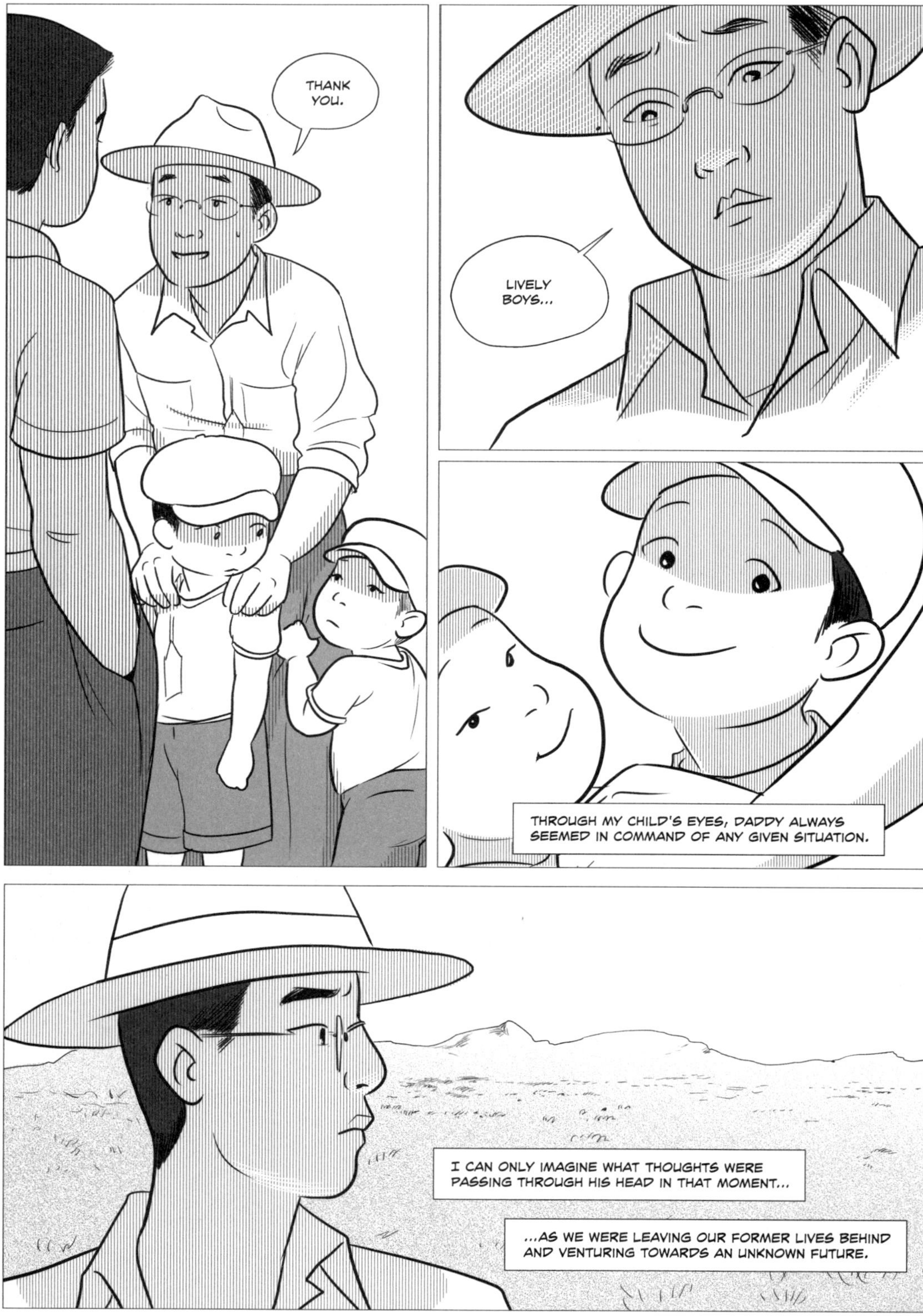
THANK YOU.
LIVELY BOYS...
THROUGH MY CHILD'S EYES, DADDY ALWAYS SEEMED IN COMMAND OF ANY GIVEN SITUATION.
I CAN ONLY IMAGINE WHAT THOUGHTS WERE PASSING THROUGH HIS HEAD IN THAT MOMENT...
...AS WE WERE LEAVING OUR FORMER LIVES BEHIND AND VENTURING TOWARDS AN UNKNOWN FUTURE.

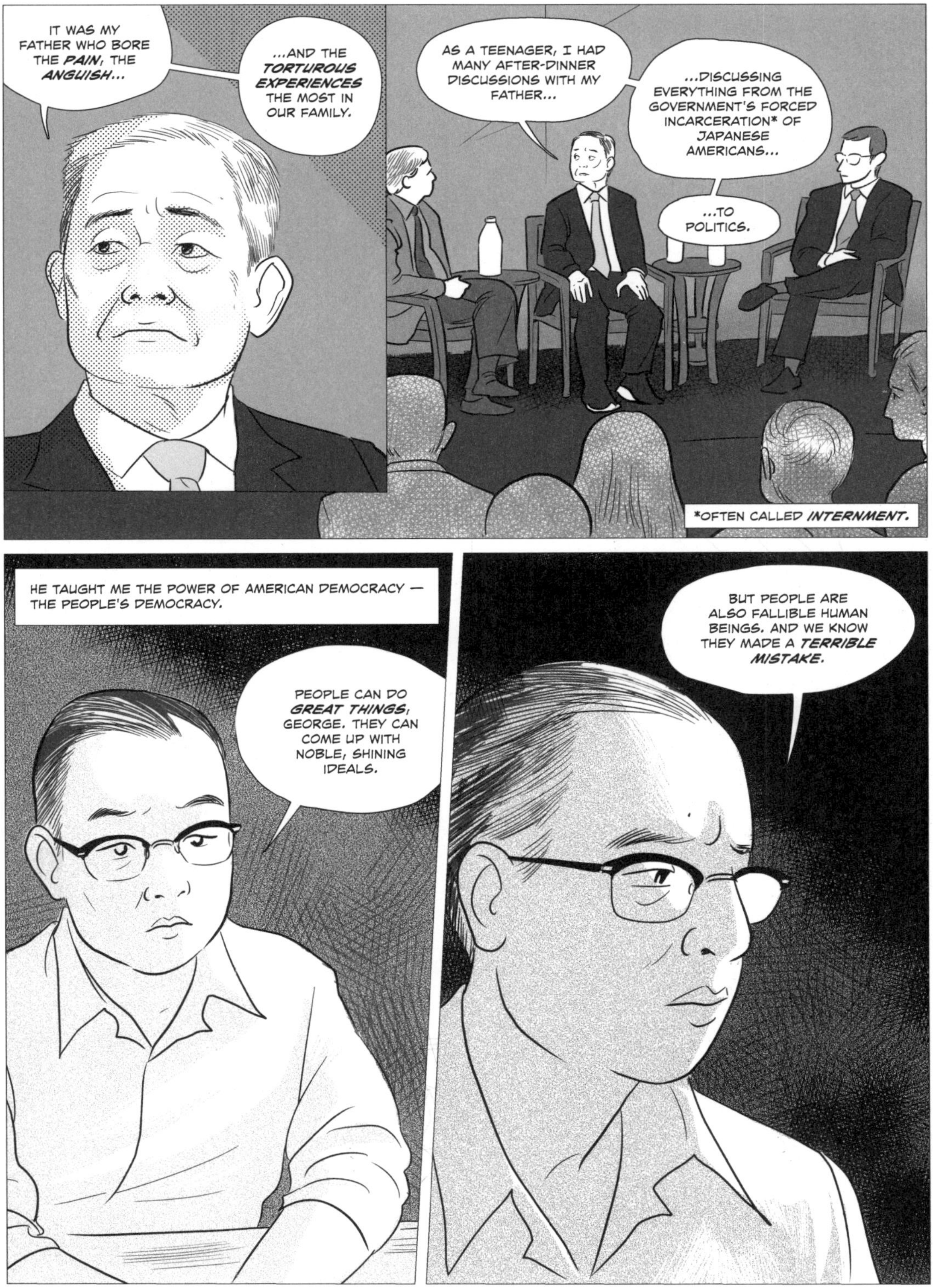
IT WAS MY FATHER WHO BORE THE PAIN, THE ANGUISH...
...AND THE TORTUROUS EXPERIENCES THE MOST IN OUR FAMILY.
AS A TEENAGER, I HAD MANY AFTER-DINNER DISCUSSIONS WITH MY FATHER...
...DISCUSSING EVERYTHING FROM THE GOVERNMENT'S FORCED INCARCERATION* OF JAPANESE AMERICANS...
...TO POLITICS.
*OFTEN CALLED INTERNMENT.
HE TAUGHT ME THE POWER OF AMERICAN DEMOCRACY — THE PEOPLE'S DEMOCRACY.
PEOPLE CAN DO GREAT THINGS, GEORGE. THEY CAN COME UP WITH NOBLE, SHINING IDEALS.
BUT PEOPLE ARE ALSO FALLIBLE HUMAN BEINGS. AND WE KNOW THEY MADE A TERRIBLE MISTAKE.

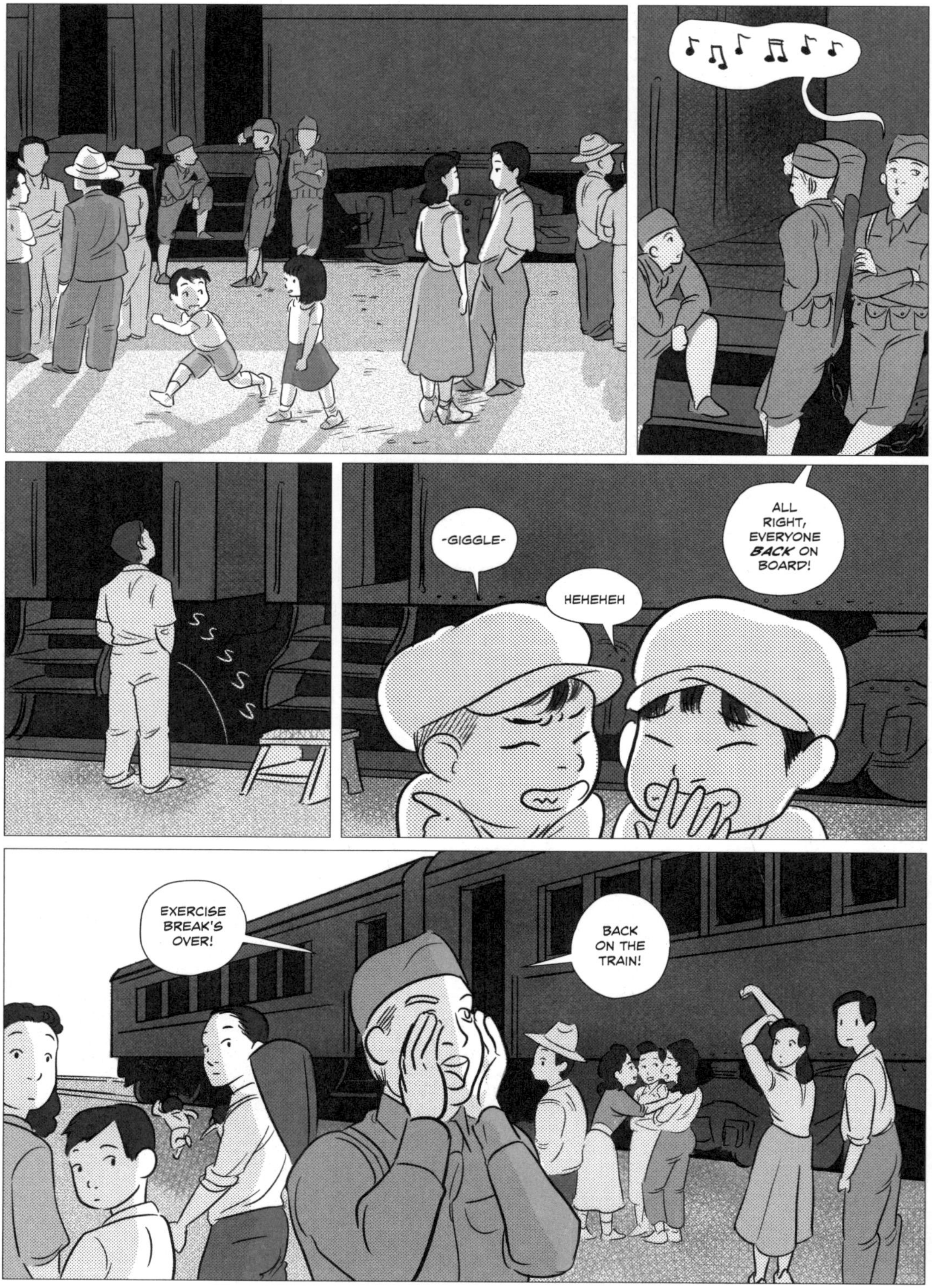

SSSSS
-GIGGLE-
HEHEHEH
ALL RIGHT, EVERYONE BACK ON BOARD!
EXERCISE BREAK'S OVER!
BACK ON THE TRAIN!

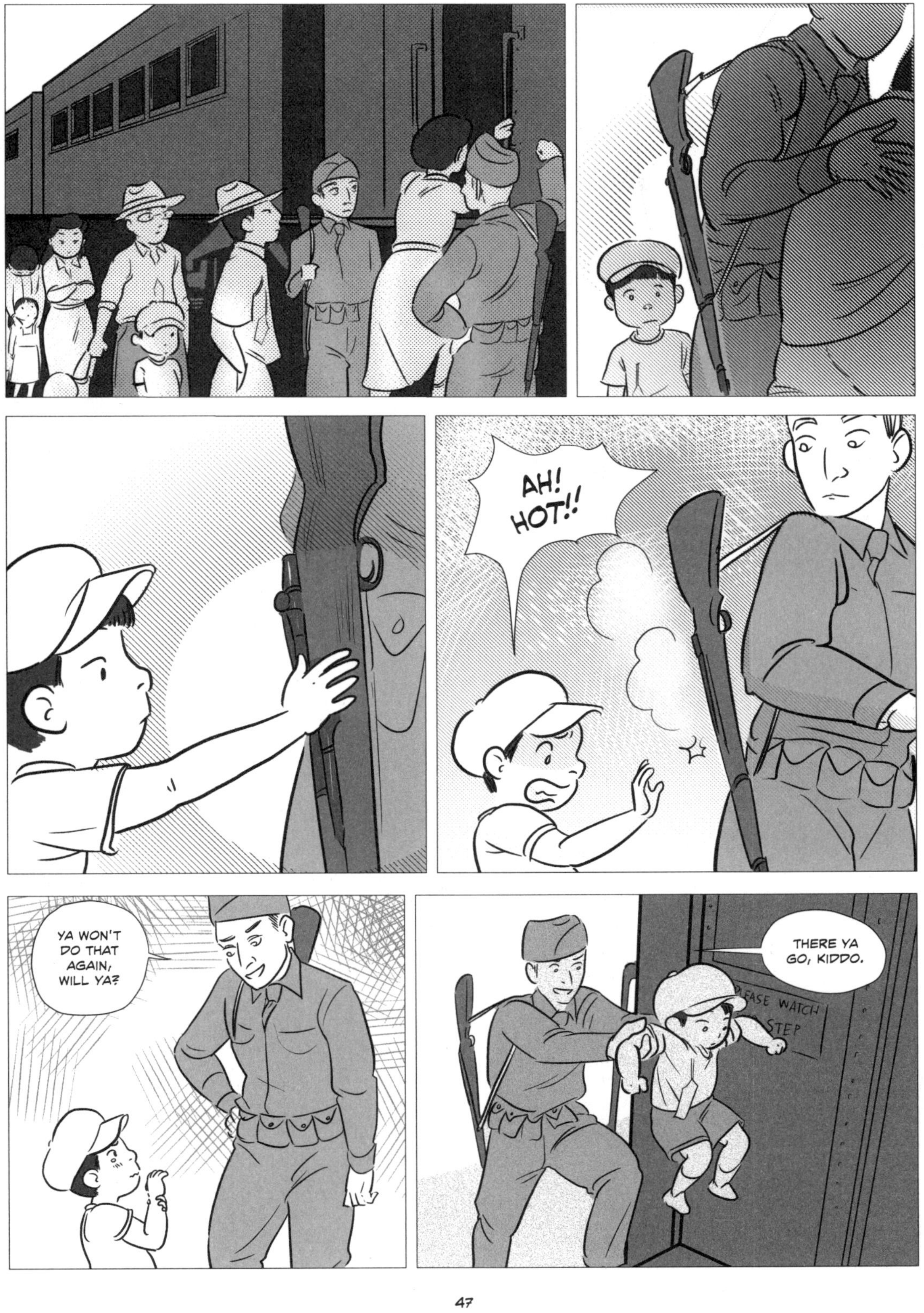
AH! HOT!!
YA WON'T DO THAT AGAIN, WILL YA?
THERE YA GO, KIDDO.

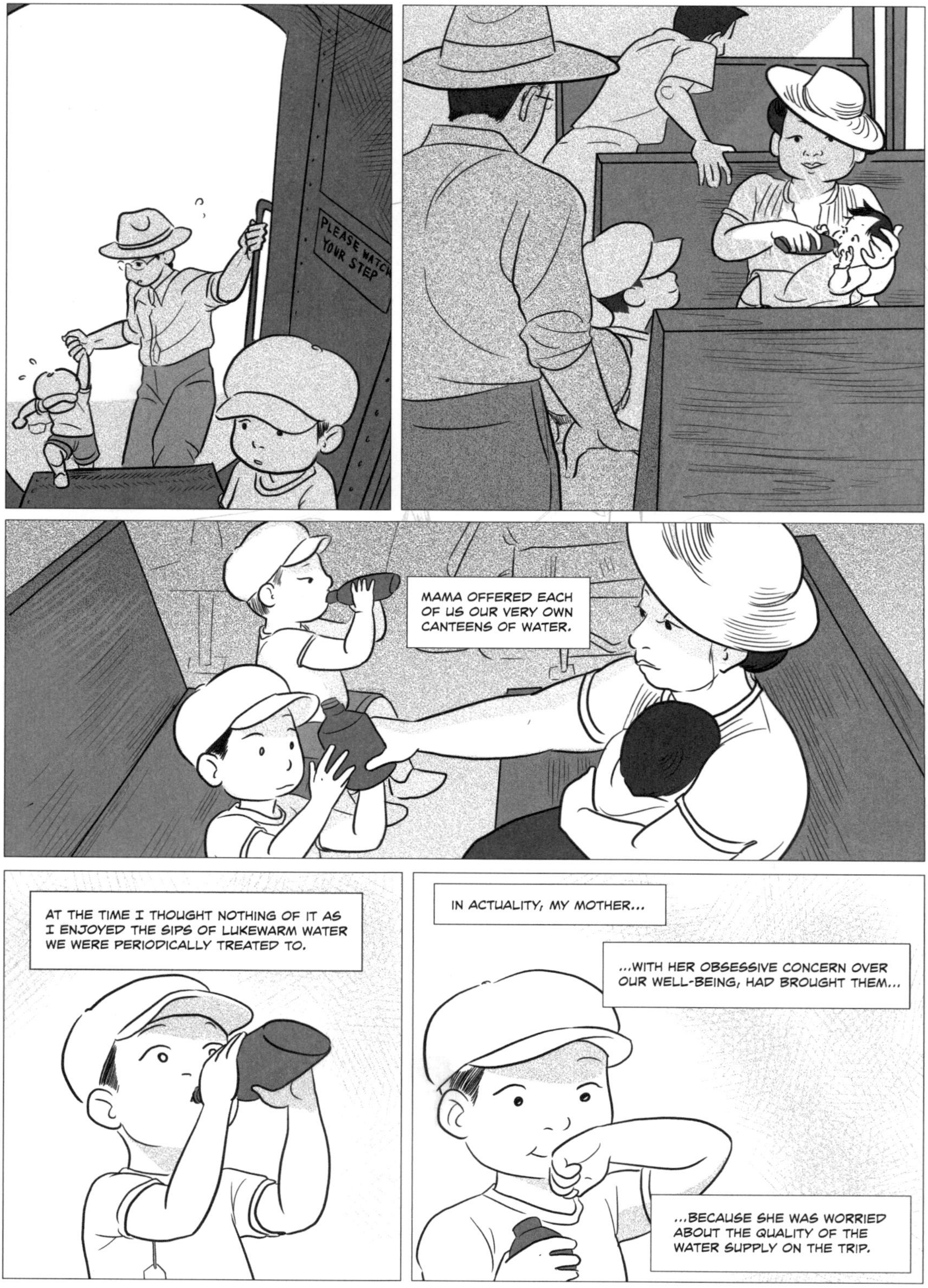
PLEASE WATCH YOUR STEP
MAMA OFFERED EACH OF US OUR VERY OWN CANTEENS OF WATER.
AT THE TIME I THOUGHT NOTHING OF IT AS I ENJOYED THE SIPS OF LUKEWARM WATER WE WERE PERIODICALLY TREATED TO.
IN ACTUALITY, MY MOTHER...
...WITH HER OBSESSIVE CONCERN OVER OUR WELL-BEING, HAD BROUGHT THEM...
...BECAUSE SHE WAS WORRIED ABOUT THE QUALITY OF THE WATER SUPPLY ON THE TRIP.

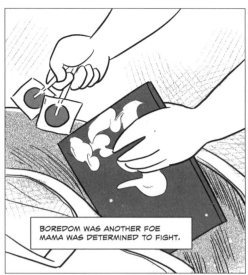

BOREDOM WAS ANOTHER FOE MAMA WAS DETERMINED TO FIGHT.

I HAVE GLOWING RECOLLECTIONS OF HER WONDERFUL BAG OF GOODIES THAT MADE THE TRIP AN UNFORGETTABLE RIDE.

SHE HAD SELFLESSLY STUFFED HER LIMITED LUGGAGE WITH SPECIAL TREATS FOR US.

THIS MADE FOR TWO STARKLY DIFFERENT JOURNEYS:

ONE, AN ADVENTURE OF DISCOVERY...

...THE OTHER, AN ANXIETY-RIDDEN VOYAGE INTO A FEARFUL UNKNOWN.

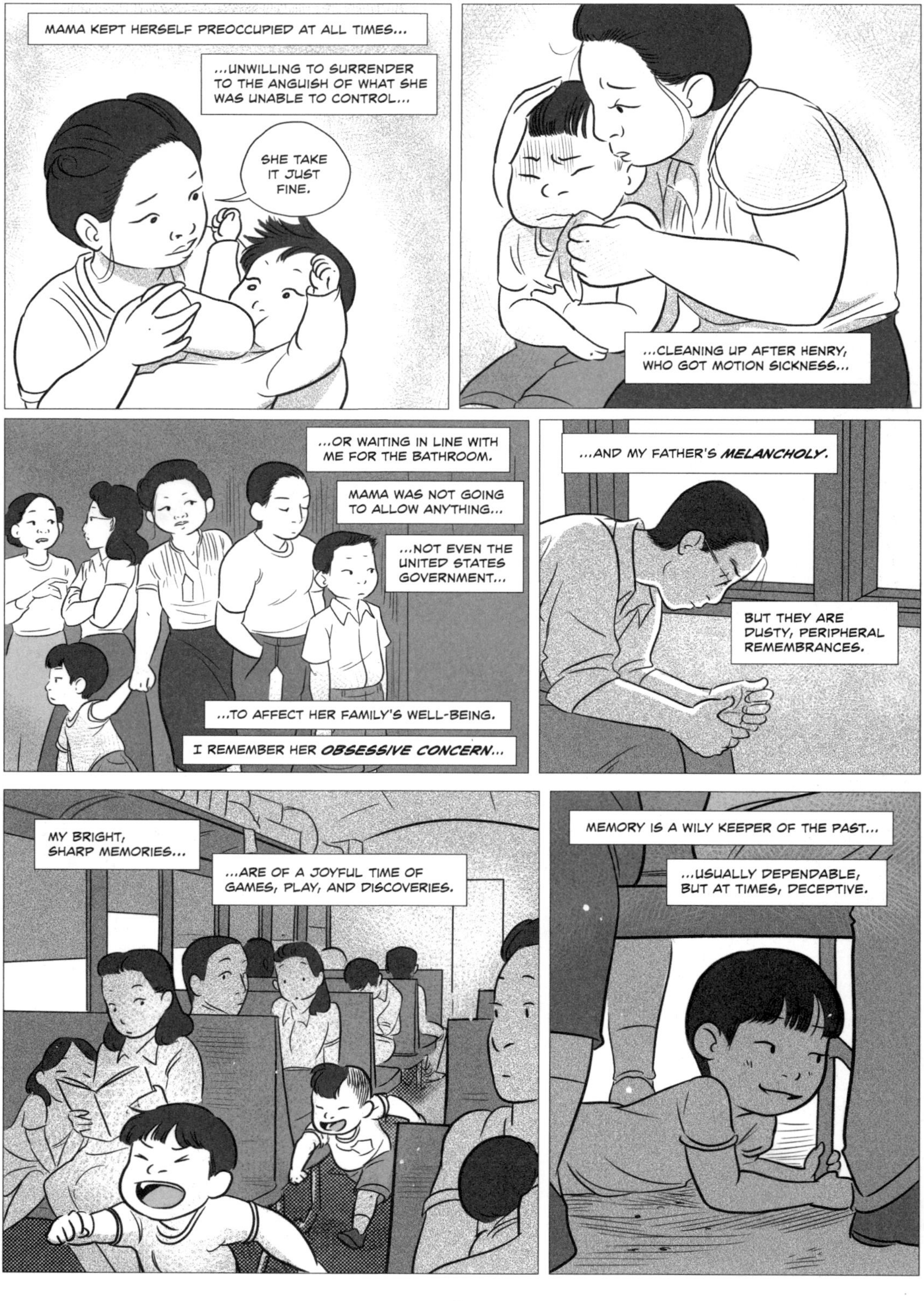
MAMA KEPT HERSELF PREOCCUPIED AT ALL TIMES...
...UNWILLING TO SURRENDER TO THE ANGUISH OF WHAT SHE WAS UNABLE TO CONTROL...
SHE TAKE IT JUST FINE.
...CLEANING UP AFTER HENRY, WHO GOT MOTION SICKNESS...
...OR WAITING IN LINE WITH ME FOR THE BATHROOM.
MAMA WAS NOT GOING TO ALLOW ANYTHING...
...NOT EVEN THE UNITED STATES GOVERNMENT...
...TO AFFECT HER FAMILY'S WELL-BEING.
I REMEMBER HER OBSESSIVE CONCERN...
...AND MY FATHER'S MELANCHOLY.
BUT THEY ARE DUSTY, PERIPHERAL REMEMBRANCES.
MY BRIGHT, SHARP MEMORIES...
...ARE OF A JOYFUL TIME OF GAMES, PLAY, AND DISCOVERIES.
MEMORY IS A WILY KEEPER OF THE PAST...
...USUALLY DEPENDABLE, BUT AT TIMES, DECEPTIVE.

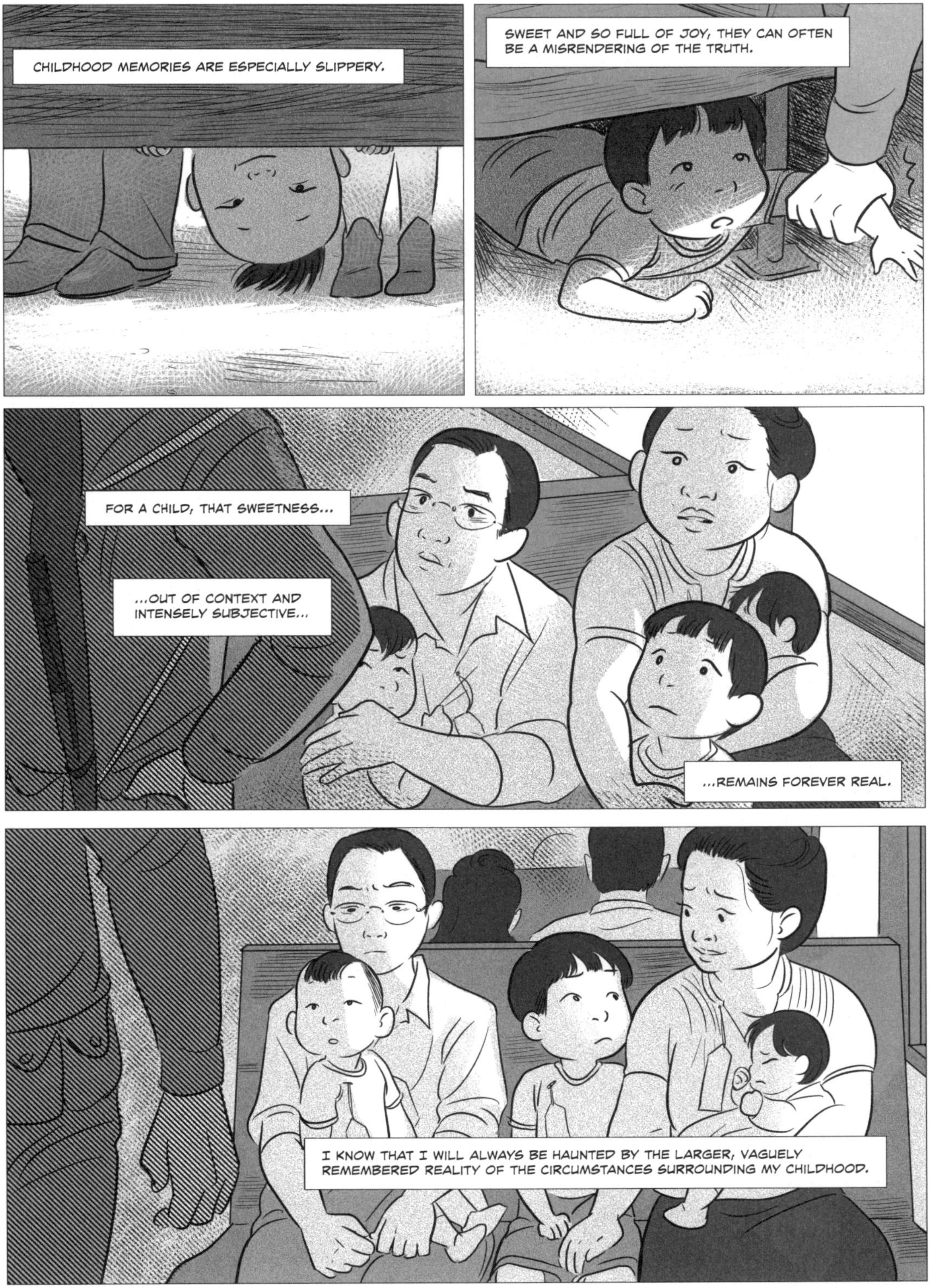
CHILDHOOD MEMORIES ARE ESPECIALLY SLIPPERY.
SWEET AND SO FULL OF JOY, THEY CAN OFTEN BE A MISRENDERING OF THE TRUTH.
FOR A CHILD, THAT SWEETNESS...
...OUT OF CONTEXT AND INTENSELY SUBJECTIVE...
...REMAINS FOREVER REAL.
I KNOW THAT I WILL ALWAYS BE HAUNTED BY THE LARGER, VAGUELY REMEMBERED REALITY OF THE CIRCUMSTANCES SURROUNDING MY CHILDHOOD.

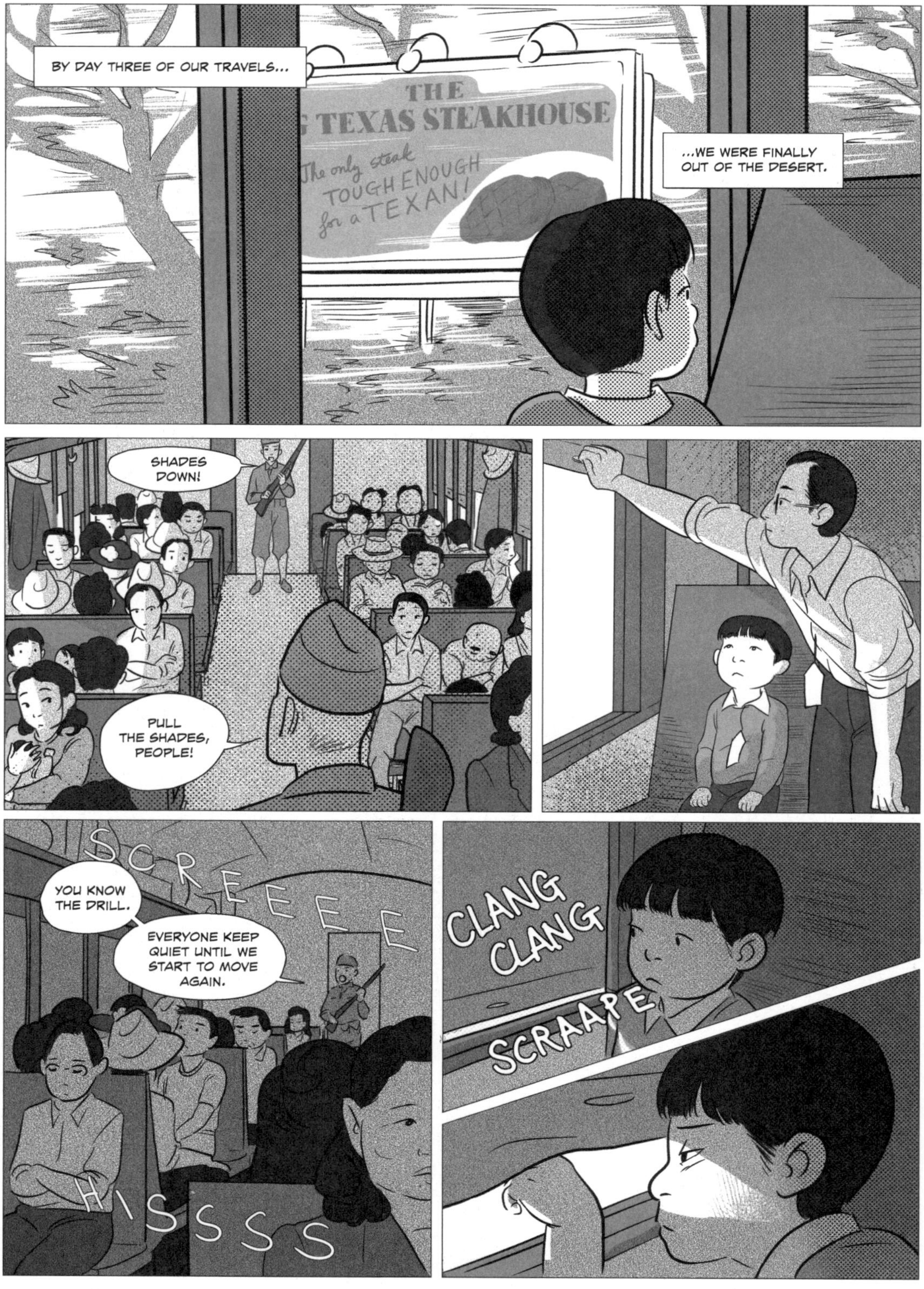
BY DAY THREE OF OUR TRAVELS...
THE
TEXAS STEAKHOUSE
The only steak
TOUGH ENOUGH
for a TEXAN!
...WE WERE FINALLY OUT OF THE DESERT.
SHADES DOWN!
PULL THE SHADES, PEOPLE!
SCREEEEE
YOU KNOW THE DRILL.
EVERYONE KEEP QUIET UNTIL WE START TO MOVE AGAIN.
HISSSSS
CLANG
CLANG
SCRAAPE

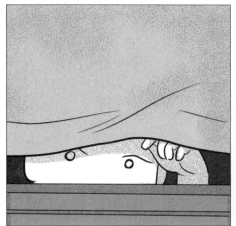

fwap!

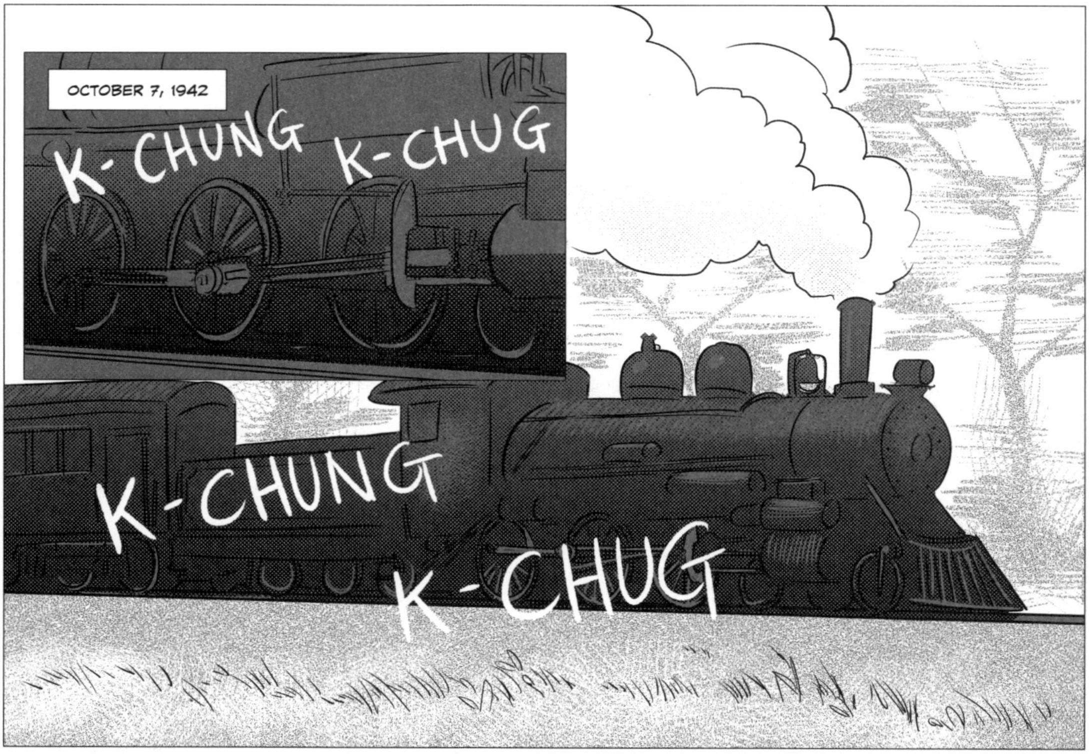
OCTOBER 7, 1942
K-CHUNG K-CHUG
K-CHUNG
K-CHUG

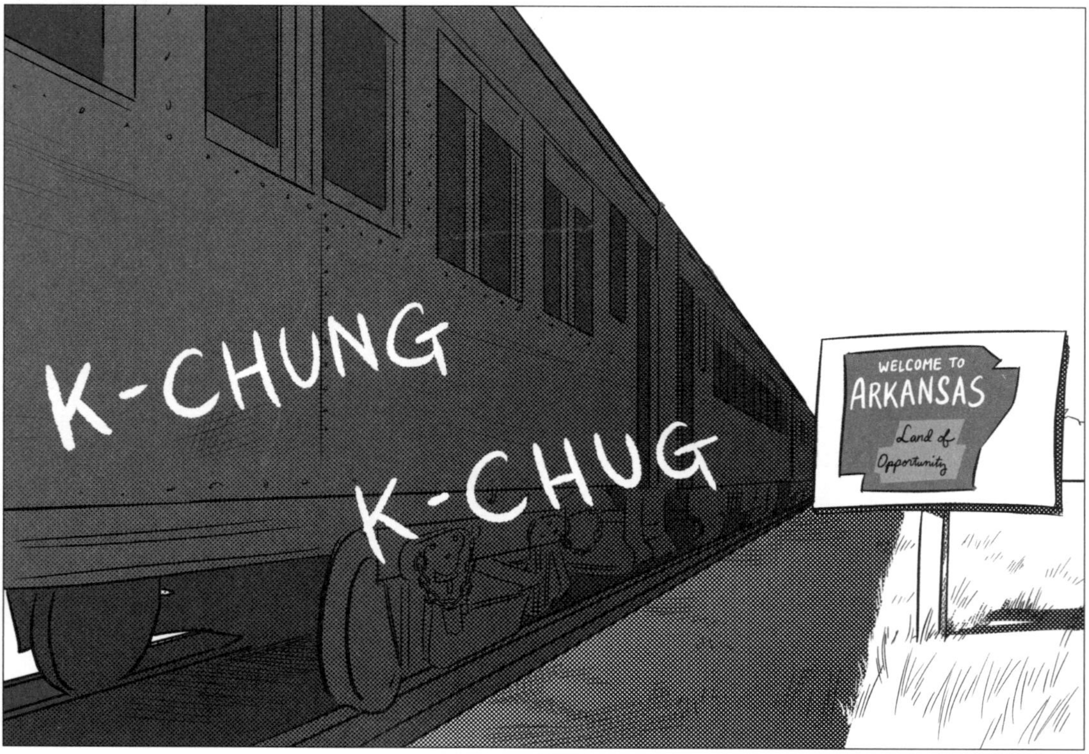
K-CHUNG
K-CHUG
WELCOME TO
ARKANSAS
Land of
Opportunity

ROAR!

RHOAR!

ROAR?

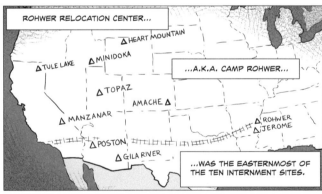

ROHWER!

ROHWER RELOCATION CENTER...

△ HEART MOUNTAIN

△ TULE LAKE △ MINIDOKA

...A.K.A. CAMP ROHWER...

△ TOPAZ

AMACHE △

△ MANZANAR

△ ROHWER
△ JEROME

△ POSTON

...WAS THE EASTERNMOST OF
THE TEN INTERNMENT SITES.

△ GILA RIVER

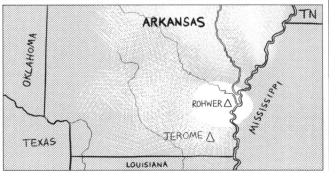

ARKANSAS

TN

OKLAHOMA

ROHWER △

MISSISSIPPI

TEXAS

JEROME △

LOUISIANA

LOOK! IT'S
IMAI-SAN,
FROM NORTH
HOLLYWOOD!

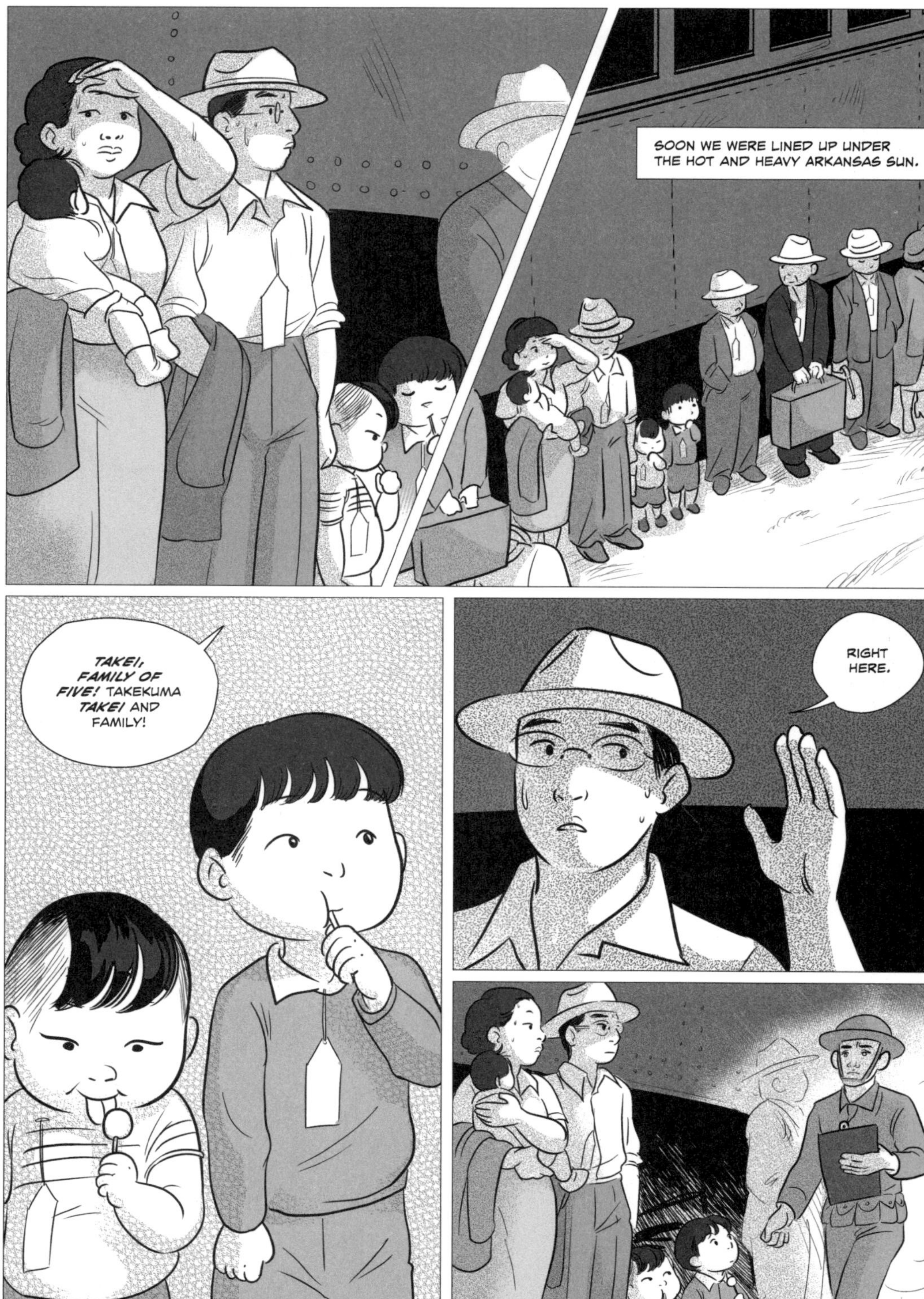

SOON WE WERE LINED UP UNDER THE HOT AND HEAVY ARKANSAS SUN.
TAKEI, FAMILY OF FIVE! TAKEKUMA *TAKEI* AND FAMILY!
RIGHT HERE.

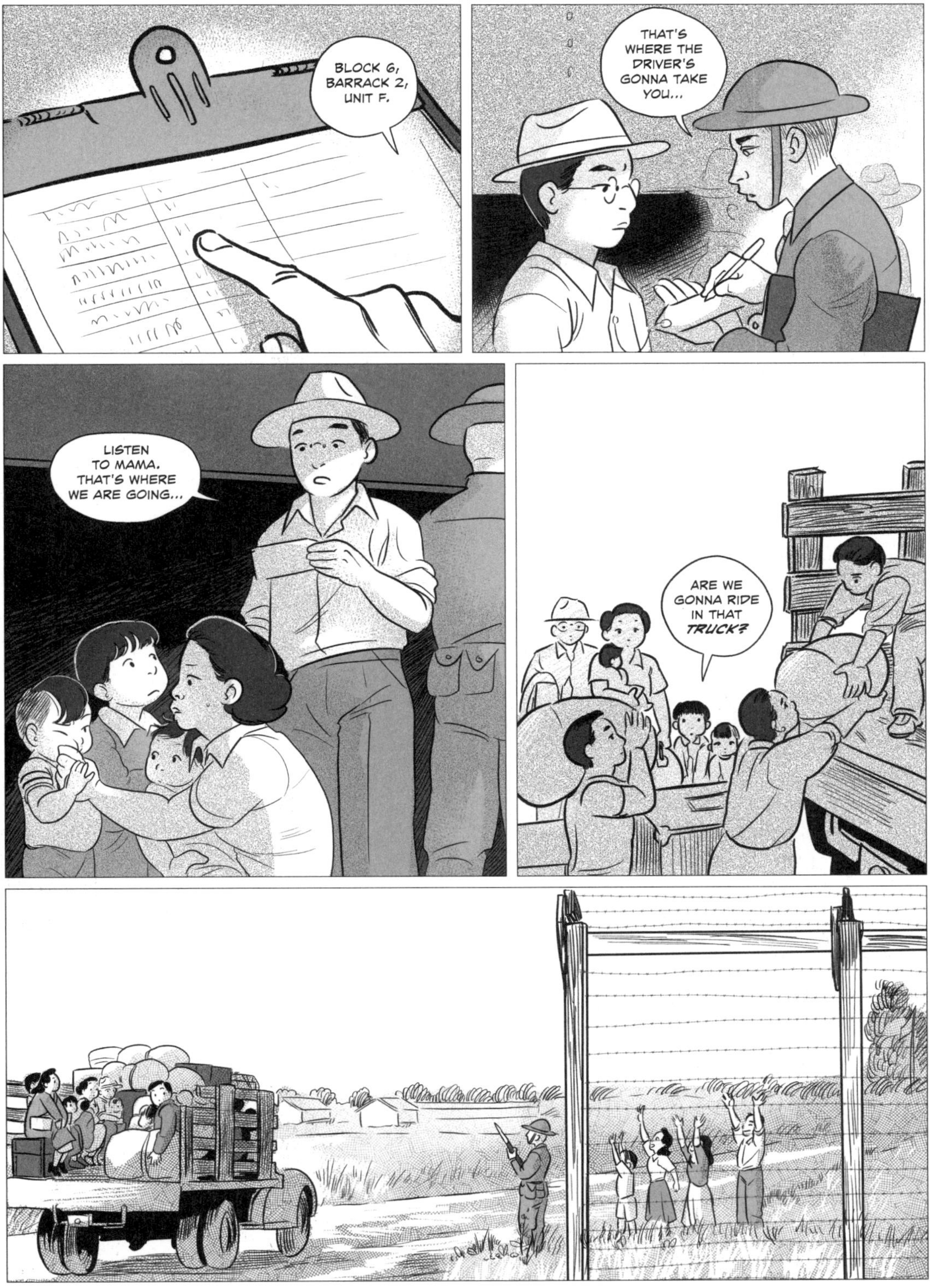
BLOCK 6, BARRACK 2, UNIT F.
THAT'S WHERE THE DRIVER'S GONNA TAKE YOU...
LISTEN TO MAMA. THAT'S WHERE WE ARE GOING...
ARE WE GONNA RIDE IN THAT *TRUCK?*

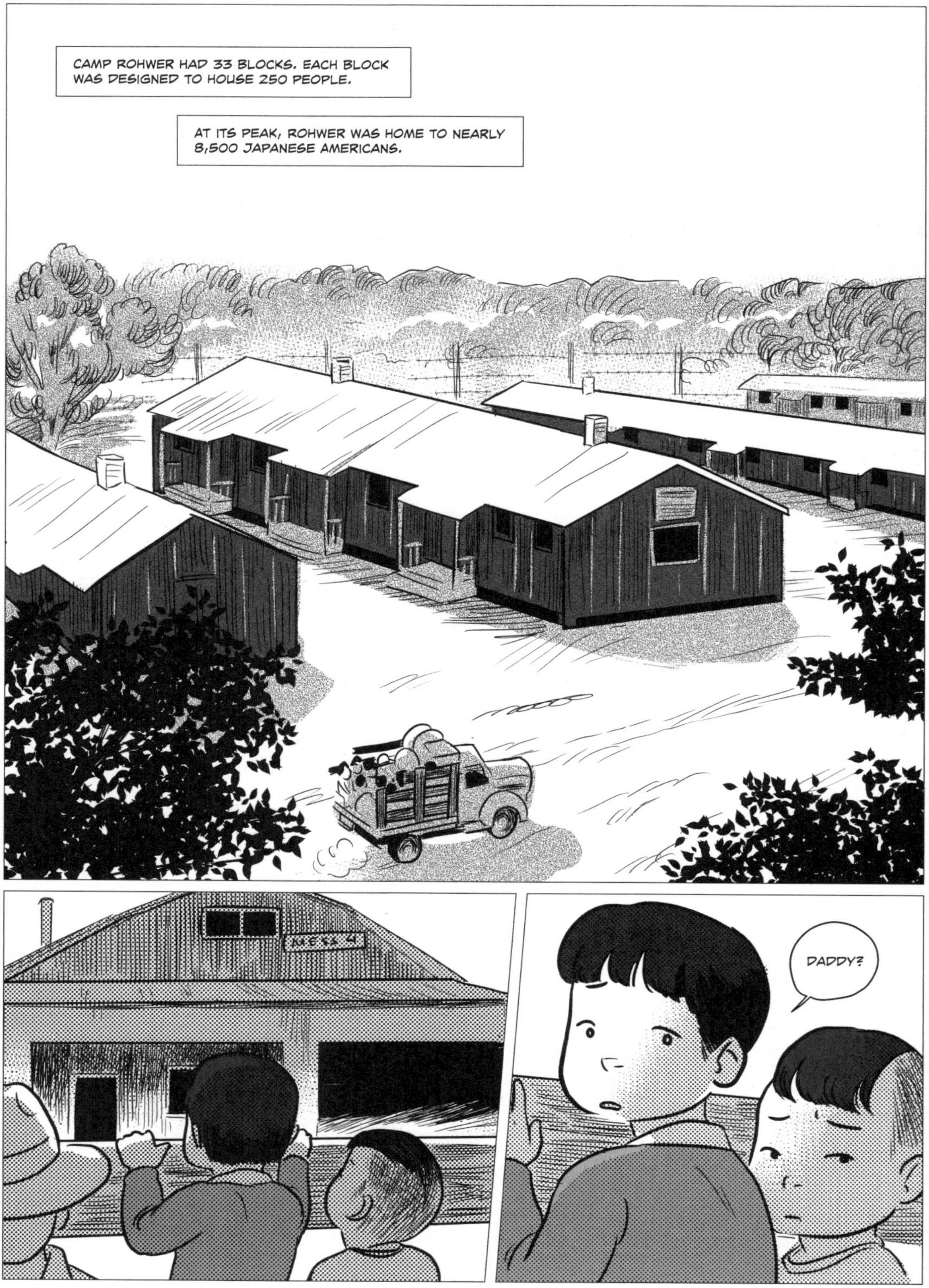
CAMP ROHWER HAD 33 BLOCKS. EACH BLOCK WAS DESIGNED TO HOUSE 250 PEOPLE.
AT ITS PEAK, ROHWER WAS HOME TO NEARLY 8,500 JAPANESE AMERICANS.
MESS 4
DADDY?

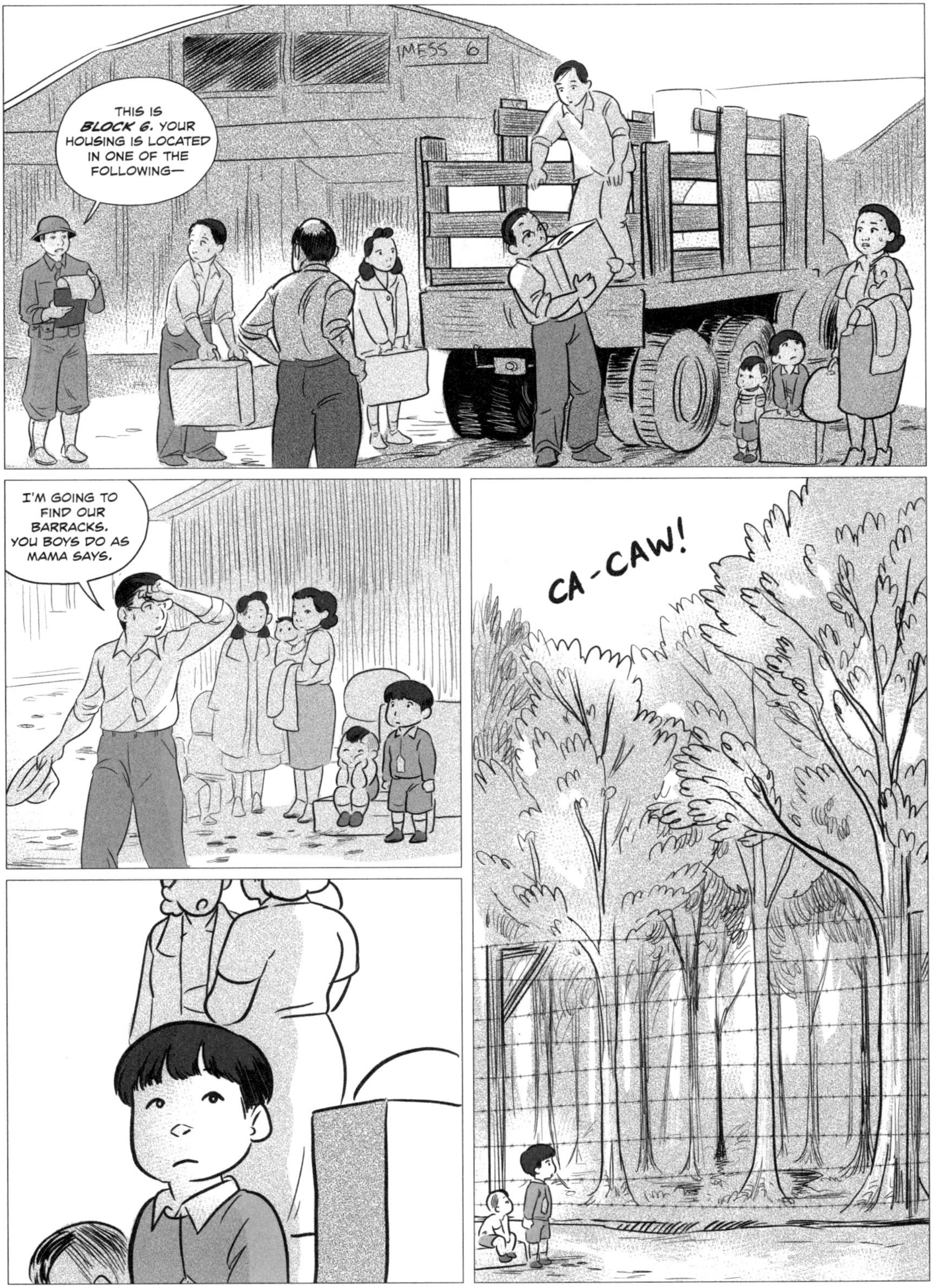
MESS 6
THIS IS BLOCK 6. YOUR HOUSING IS LOCATED IN ONE OF THE FOLLOWING—
I'M GOING TO FIND OUR BARRACKS. YOU BOYS DO AS MAMA SAYS.
CA-CAW!

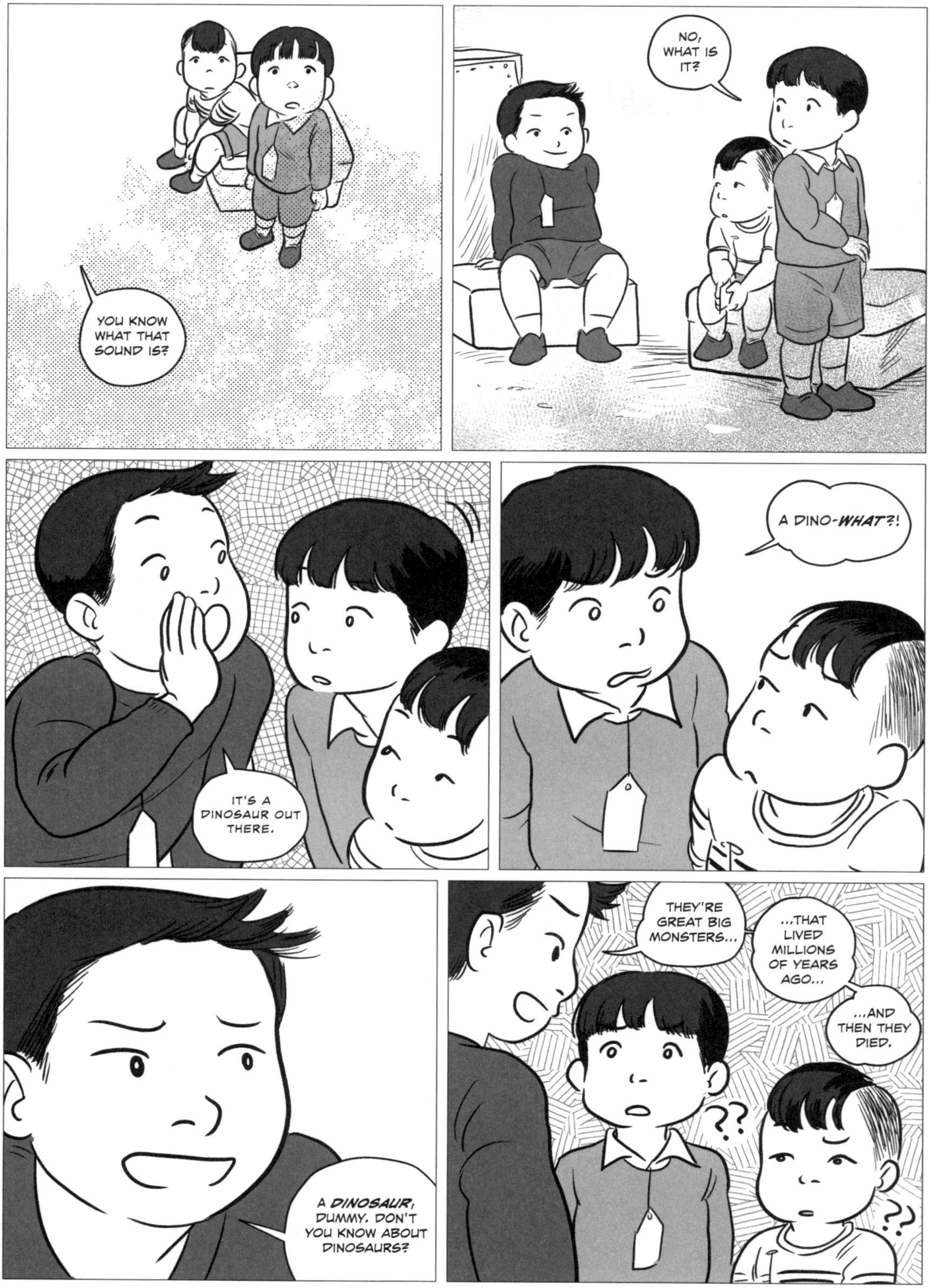
YOU KNOW WHAT THAT SOUND IS?
NO, WHAT IS IT?
IT'S A DINOSAUR OUT THERE.
A DINO-*WHAT*?!
A ***DINOSAUR***, DUMMY. DON'T YOU KNOW ABOUT DINOSAURS?
THEY'RE GREAT BIG MONSTERS...
...THAT LIVED MILLIONS OF YEARS AGO...
...AND THEN THEY DIED.
??
??

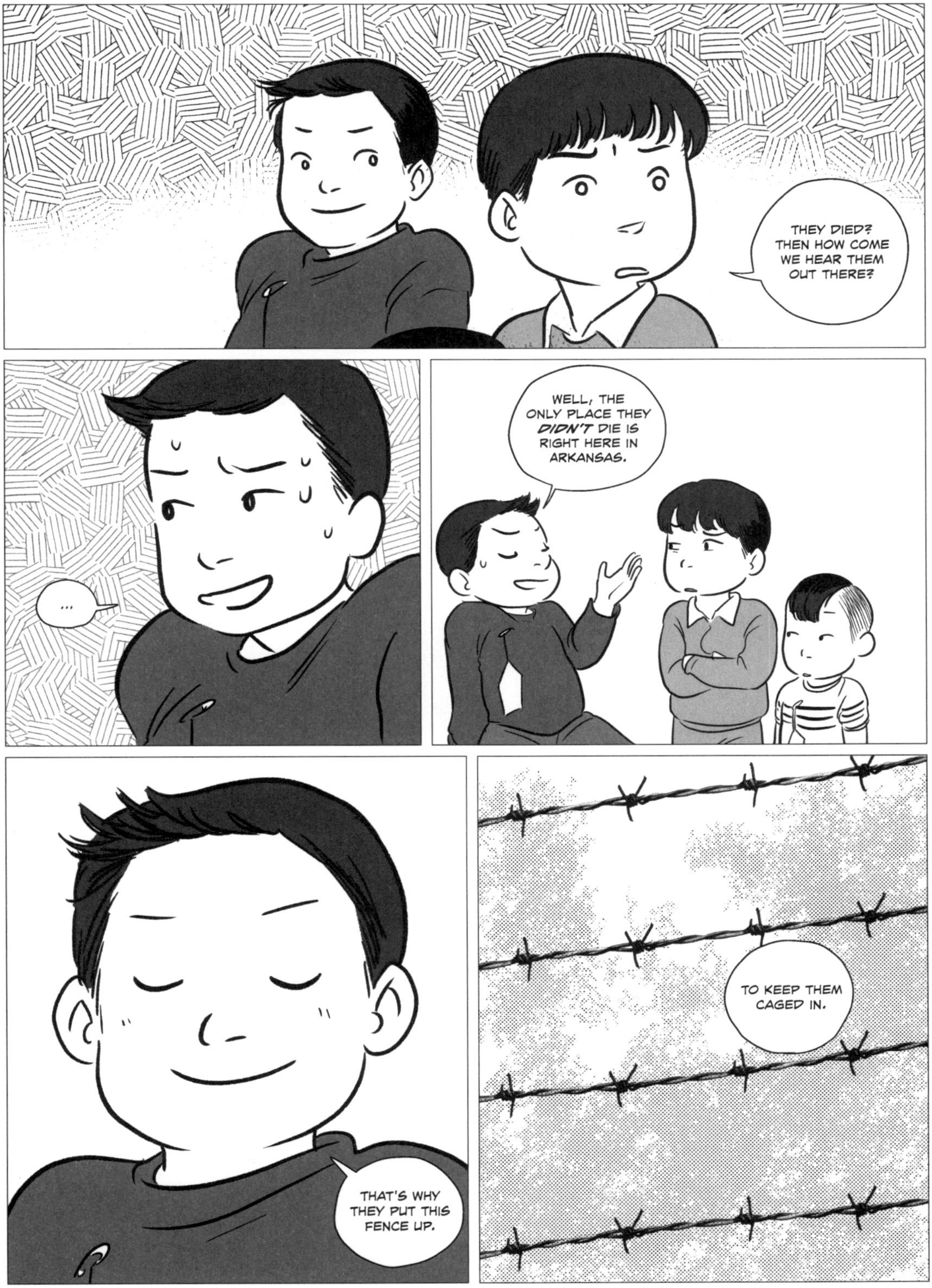
THEY DIED? THEN HOW COME WE HEAR THEM OUT THERE?
...
WELL, THE ONLY PLACE THEY *DIDN'T* DIE IS RIGHT HERE IN ARKANSAS.
THAT'S WHY THEY PUT THIS FENCE UP.
TO KEEP THEM CAGED IN.

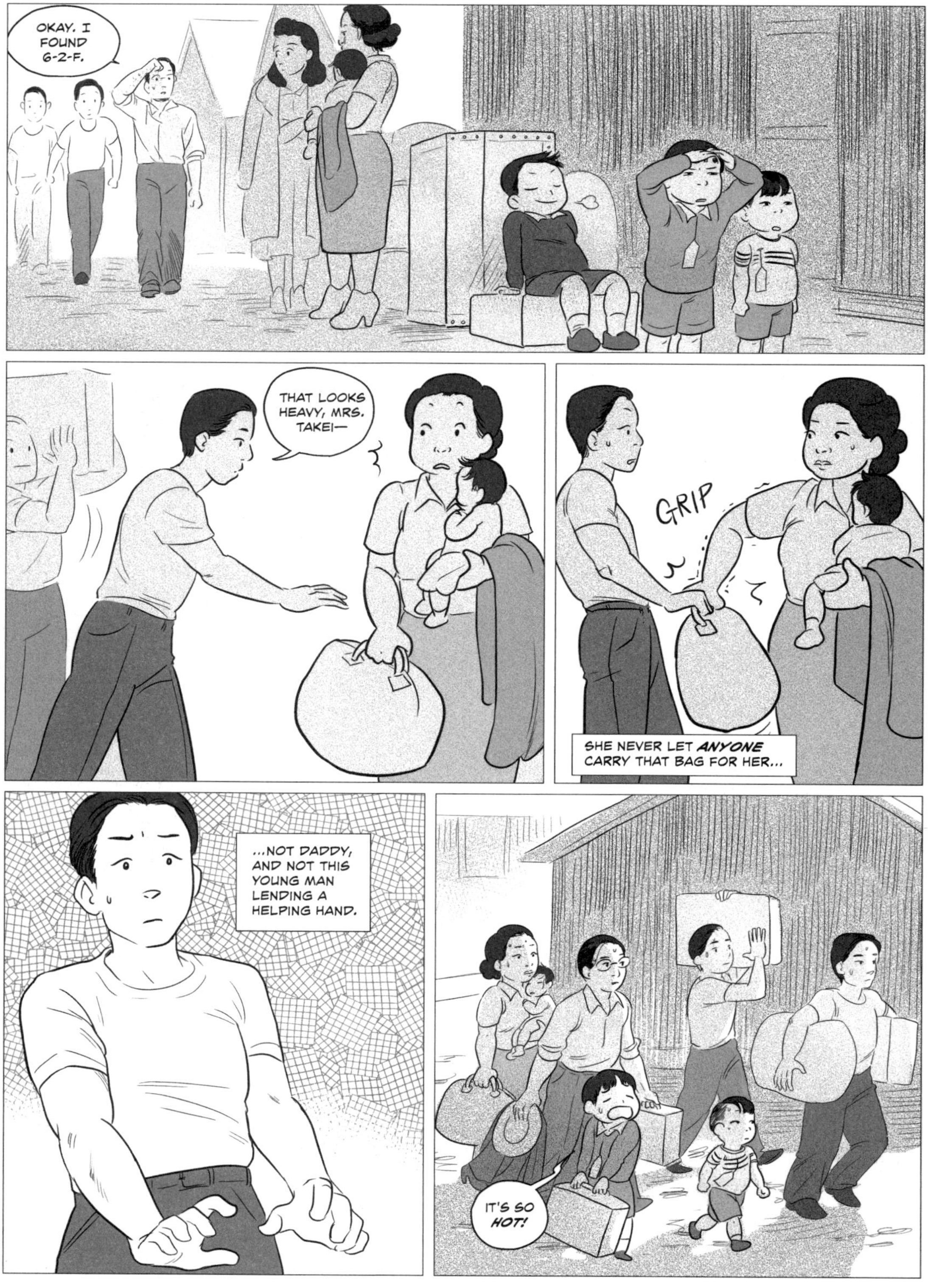
OKAY. I FOUND 6-2-F.
THAT LOOKS HEAVY, MRS. TAKEI—
GRIP
SHE NEVER LET ANYONE CARRY THAT BAG FOR HER...
...NOT DADDY, AND NOT THIS YOUNG MAN LENDING A HELPING HAND.
IT'S SO HOT!

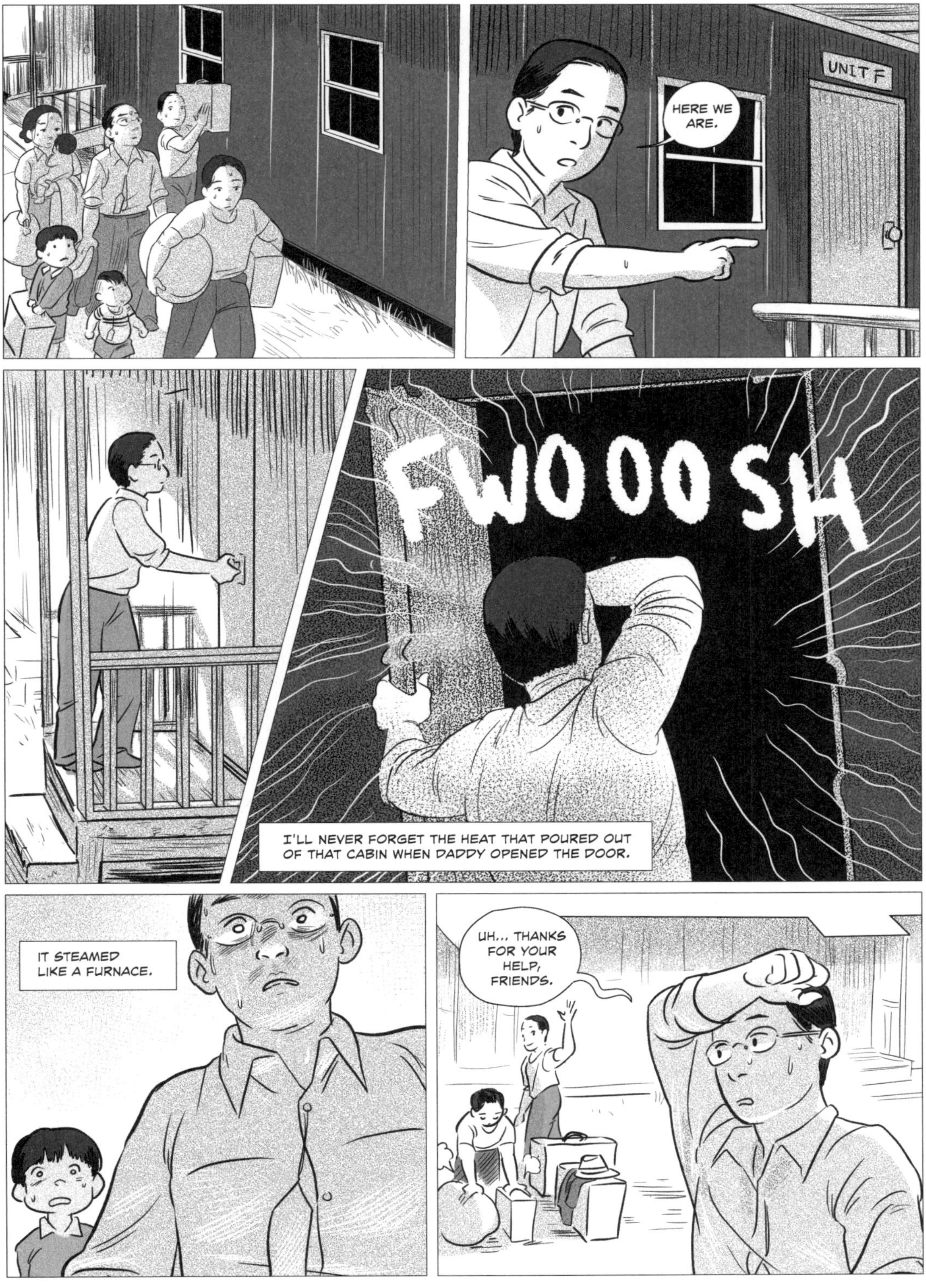
UNIT F
HERE WE ARE.
FWOOOSH
I'LL NEVER FORGET THE HEAT THAT POURED OUT OF THAT CABIN WHEN DADDY OPENED THE DOOR.
IT STEAMED LIKE A FURNACE.
UH... THANKS FOR YOUR HELP, FRIENDS.

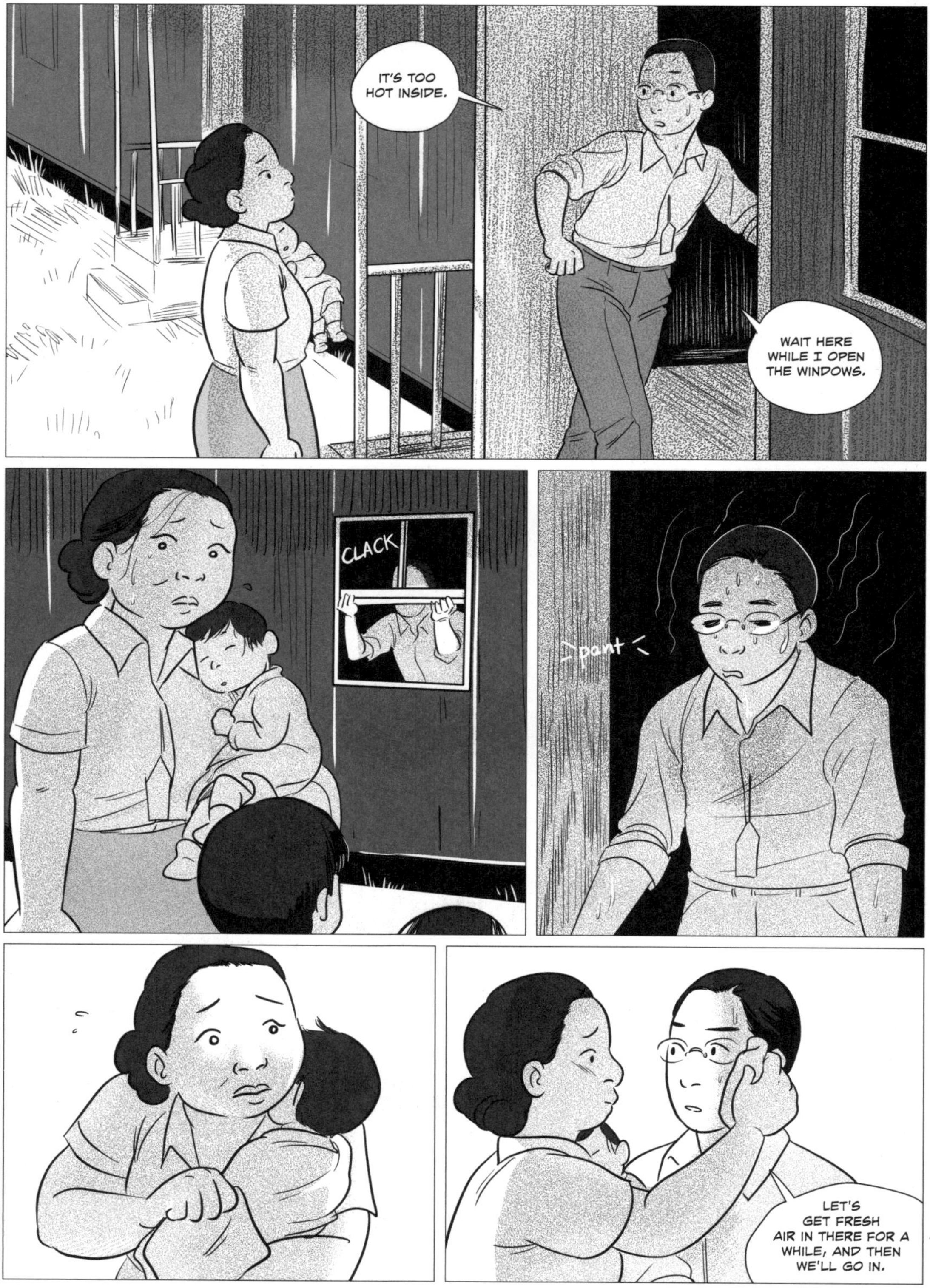
IT'S TOO HOT INSIDE.
WAIT HERE WHILE I OPEN THE WINDOWS.
CLACK
pant
LET'S GET FRESH AIR IN THERE FOR A WHILE, AND THEN WE'LL GO IN.

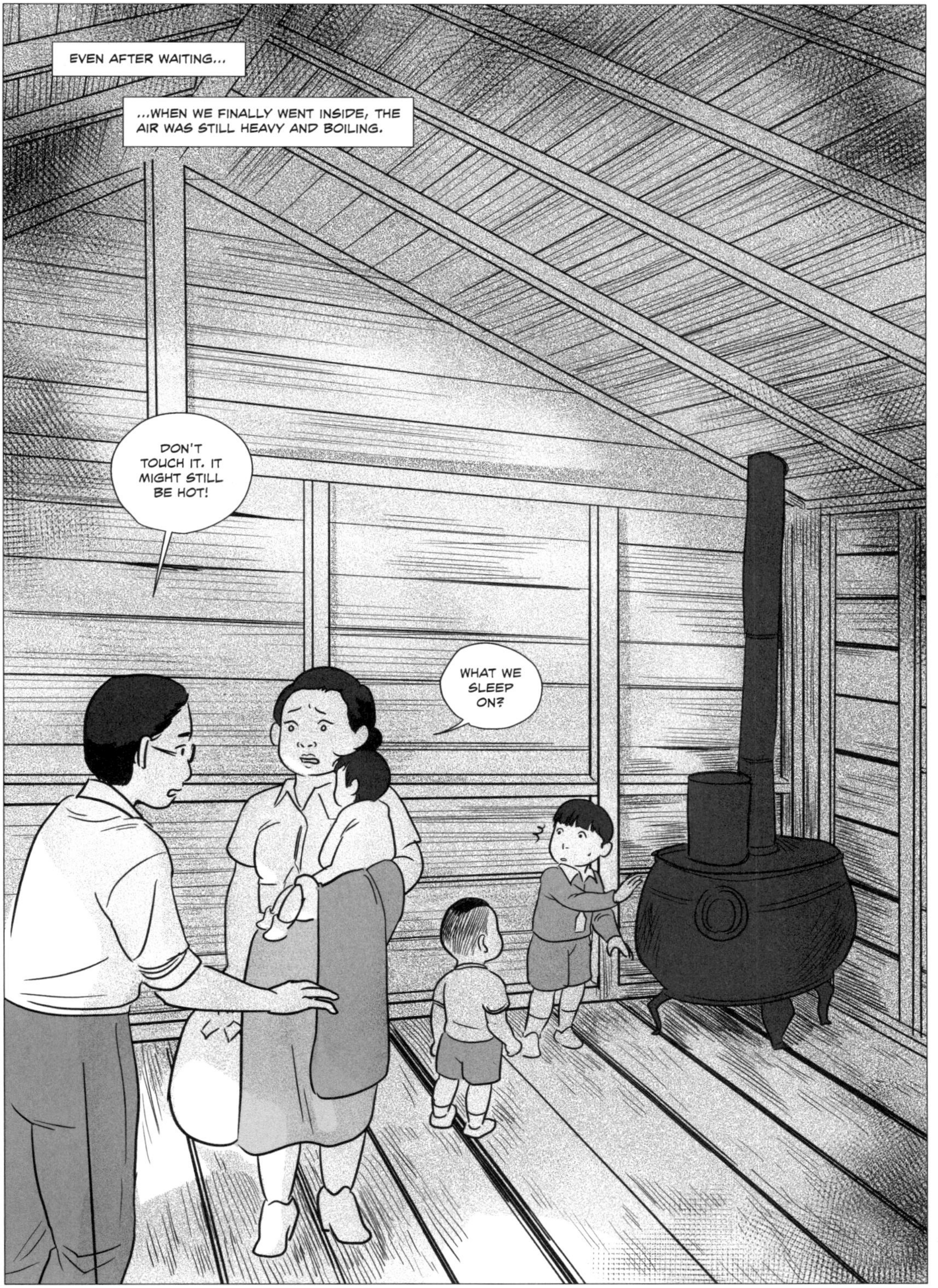
EVEN AFTER WAITING...
...WHEN WE FINALLY WENT INSIDE, THE AIR WAS STILL HEAVY AND BOILING.
DON'T TOUCH IT. IT MIGHT STILL BE HOT!
WHAT WE SLEEP ON?

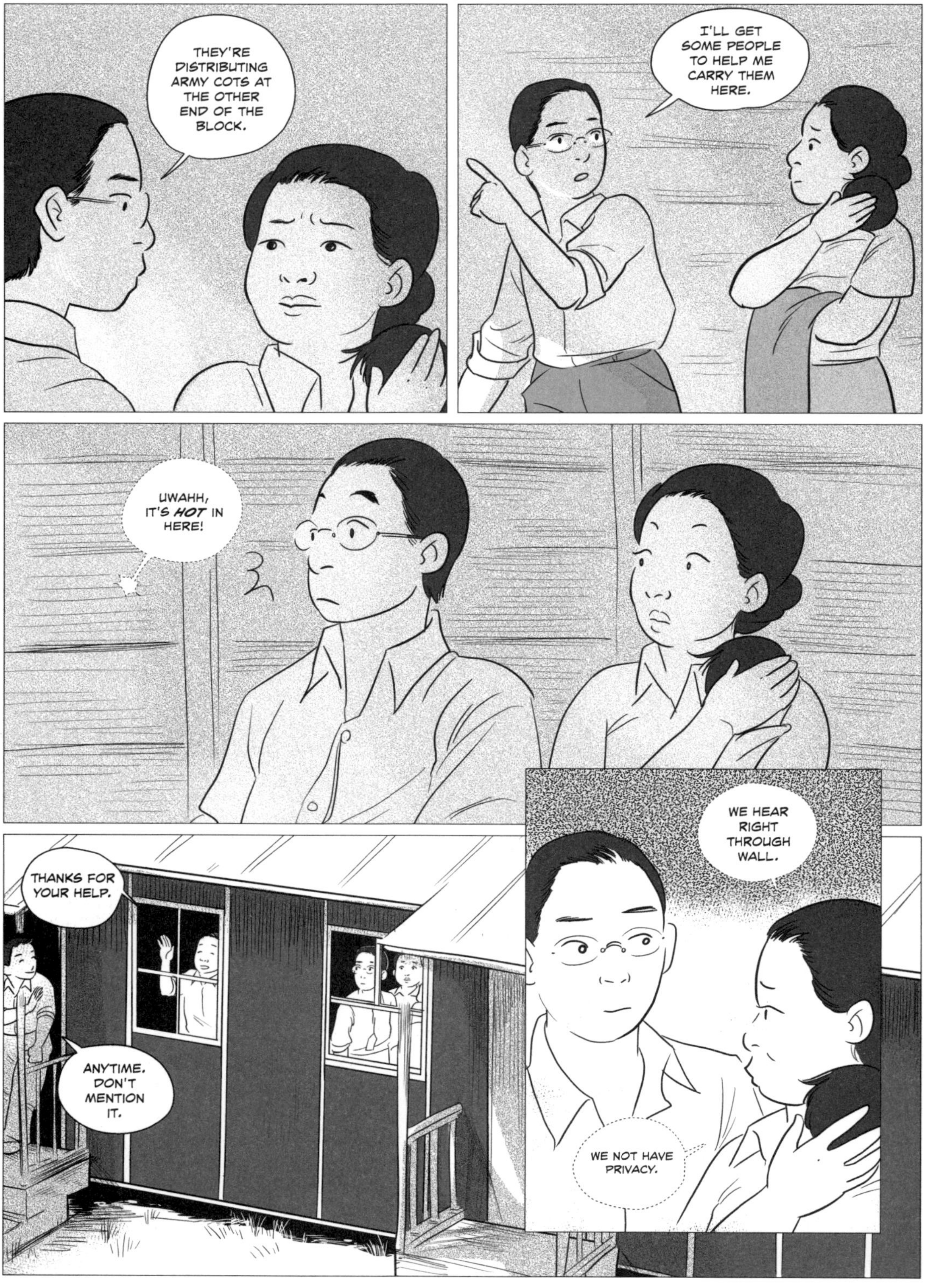
THEY'RE DISTRIBUTING ARMY COTS AT THE OTHER END OF THE BLOCK.
I'LL GET SOME PEOPLE TO HELP ME CARRY THEM HERE.
UWAHH, IT'S *HOT* IN HERE!
THANKS FOR YOUR HELP.
ANYTIME. DON'T MENTION IT.
WE HEAR RIGHT THROUGH WALL.
WE NOT HAVE PRIVACY.

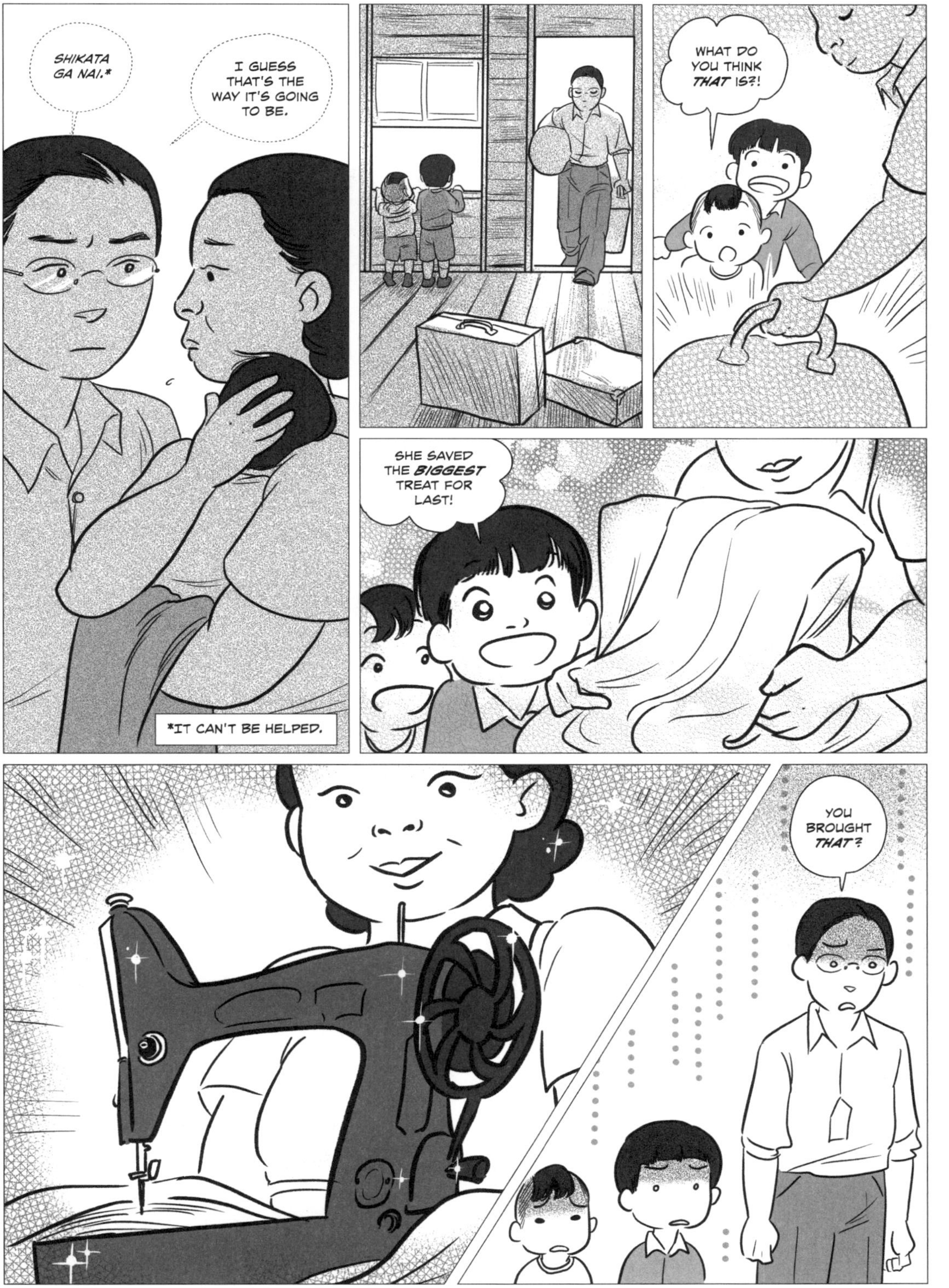
SHIKATA GA NAI.*
I GUESS THAT'S THE WAY IT'S GOING TO BE.
*IT CAN'T BE HELPED.
WHAT DO YOU THINK THAT IS?!
SHE SAVED THE BIGGEST TREAT FOR LAST!
YOU BROUGHT THAT?

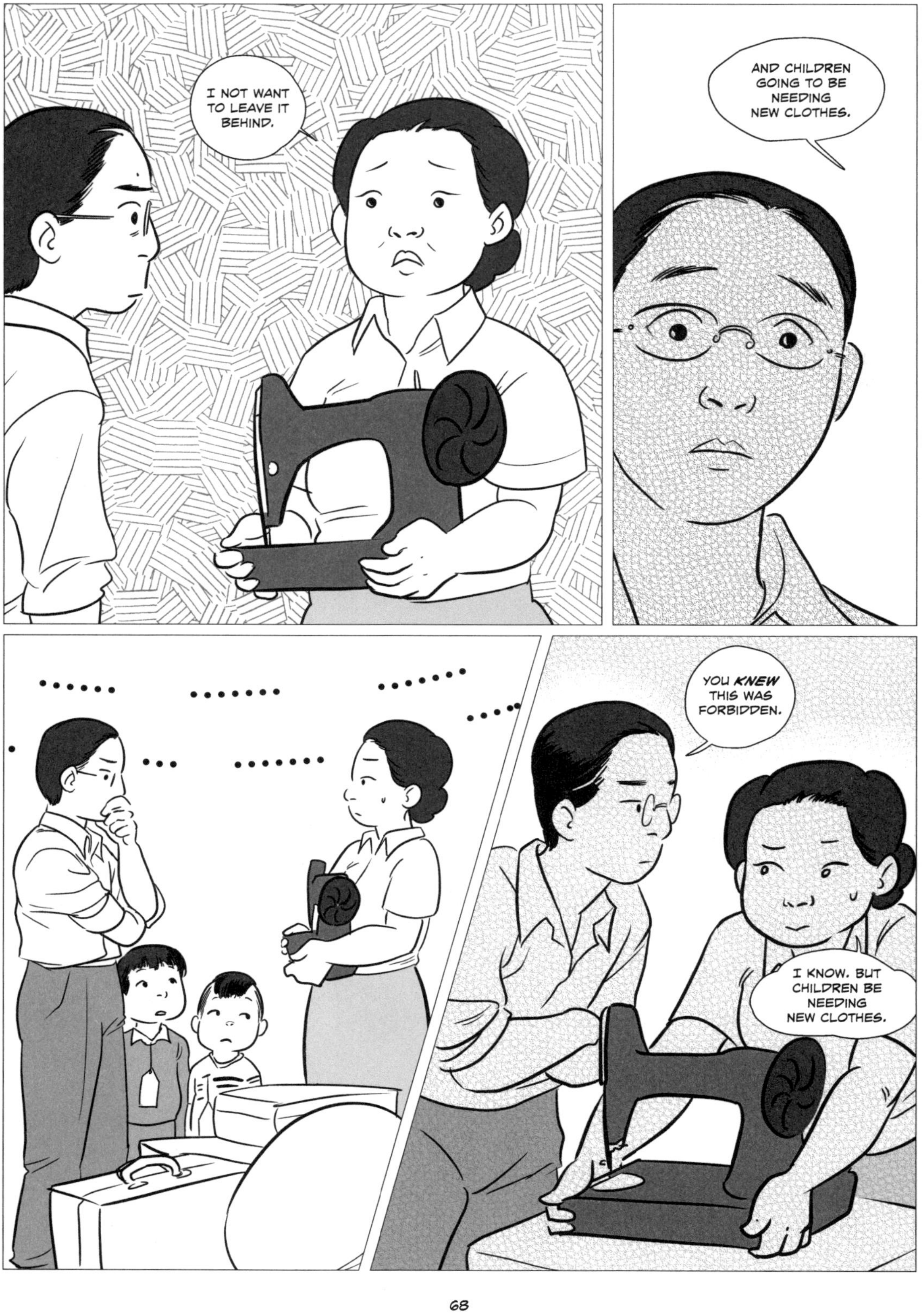
I NOT WANT TO LEAVE IT BEHIND.
AND CHILDREN GOING TO BE NEEDING NEW CLOTHES.
.....
....
....
.....
.
...
....
YOU **KNEW** THIS WAS FORBIDDEN.
I KNOW. BUT CHILDREN BE NEEDING NEW CLOTHES.

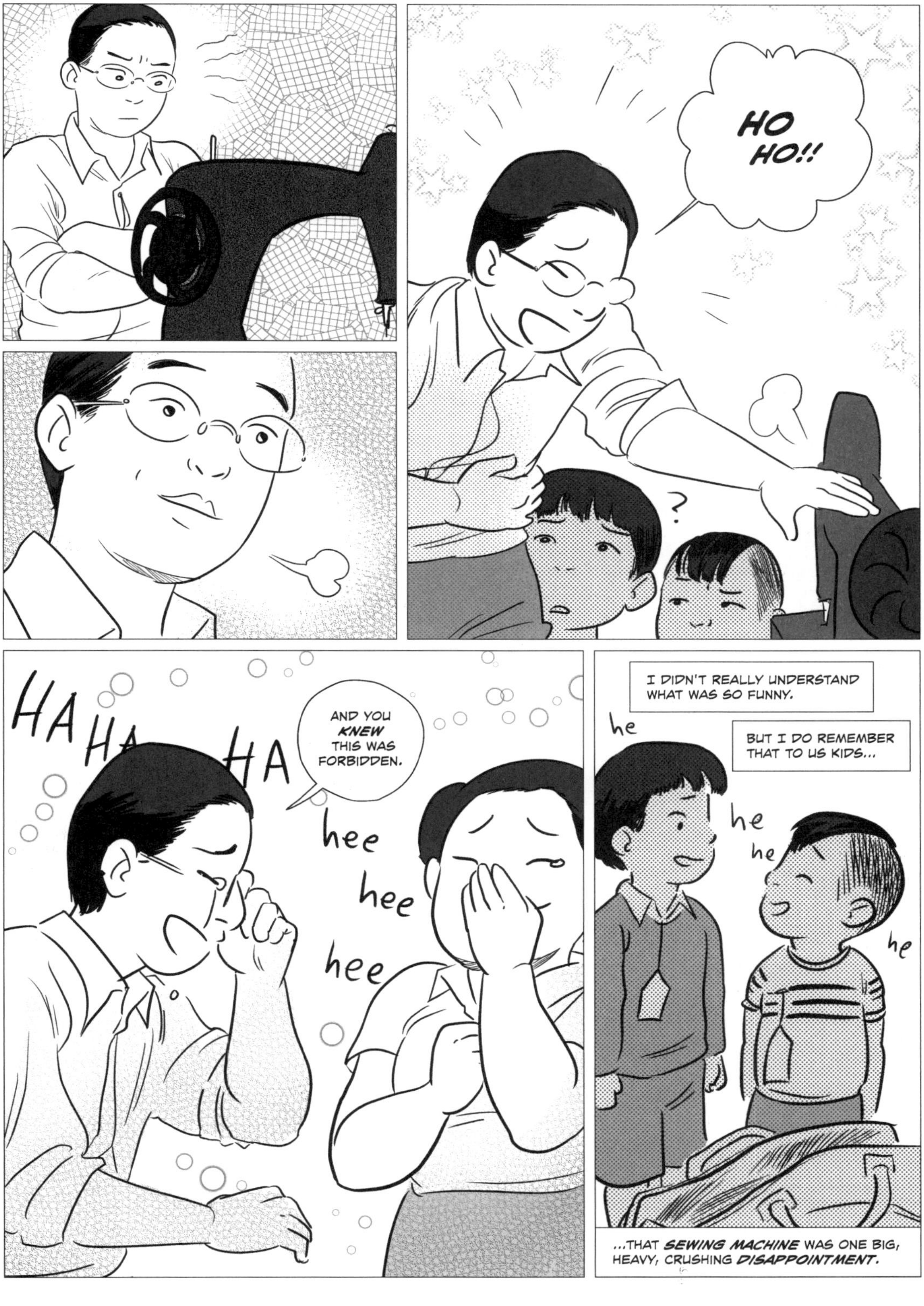
HO HO!!
?
HA HA HA
AND YOU KNEW THIS WAS FORBIDDEN.
hee hee hee
I DIDN'T REALLY UNDERSTAND WHAT WAS SO FUNNY.
BUT I DO REMEMBER THAT TO US KIDS...
he
he he
he
...THAT SEWING MACHINE WAS ONE BIG, HEAVY, CRUSHING DISAPPOINTMENT.

SETTING UP OUR NEW LIFE IN ROHWER IMMEDIATELY BECAME PRIORITY NUMBER ONE.

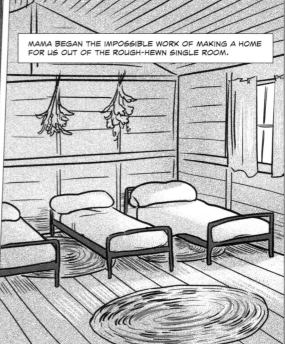

MAMA BEGAN THE IMPOSSIBLE WORK OF MAKING A HOME FOR US OUT OF THE ROUGH-HEWN SINGLE ROOM.

WHIRRRRR
WHIRRRR
WHIRR

SHE RAN UP CURTAINS MADE FROM GOVERNMENT SURPLUS FABRICS.

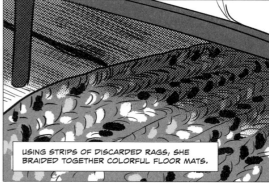

USING STRIPS OF DISCARDED RAGS, SHE BRAIDED TOGETHER COLORFUL FLOOR MATS.

70

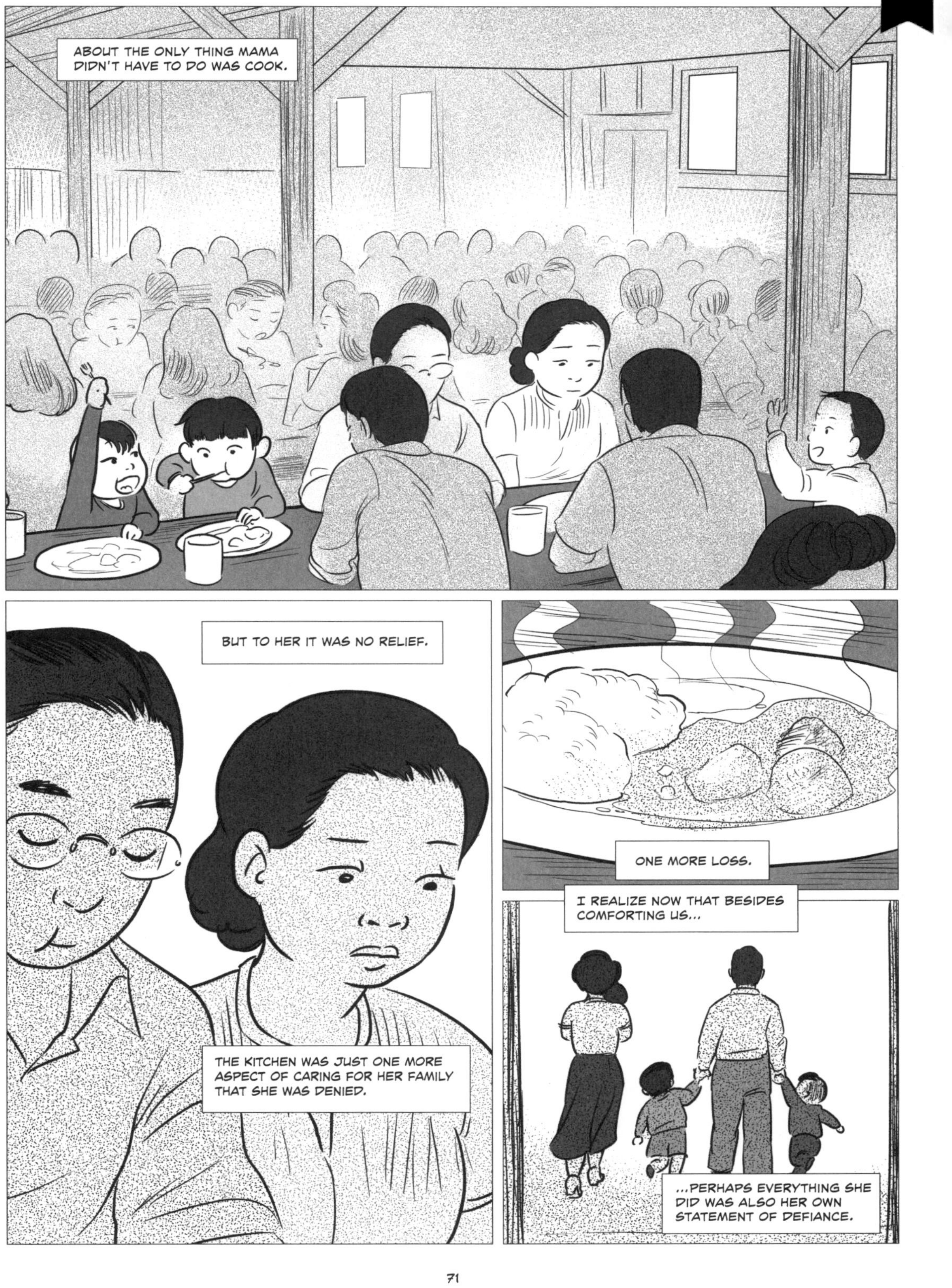
ABOUT THE ONLY THING MAMA DIDN'T HAVE TO DO WAS COOK.
BUT TO HER IT WAS NO RELIEF.
THE KITCHEN WAS JUST ONE MORE ASPECT OF CARING FOR HER FAMILY THAT SHE WAS DENIED.
ONE MORE LOSS.
I REALIZE NOW THAT BESIDES COMFORTING US...
...PERHAPS EVERYTHING SHE DID WAS ALSO HER OWN STATEMENT OF DEFIANCE.

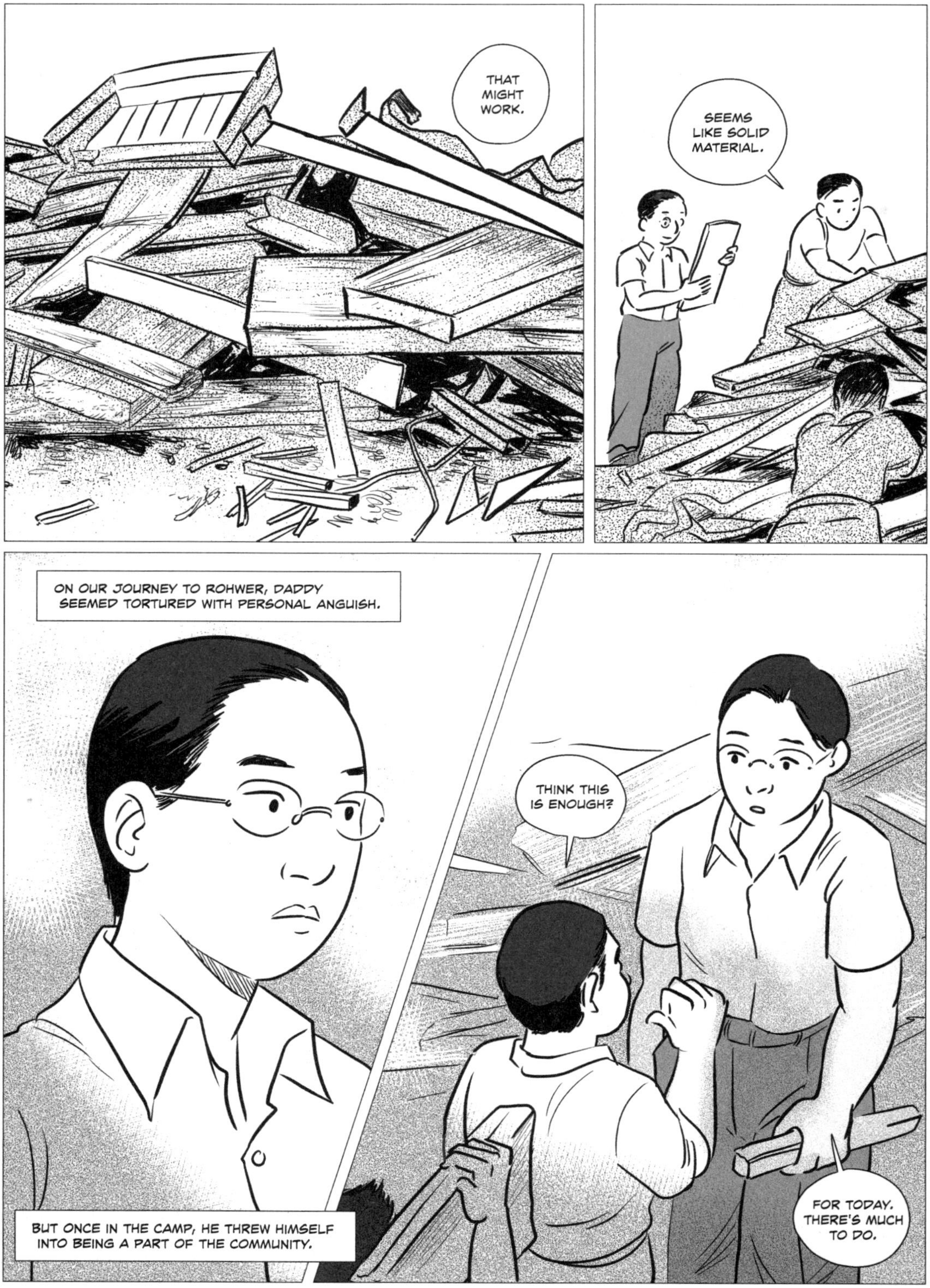
THAT MIGHT WORK.
SEEMS LIKE SOLID MATERIAL.
ON OUR JOURNEY TO ROHWER, DADDY SEEMED TORTURED WITH PERSONAL ANGUISH.
BUT ONCE IN THE CAMP, HE THREW HIMSELF INTO BEING A PART OF THE COMMUNITY.
THINK THIS IS ENOUGH?
FOR TODAY. THERE'S MUCH TO DO.

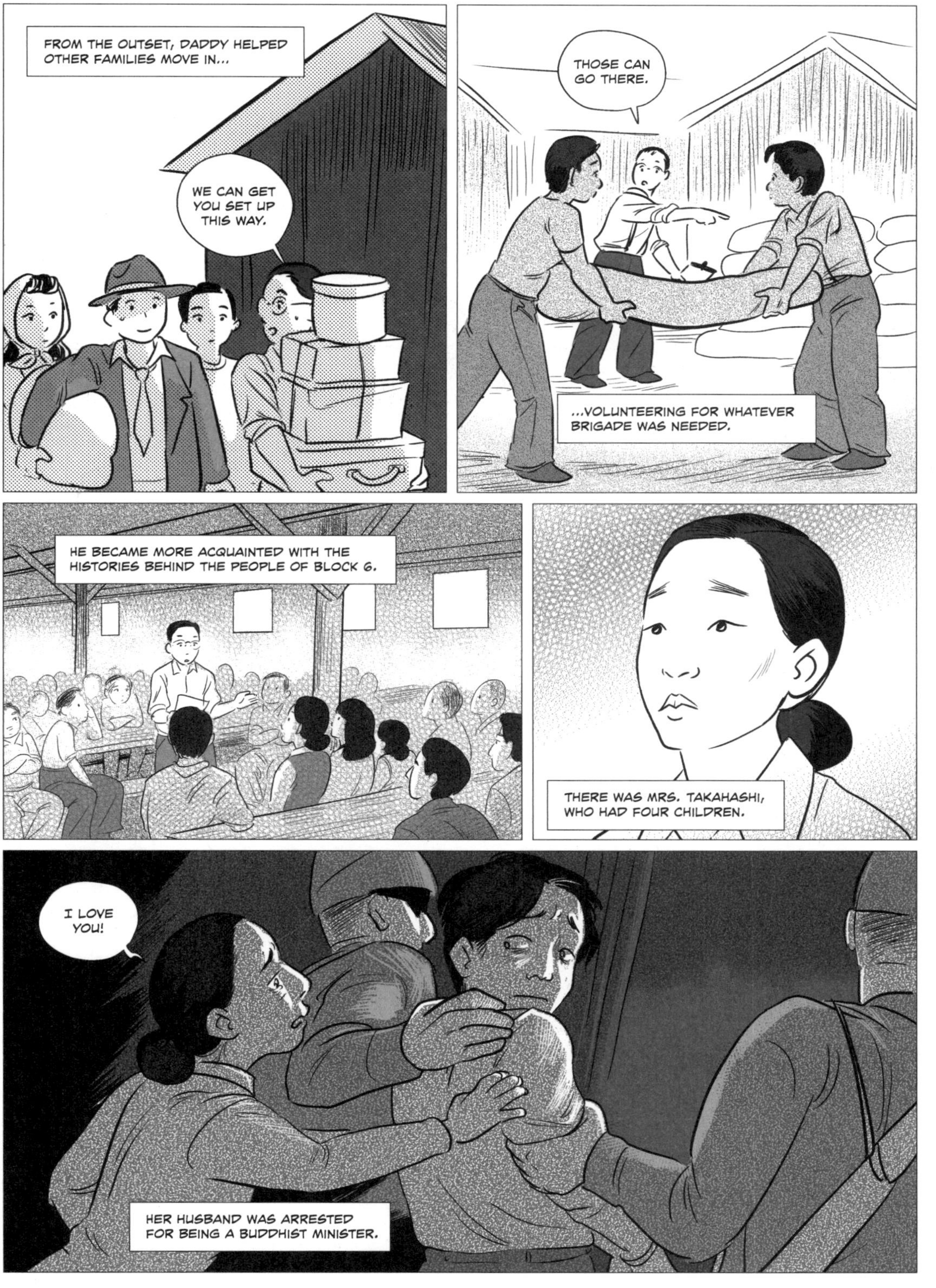
FROM THE OUTSET, DADDY HELPED OTHER FAMILIES MOVE IN...
WE CAN GET YOU SET UP THIS WAY.
THOSE CAN GO THERE.
...VOLUNTEERING FOR WHATEVER BRIGADE WAS NEEDED.
HE BECAME MORE ACQUAINTED WITH THE HISTORIES BEHIND THE PEOPLE OF BLOCK 6.
THERE WAS MRS. TAKAHASHI, WHO HAD FOUR CHILDREN.
I LOVE YOU!
HER HUSBAND WAS ARRESTED FOR BEING A BUDDHIST MINISTER.

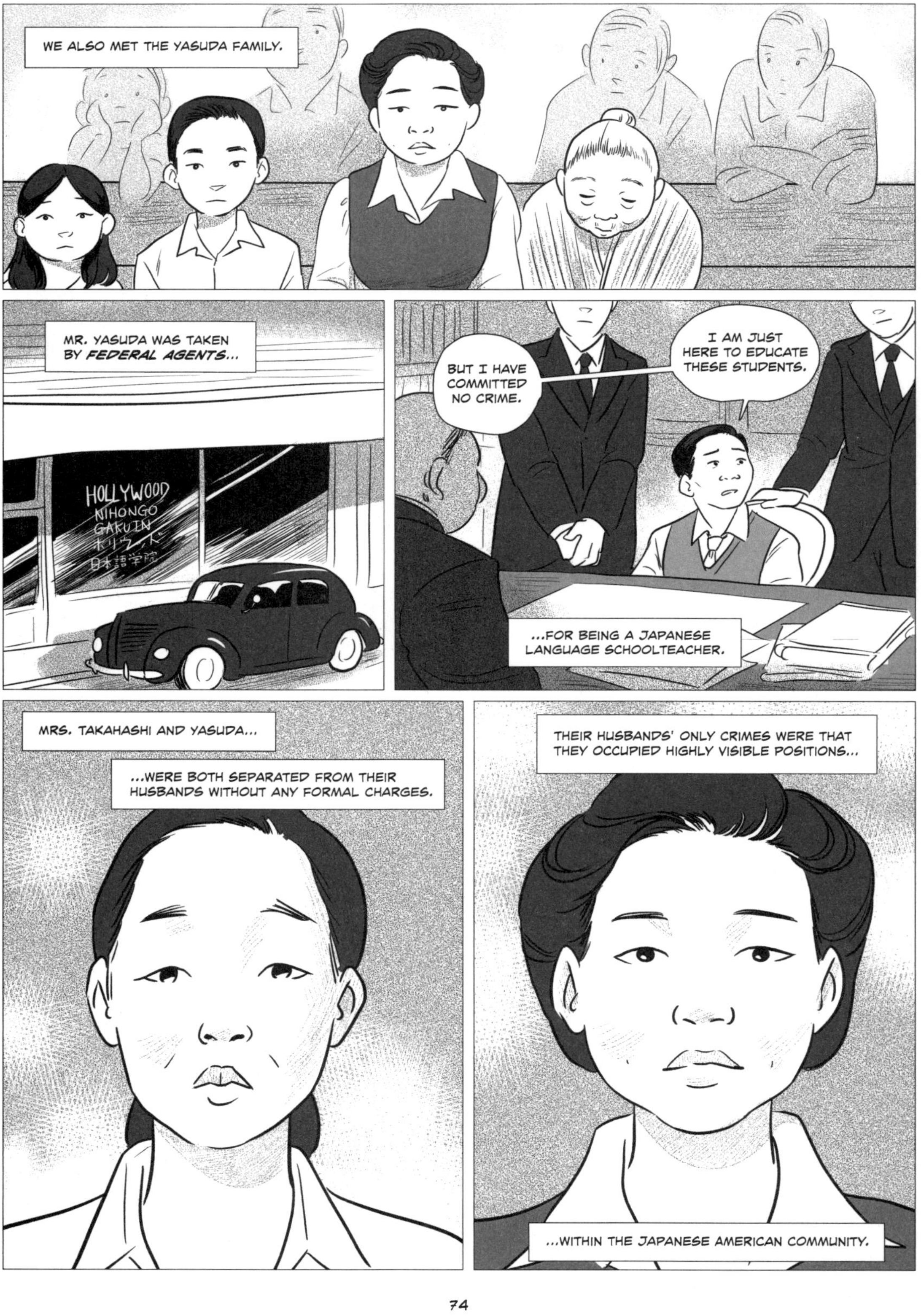
WE ALSO MET THE YASUDA FAMILY.
MR. YASUDA WAS TAKEN BY *FEDERAL AGENTS*...
HOLLYWOOD NIHONGO GAKUIN
日本語学院
BUT I HAVE COMMITTED NO CRIME.
I AM JUST HERE TO EDUCATE THESE STUDENTS.
...FOR BEING A JAPANESE LANGUAGE SCHOOLTEACHER.
MRS. TAKAHASHI AND YASUDA...
...WERE BOTH SEPARATED FROM THEIR HUSBANDS WITHOUT ANY FORMAL CHARGES.
THEIR HUSBANDS' ONLY CRIMES WERE THAT THEY OCCUPIED HIGHLY VISIBLE POSITIONS...
...WITHIN THE JAPANESE AMERICAN COMMUNITY.

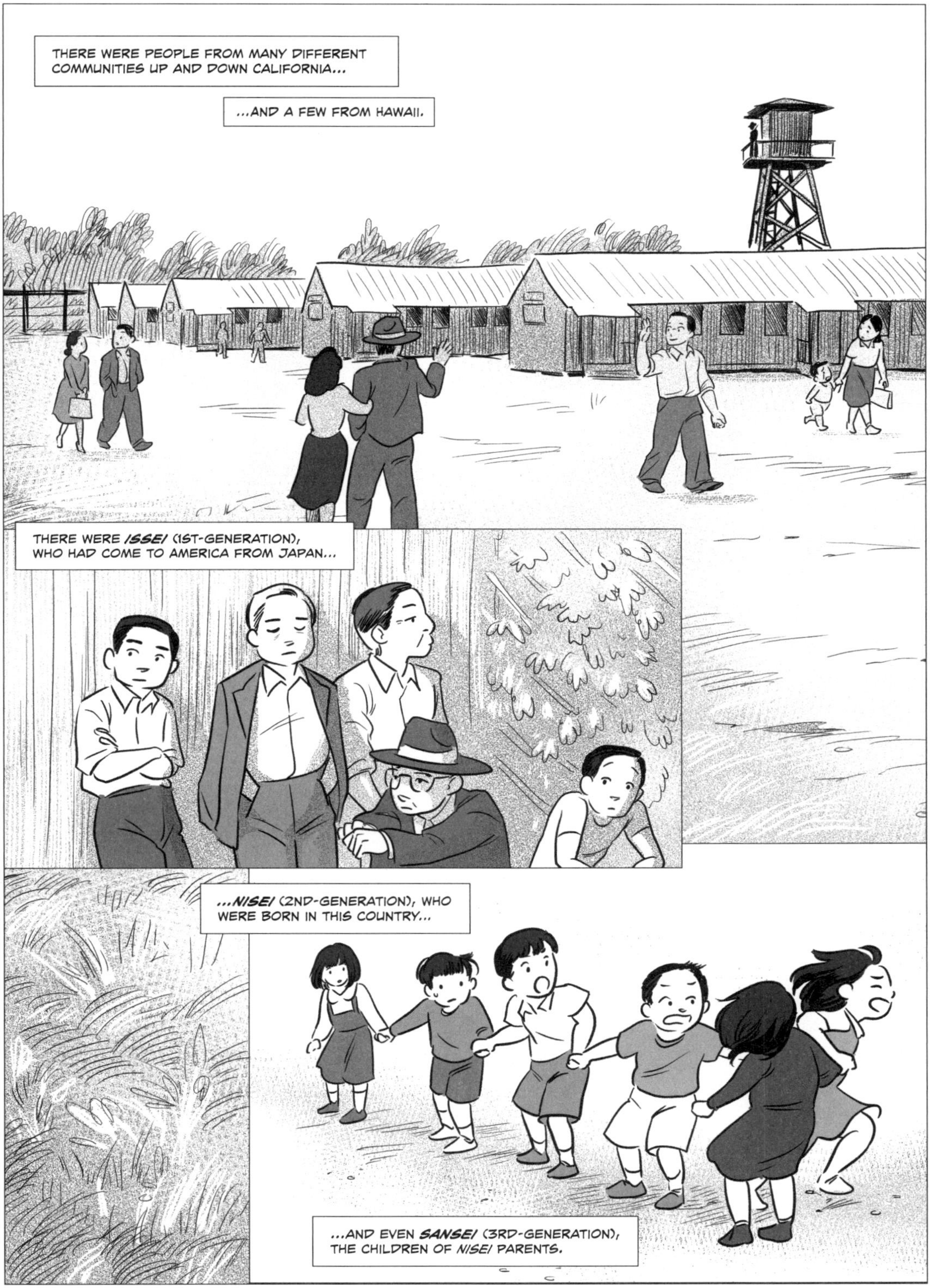
THERE WERE PEOPLE FROM MANY DIFFERENT COMMUNITIES UP AND DOWN CALIFORNIA...
...AND A FEW FROM HAWAII.
THERE WERE *ISSEI* (1ST-GENERATION), WHO HAD COME TO AMERICA FROM JAPAN...
...*NISEI* (2ND-GENERATION), WHO WERE BORN IN THIS COUNTRY...
...AND EVEN *SANSEI* (3RD-GENERATION), THE CHILDREN OF *NISEI* PARENTS.

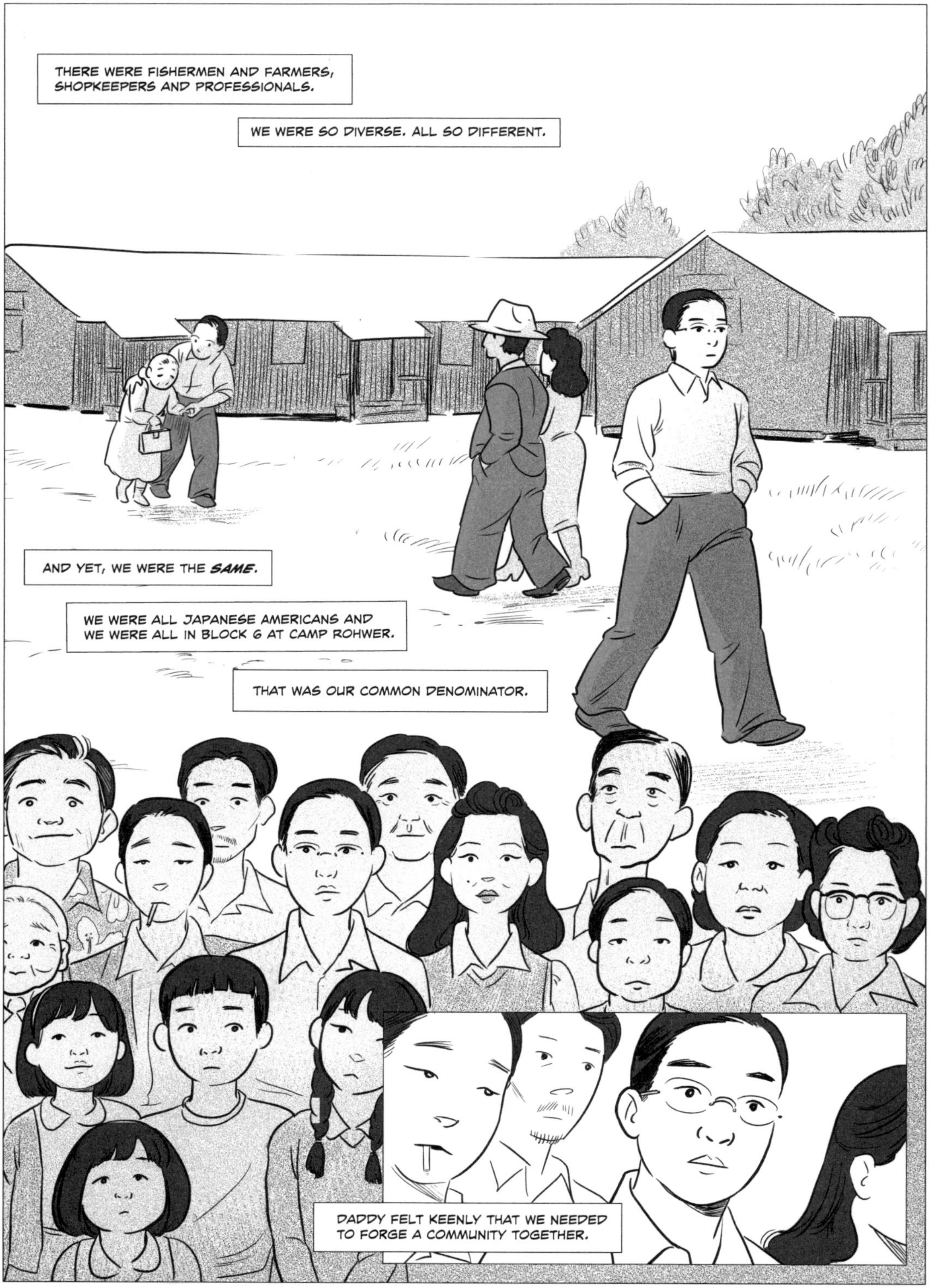
THERE WERE FISHERMEN AND FARMERS, SHOPKEEPERS AND PROFESSIONALS.
WE WERE SO DIVERSE. ALL SO DIFFERENT.
AND YET, WE WERE THE *SAME.*
WE WERE ALL JAPANESE AMERICANS AND WE WERE ALL IN BLOCK 6 AT CAMP ROHWER.
THAT WAS OUR COMMON DENOMINATOR.
DADDY FELT KEENLY THAT WE NEEDED TO FORGE A COMMUNITY TOGETHER.

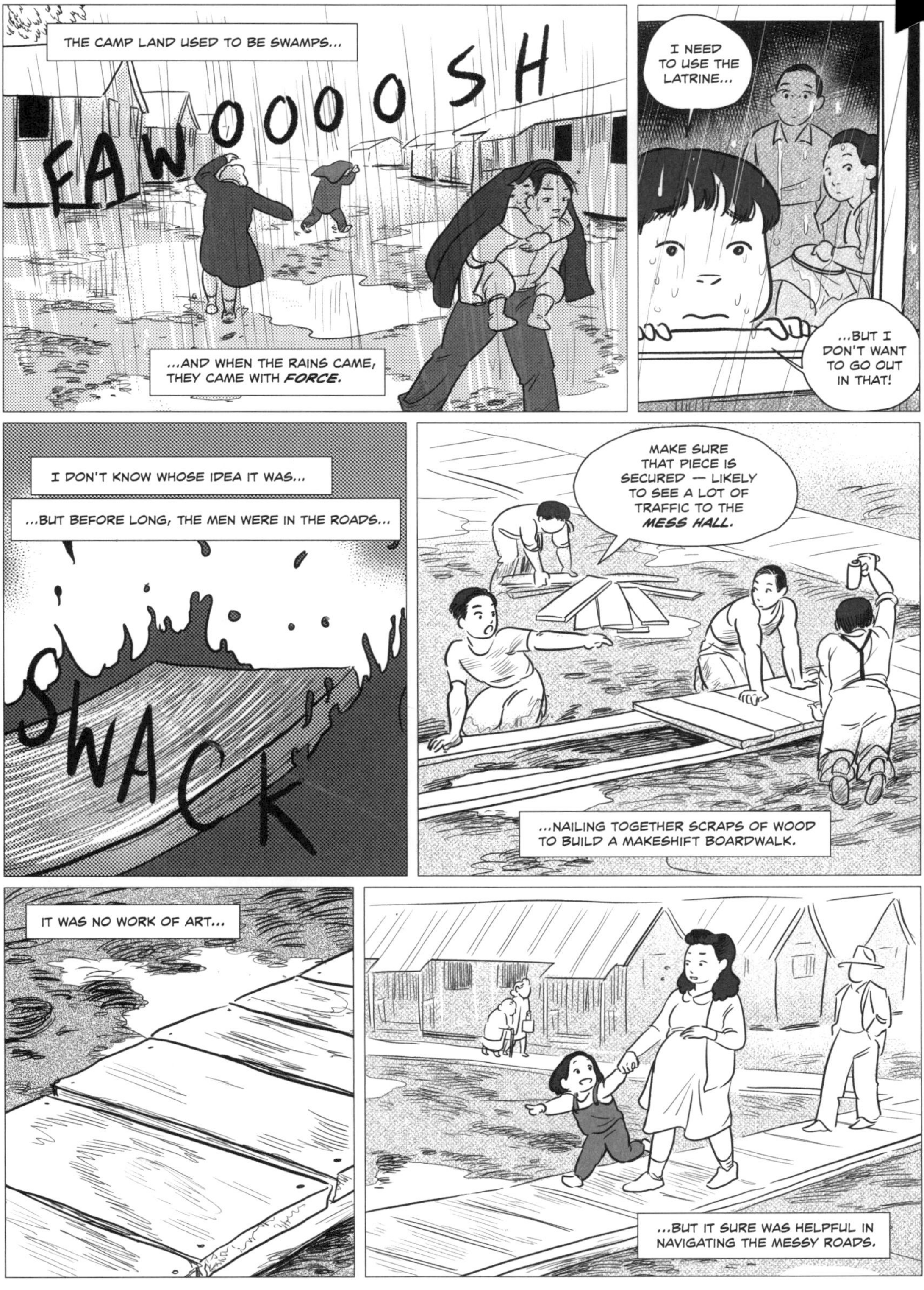

THE CAMP LAND USED TO BE SWAMPS...
FAWOOOOSH
...AND WHEN THE RAINS CAME, THEY CAME WITH FORCE.
I NEED TO USE THE LATRINE...
...BUT I DON'T WANT TO GO OUT IN THAT!
I DON'T KNOW WHOSE IDEA IT WAS...
...BUT BEFORE LONG, THE MEN WERE IN THE ROADS...
SWACK
MAKE SURE THAT PIECE IS SECURED — LIKELY TO SEE A LOT OF TRAFFIC TO THE MESS HALL.
...NAILING TOGETHER SCRAPS OF WOOD TO BUILD A MAKESHIFT BOARDWALK.
IT WAS NO WORK OF ART...
...BUT IT SURE WAS HELPFUL IN NAVIGATING THE MESSY ROADS.

THIS IS UNACCEPTABLE!

BUT PROBLEMS AND COMPLAINTS WERE INEVITABLE...

WE NEED MORE PRIVACY!

SOMEONE MUST SPEAK WITH THE GUARDS!

...AND THEY IMMEDIATELY STARTED CROPPING UP.

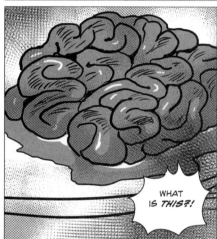

WHAT IS *THIS*?!

I *CANNOT* EAT THIS!

THERE WAS A CLEAR NEED FOR SOMEONE TO BE A REPRESENTATIVE OF OUR COMMUNITY.

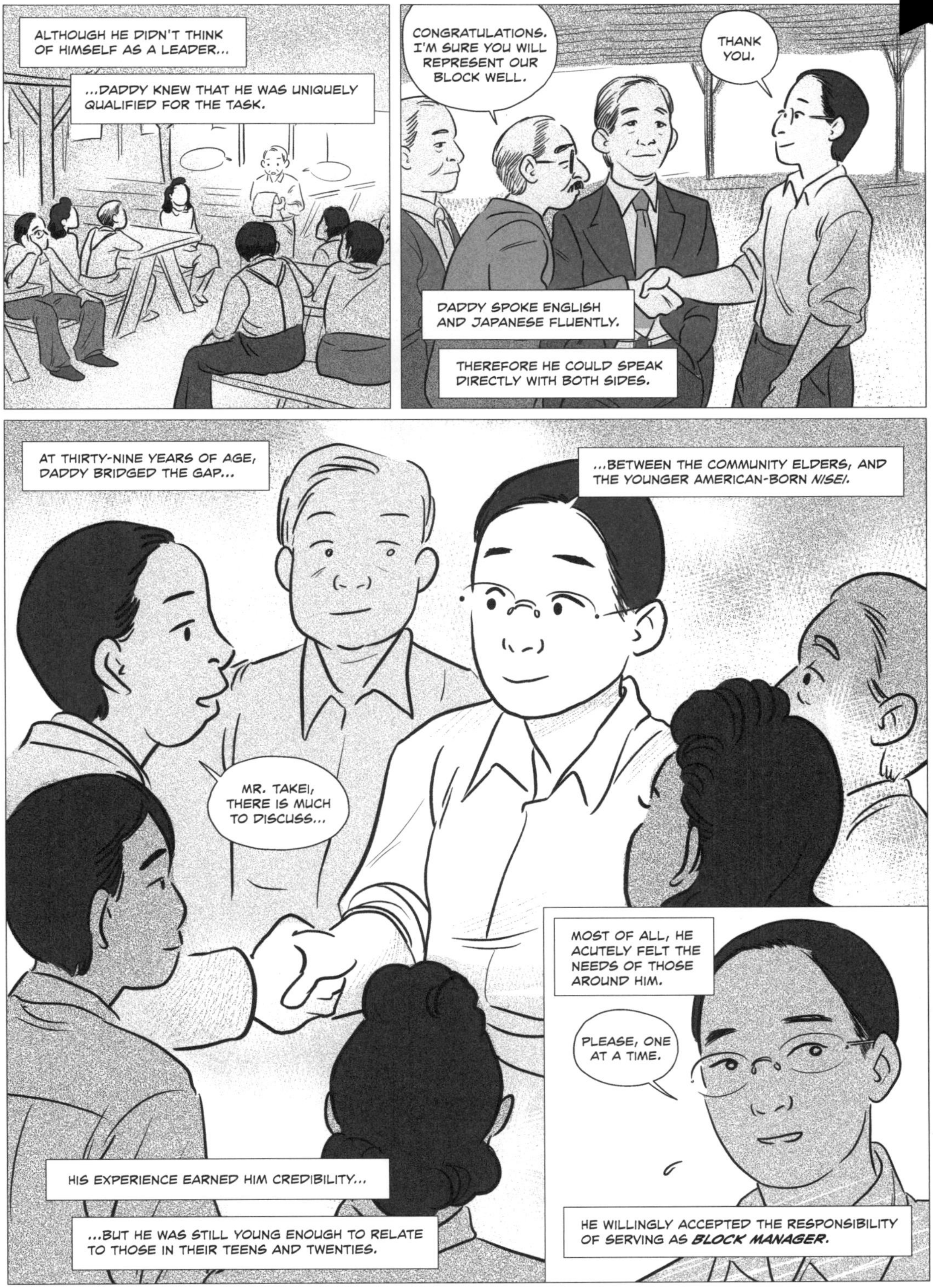

ALTHOUGH HE DIDN'T THINK OF HIMSELF AS A LEADER...
...DADDY KNEW THAT HE WAS UNIQUELY QUALIFIED FOR THE TASK.
CONGRATULATIONS. I'M SURE YOU WILL REPRESENT OUR BLOCK WELL.
THANK YOU.
DADDY SPOKE ENGLISH AND JAPANESE FLUENTLY.
THEREFORE HE COULD SPEAK DIRECTLY WITH BOTH SIDES.
AT THIRTY-NINE YEARS OF AGE, DADDY BRIDGED THE GAP...
...BETWEEN THE COMMUNITY ELDERS, AND THE YOUNGER AMERICAN-BORN *NISEI*.
MR. TAKEI, THERE IS MUCH TO DISCUSS...
HIS EXPERIENCE EARNED HIM CREDIBILITY...
...BUT HE WAS STILL YOUNG ENOUGH TO RELATE TO THOSE IN THEIR TEENS AND TWENTIES.
MOST OF ALL, HE ACUTELY FELT THE NEEDS OF THOSE AROUND HIM.
PLEASE, ONE AT A TIME.
HE WILLINGLY ACCEPTED THE RESPONSIBILITY OF SERVING AS ***BLOCK MANAGER***.

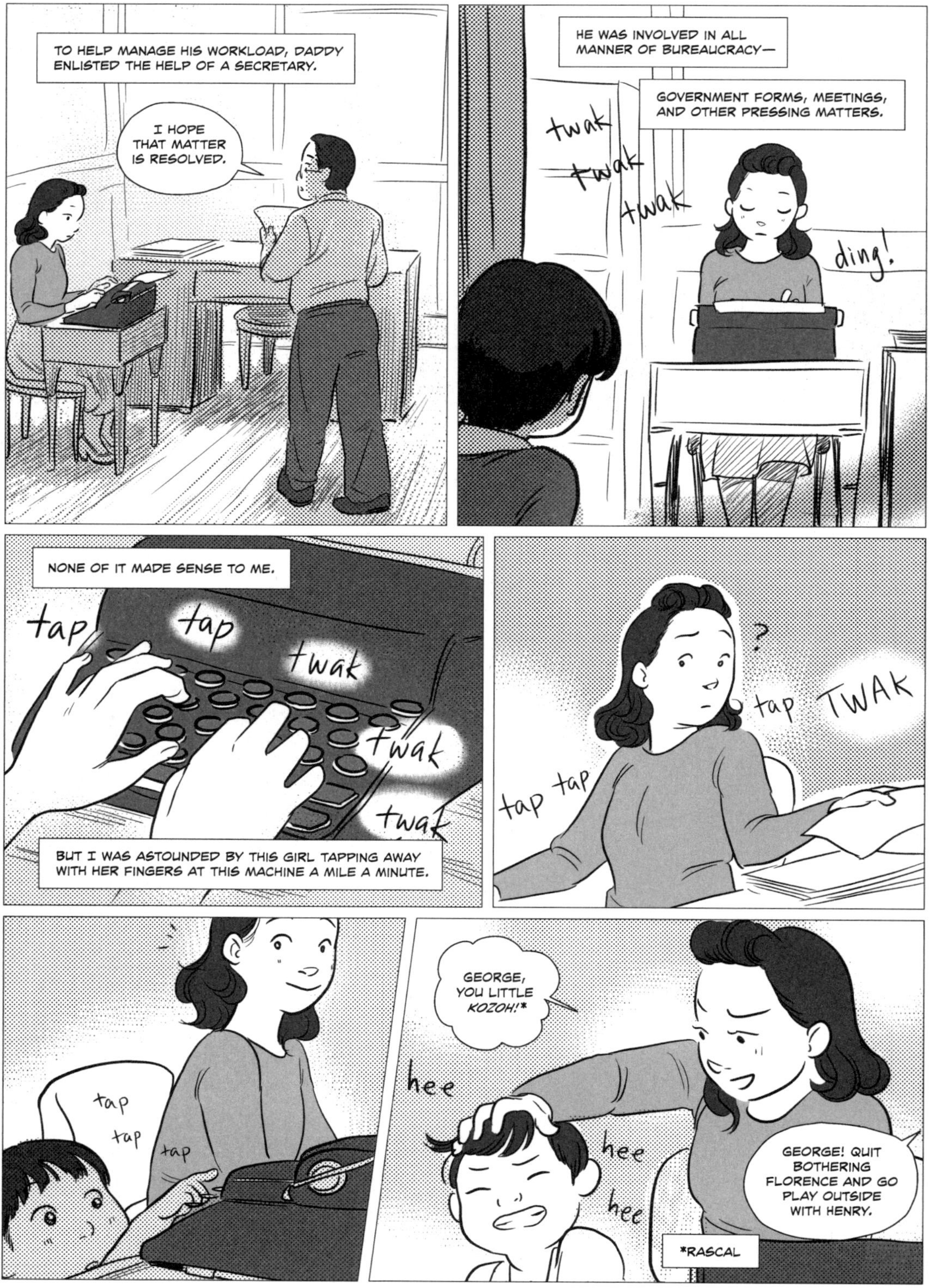
TO HELP MANAGE HIS WORKLOAD, DADDY ENLISTED THE HELP OF A SECRETARY.
I HOPE THAT MATTER IS RESOLVED.
HE WAS INVOLVED IN ALL MANNER OF BUREAUCRACY—
GOVERNMENT FORMS, MEETINGS, AND OTHER PRESSING MATTERS.
twak
twak
twak
ding!
NONE OF IT MADE SENSE TO ME.
tap
tap
twak
twak
twak
BUT I WAS ASTOUNDED BY THIS GIRL TAPPING AWAY WITH HER FINGERS AT THIS MACHINE A MILE A MINUTE.
?
tap
TWAK
tap tap
tap
tap
tap
GEORGE, YOU LITTLE *KOZOH!**
hee
hee
hee
GEORGE! QUIT BOTHERING FLORENCE AND GO PLAY OUTSIDE WITH HENRY.
*RASCAL

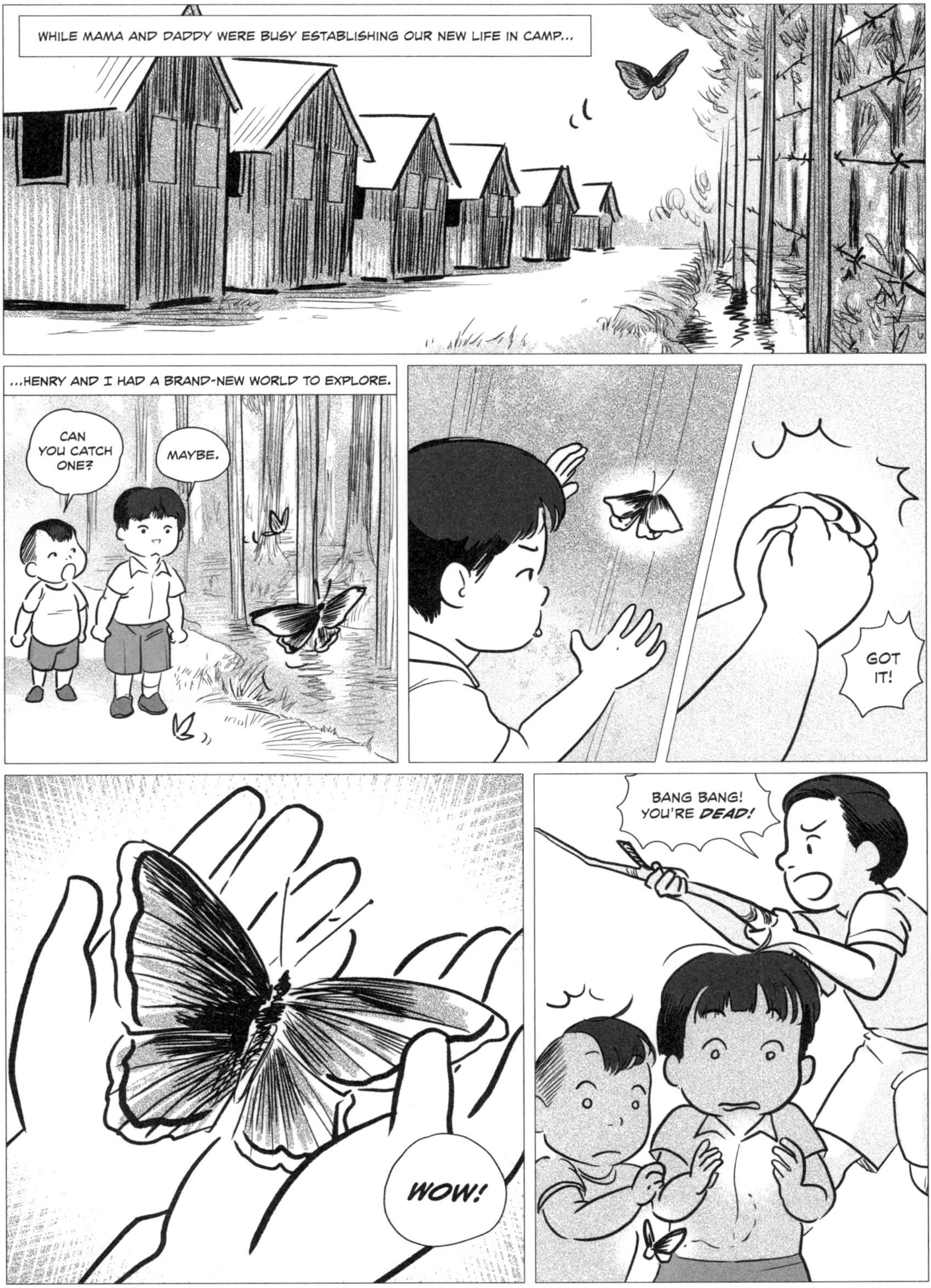

WHILE MAMA AND DADDY WERE BUSY ESTABLISHING OUR NEW LIFE IN CAMP...
...HENRY AND I HAD A BRAND-NEW WORLD TO EXPLORE.
CAN YOU CATCH ONE?
MAYBE.
GOT IT!
WOW!
BANG BANG! YOU'RE *DEAD!*

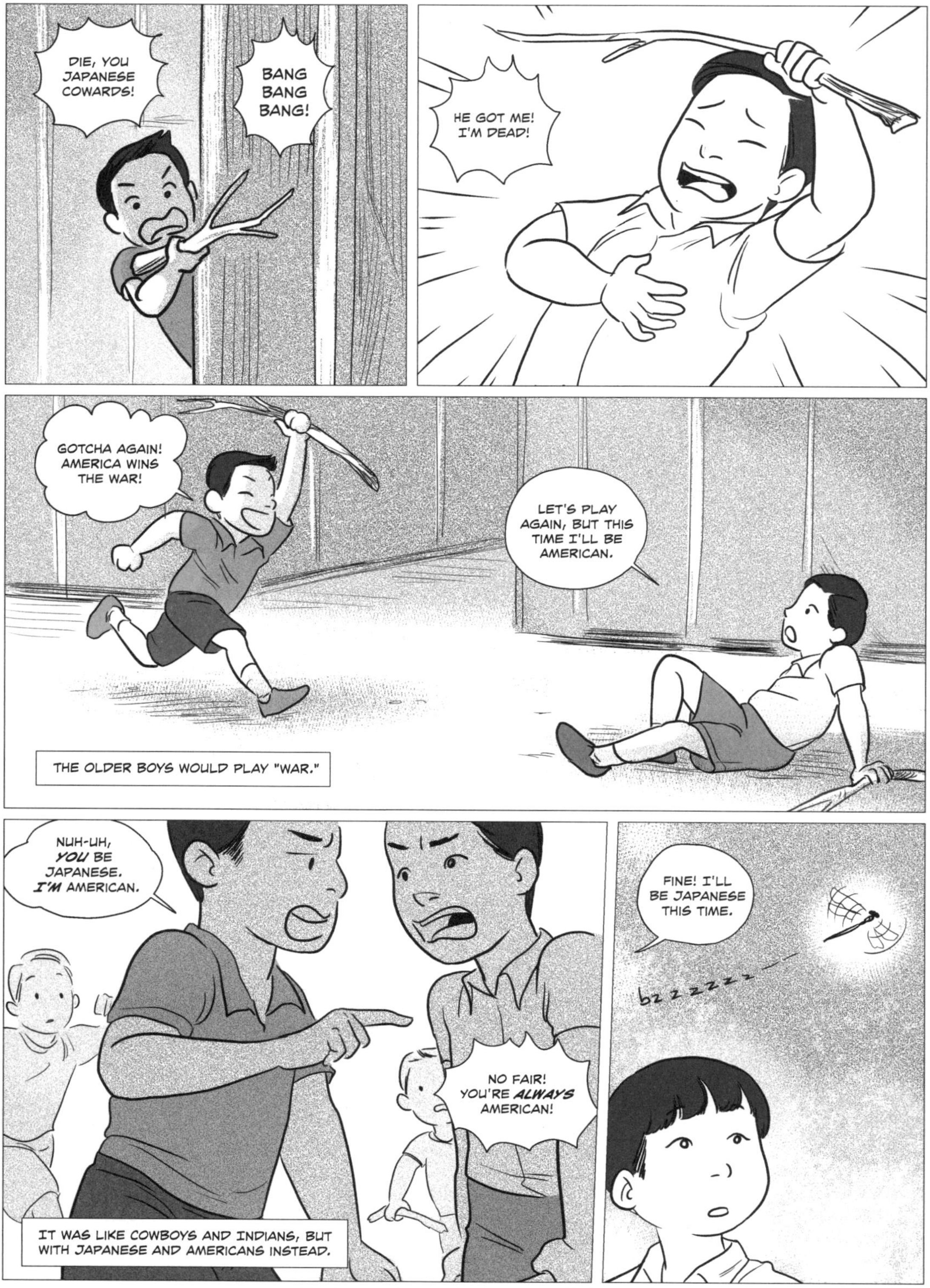
DIE, YOU JAPANESE COWARDS!
BANG BANG BANG!
HE GOT ME! I'M DEAD!
GOTCHA AGAIN! AMERICA WINS THE WAR!
LET'S PLAY AGAIN, BUT THIS TIME I'LL BE AMERICAN.
THE OLDER BOYS WOULD PLAY "WAR."
NUH-UH, ***YOU*** BE JAPANESE. ***I'M*** AMERICAN.
NO FAIR! YOU'RE ***ALWAYS*** AMERICAN!
IT WAS LIKE COWBOYS AND INDIANS, BUT WITH JAPANESE AND AMERICANS INSTEAD.
FINE! I'LL BE JAPANESE THIS TIME.
bzzzzzz

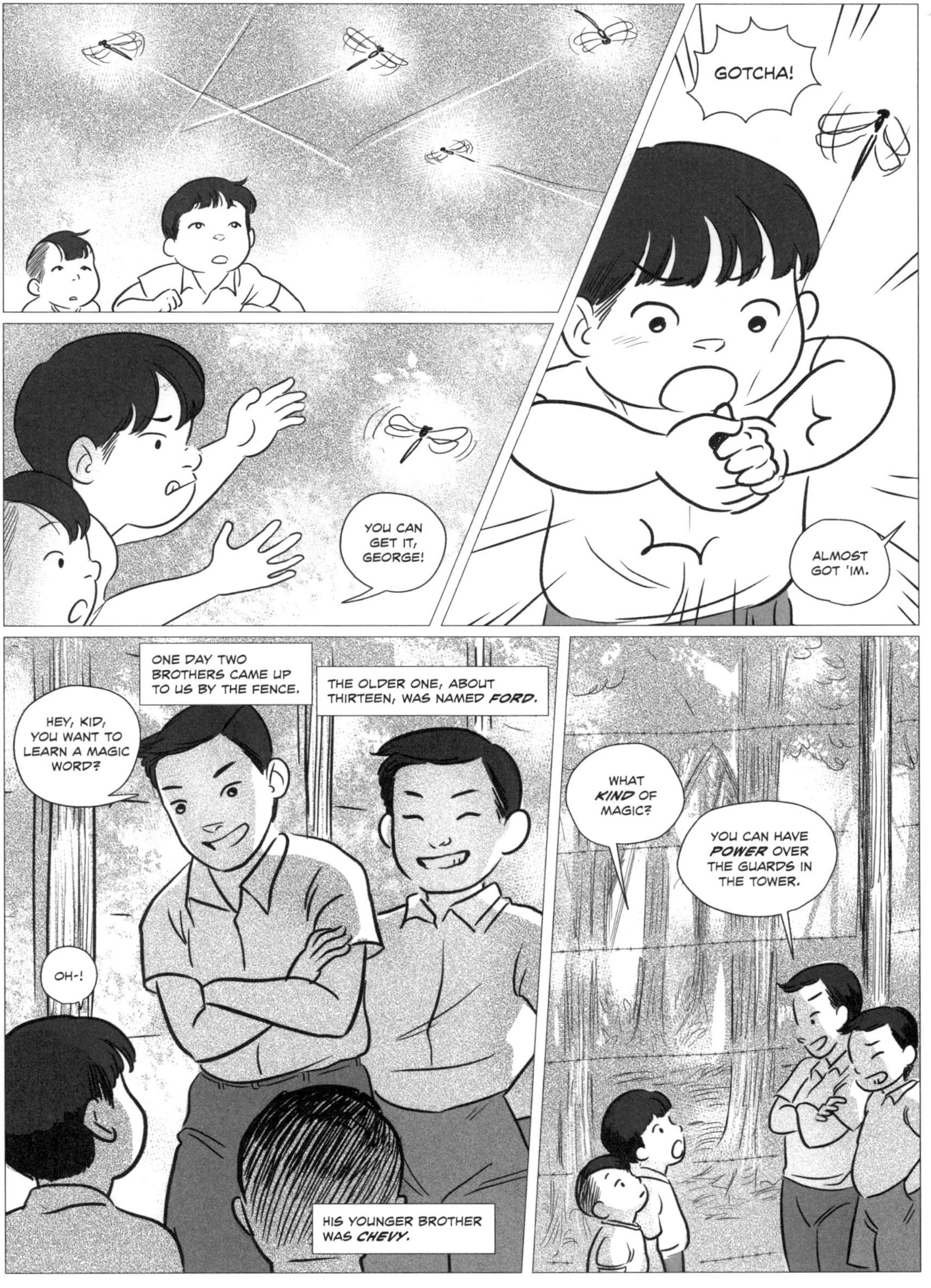
GOTCHA!
YOU CAN GET IT, GEORGE!
ALMOST GOT 'IM.
ONE DAY TWO BROTHERS CAME UP TO US BY THE FENCE.
THE OLDER ONE, ABOUT THIRTEEN, WAS NAMED *FORD*.
HEY, KID, YOU WANT TO LEARN A MAGIC WORD?
OH-!
HIS YOUNGER BROTHER WAS *CHEVY*.
WHAT *KIND* OF MAGIC?
YOU CAN HAVE *POWER* OVER THE GUARDS IN THE TOWER.

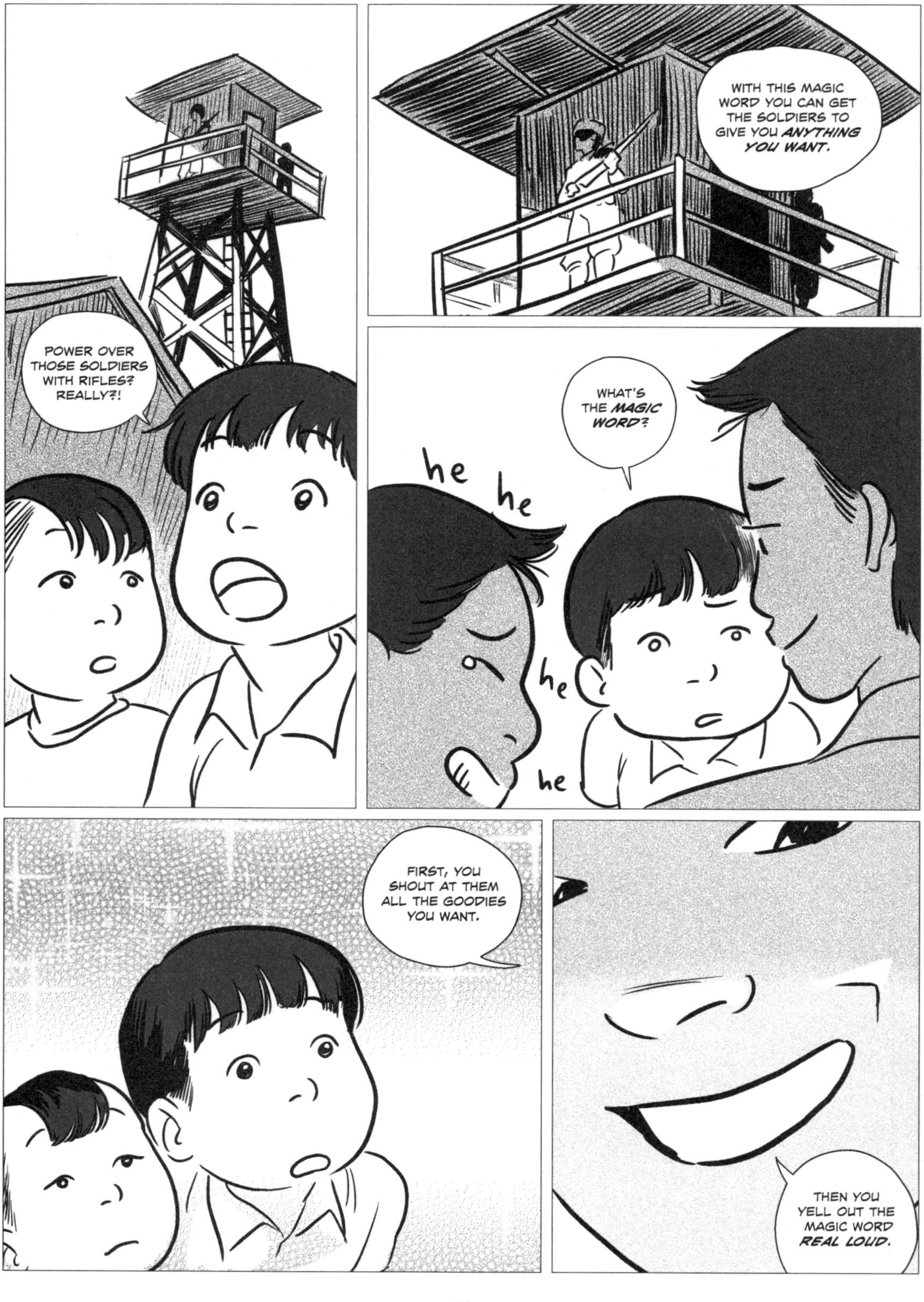
WITH THIS MAGIC WORD YOU CAN GET THE SOLDIERS TO GIVE YOU ANYTHING YOU WANT.
POWER OVER THOSE SOLDIERS WITH RIFLES? REALLY?!
WHAT'S THE MAGIC WORD?
he he he he
FIRST, YOU SHOUT AT THEM ALL THE GOODIES YOU WANT.
THEN YOU YELL OUT THE MAGIC WORD REAL LOUD.

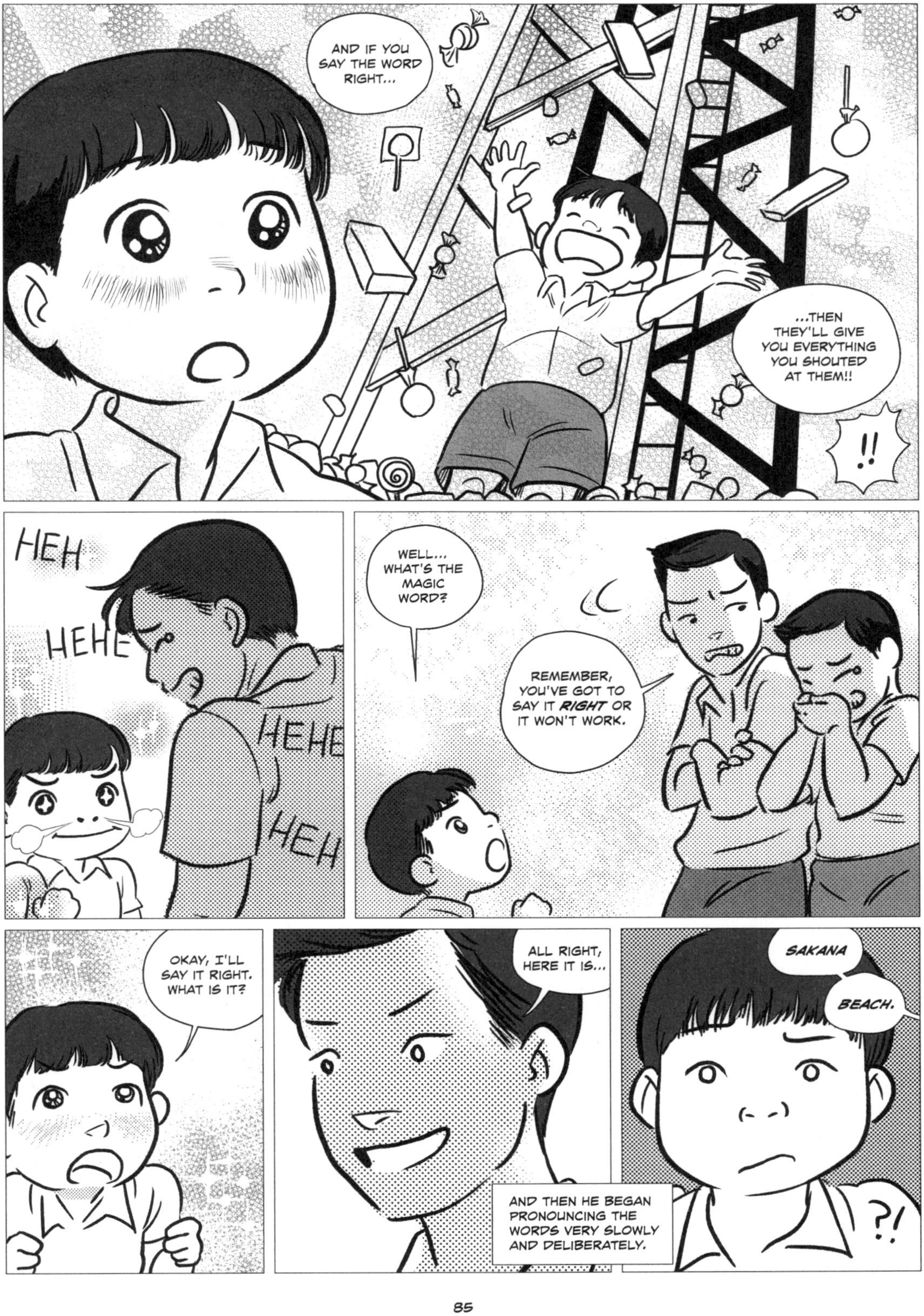
AND IF YOU SAY THE WORD RIGHT...
...THEN THEY'LL GIVE YOU EVERYTHING YOU SHOUTED AT THEM!!
!!
HEH
HEHE
HEHE
HEH
WELL... WHAT'S THE MAGIC WORD?
REMEMBER, YOU'VE GOT TO SAY IT RIGHT OR IT WON'T WORK.
OKAY, I'LL SAY IT RIGHT. WHAT IS IT?
ALL RIGHT, HERE IT IS...
AND THEN HE BEGAN PRONOUNCING THE WORDS VERY SLOWLY AND DELIBERATELY.
SAKANA
BEACH.
?!

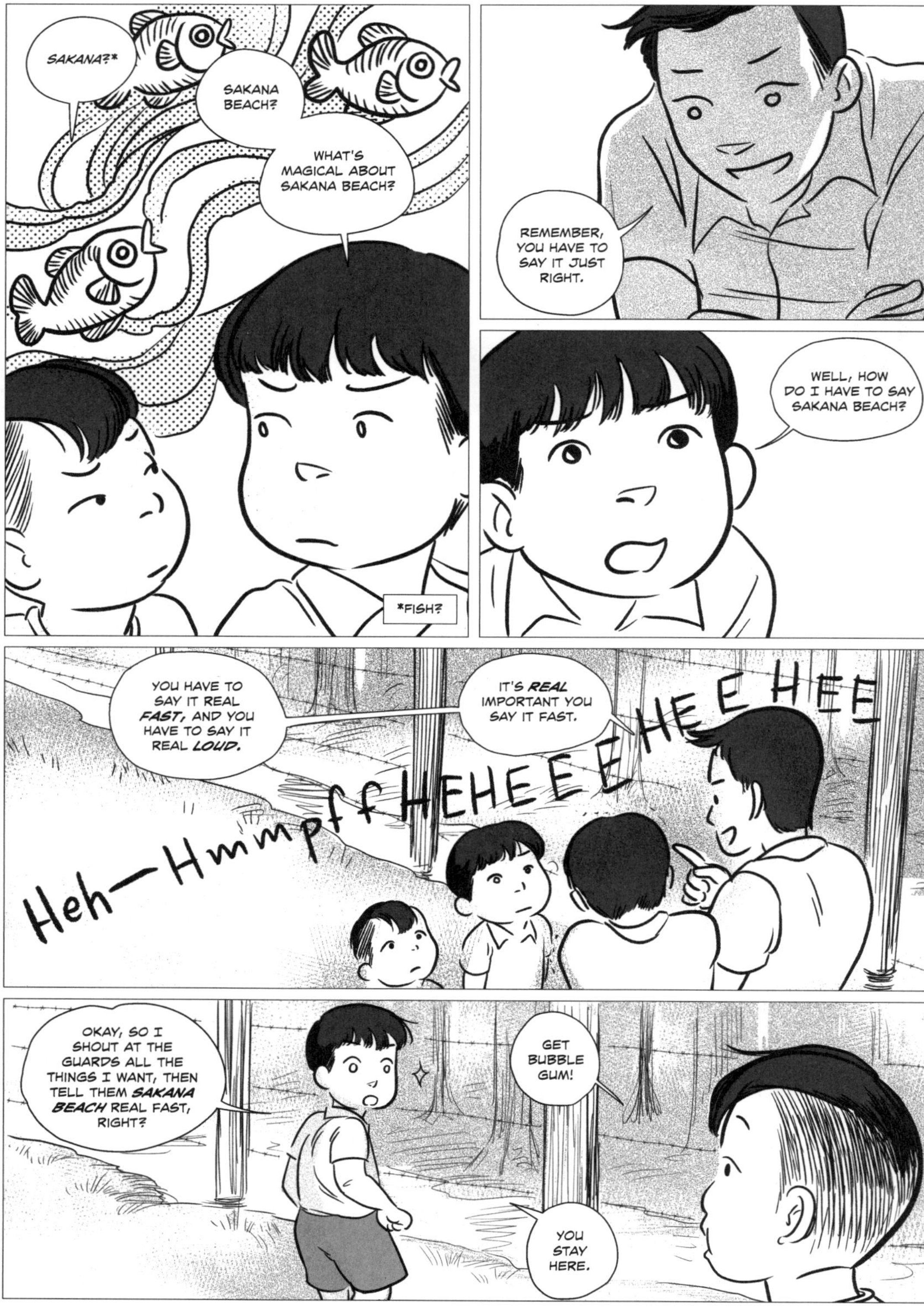

SAKANA?*
SAKANA BEACH?
WHAT'S MAGICAL ABOUT SAKANA BEACH?
*FISH?
REMEMBER, YOU HAVE TO SAY IT JUST RIGHT.
WELL, HOW DO I HAVE TO SAY SAKANA BEACH?
YOU HAVE TO SAY IT REAL FAST, AND YOU HAVE TO SAY IT REAL LOUD.
IT'S REAL IMPORTANT YOU SAY IT FAST.
Heh—HmmpffHEHEEEHEEHEE
OKAY, SO I SHOUT AT THE GUARDS ALL THE THINGS I WANT, THEN TELL THEM SAKANA BEACH REAL FAST, RIGHT?
GET BUBBLE GUM!
YOU STAY HERE.

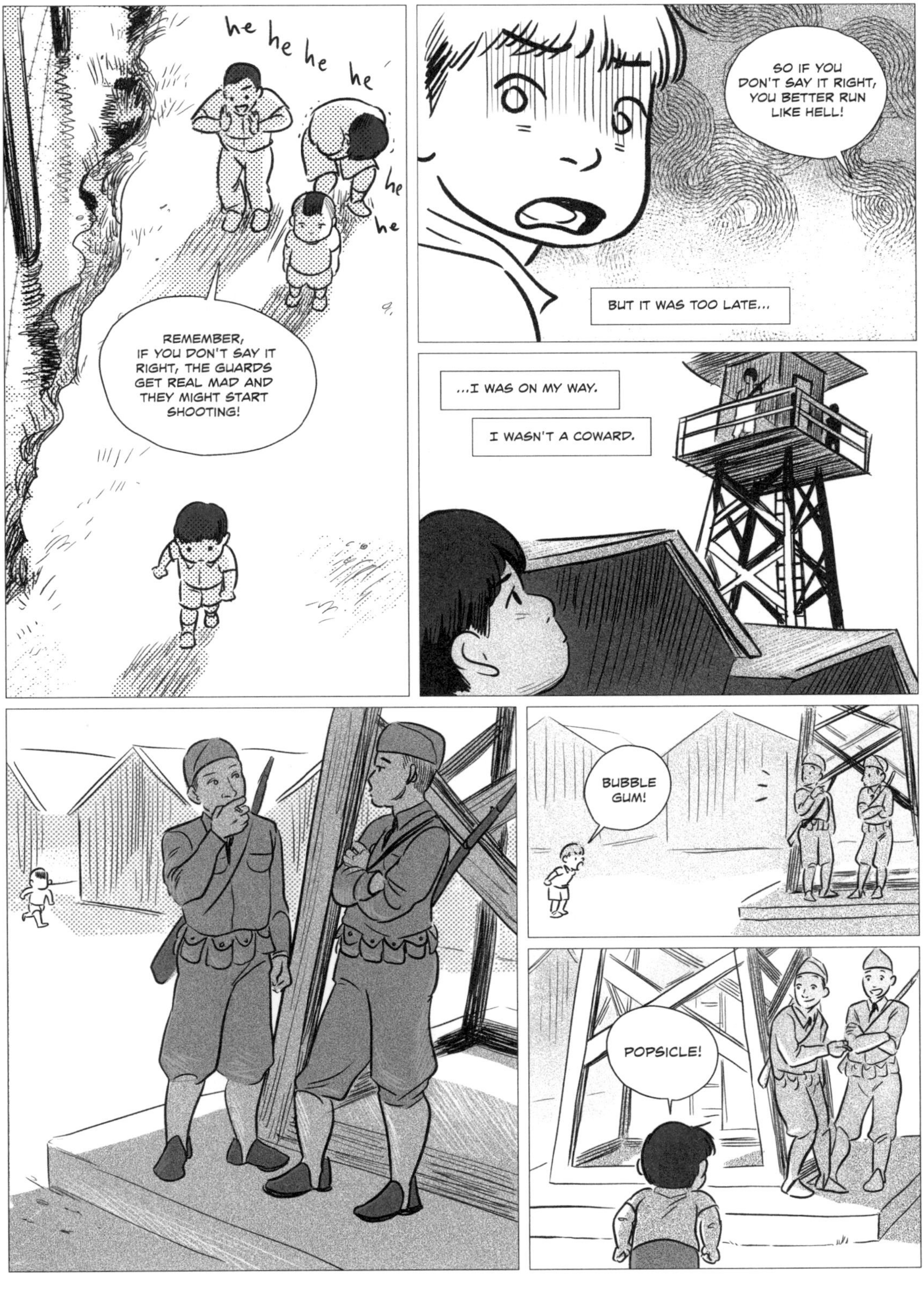
he he he he
he he
REMEMBER, IF YOU DON'T SAY IT RIGHT, THE GUARDS GET REAL MAD AND THEY MIGHT START SHOOTING!
SO IF YOU DON'T SAY IT RIGHT, YOU BETTER RUN LIKE HELL!
BUT IT WAS TOO LATE...
...I WAS ON MY WAY.
I WASN'T A COWARD.
BUBBLE GUM!
POPSICLE!

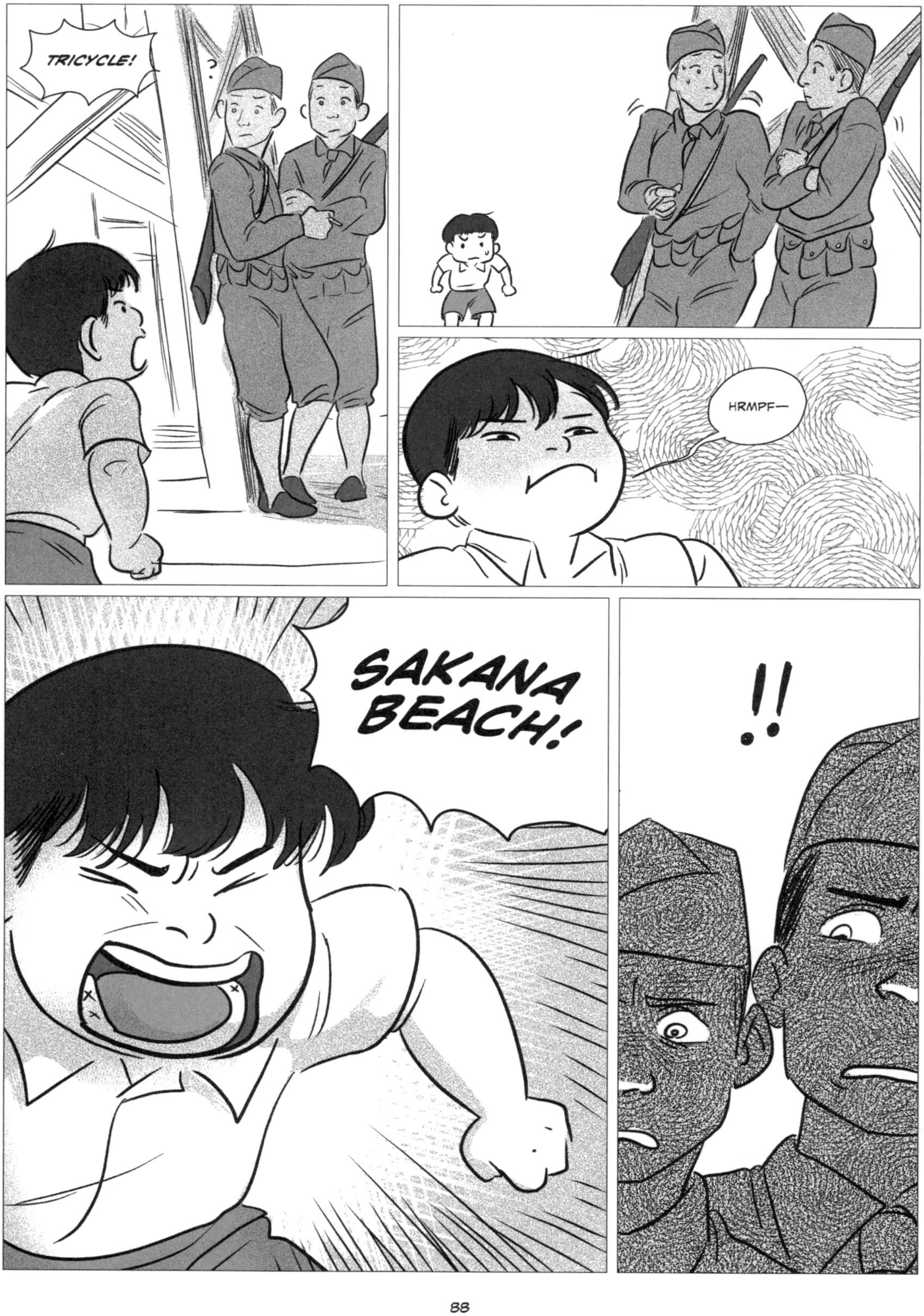
TRICYCLE!
?
HRMPF—
SAKANA BEACH!
!!

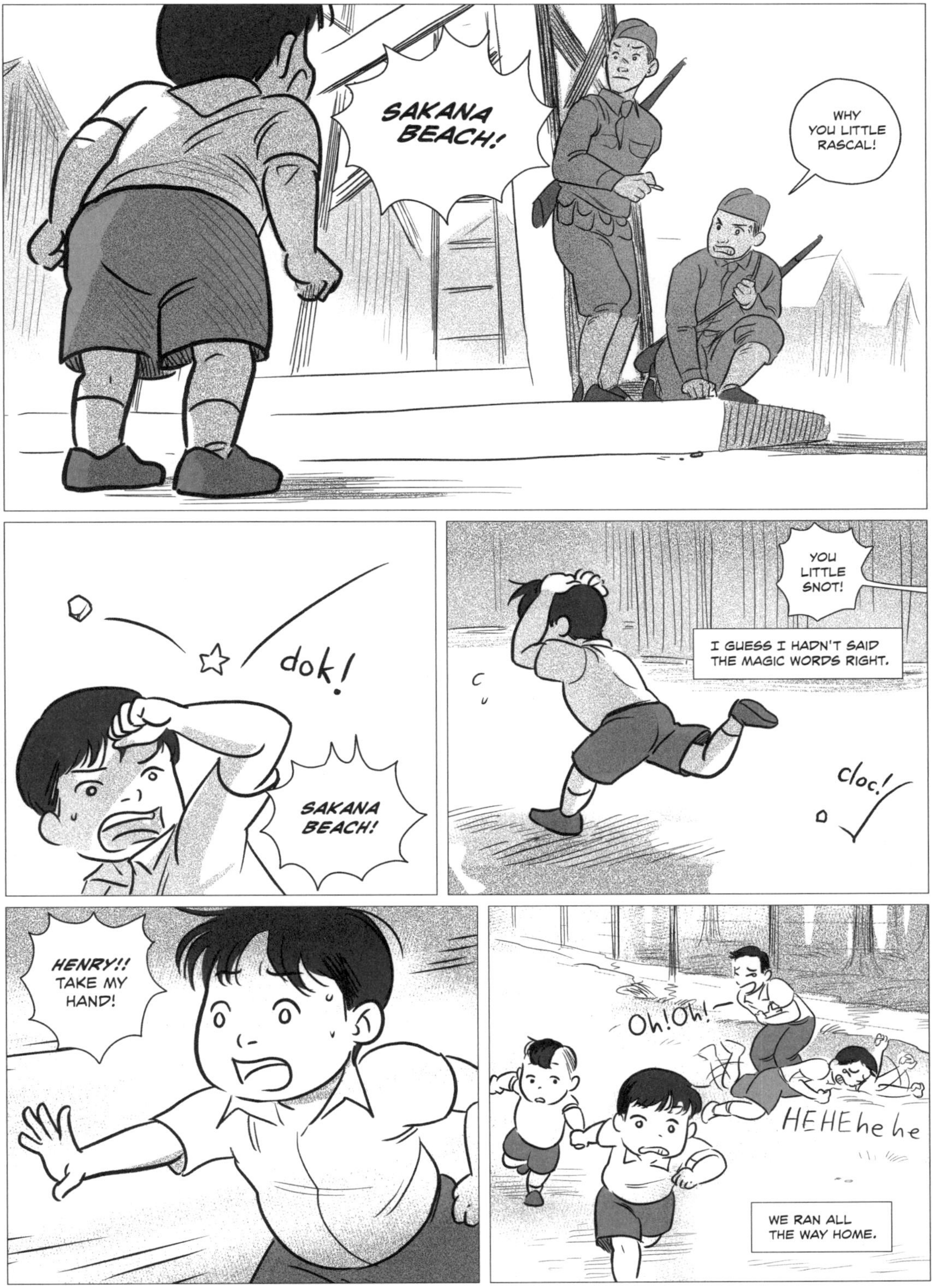
SAKANA BEACH!
WHY YOU LITTLE RASCAL!
dok!
SAKANA BEACH!
YOU LITTLE SNOT!
I GUESS I HADN'T SAID THE MAGIC WORDS RIGHT.
cloc!
HENRY!! TAKE MY HAND!
Oh! Oh!
HEHEhehe
WE RAN ALL THE WAY HOME.

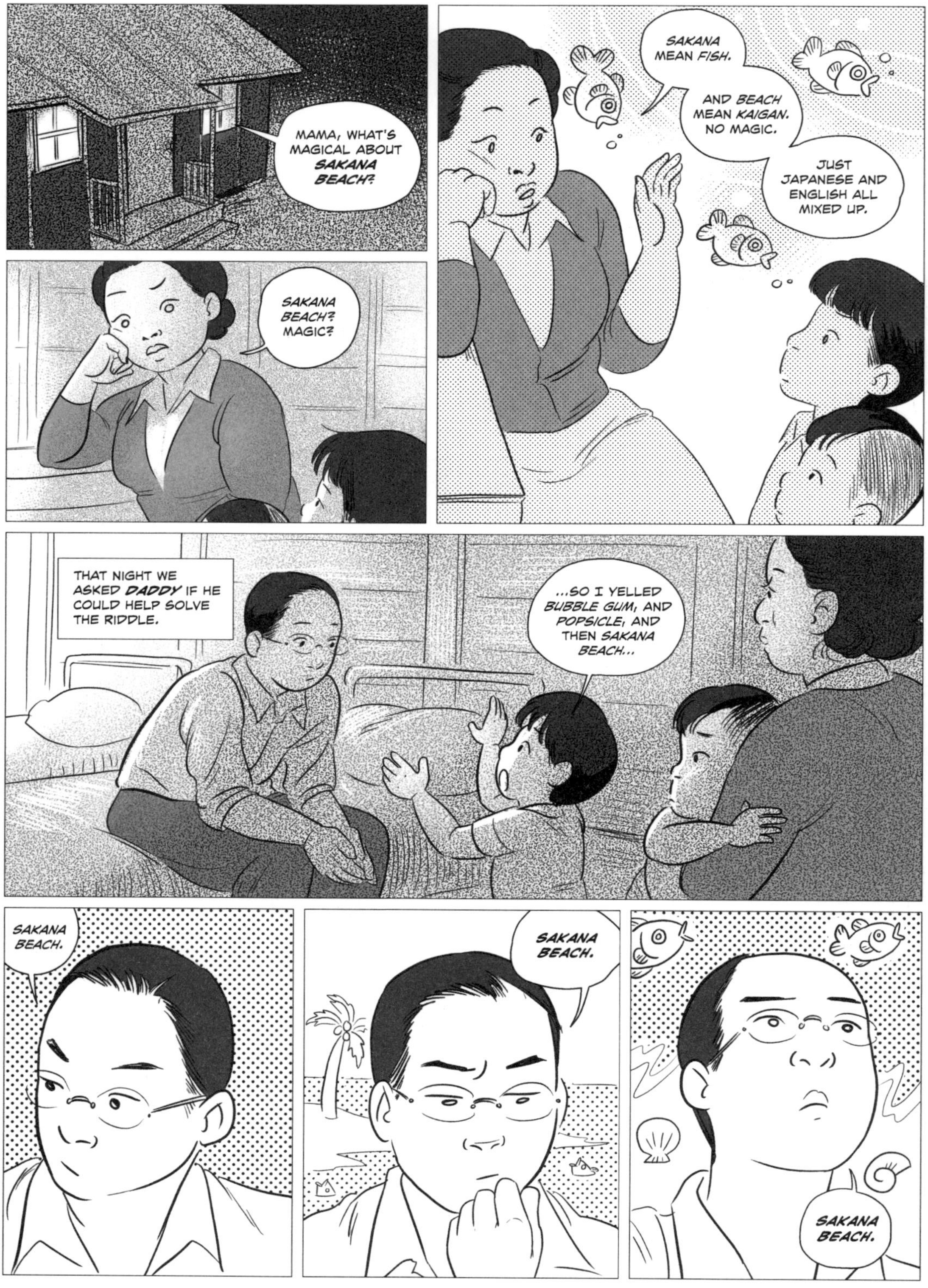

MAMA, WHAT'S MAGICAL ABOUT SAKANA BEACH?
SAKANA BEACH? MAGIC?
SAKANA MEAN FISH.
AND BEACH MEAN KAIGAN. NO MAGIC.
JUST JAPANESE AND ENGLISH ALL MIXED UP.
THAT NIGHT WE ASKED DADDY IF HE COULD HELP SOLVE THE RIDDLE.
...SO I YELLED BUBBLE GUM, AND POPSICLE, AND THEN SAKANA BEACH...
SAKANA BEACH.
SAKANA BEACH.
SAKANA BEACH.

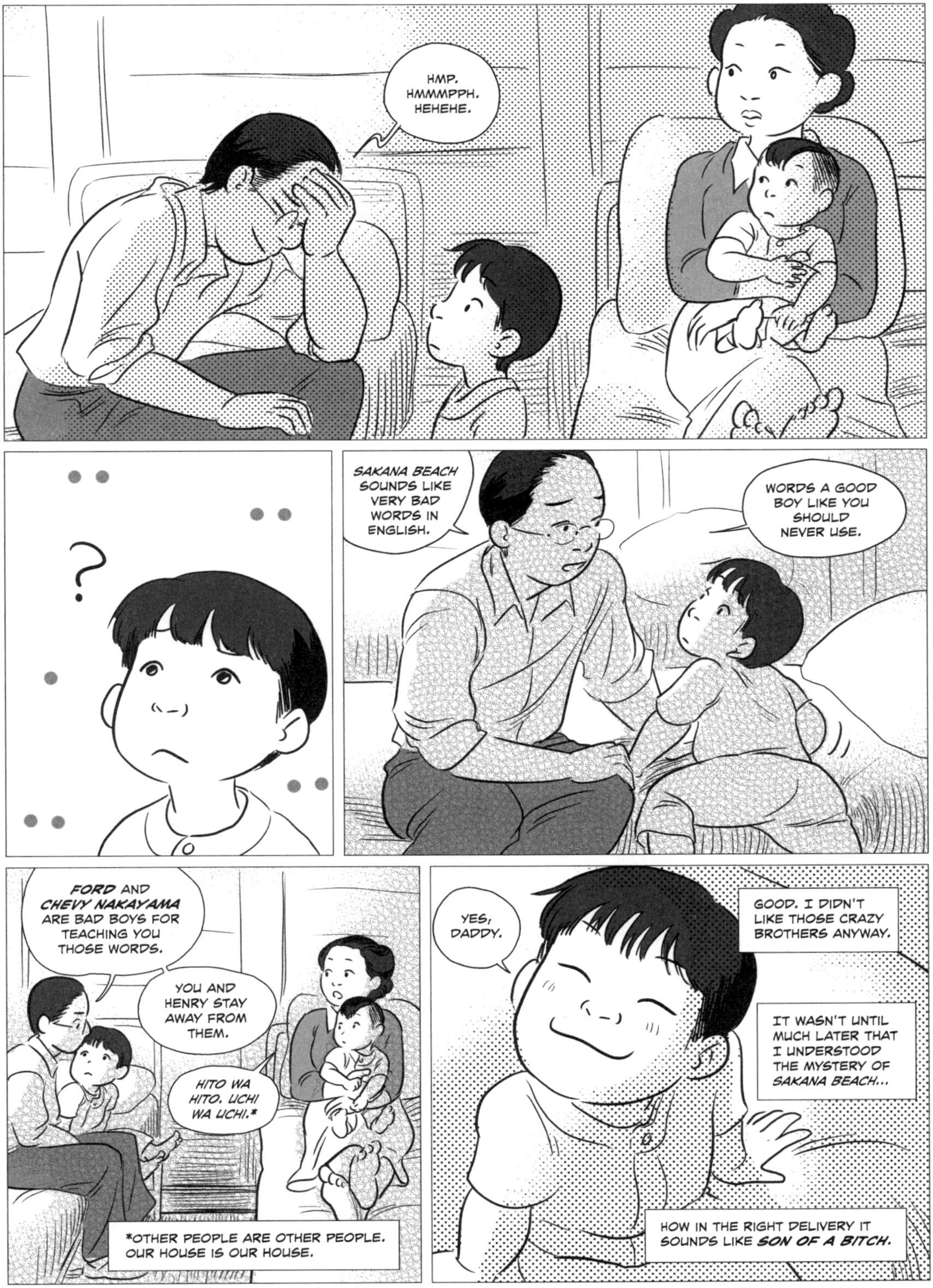
HMP. HMMMPPH. HEHEHE.
SAKANA BEACH SOUNDS LIKE VERY BAD WORDS IN ENGLISH.
WORDS A GOOD BOY LIKE YOU SHOULD NEVER USE.
FORD AND CHEVY NAKAYAMA ARE BAD BOYS FOR TEACHING YOU THOSE WORDS.
YOU AND HENRY STAY AWAY FROM THEM.
HITO WA HITO. UCHI WA UCHI.*
*OTHER PEOPLE ARE OTHER PEOPLE. OUR HOUSE IS OUR HOUSE.
YES, DADDY.
GOOD. I DIDN'T LIKE THOSE CRAZY BROTHERS ANYWAY.
IT WASN'T UNTIL MUCH LATER THAT I UNDERSTOOD THE MYSTERY OF SAKANA BEACH...
HOW IN THE RIGHT DELIVERY IT SOUNDS LIKE SON OF A BITCH.

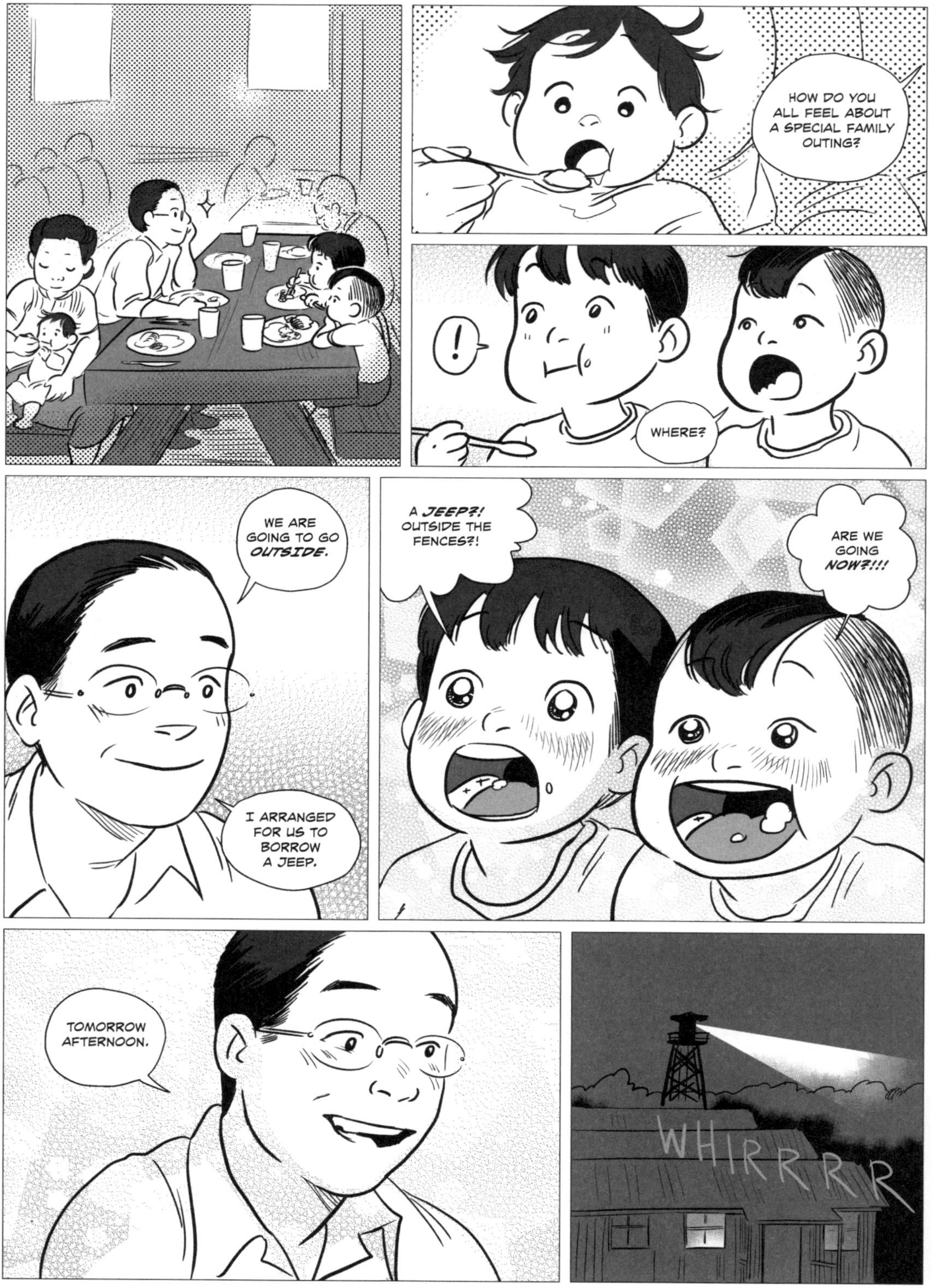
HOW DO YOU ALL FEEL ABOUT A SPECIAL FAMILY OUTING?
!
WHERE?
WE ARE GOING TO GO *OUTSIDE*.
I ARRANGED FOR US TO BORROW A JEEP.
A *JEEP?!* OUTSIDE THE FENCES?!
ARE WE GOING *NOW?!!!*
TOMORROW AFTERNOON.
WHIRRRR

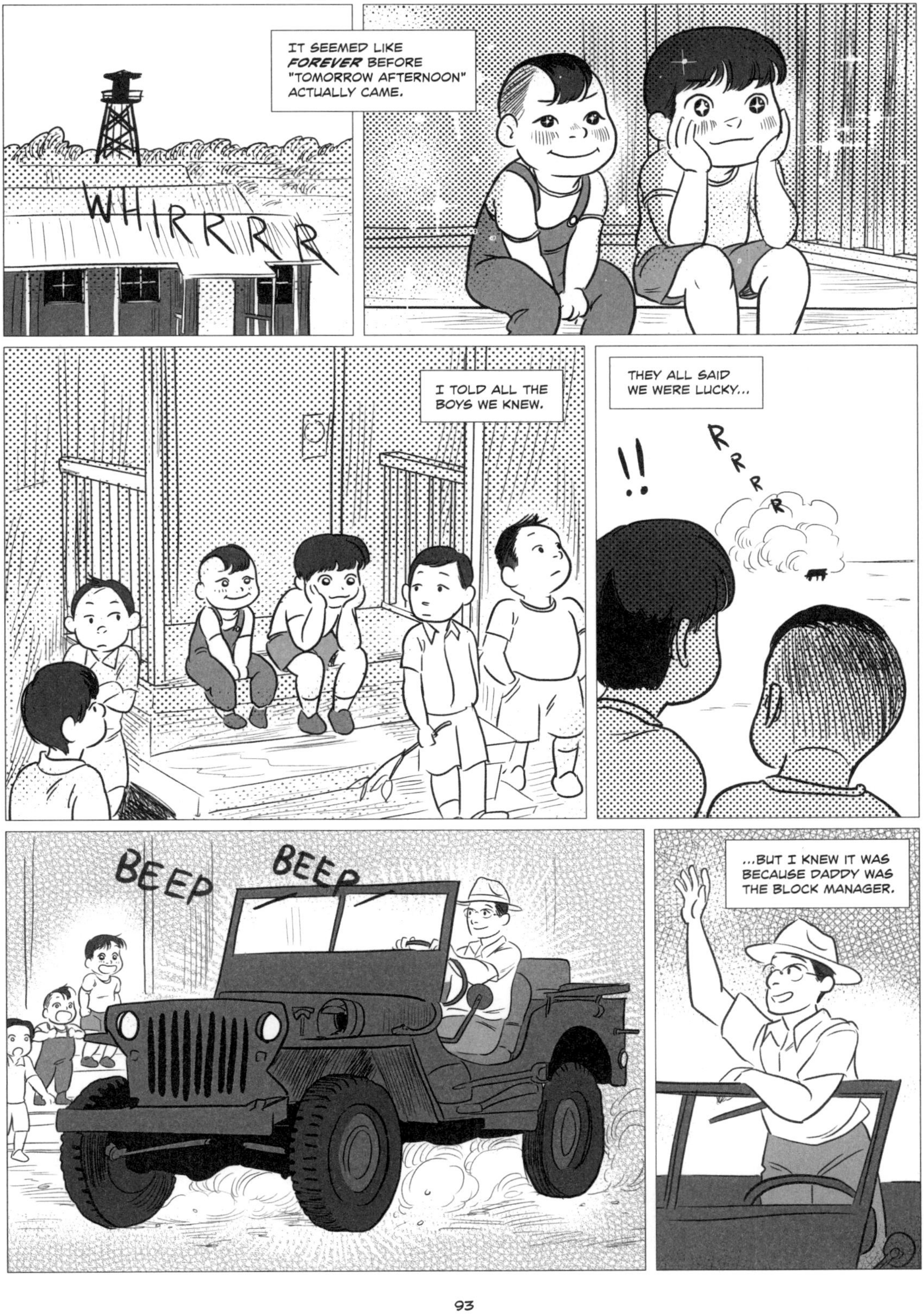
WHIRRRRR
IT SEEMED LIKE *FOREVER* BEFORE "TOMORROW AFTERNOON" ACTUALLY CAME.
I TOLD ALL THE BOYS WE KNEW.
THEY ALL SAID WE WERE LUCKY...
!!
RRRR
BEEP BEEP
...BUT I KNEW IT WAS BECAUSE DADDY WAS THE BLOCK MANAGER.

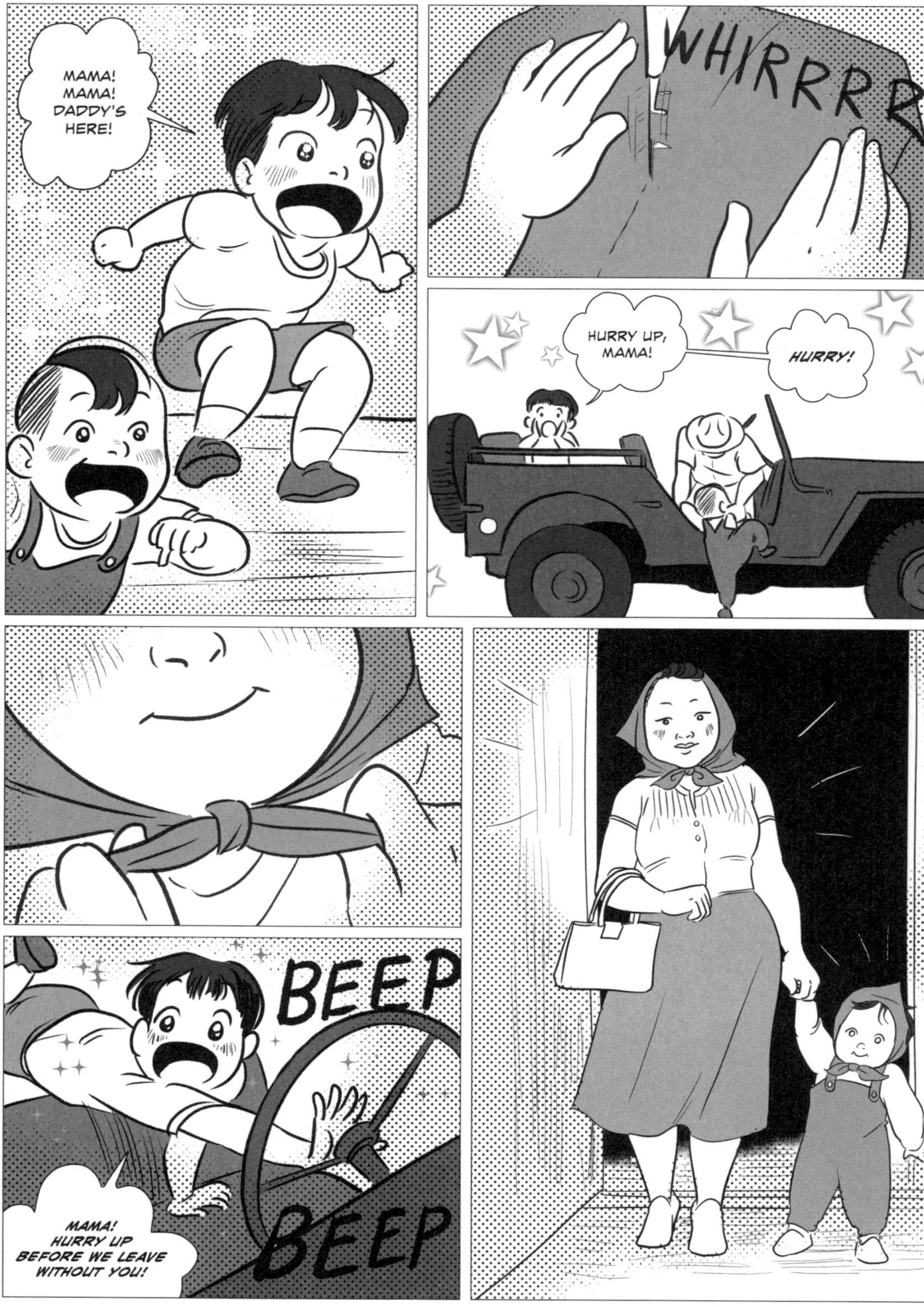
MAMA! MAMA! DADDY'S HERE!
WHIRRRR
HURRY UP, MAMA!
HURRY!
BEEP
BEEP
MAMA! HURRY UP BEFORE WE LEAVE WITHOUT YOU!

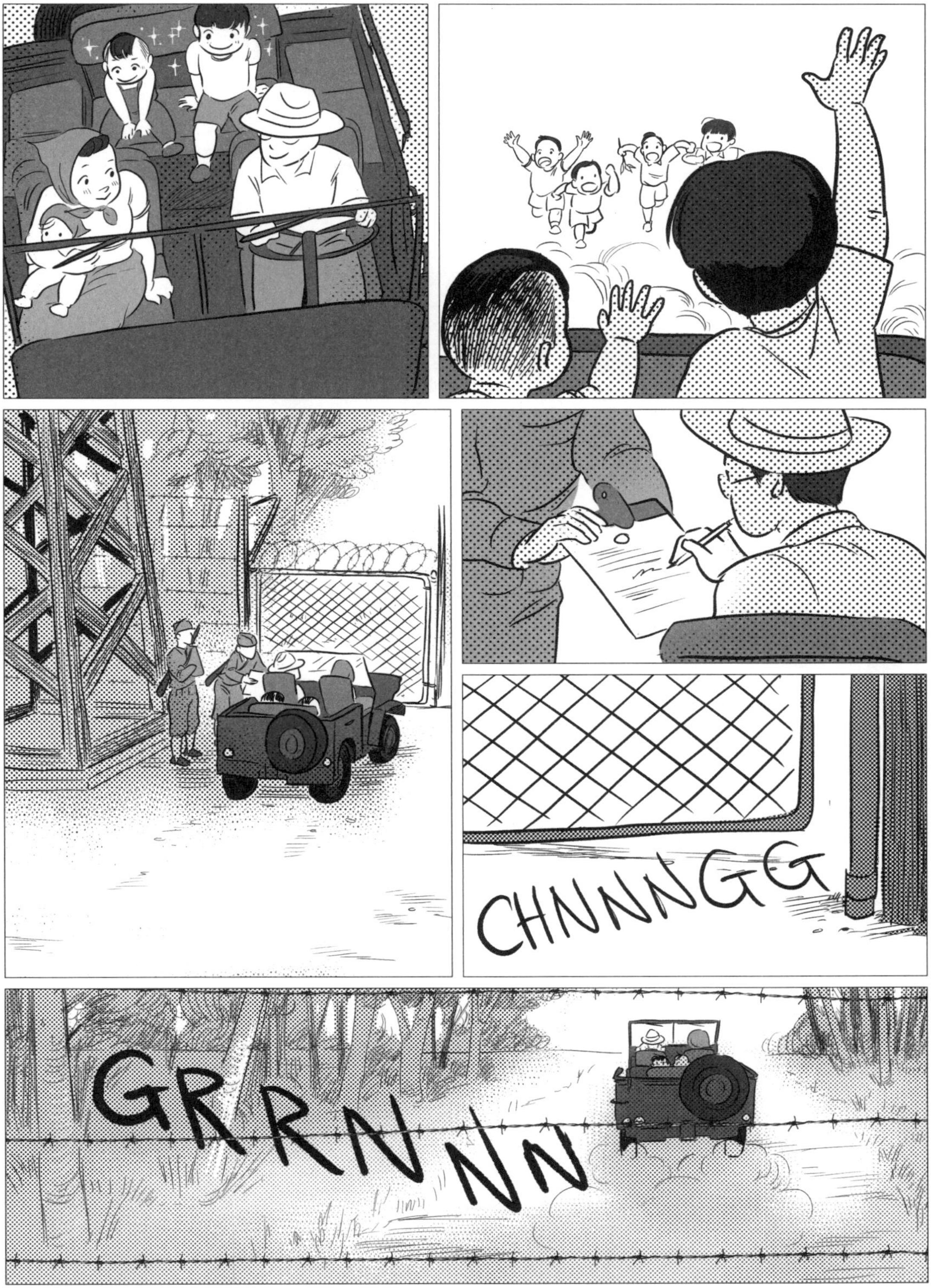
CHNNNGG
GRRRNNN

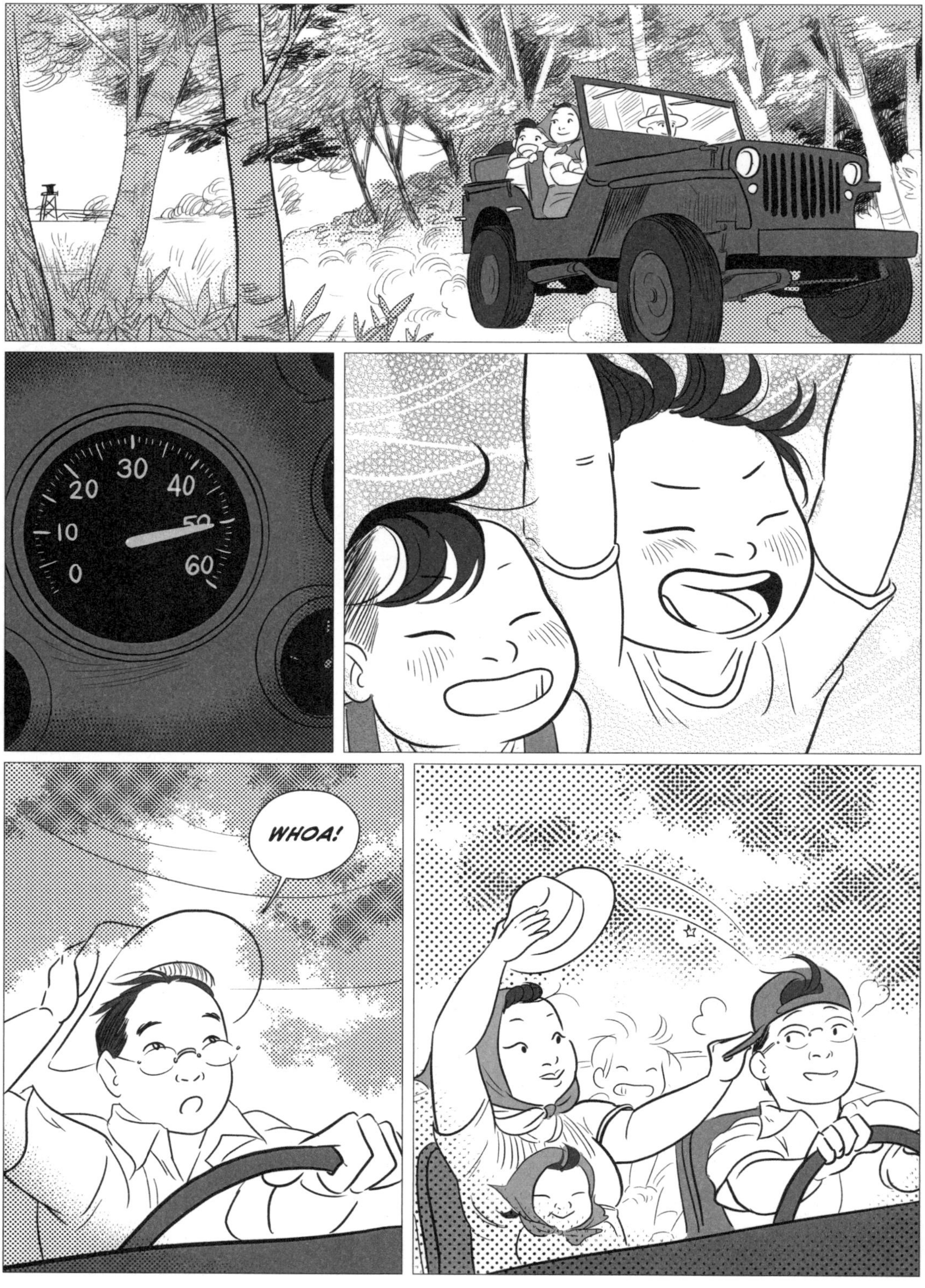
WHOA!

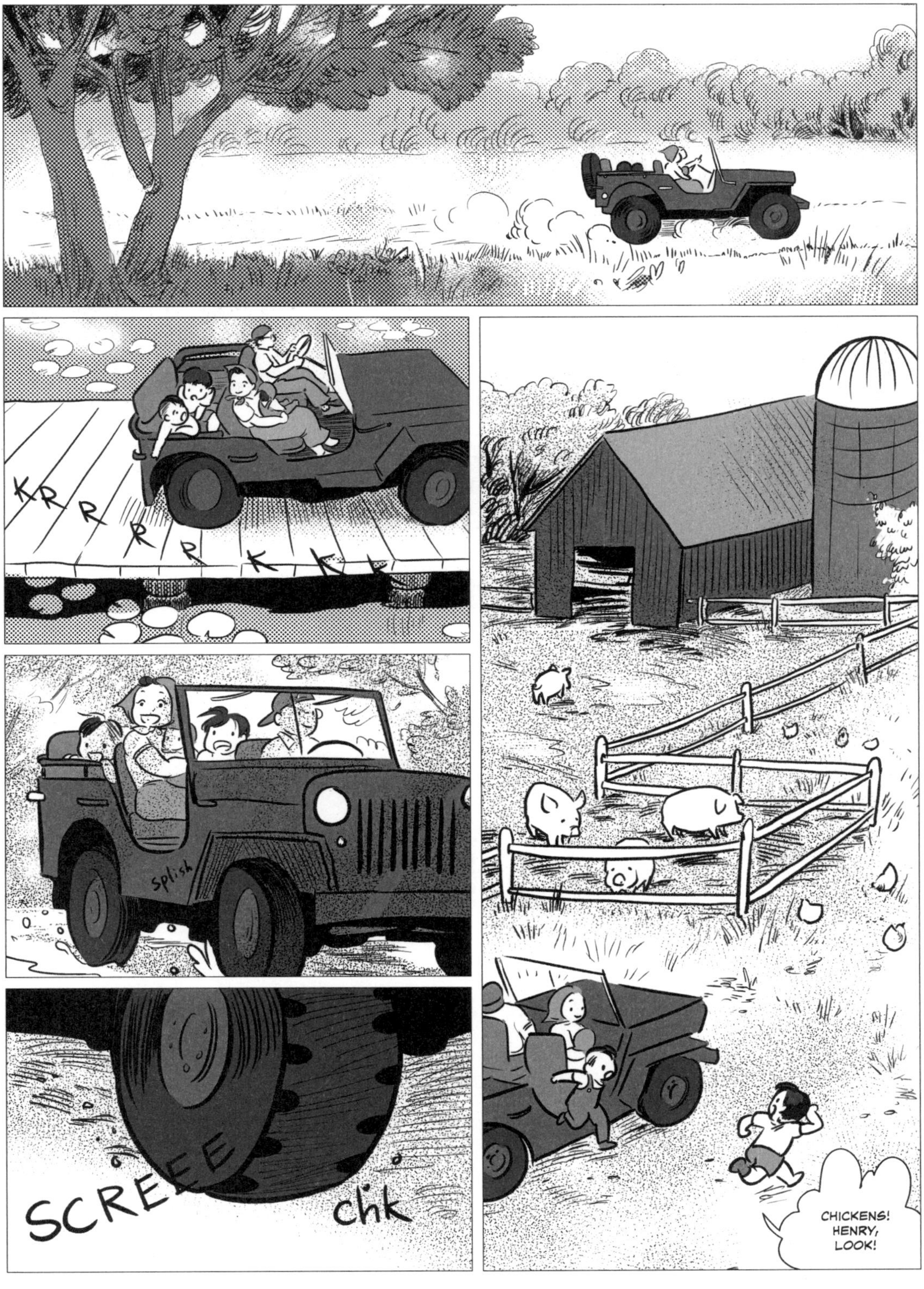
KRRRRRKKK
splish
SCREEE
chk
CHICKENS! HENRY, LOOK!

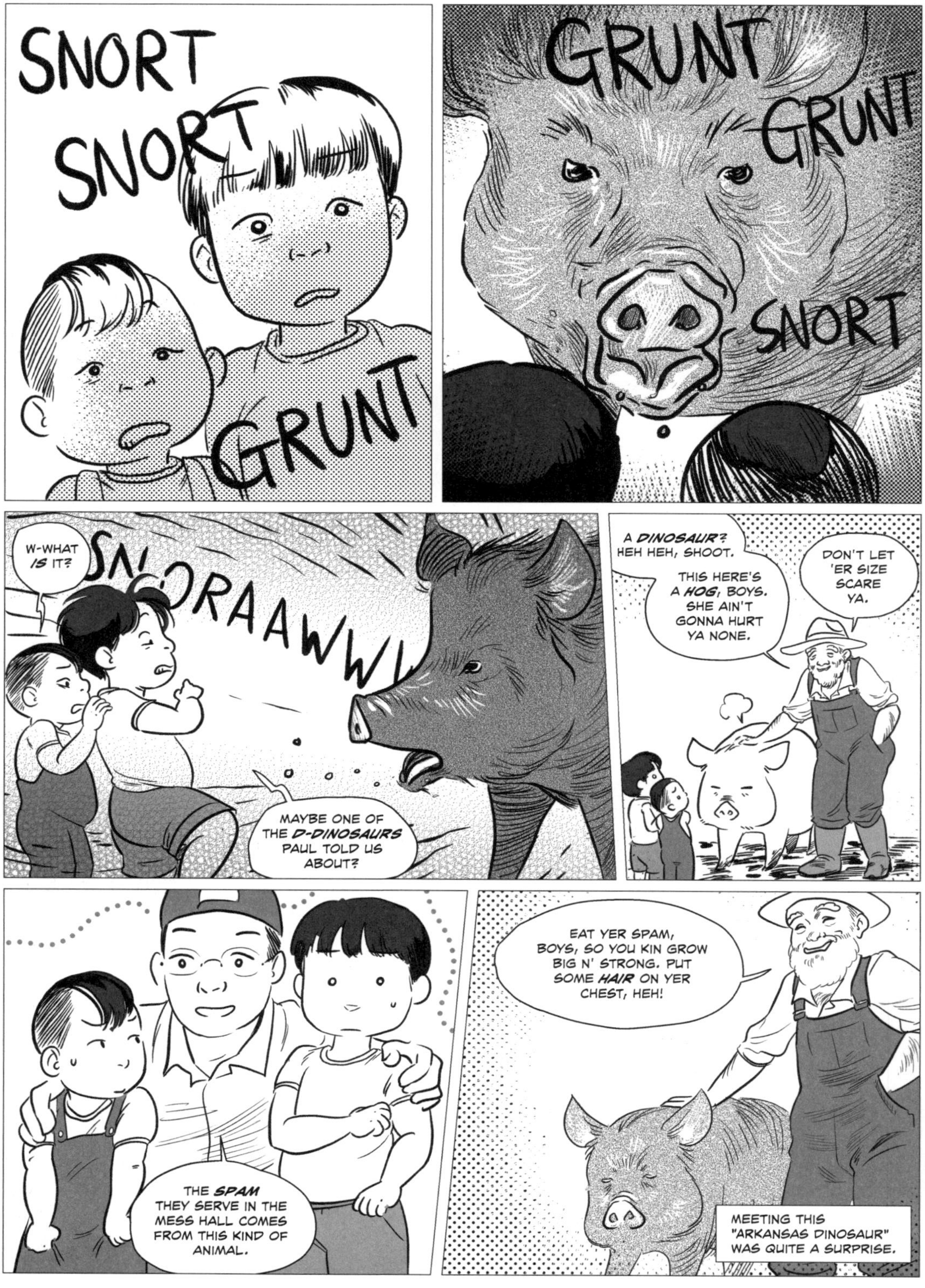
SNORT
SNORT
GRUNT
GRUNT
GRUNT
SNORT
W-WHAT *IS* IT?
SNORAAWWL
MAYBE ONE OF THE *D-DINOSAURS* PAUL TOLD US ABOUT?
A *DINOSAUR*? HEH HEH, SHOOT.
THIS HERE'S A *HOG*, BOYS. SHE AIN'T GONNA HURT YA NONE.
DON'T LET 'ER SIZE SCARE YA.
THE *SPAM* THEY SERVE IN THE MESS HALL COMES FROM THIS KIND OF ANIMAL.
EAT YER SPAM, BOYS, SO YOU KIN GROW BIG N' STRONG. PUT SOME *HAIR* ON YER CHEST, HEH!
MEETING THIS "ARKANSAS DINOSAUR" WAS QUITE A SURPRISE.

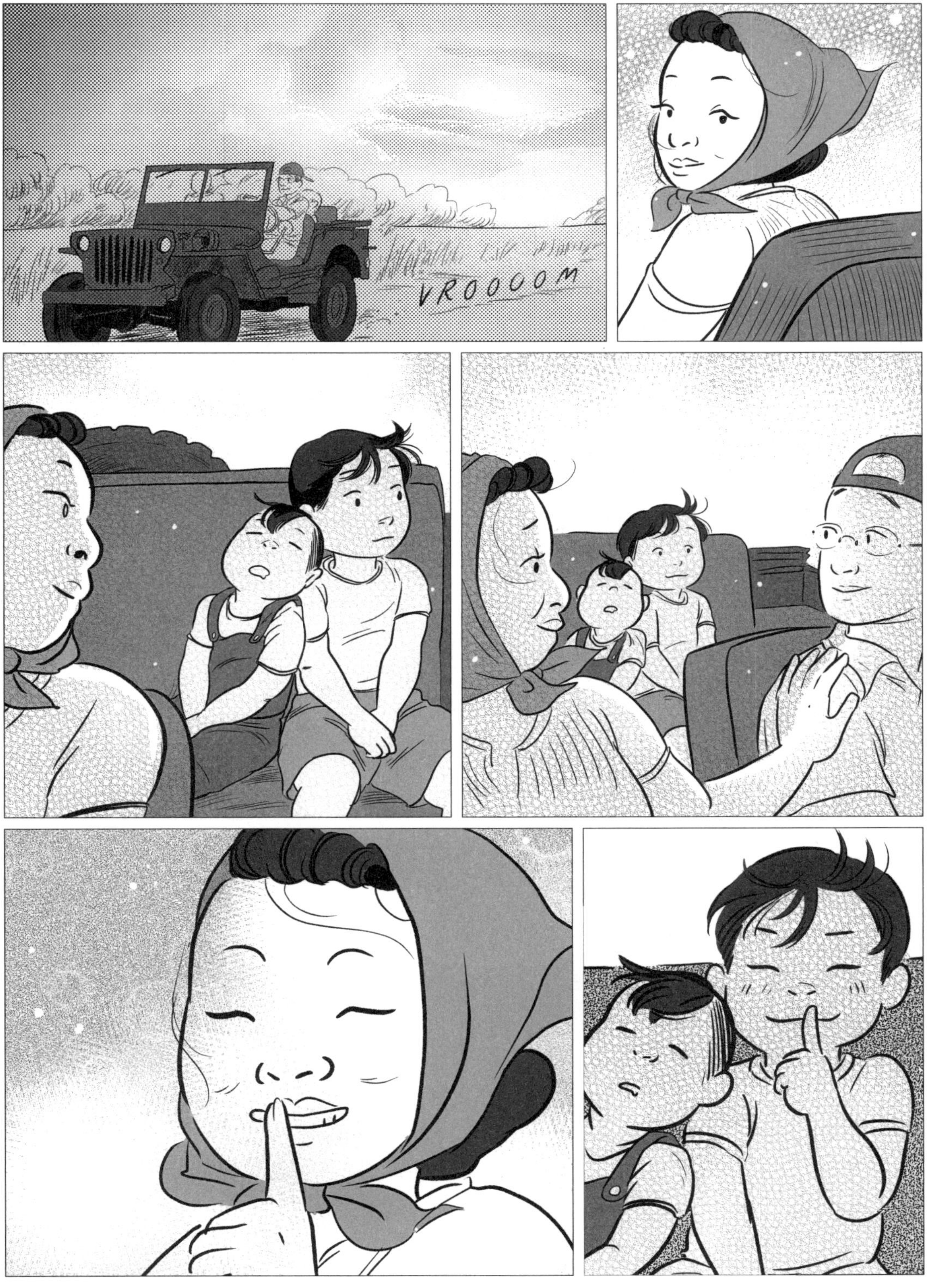
VROOOOM

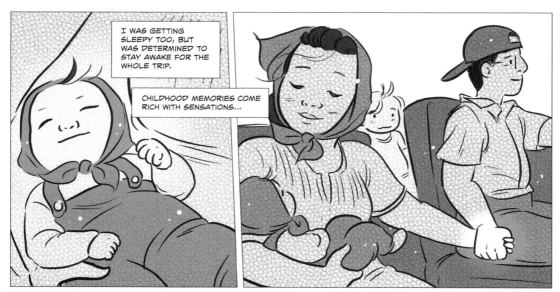

I WAS GETTING SLEEPY TOO, BUT WAS DETERMINED TO STAY AWAKE FOR THE WHOLE TRIP.

CHILDHOOD MEMORIES COME RICH WITH SENSATIONS...

...FRAGRANCES, SOUNDS, COLORS, AND ESPECIALLY TEMPERATURES.

THAT GOLDEN AFTERNOON WHEN DADDY TOOK THE FAMILY ON THAT WONDERFUL JEEP RIDE...

...IS A FOND MEMORY THAT GLOWS RADIANTLY WITH *WARMTH*.

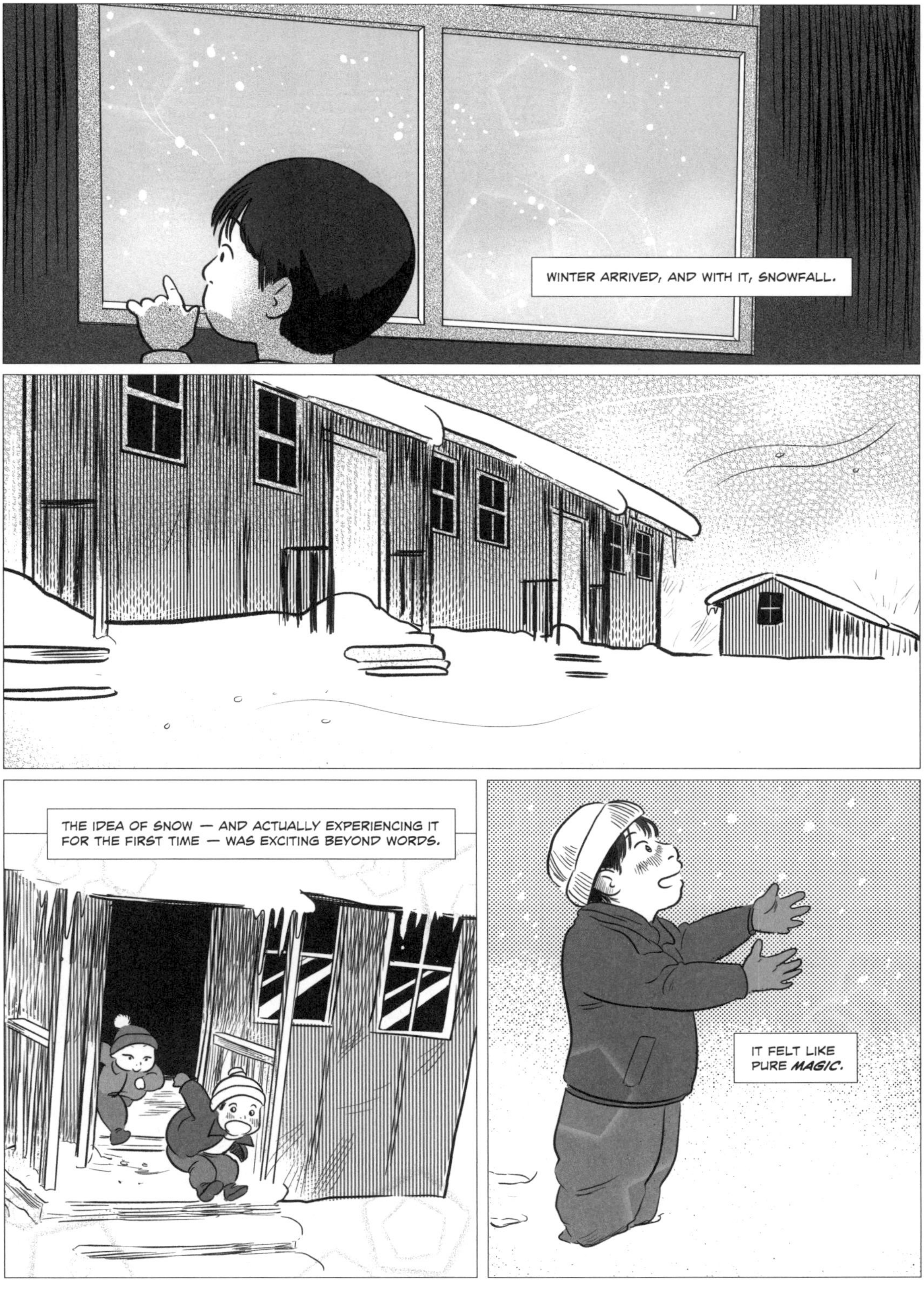
WINTER ARRIVED, AND WITH IT, SNOWFALL.
THE IDEA OF SNOW — AND ACTUALLY EXPERIENCING IT FOR THE FIRST TIME — WAS EXCITING BEYOND WORDS.
IT FELT LIKE PURE *MAGIC.*

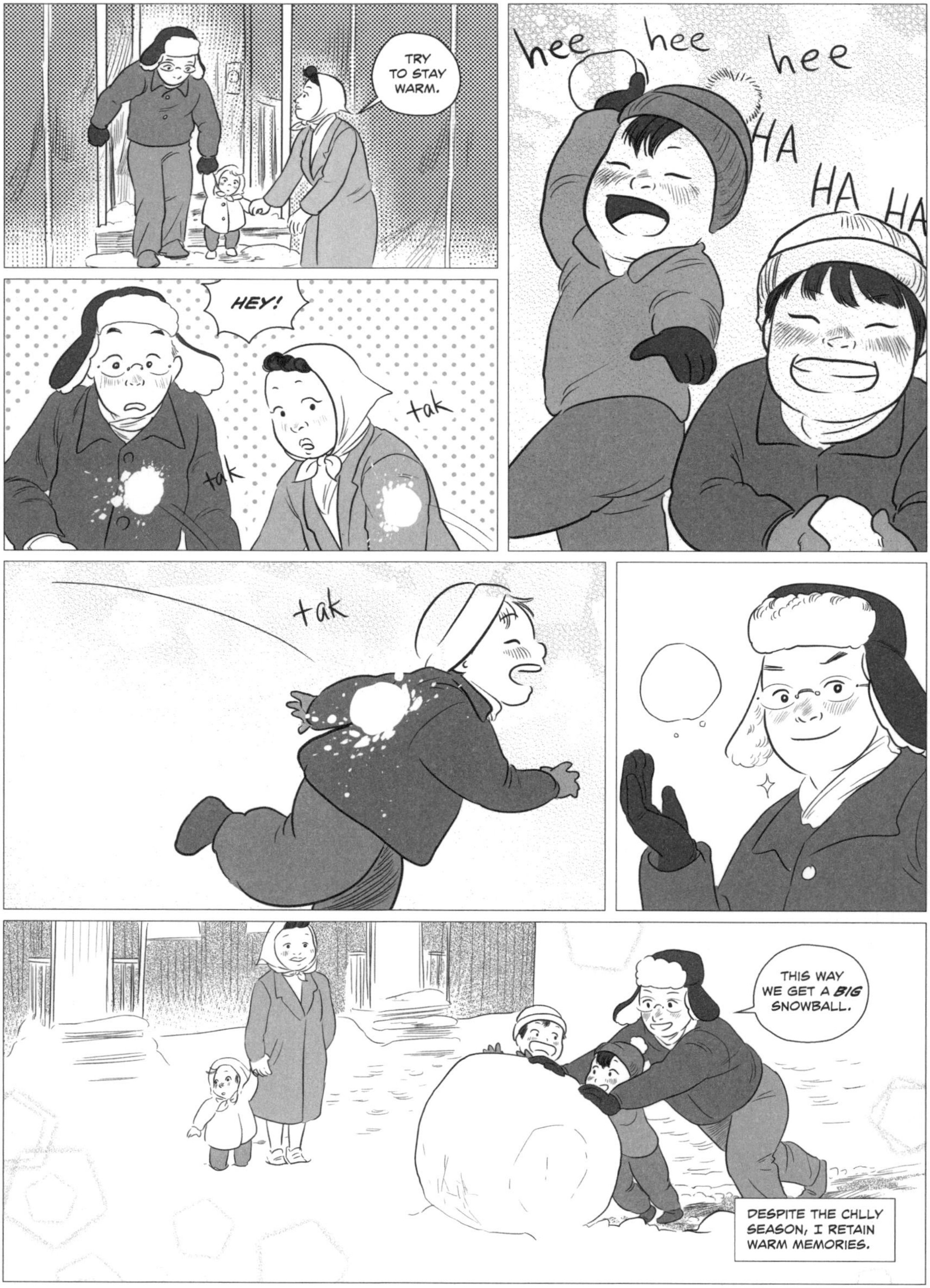
TRY TO STAY WARM.
hee hee hee
HA HA HA
HEY!
tak
tak
tak
THIS WAY WE GET A *BIG* SNOWBALL.
DESPITE THE CHLLY SEASON, I RETAIN WARM MEMORIES.

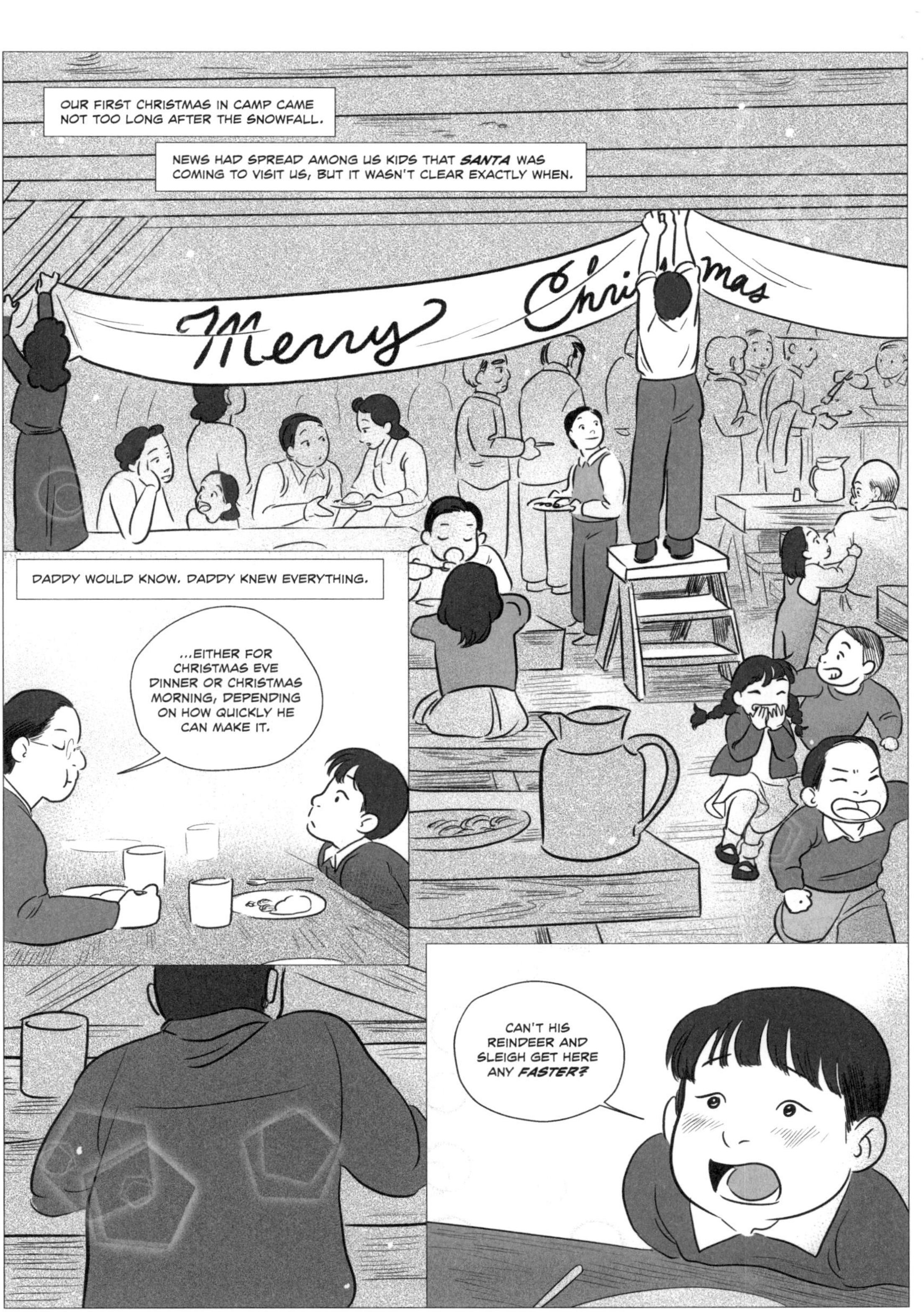
OUR FIRST CHRISTMAS IN CAMP CAME NOT TOO LONG AFTER THE SNOWFALL.
NEWS HAD SPREAD AMONG US KIDS THAT *SANTA* WAS COMING TO VISIT US, BUT IT WASN'T CLEAR EXACTLY WHEN.
Merry Christmas
DADDY WOULD KNOW. DADDY KNEW EVERYTHING.
...EITHER FOR CHRISTMAS EVE DINNER OR CHRISTMAS MORNING, DEPENDING ON HOW QUICKLY HE CAN MAKE IT.
CAN'T HIS REINDEER AND SLEIGH GET HERE ANY *FASTER?*

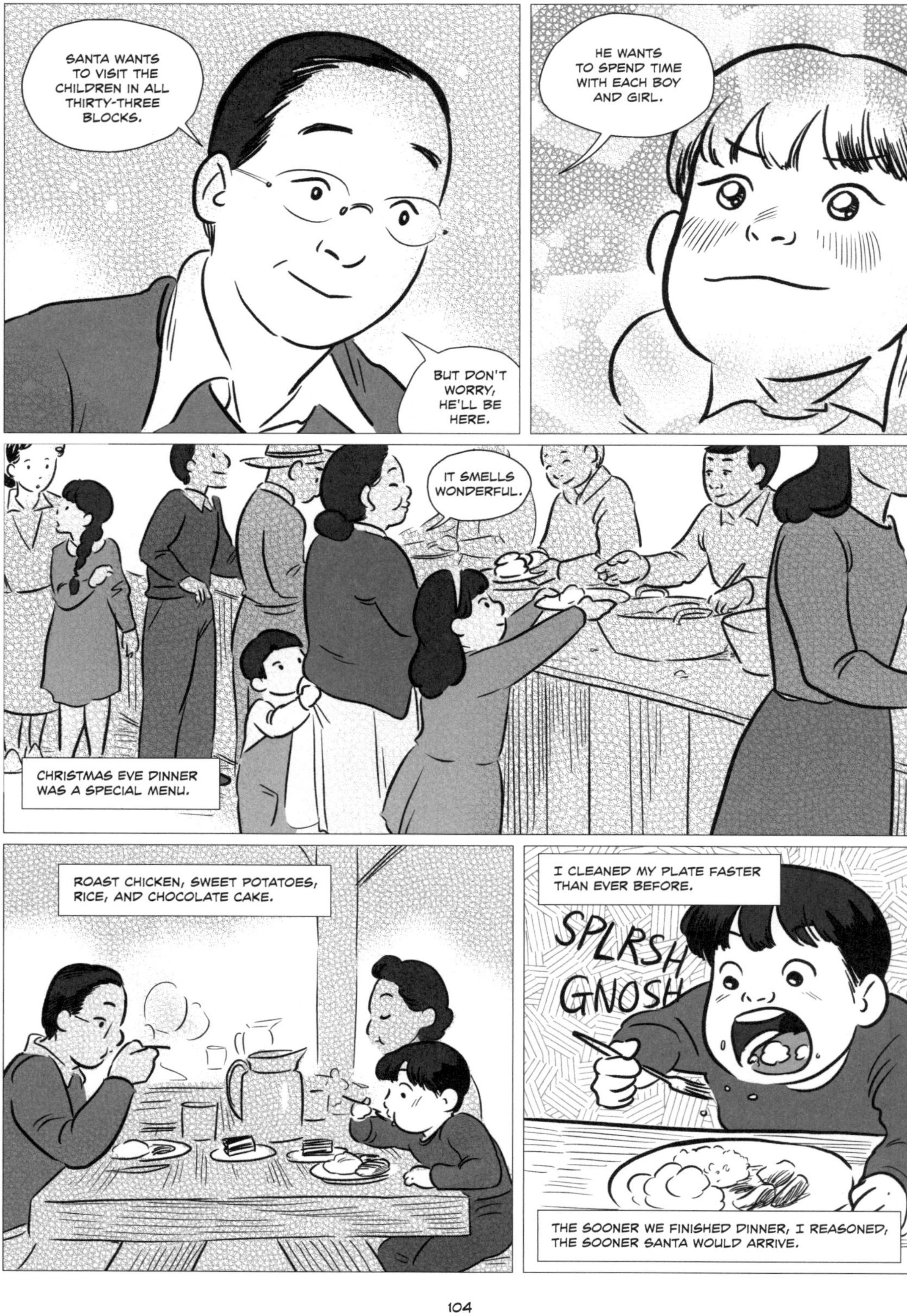
SANTA WANTS TO VISIT THE CHILDREN IN ALL THIRTY-THREE BLOCKS.
BUT DON'T WORRY, HE'LL BE HERE.
HE WANTS TO SPEND TIME WITH EACH BOY AND GIRL.
IT SMELLS WONDERFUL.
CHRISTMAS EVE DINNER WAS A SPECIAL MENU.
ROAST CHICKEN, SWEET POTATOES, RICE, AND CHOCOLATE CAKE.
I CLEANED MY PLATE FASTER THAN EVER BEFORE.
SPLRSH
GNOSH
THE SOONER WE FINISHED DINNER, I REASONED, THE SOONER SANTA WOULD ARRIVE.

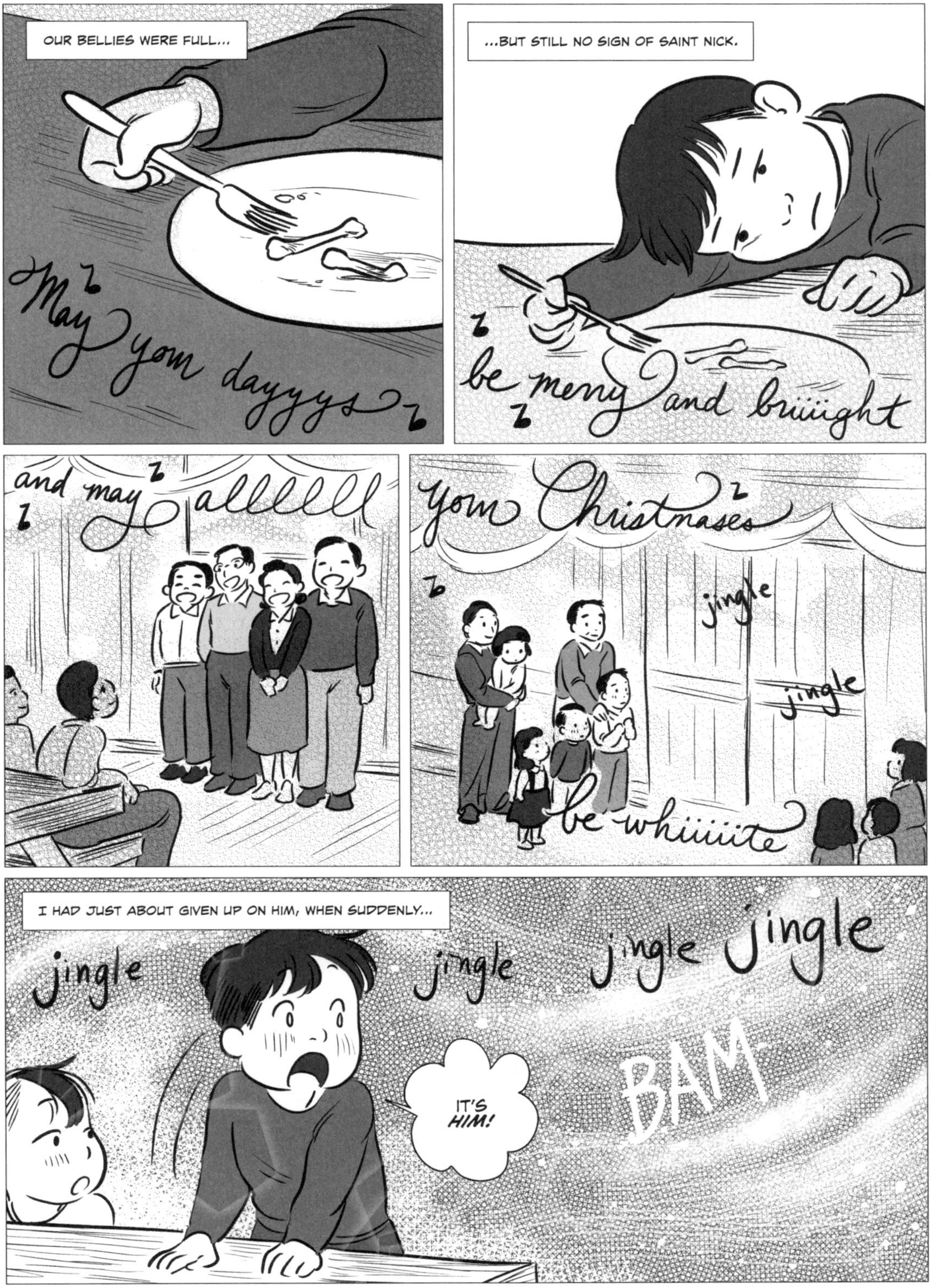
OUR BELLIES WERE FULL...
May your dayyys
...BUT STILL NO SIGN OF SAINT NICK.
be merry and briiiight
and may allllll
your Christmases
jingle
jingle
be whiiiiite
I HAD JUST ABOUT GIVEN UP ON HIM, WHEN SUDDENLY...
jingle
jingle
jingle jingle
IT'S HIM!
BAM

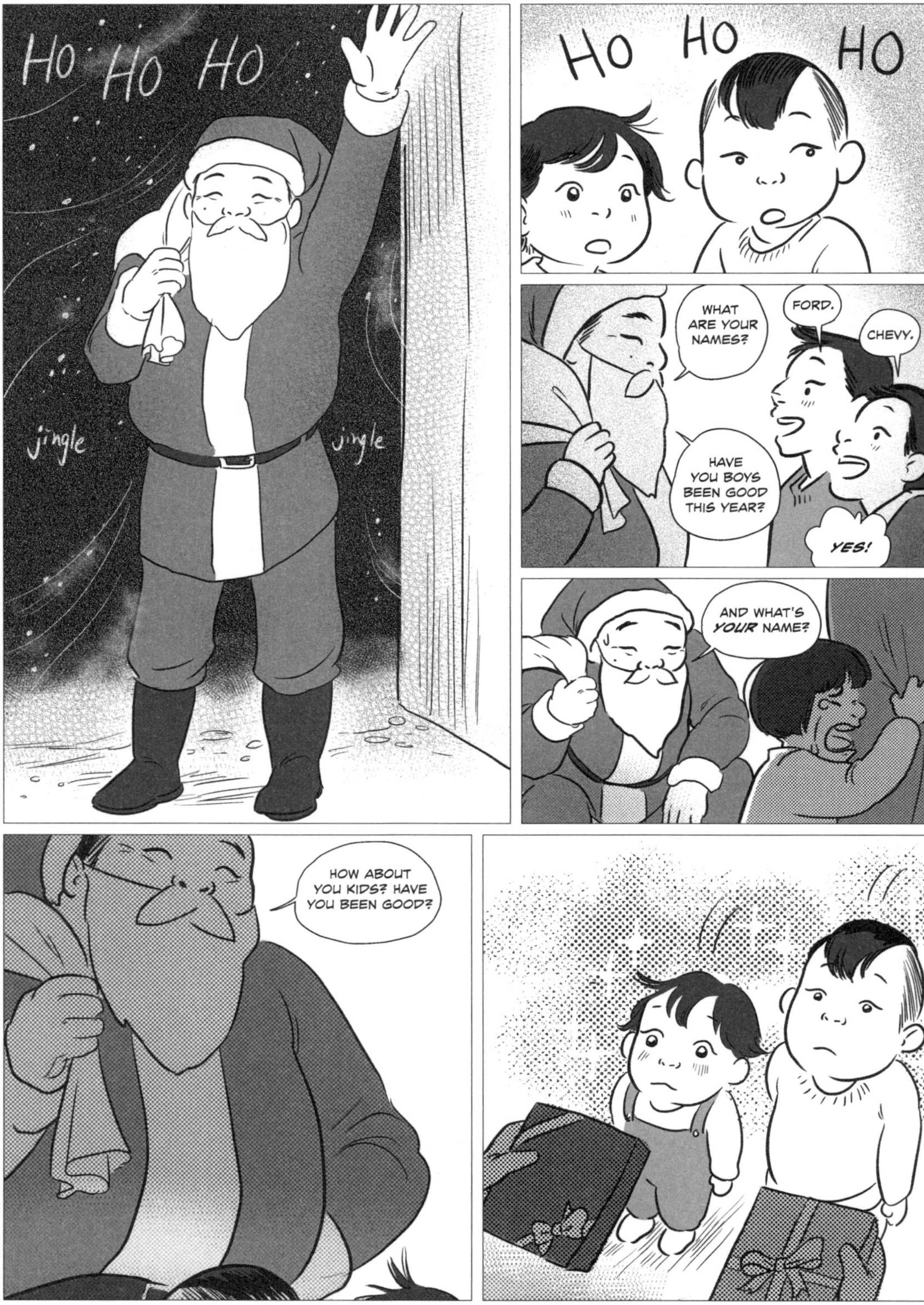
HO HO HO
jingle
jingle
HO HO HO
WHAT ARE YOUR NAMES?
FORD.
CHEVY.
HAVE YOU BOYS BEEN GOOD THIS YEAR?
YES!
AND WHAT'S *YOUR* NAME?
HOW ABOUT YOU KIDS? HAVE YOU BEEN GOOD?

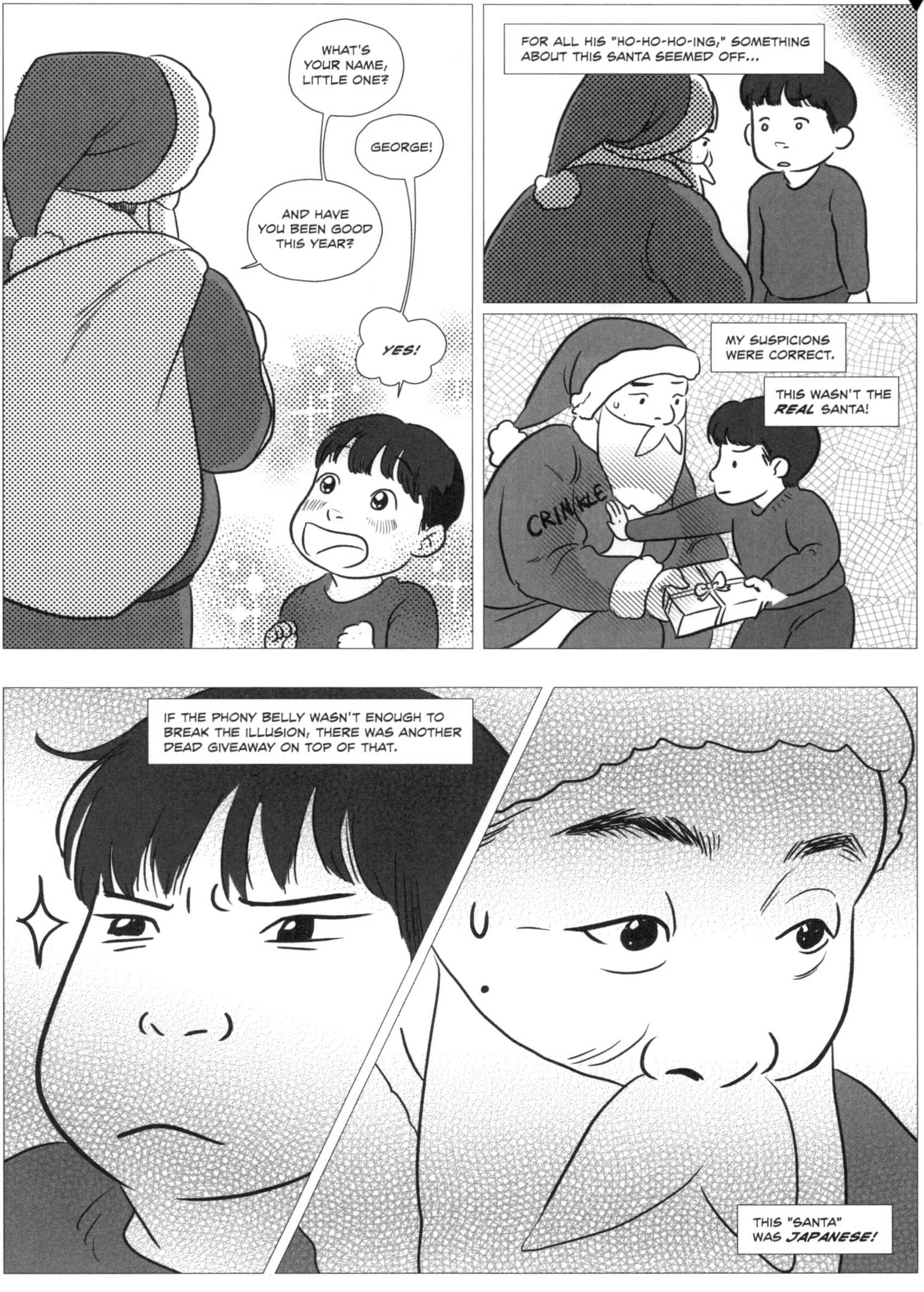
WHAT'S YOUR NAME, LITTLE ONE?
GEORGE!
AND HAVE YOU BEEN GOOD THIS YEAR?
YES!
FOR ALL HIS "HO-HO-HO-ING," SOMETHING ABOUT THIS SANTA SEEMED OFF...
MY SUSPICIONS WERE CORRECT.
THIS WASN'T THE *REAL* SANTA!
CRINKLE
IF THE PHONY BELLY WASN'T ENOUGH TO BREAK THE ILLUSION, THERE WAS ANOTHER DEAD GIVEAWAY ON TOP OF THAT.
THIS "SANTA" WAS ***JAPANESE!***

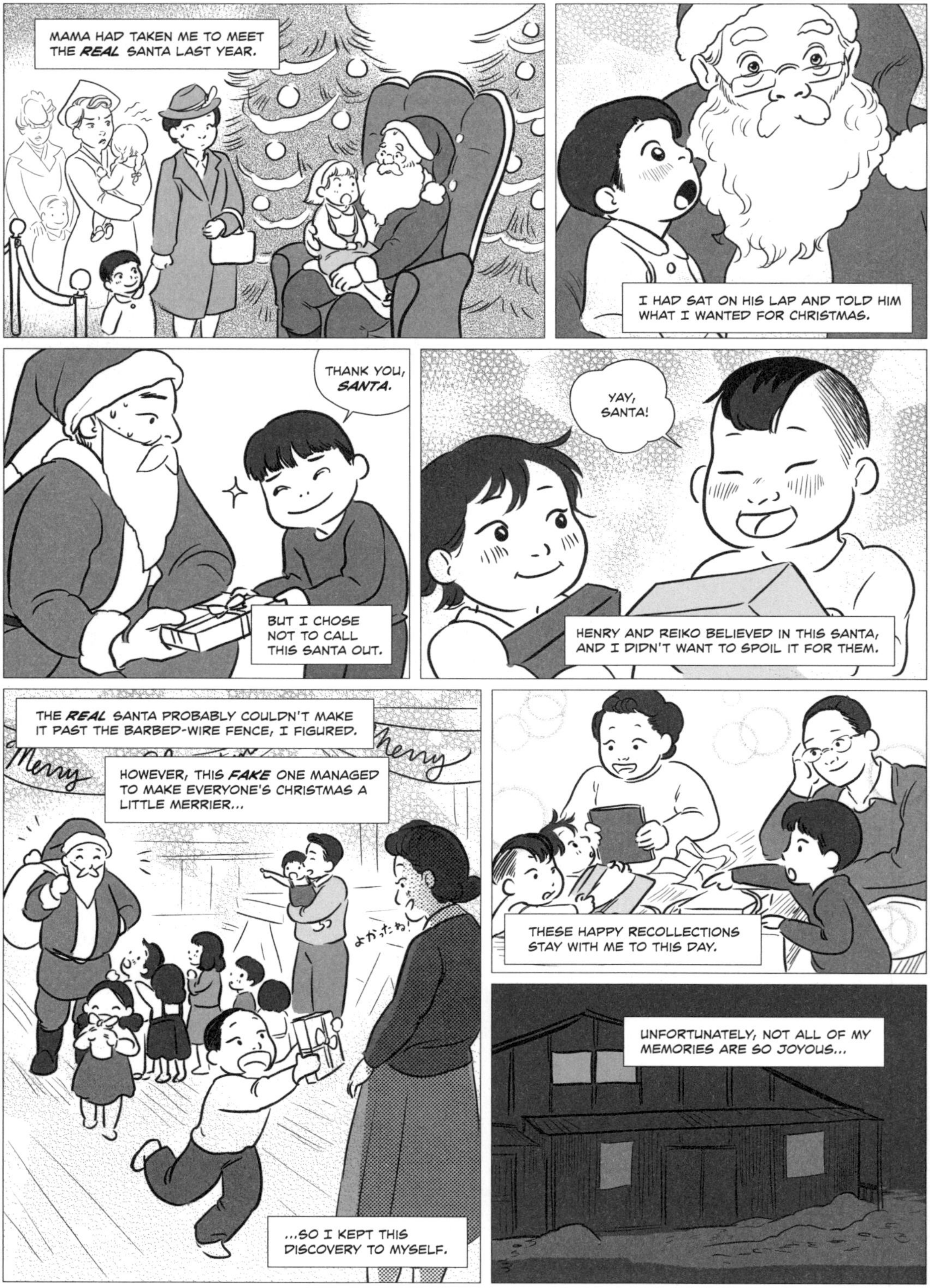
MAMA HAD TAKEN ME TO MEET THE **REAL** SANTA LAST YEAR.
I HAD SAT ON HIS LAP AND TOLD HIM WHAT I WANTED FOR CHRISTMAS.
THANK YOU, **SANTA.**
BUT I CHOSE NOT TO CALL THIS SANTA OUT.
YAY, SANTA!
HENRY AND REIKO BELIEVED IN THIS SANTA, AND I DIDN'T WANT TO SPOIL IT FOR THEM.
THE **REAL** SANTA PROBABLY COULDN'T MAKE IT PAST THE BARBED-WIRE FENCE, I FIGURED.
Merry
Merry
HOWEVER, THIS **FAKE** ONE MANAGED TO MAKE EVERYONE'S CHRISTMAS A LITTLE MERRIER...
よかったね!
...SO I KEPT THIS DISCOVERY TO MYSELF.
THESE HAPPY RECOLLECTIONS STAY WITH ME TO THIS DAY.
UNFORTUNATELY, NOT ALL OF MY MEMORIES ARE SO JOYOUS...

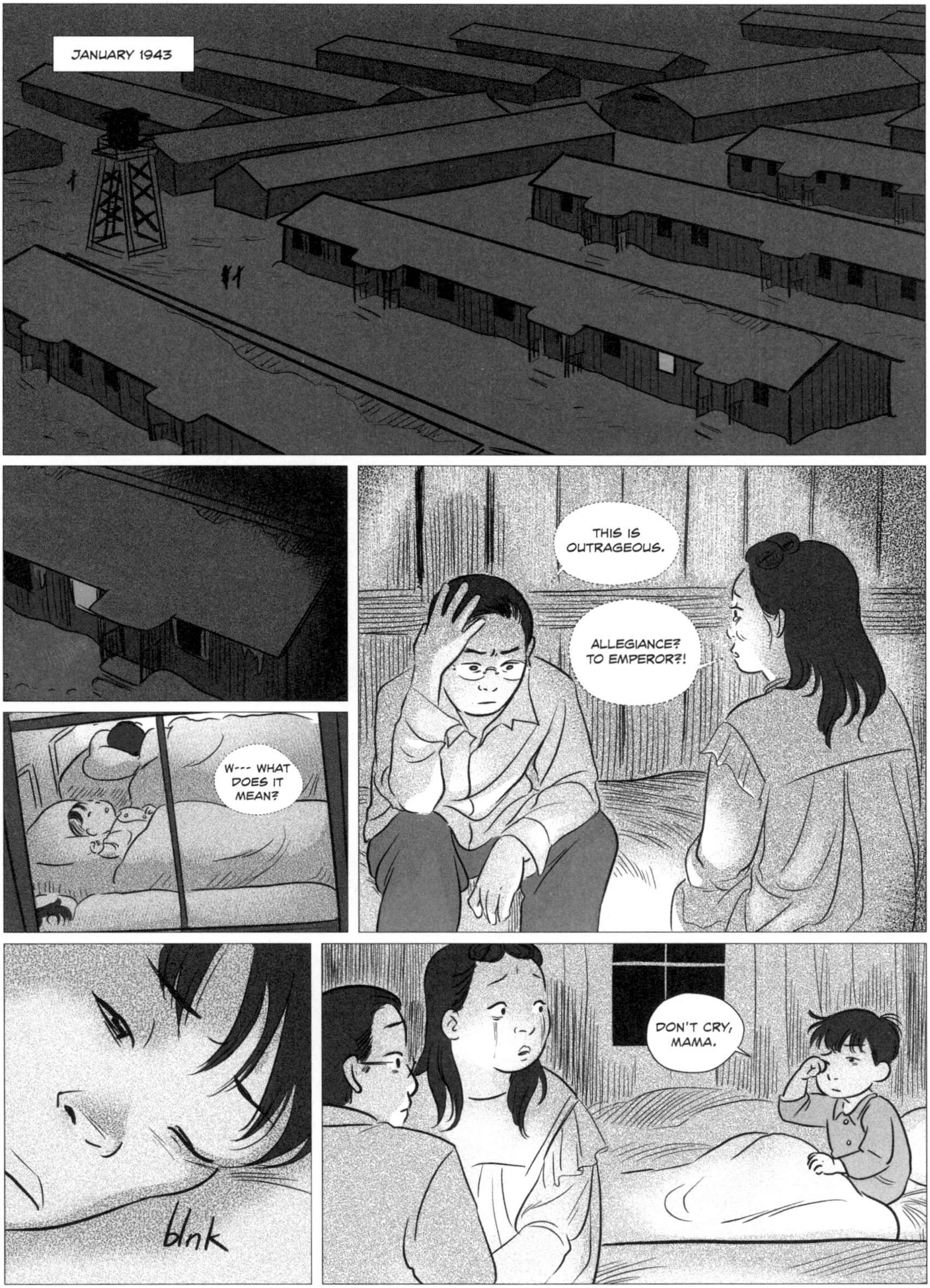
JANUARY 1943
W--- WHAT DOES IT MEAN?
THIS IS OUTRAGEOUS.
ALLEGIANCE? TO EMPEROR?!
blnk
DON'T CRY, MAMA.

IT'S ALL RIGHT. GO BACK TO SLEEP.

GEORGE!

MAMA AND I WERE TALKING ABOUT GROWN-UP THINGS.

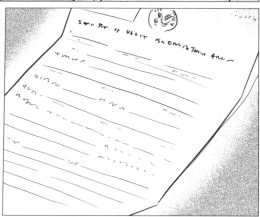

FROM THE MOMENT THE WAR BEGAN, OUR *LOYALTY* AS AMERICANS WAS CONSTANTLY UNDER SUSPICION.

GENERAL JOHN L. DEWITT, COMMANDING GENERAL OF THE WESTERN THEATER OF OPERATION

A *JAP* IS A *JAP*...

IT MAKES NO DIFFERENCE WHETHER HE IS THEORETICALLY AN AMERICAN CITIZEN; HE IS STILL A JAPANESE.

SENATOR TOM STEWART (D-TN)

THEY CANNOT BE ASSIMILATED.

THERE IS NOT A SINGLE JAPANESE IN THIS COUNTRY WHO WOULD NOT STAB YOU IN THE BACK.

NEVER MIND THAT IN THE EARLY DAYS OF THE WAR, JAPANESE AMERICANS SHOWED UP IN GREAT NUMBERS TO REGISTER FOR MILITARY SERVICE.

U.S. ARMY RECRUITING SERVICES

JOIN THE ARMY

THE CALL TO DUTY

JOIN NOW!

your country needs you

NATIONAL SERVICE It's up to you

JOIN THE ARMY

THE CALL TO DUTY

THIS WAS AN ACT OF PATRIOTISM, BUT IT WAS MET WITH A SLAP IN THE FACE.

NATIONAL SERVICE It's up to you!

JOIN NOW!

your country needs you

THEY WERE DENIED MILITARY SERVICE AND CATEGORIZED AS *4-C: ENEMY ALIENS.*

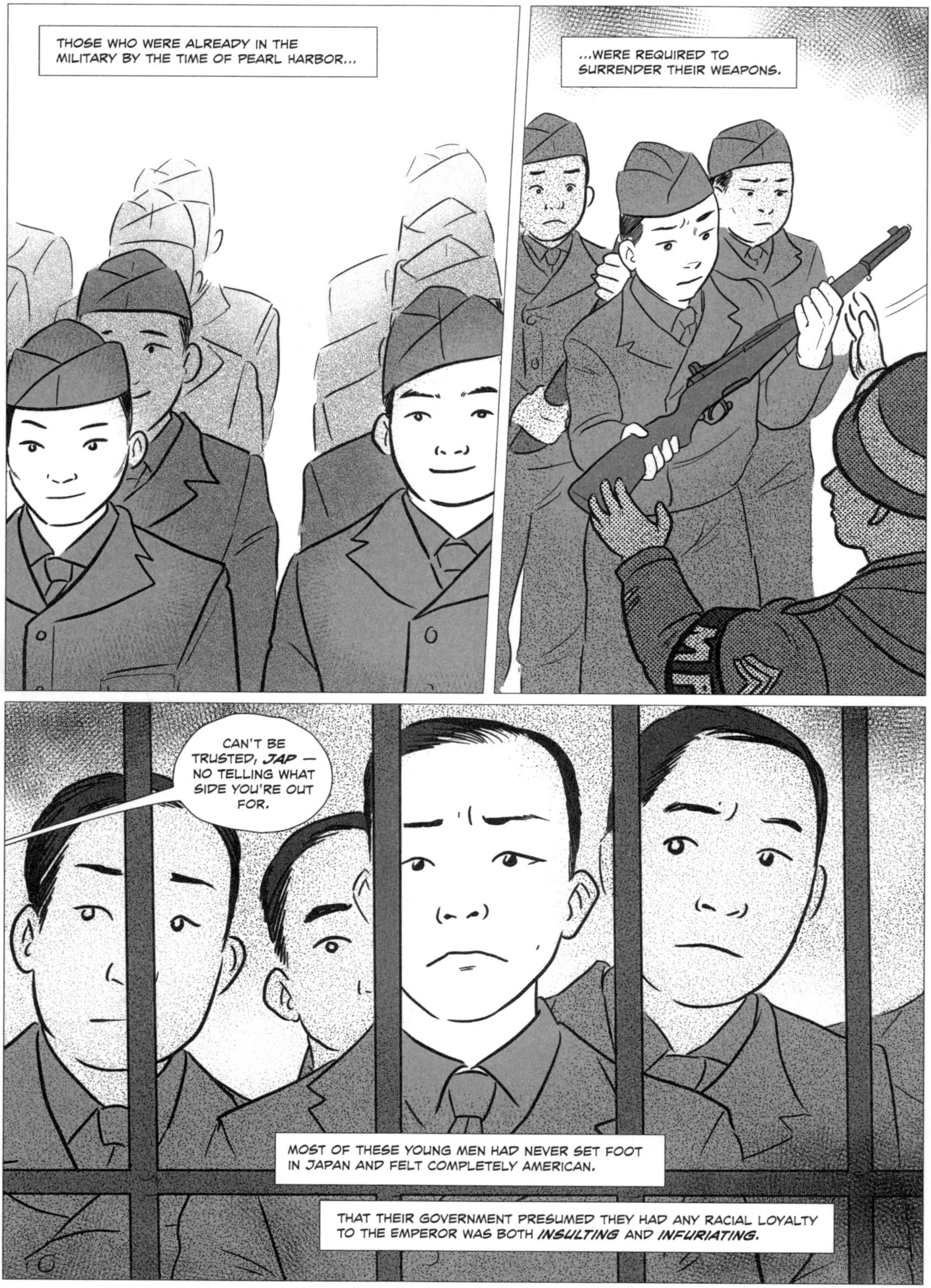
THOSE WHO WERE ALREADY IN THE MILITARY BY THE TIME OF PEARL HARBOR...
...WERE REQUIRED TO SURRENDER THEIR WEAPONS.
CAN'T BE TRUSTED, *JAP* — NO TELLING WHAT SIDE YOU'RE OUT FOR.
MOST OF THESE YOUNG MEN HAD NEVER SET FOOT IN JAPAN AND FELT COMPLETELY AMERICAN.
THAT THEIR GOVERNMENT PRESUMED THEY HAD ANY RACIAL LOYALTY TO THE EMPEROR WAS BOTH *INSULTING* AND *INFURIATING.*

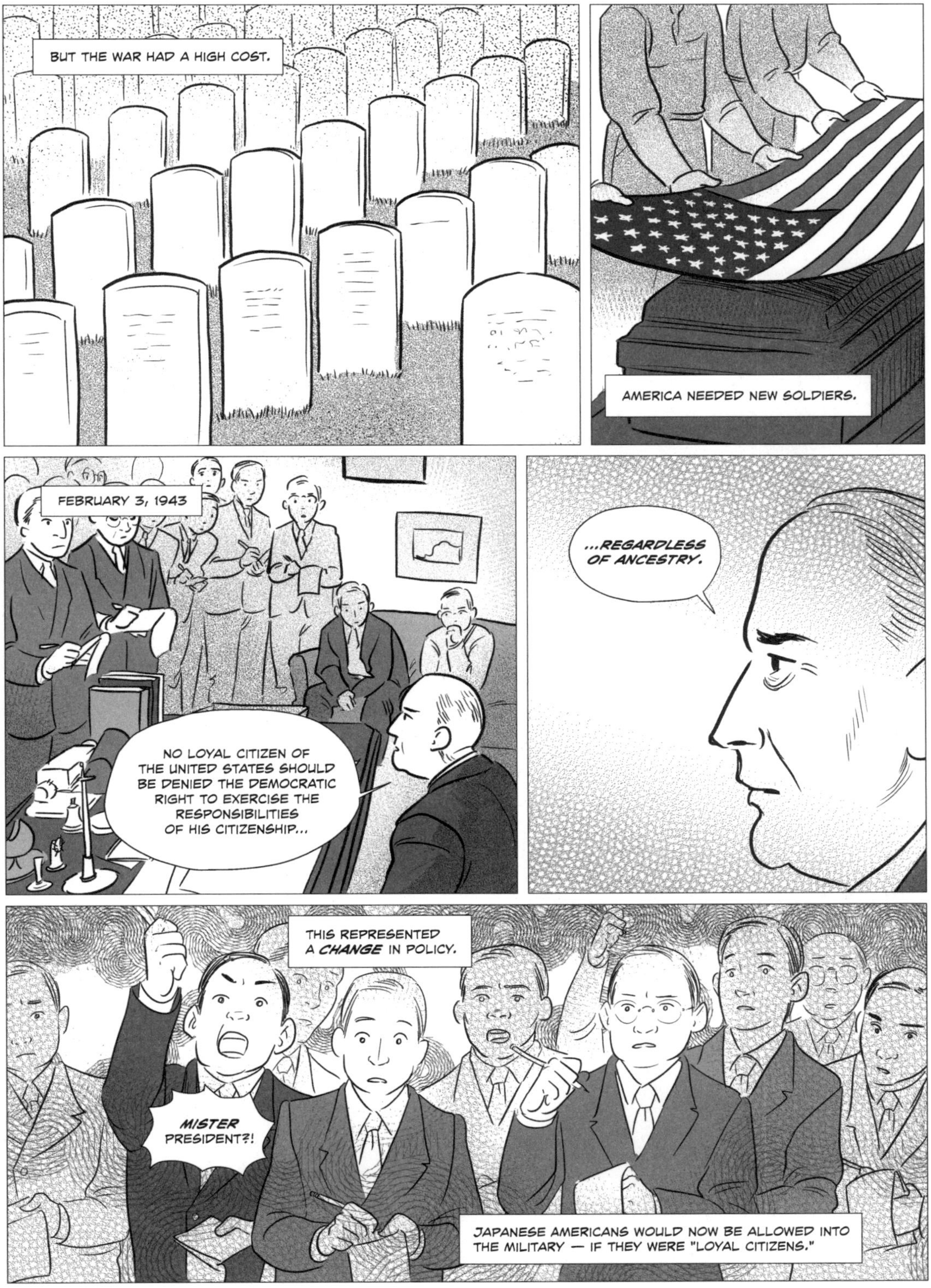
BUT THE WAR HAD A HIGH COST.
AMERICA NEEDED NEW SOLDIERS.
FEBRUARY 3, 1943
NO LOYAL CITIZEN OF THE UNITED STATES SHOULD BE DENIED THE DEMOCRATIC RIGHT TO EXERCISE THE RESPONSIBILITIES OF HIS CITIZENSHIP...
...REGARDLESS OF ANCESTRY.
THIS REPRESENTED A CHANGE IN POLICY.
MISTER PRESIDENT?!
JAPANESE AMERICANS WOULD NOW BE ALLOWED INTO THE MILITARY — IF THEY WERE "LOYAL CITIZENS."

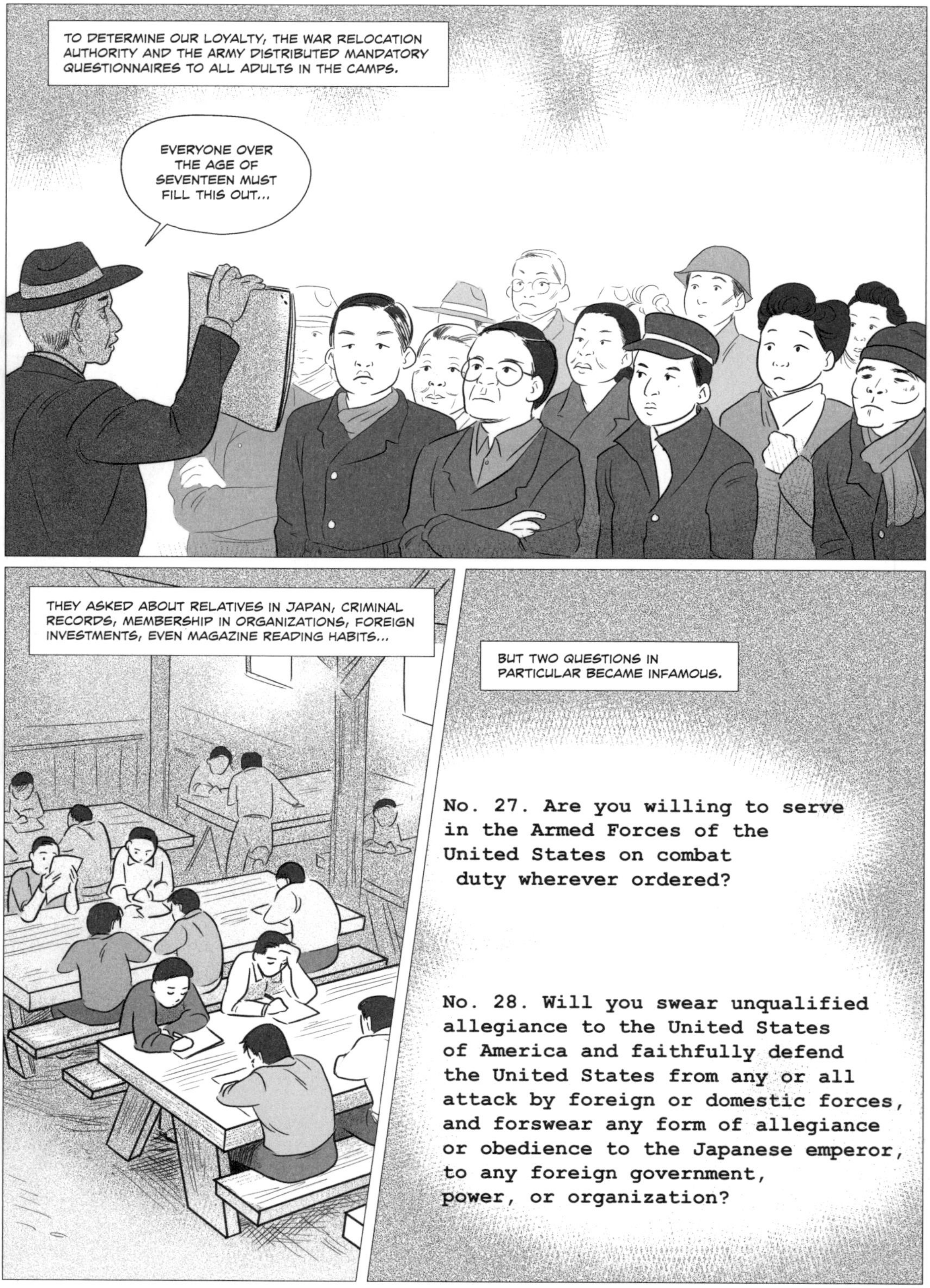
TO DETERMINE OUR LOYALTY, THE WAR RELOCATION AUTHORITY AND THE ARMY DISTRIBUTED MANDATORY QUESTIONNAIRES TO ALL ADULTS IN THE CAMPS.
EVERYONE OVER THE AGE OF SEVENTEEN MUST FILL THIS OUT...
THEY ASKED ABOUT RELATIVES IN JAPAN, CRIMINAL RECORDS, MEMBERSHIP IN ORGANIZATIONS, FOREIGN INVESTMENTS, EVEN MAGAZINE READING HABITS...
BUT TWO QUESTIONS IN PARTICULAR BECAME INFAMOUS.
No. 27. Are you willing to serve in the Armed Forces of the United States on combat duty wherever ordered?
No. 28. Will you swear unqualified allegiance to the United States of America and faithfully defend the United States from any or all attack by foreign or domestic forces, and forswear any form of allegiance or obedience to the Japanese emperor, to any foreign government, power, or organization?

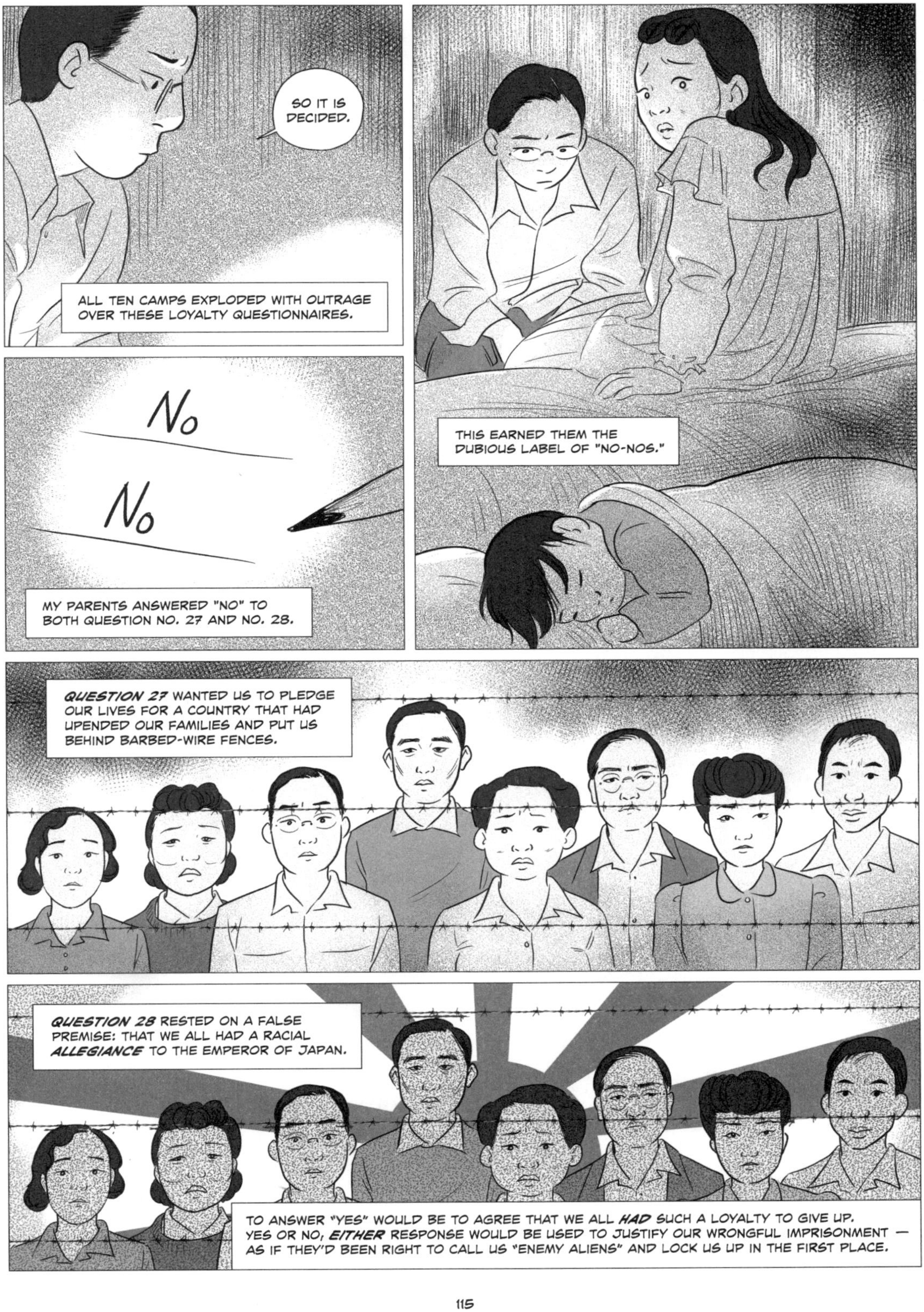
SO IT IS DECIDED.
ALL TEN CAMPS EXPLODED WITH OUTRAGE OVER THESE LOYALTY QUESTIONNAIRES.
No
No
MY PARENTS ANSWERED "NO" TO BOTH QUESTION NO. 27 AND NO. 28.
THIS EARNED THEM THE DUBIOUS LABEL OF "NO-NOS."
QUESTION 27 WANTED US TO PLEDGE OUR LIVES FOR A COUNTRY THAT HAD UPENDED OUR FAMILIES AND PUT US BEHIND BARBED-WIRE FENCES.
QUESTION 28 RESTED ON A FALSE PREMISE: THAT WE ALL HAD A RACIAL ALLEGIANCE TO THE EMPEROR OF JAPAN.
TO ANSWER "YES" WOULD BE TO AGREE THAT WE ALL HAD SUCH A LOYALTY TO GIVE UP. YES OR NO, EITHER RESPONSE WOULD BE USED TO JUSTIFY OUR WRONGFUL IMPRISONMENT — AS IF THEY'D BEEN RIGHT TO CALL US "ENEMY ALIENS" AND LOCK US UP IN THE FIRST PLACE.

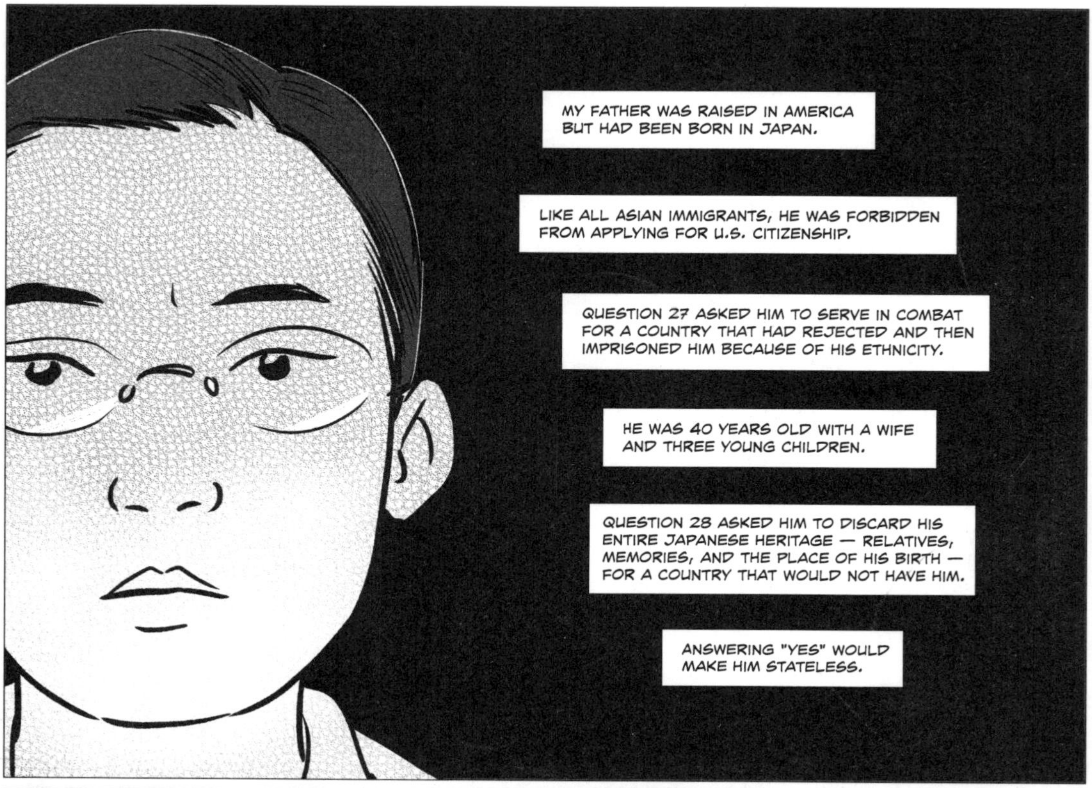
MY FATHER WAS RAISED IN AMERICA BUT HAD BEEN BORN IN JAPAN.
LIKE ALL ASIAN IMMIGRANTS, HE WAS FORBIDDEN FROM APPLYING FOR U.S. CITIZENSHIP.
QUESTION 27 ASKED HIM TO SERVE IN COMBAT FOR A COUNTRY THAT HAD REJECTED AND THEN IMPRISONED HIM BECAUSE OF HIS ETHNICITY.
HE WAS 40 YEARS OLD WITH A WIFE AND THREE YOUNG CHILDREN.
QUESTION 28 ASKED HIM TO DISCARD HIS ENTIRE JAPANESE HERITAGE — RELATIVES, MEMORIES, AND THE PLACE OF HIS BIRTH — FOR A COUNTRY THAT WOULD NOT HAVE HIM.
ANSWERING "YES" WOULD MAKE HIM STATELESS.

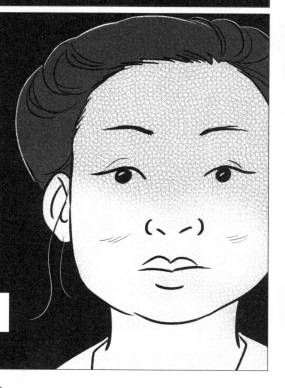

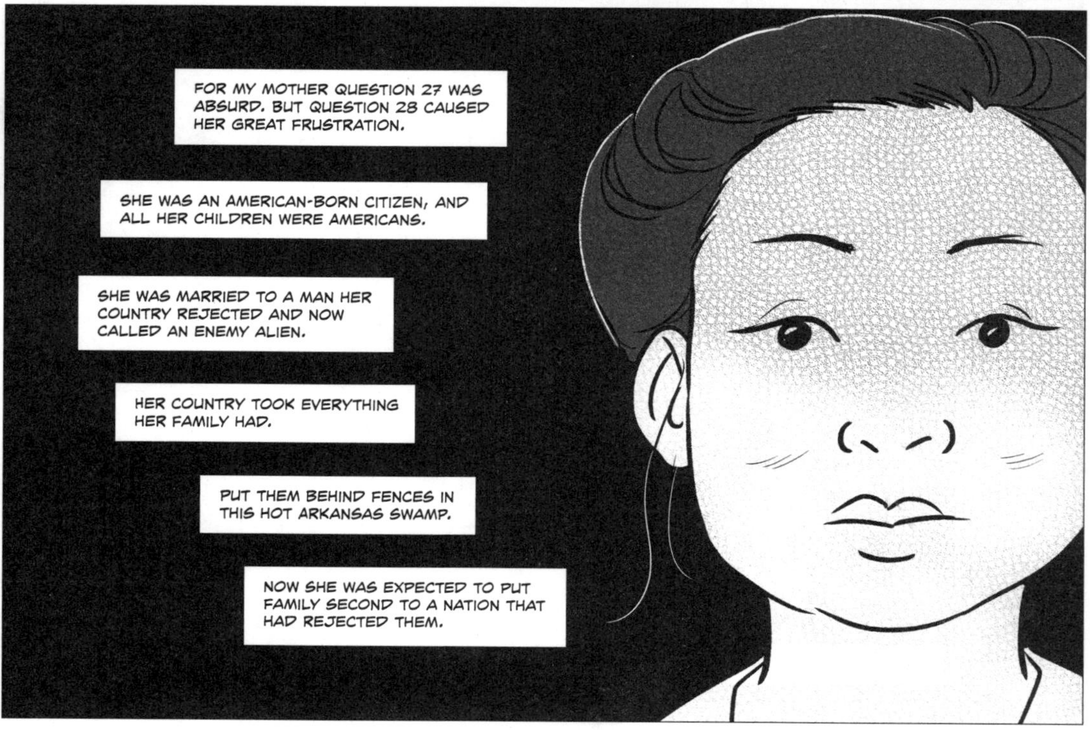
FOR MY MOTHER QUESTION 27 WAS ABSURD. BUT QUESTION 28 CAUSED HER GREAT FRUSTRATION.
SHE WAS AN AMERICAN-BORN CITIZEN, AND ALL HER CHILDREN WERE AMERICANS.
SHE WAS MARRIED TO A MAN HER COUNTRY REJECTED AND NOW CALLED AN ENEMY ALIEN.
HER COUNTRY TOOK EVERYTHING HER FAMILY HAD.
PUT THEM BEHIND FENCES IN THIS HOT ARKANSAS SWAMP.
NOW SHE WAS EXPECTED TO PUT FAMILY SECOND TO A NATION THAT HAD REJECTED THEM.

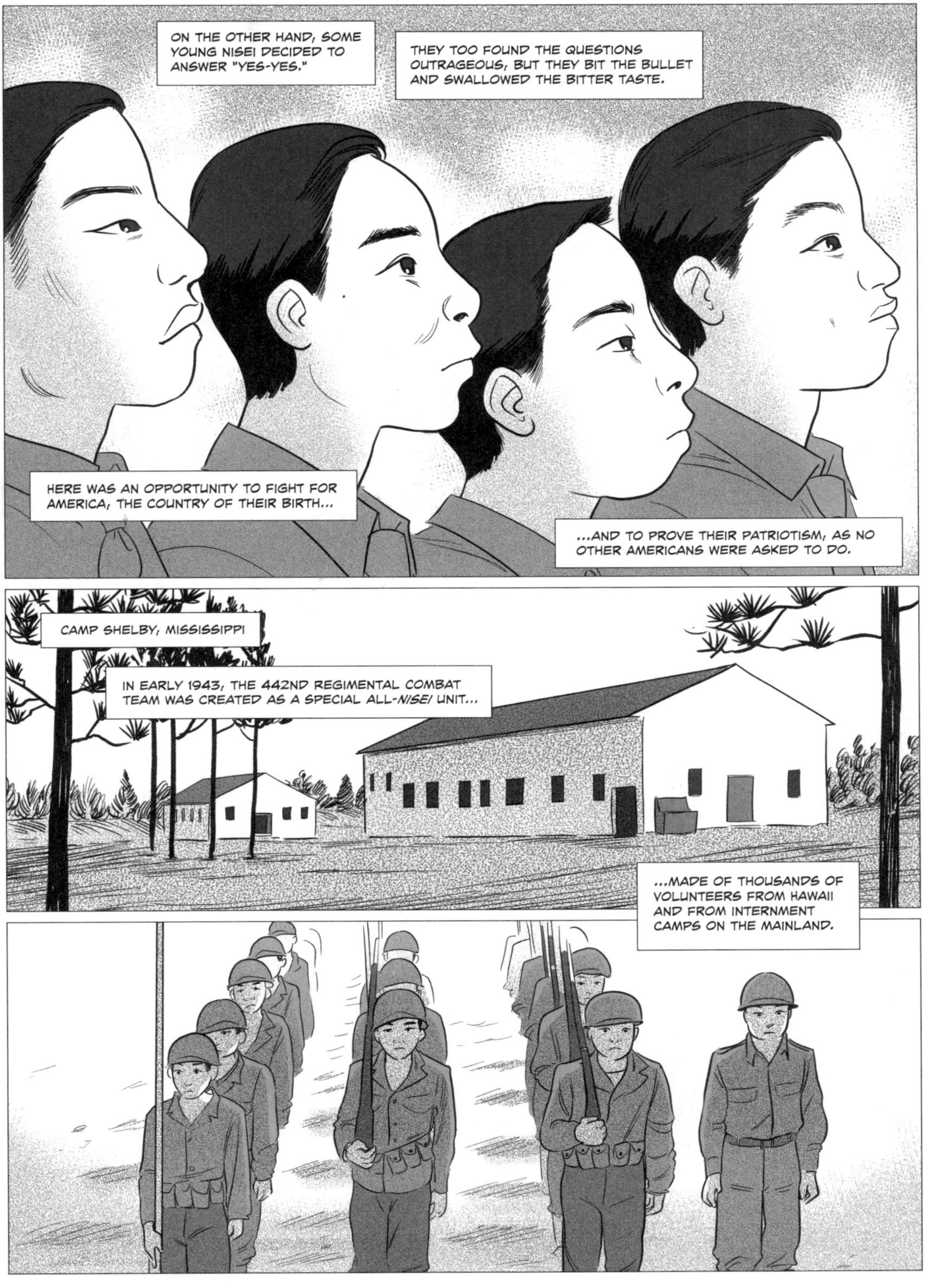
ON THE OTHER HAND, SOME YOUNG NISEI DECIDED TO ANSWER "YES-YES."
THEY TOO FOUND THE QUESTIONS OUTRAGEOUS, BUT THEY BIT THE BULLET AND SWALLOWED THE BITTER TASTE.
HERE WAS AN OPPORTUNITY TO FIGHT FOR AMERICA, THE COUNTRY OF THEIR BIRTH...
...AND TO PROVE THEIR PATRIOTISM, AS NO OTHER AMERICANS WERE ASKED TO DO.
CAMP SHELBY, MISSISSIPPI
IN EARLY 1943, THE 442ND REGIMENTAL COMBAT TEAM WAS CREATED AS A SPECIAL ALL-*NISEI* UNIT...
...MADE OF THOUSANDS OF VOLUNTEERS FROM HAWAII AND FROM INTERNMENT CAMPS ON THE MAINLAND.

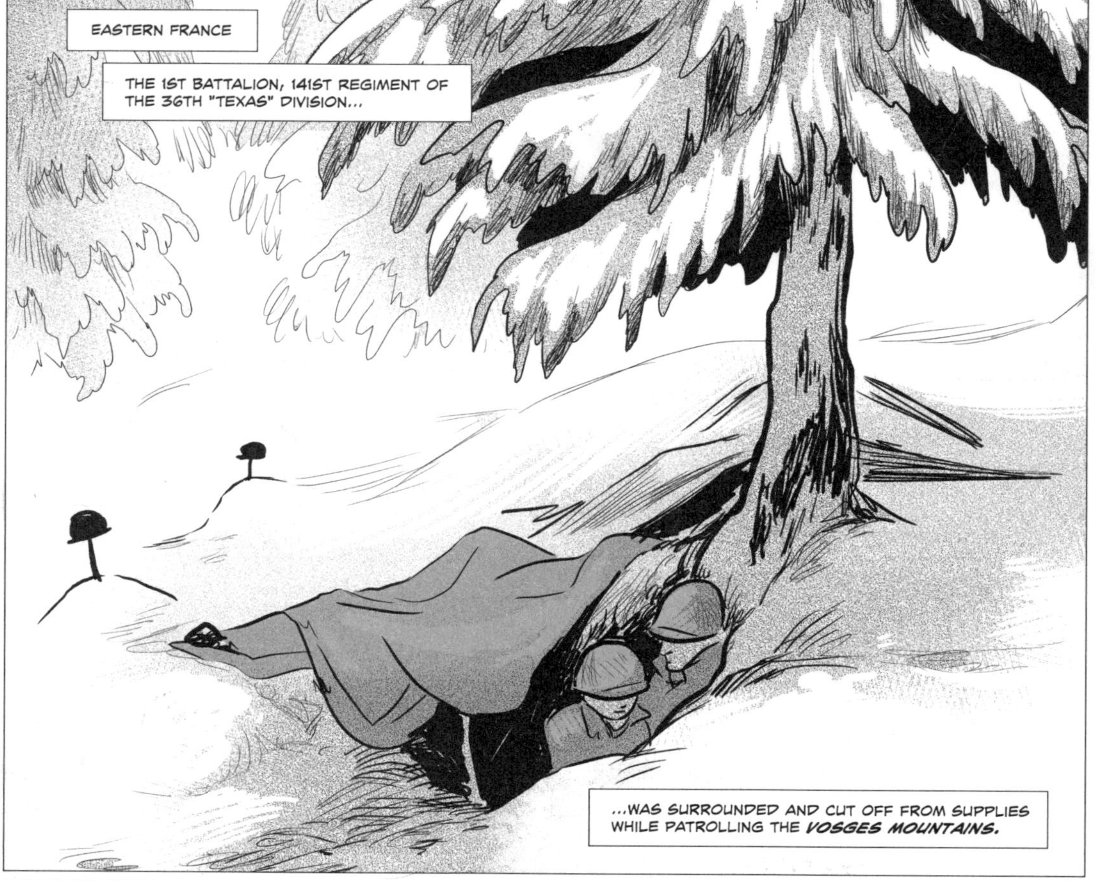
EASTERN FRANCE
THE 1ST BATTALION, 141ST REGIMENT OF THE 36TH "TEXAS" DIVISION...
...WAS SURROUNDED AND CUT OFF FROM SUPPLIES WHILE PATROLLING THE *VOSGES MOUNTAINS.*

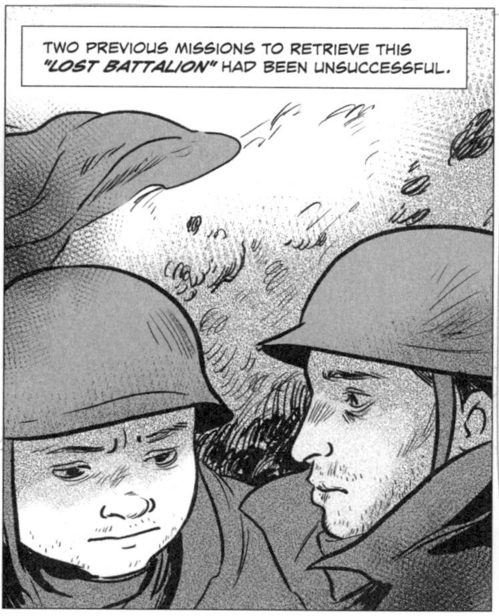
TWO PREVIOUS MISSIONS TO RETRIEVE THIS *"LOST BATTALION"* HAD BEEN UNSUCCESSFUL.

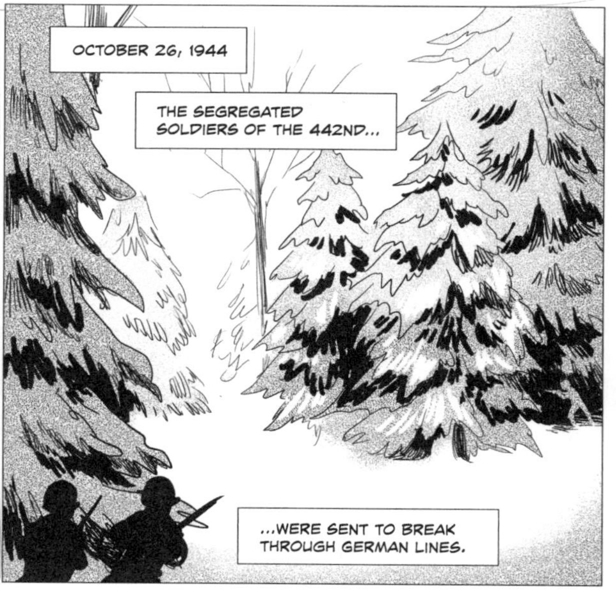
OCTOBER 26, 1944
THE SEGREGATED SOLDIERS OF THE 442ND...
...WERE SENT TO BREAK THROUGH GERMAN LINES.

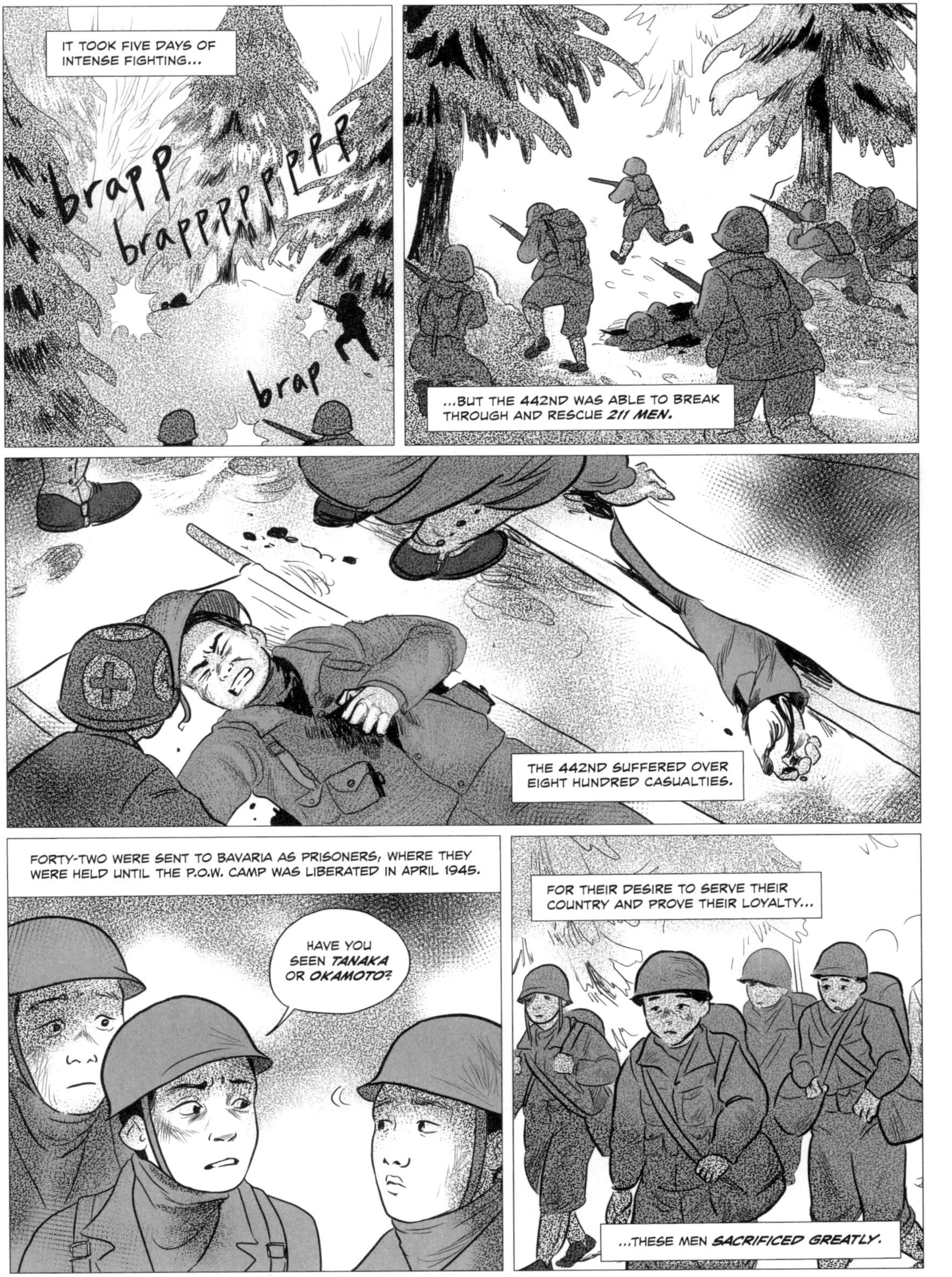
IT TOOK FIVE DAYS OF INTENSE FIGHTING...
brapp
brappppppppp
brap
...BUT THE 442ND WAS ABLE TO BREAK THROUGH AND RESCUE 211 MEN.
THE 442ND SUFFERED OVER EIGHT HUNDRED CASUALTIES.
FORTY-TWO WERE SENT TO BAVARIA AS PRISONERS, WHERE THEY WERE HELD UNTIL THE P.O.W. CAMP WAS LIBERATED IN APRIL 1945.
HAVE YOU SEEN TANAKA OR OKAMOTO?
FOR THEIR DESIRE TO SERVE THEIR COUNTRY AND PROVE THEIR LOYALTY...
...THESE MEN SACRIFICED GREATLY.

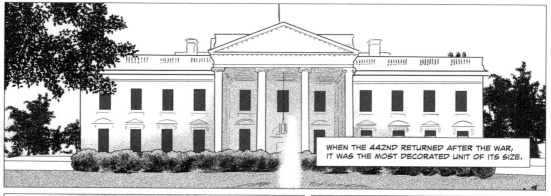

WHEN THE 442ND RETURNED AFTER THE WAR, IT WAS THE MOST DECORATED UNIT OF ITS SIZE.

PRESIDENT *TRUMAN* HONORED DOZENS OF ITS MEMBERS WITH THE *DISTINGUISHED SERVICE CROSS...*

YOU FOUGHT NOT ONLY THE ENEMY, BUT YOU FOUGHT PREJUDICE— AND YOU HAVE WON.

JULY 15, 1946

...THE *SECOND-HIGHEST* HONOR THAT COULD BE AWARDED.

MANY YEARS LATER, THE GOVERNMENT RECOGNIZED THEIR INCREDIBLE HEROISM WITH AN UPGRADE TO THE *CONGRESSIONAL MEDAL OF HONOR.*

AMERICA OWES AN *UNREPAYABLE* DEBT TO YOU...

JULY 21, 2000

PRESIDENT *CLINTON* HAD APPOINTED ME TO THE JAPAN-U.S. FRIENDSHIP COMMISSION, AND I WAS INVITED TO THE CEREMONY...

...TO WITNESS THE SURVIVING MEMBERS FINALLY RECEIVE OUR NATION'S HIGHEST MILITARY AWARD.

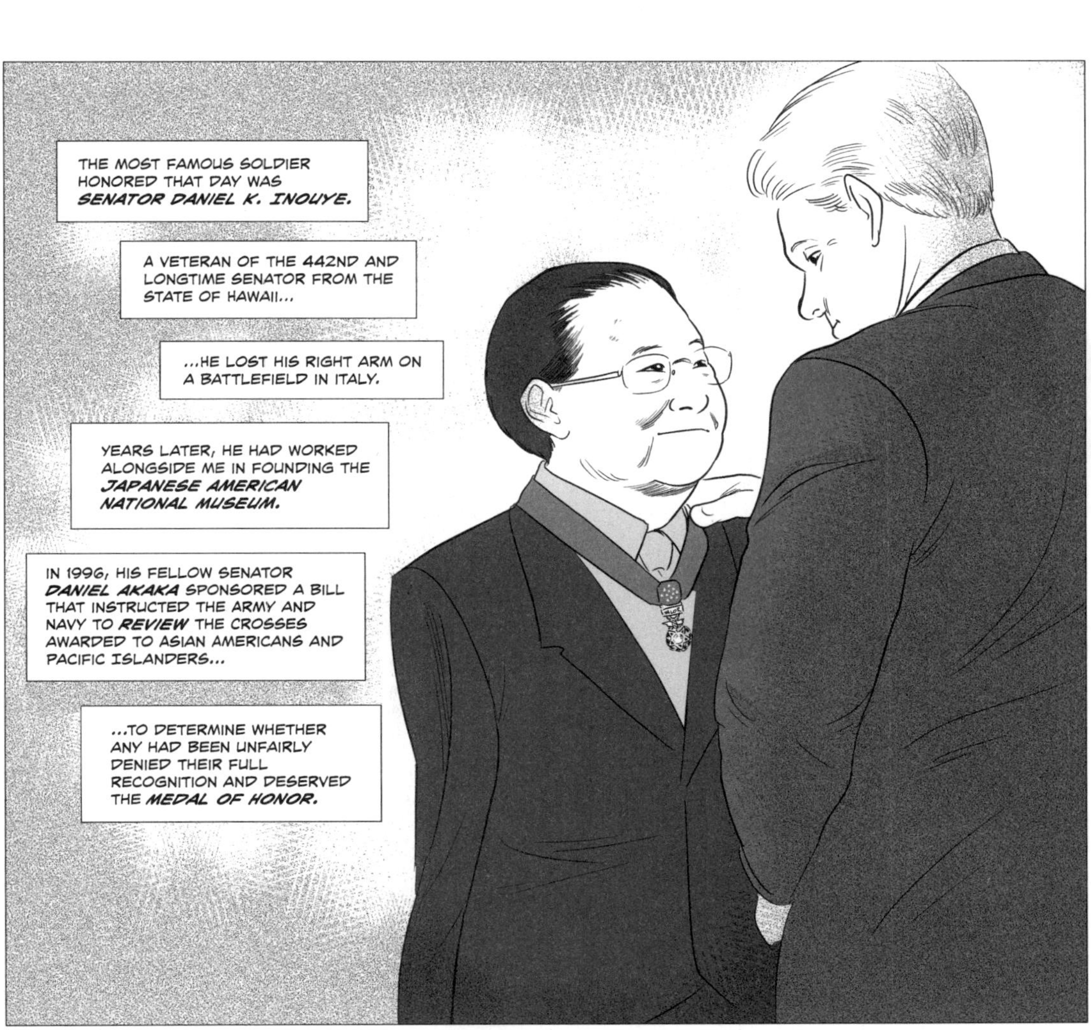
THE MOST FAMOUS SOLDIER HONORED THAT DAY WAS *SENATOR DANIEL K. INOUYE.*
A VETERAN OF THE 442ND AND LONGTIME SENATOR FROM THE STATE OF HAWAII...
...HE LOST HIS RIGHT ARM ON A BATTLEFIELD IN ITALY.
YEARS LATER, HE HAD WORKED ALONGSIDE ME IN FOUNDING THE *JAPANESE AMERICAN NATIONAL MUSEUM.*
IN 1996, HIS FELLOW SENATOR *DANIEL AKAKA* SPONSORED A BILL THAT INSTRUCTED THE ARMY AND NAVY TO *REVIEW* THE CROSSES AWARDED TO ASIAN AMERICANS AND PACIFIC ISLANDERS...
...TO DETERMINE WHETHER ANY HAD BEEN UNFAIRLY DENIED THEIR FULL RECOGNITION AND DESERVED THE *MEDAL OF HONOR.*

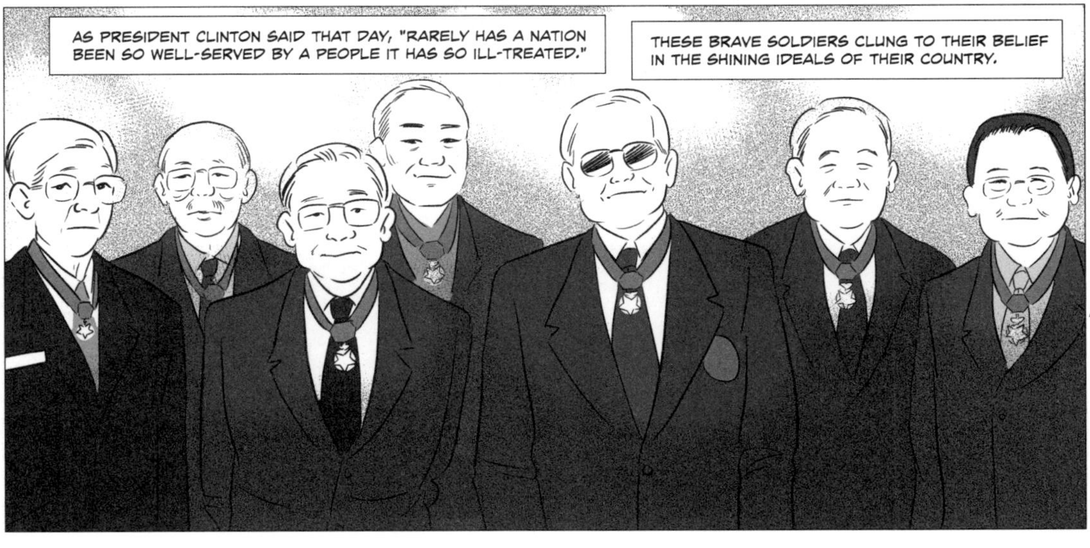
AS PRESIDENT CLINTON SAID THAT DAY, "RARELY HAS A NATION BEEN SO WELL-SERVED BY A PEOPLE IT HAS SO ILL-TREATED."
THESE BRAVE SOLDIERS CLUNG TO THEIR BELIEF IN THE SHINING IDEALS OF THEIR COUNTRY.

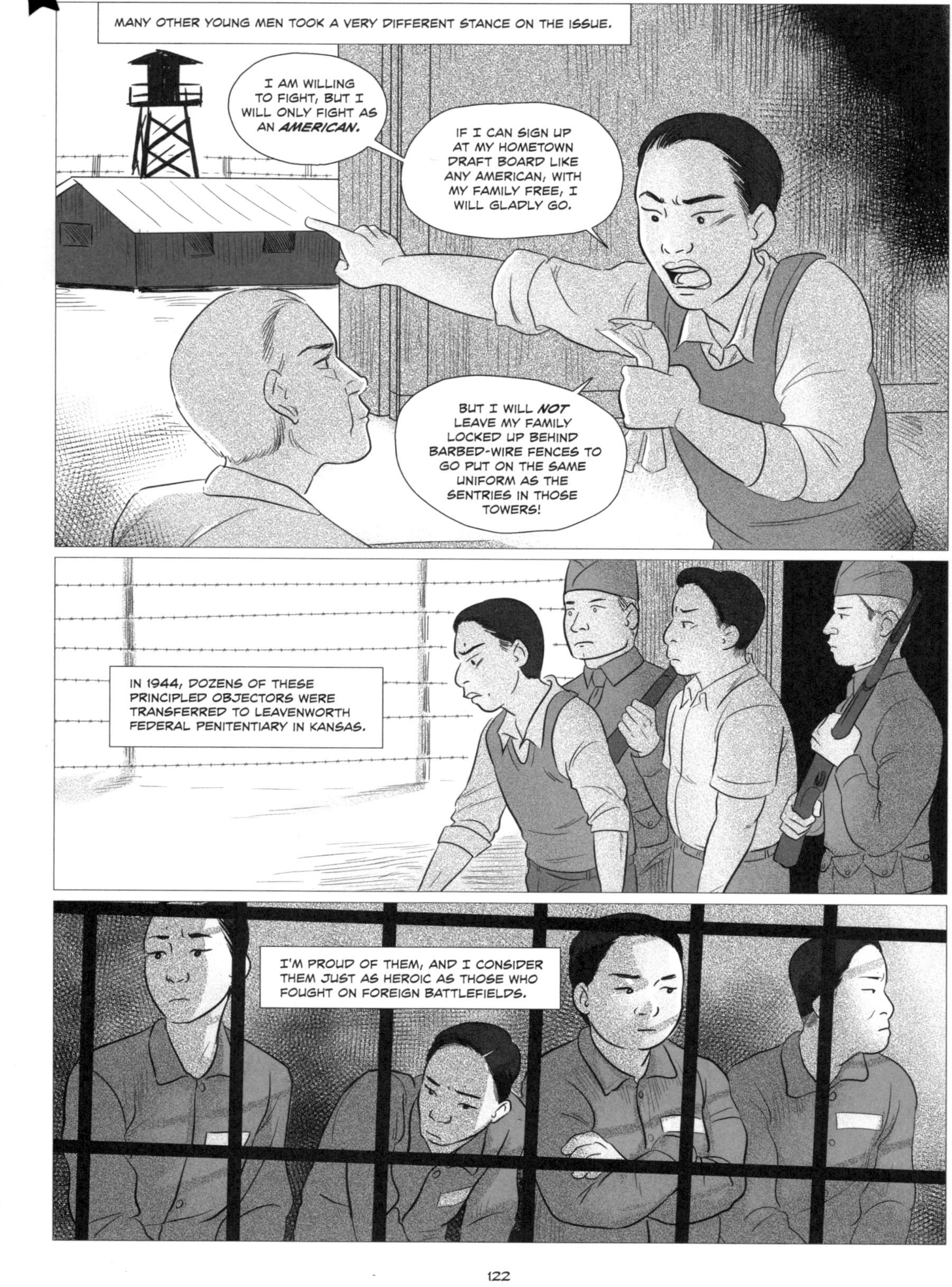
MANY OTHER YOUNG MEN TOOK A VERY DIFFERENT STANCE ON THE ISSUE.
I AM WILLING TO FIGHT, BUT I WILL ONLY FIGHT AS AN ***AMERICAN.***
IF I CAN SIGN UP AT MY HOMETOWN DRAFT BOARD LIKE ANY AMERICAN, WITH MY FAMILY FREE, I WILL GLADLY GO.
BUT I WILL ***NOT*** LEAVE MY FAMILY LOCKED UP BEHIND BARBED-WIRE FENCES TO GO PUT ON THE SAME UNIFORM AS THE SENTRIES IN THOSE TOWERS!
IN 1944, DOZENS OF THESE PRINCIPLED OBJECTORS WERE TRANSFERRED TO LEAVENWORTH FEDERAL PENITENTIARY IN KANSAS.
I'M PROUD OF THEM, AND I CONSIDER THEM JUST AS HEROIC AS THOSE WHO FOUGHT ON FOREIGN BATTLEFIELDS.

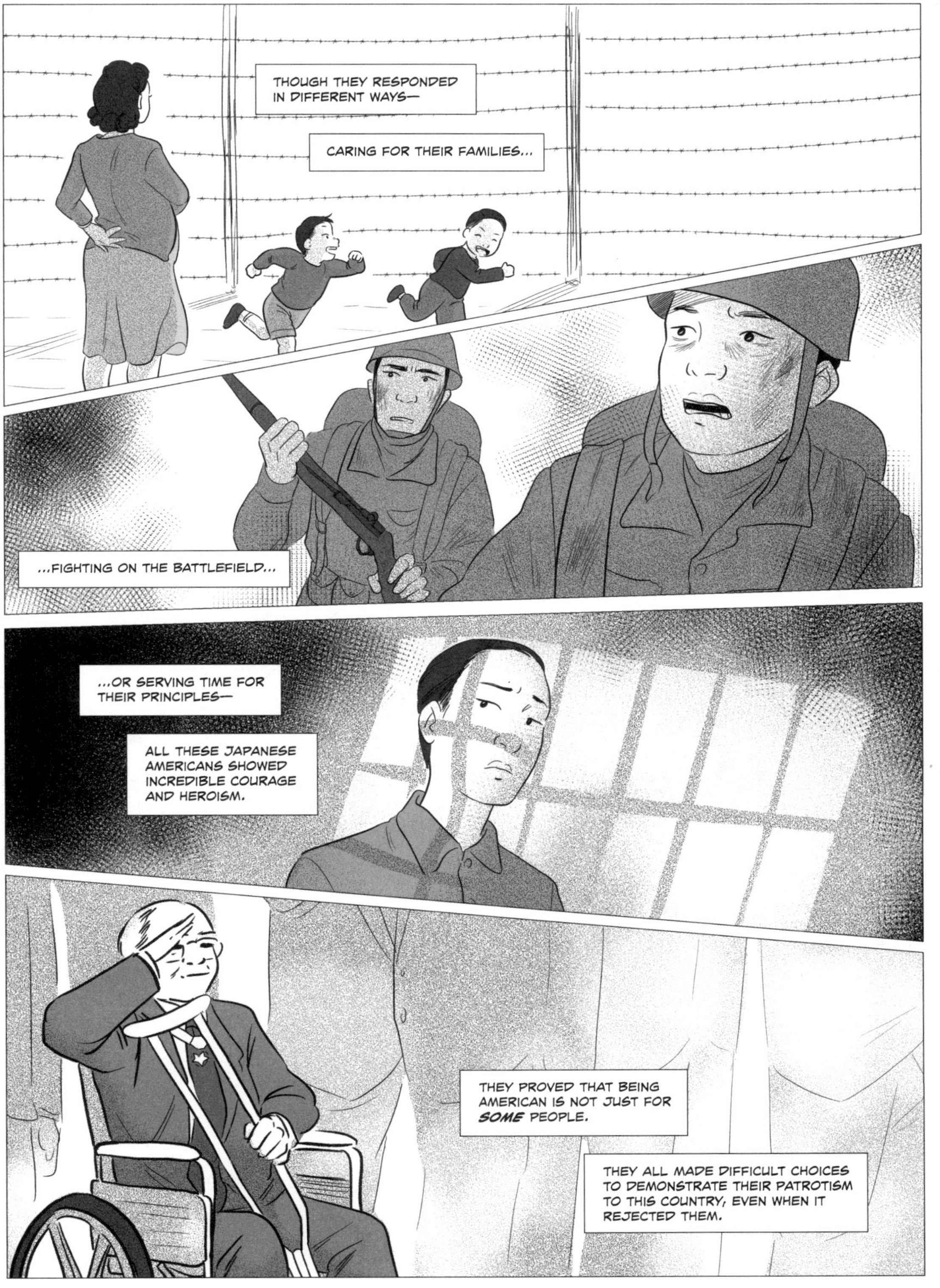
THOUGH THEY RESPONDED IN DIFFERENT WAYS—
CARING FOR THEIR FAMILIES...
...FIGHTING ON THE BATTLEFIELD...
...OR SERVING TIME FOR THEIR PRINCIPLES—
ALL THESE JAPANESE AMERICANS SHOWED INCREDIBLE COURAGE AND HEROISM.
THEY PROVED THAT BEING AMERICAN IS NOT JUST FOR *SOME* PEOPLE.
THEY ALL MADE DIFFICULT CHOICES TO DEMONSTRATE THEIR PATRIOTISM TO THIS COUNTRY, EVEN WHEN IT REJECTED THEM.

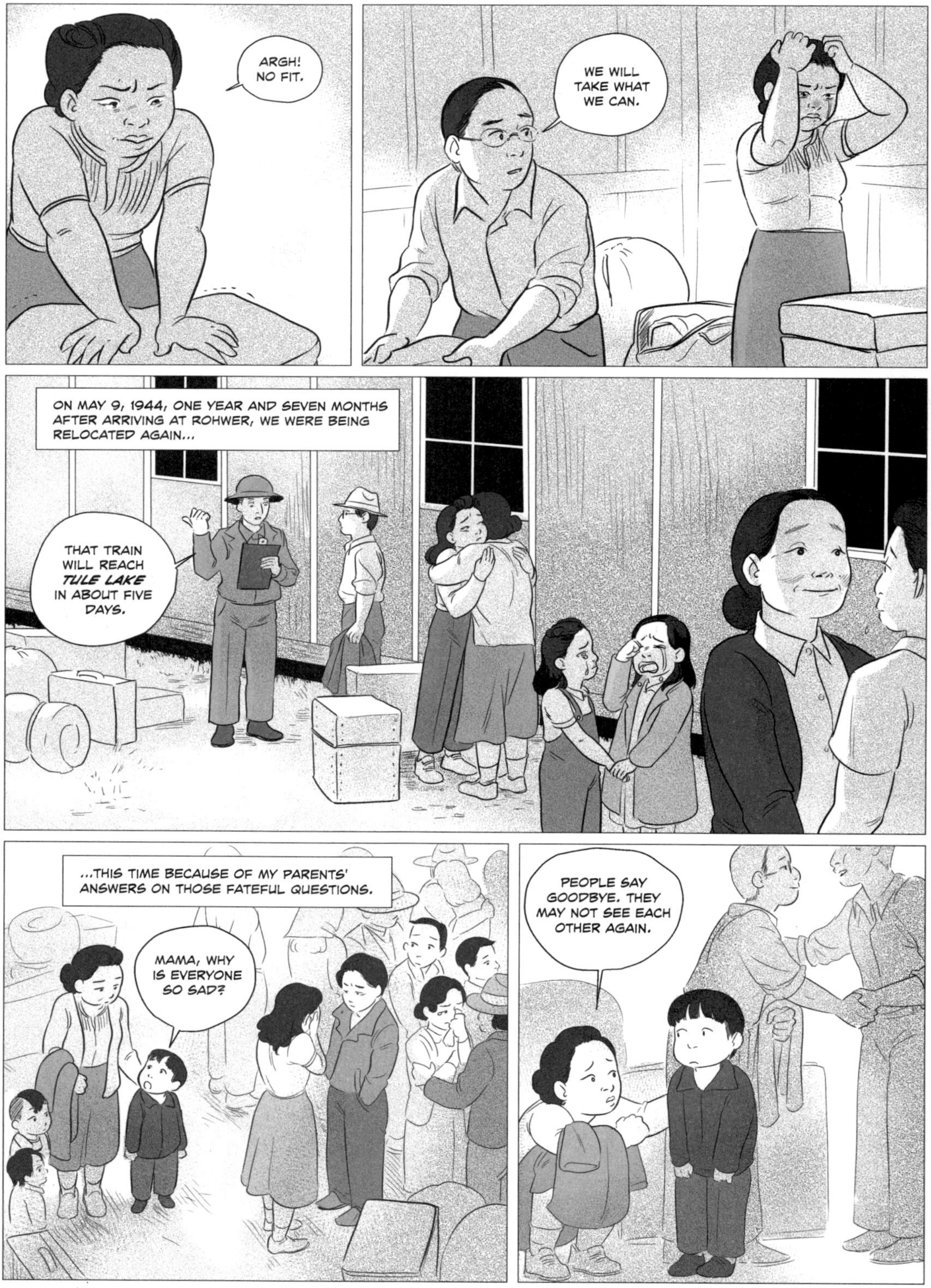
ARGH! NO FIT.
WE WILL TAKE WHAT WE CAN.
ON MAY 9, 1944, ONE YEAR AND SEVEN MONTHS AFTER ARRIVING AT ROHWER, WE WERE BEING RELOCATED AGAIN...
THAT TRAIN WILL REACH *TULE LAKE* IN ABOUT FIVE DAYS.
...THIS TIME BECAUSE OF MY PARENTS' ANSWERS ON THOSE FATEFUL QUESTIONS.
MAMA, WHY IS EVERYONE SO SAD?
PEOPLE SAY GOODBYE. THEY MAY NOT SEE EACH OTHER AGAIN.

CHOO

CHOOOO

I REMEMBER LOOKING OUT THAT TRAIN WINDOW.

I SAW THE SAD FACES OF PEOPLE WHO HAD BECOME FRIENDS.

THOSE BLACK BARRACKS HAD BECOME HOME.

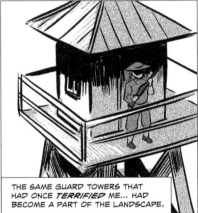

THE SAME GUARD TOWERS THAT HAD ONCE *TERRIFIED* ME... HAD BECOME A PART OF THE LANDSCAPE.

AHNNNGG

HUSH NOW. NO CRY.

HNNNG

HPPHPP

AS THE TRAIN PULLED AWAY FROM THE PLATFORM AND THE LIFE WE'D COME TO KNOW...

...FEAR OF THE UNKNOWN BECAME *UNBEARABLE*.

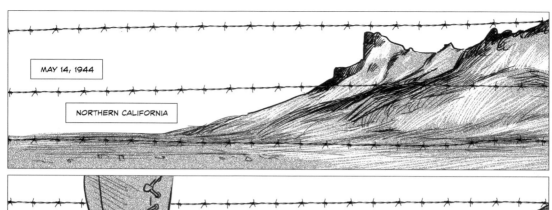

MAY 14, 1944

NORTHERN CALIFORNIA

krnnch

four!

hup, two, three, four!

hup, two, three, four! hup, two, thr

KRNCH

KRNCH KRNCH

CAMP TULE LAKE WAS A LOT DIFFERENT THAN ROHWER.

NOT ONE LAYER OF BARBED-WIRE FENCE, BUT THREE.

THE GOVERNMENT HAD CONVERTED IT INTO A MAXIMUM-SECURITY SEGREGATION CAMP FOR DISLOYALS...

...GUARDED BY BATTLE-READY TROOPS...

...MACHINE-GUN TOWERS...

...AND EVEN TANKS.

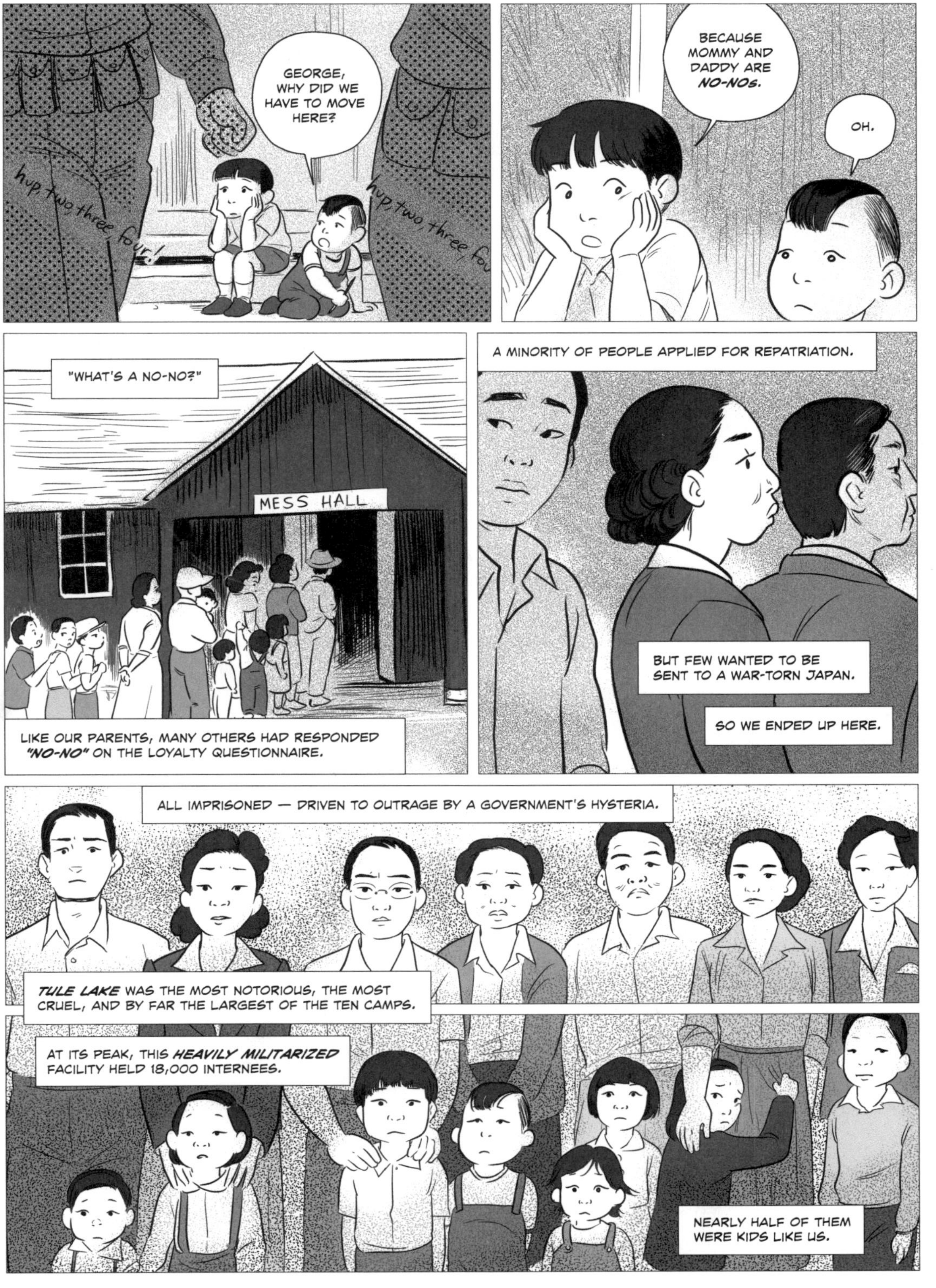

hup two, three four!
GEORGE, WHY DID WE HAVE TO MOVE HERE?
hup two, three, fou
BECAUSE MOMMY AND DADDY ARE ***NO-NOs.***
OH.
"WHAT'S A NO-NO?"
MESS HALL
LIKE OUR PARENTS, MANY OTHERS HAD RESPONDED ***"NO-NO"*** ON THE LOYALTY QUESTIONNAIRE.
A MINORITY OF PEOPLE APPLIED FOR REPATRIATION.
BUT FEW WANTED TO BE SENT TO A WAR-TORN JAPAN.
SO WE ENDED UP HERE.
ALL IMPRISONED — DRIVEN TO OUTRAGE BY A GOVERNMENT'S HYSTERIA.
TULE LAKE WAS THE MOST NOTORIOUS, THE MOST CRUEL, AND BY FAR THE LARGEST OF THE TEN CAMPS.
AT ITS PEAK, THIS ***HEAVILY MILITARIZED*** FACILITY HELD 18,000 INTERNEES.
NEARLY HALF OF THEM WERE KIDS LIKE US.

CLANG!

CLANG!

CLANG!

CLANG!

BREAKFAST!

WHILE I THOUGHT LIVING ACROSS FROM THE MESS HALL WAS GREAT, MAMA *HATED* IT.

CAN WE LINE UP?

IT SO *LOUD!* WE GET NO PEACE.

BUT WE HAVE TWO ROOMS. BETTER FOR US.

THEY WERE *BOTH* RIGHT, OF COURSE.

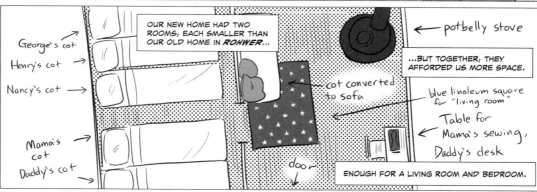

George's cot →

Henry's cot →

Nancy's cot →

Mama's cot →

Daddy's cot →

OUR NEW HOME HAD TWO ROOMS, EACH SMALLER THAN OUR OLD HOME IN *ROHWER*...

← potbelly stove

...BUT TOGETHER, THEY AFFORDED US MORE SPACE.

cot converted to sofa

blue linoleum square for "living room"

Table for Mama's sewing, Daddy's desk

door

ENOUGH FOR A LIVING ROOM AND BEDROOM.

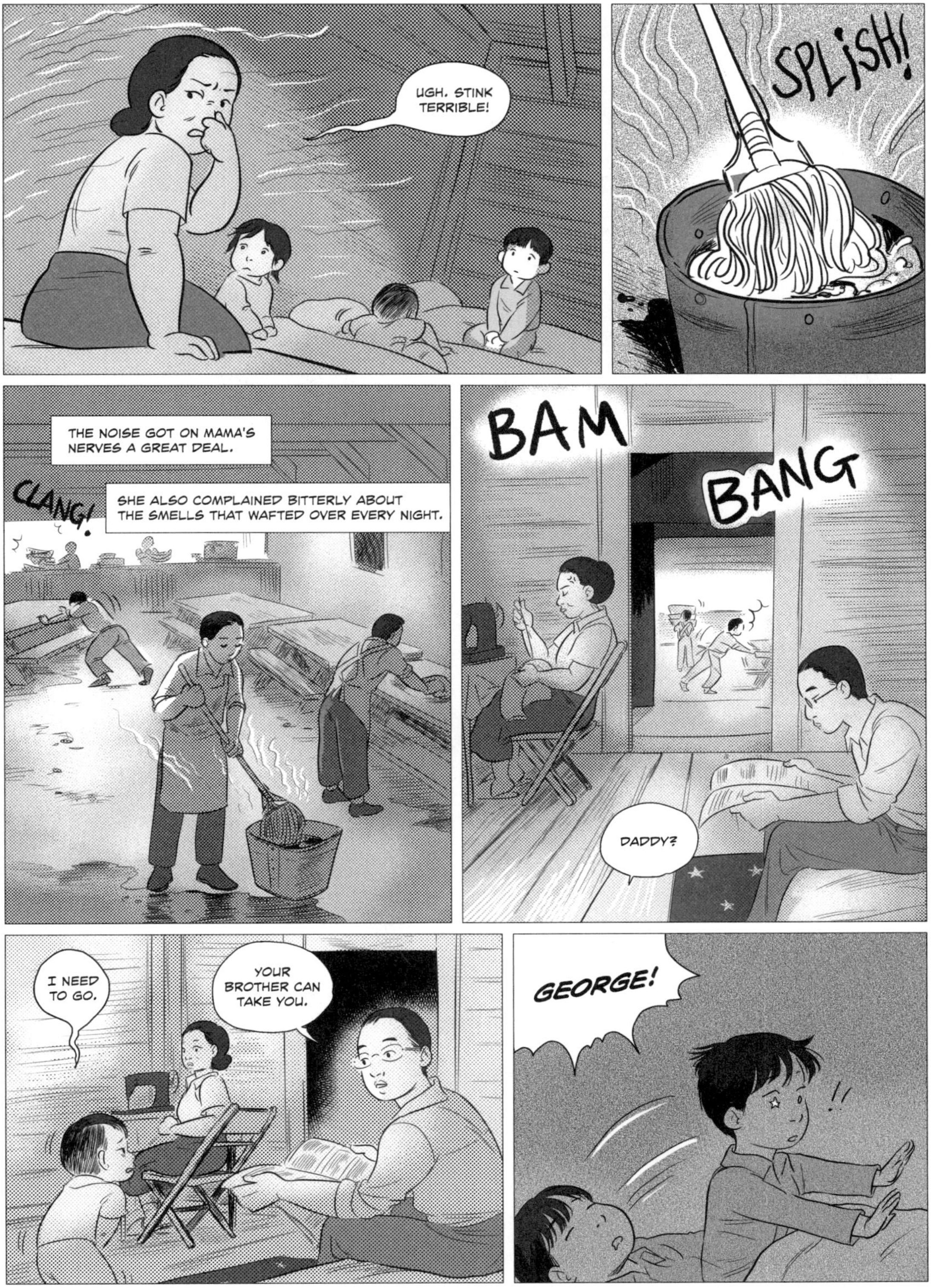
UGH. STINK TERRIBLE!
SPLISH!
THE NOISE GOT ON MAMA'S NERVES A GREAT DEAL.
CLANG!
SHE ALSO COMPLAINED BITTERLY ABOUT THE SMELLS THAT WAFTED OVER EVERY NIGHT.
BAM
BANG
DADDY?
I NEED TO GO.
YOUR BROTHER CAN TAKE YOU.
GEORGE!

COME ON!

OUCH! DON'T PULL SO HARD!

WE DIDN'T MAKE IT IN TIME.

Snnfff

SEE? TOILET SO FAR AWAY NOW.

THERE ARE TRADE-OFFS.

FROM THEN ON, MY MOTHER COLLECTED COFFEE CANS TO KEEP IN THE BEDROOM.

EDW
COFF
REGULAR G

GOOD MORN
COFFE

MAX
H
OF

JUST IN CASE.

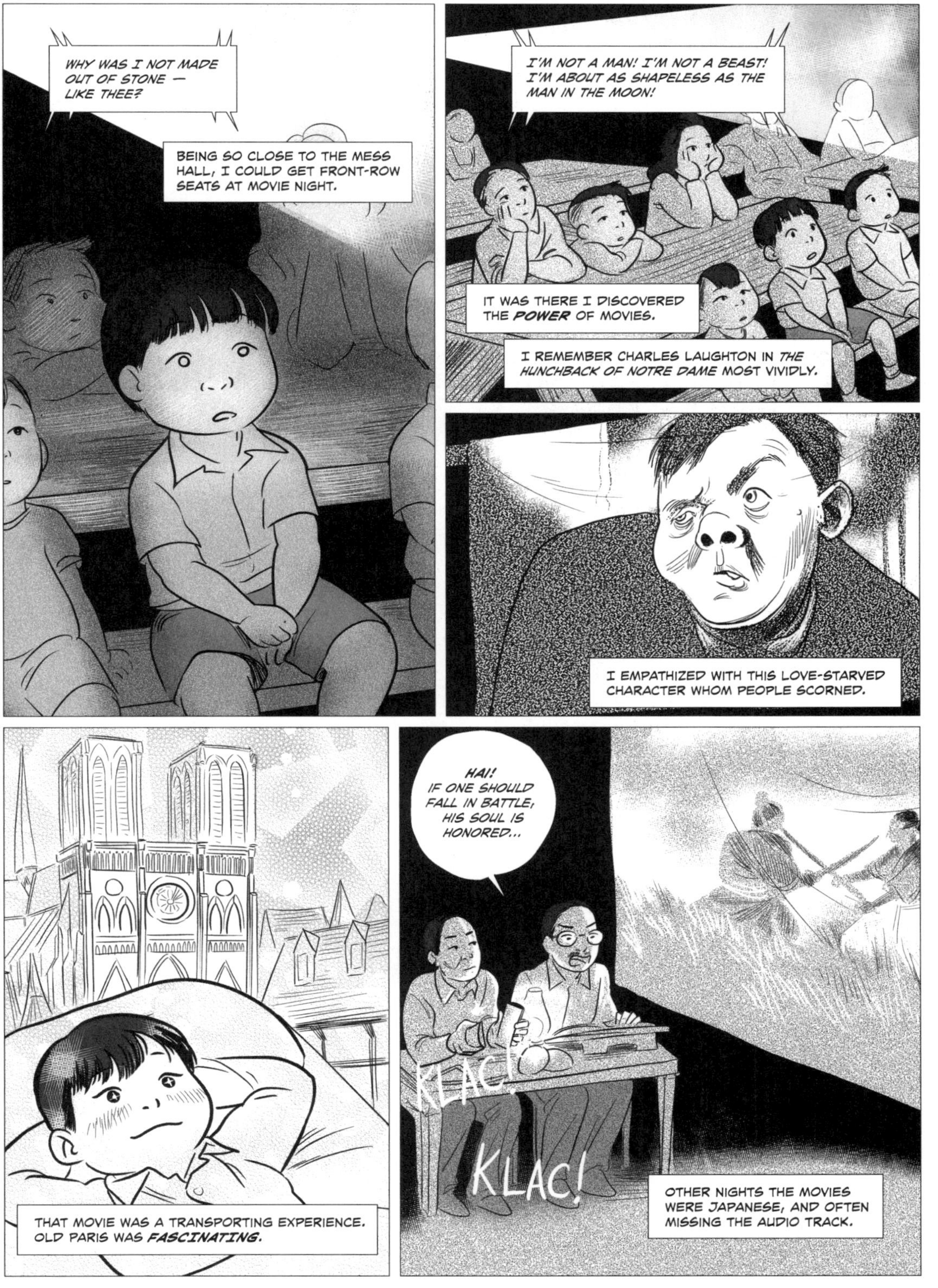
WHY WAS I NOT MADE OUT OF STONE — LIKE THEE?
BEING SO CLOSE TO THE MESS HALL, I COULD GET FRONT-ROW SEATS AT MOVIE NIGHT.
I'M NOT A MAN! I'M NOT A BEAST! I'M ABOUT AS SHAPELESS AS THE MAN IN THE MOON!
IT WAS THERE I DISCOVERED THE *POWER* OF MOVIES.
I REMEMBER CHARLES LAUGHTON IN *THE HUNCHBACK OF NOTRE DAME* MOST VIVIDLY.
I EMPATHIZED WITH THIS LOVE-STARVED CHARACTER WHOM PEOPLE SCORNED.
THAT MOVIE WAS A TRANSPORTING EXPERIENCE. OLD PARIS WAS *FASCINATING*.
HAI! IF ONE SHOULD FALL IN BATTLE, HIS SOUL IS HONORED...
KLAC!
KLAC!
OTHER NIGHTS THE MOVIES WERE JAPANESE, AND OFTEN MISSING THE AUDIO TRACK.

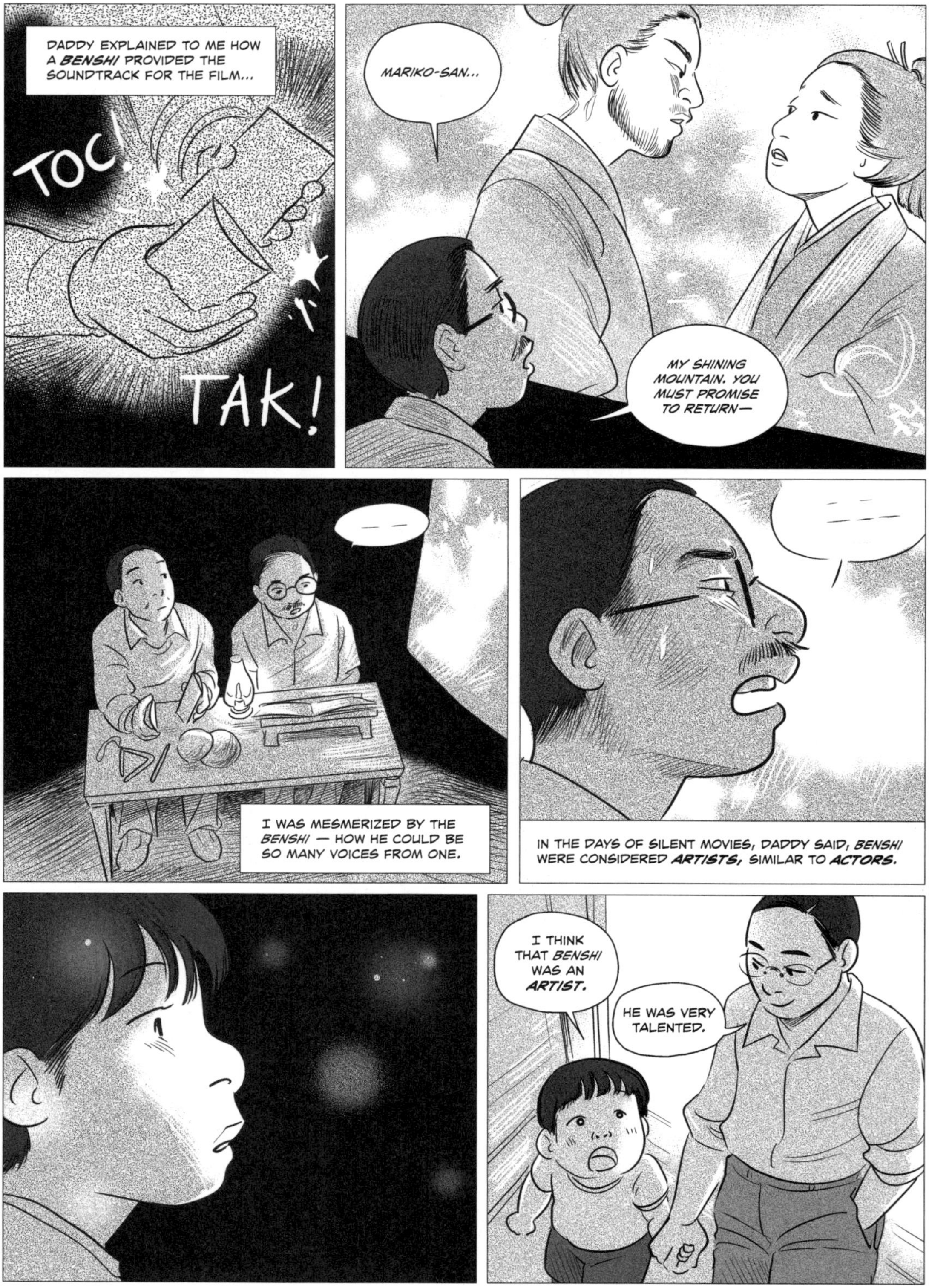
DADDY EXPLAINED TO ME HOW A *BENSHI* PROVIDED THE SOUNDTRACK FOR THE FILM...
TOC!
TAK!
MARIKO-SAN...
MY SHINING MOUNTAIN. YOU MUST PROMISE TO RETURN—
I WAS MESMERIZED BY THE *BENSHI* — HOW HE COULD BE SO MANY VOICES FROM ONE.
IN THE DAYS OF SILENT MOVIES, DADDY SAID, *BENSHI* WERE CONSIDERED ***ARTISTS,*** SIMILAR TO ***ACTORS.***
I THINK THAT *BENSHI* WAS AN ***ARTIST.***
HE WAS VERY TALENTED.

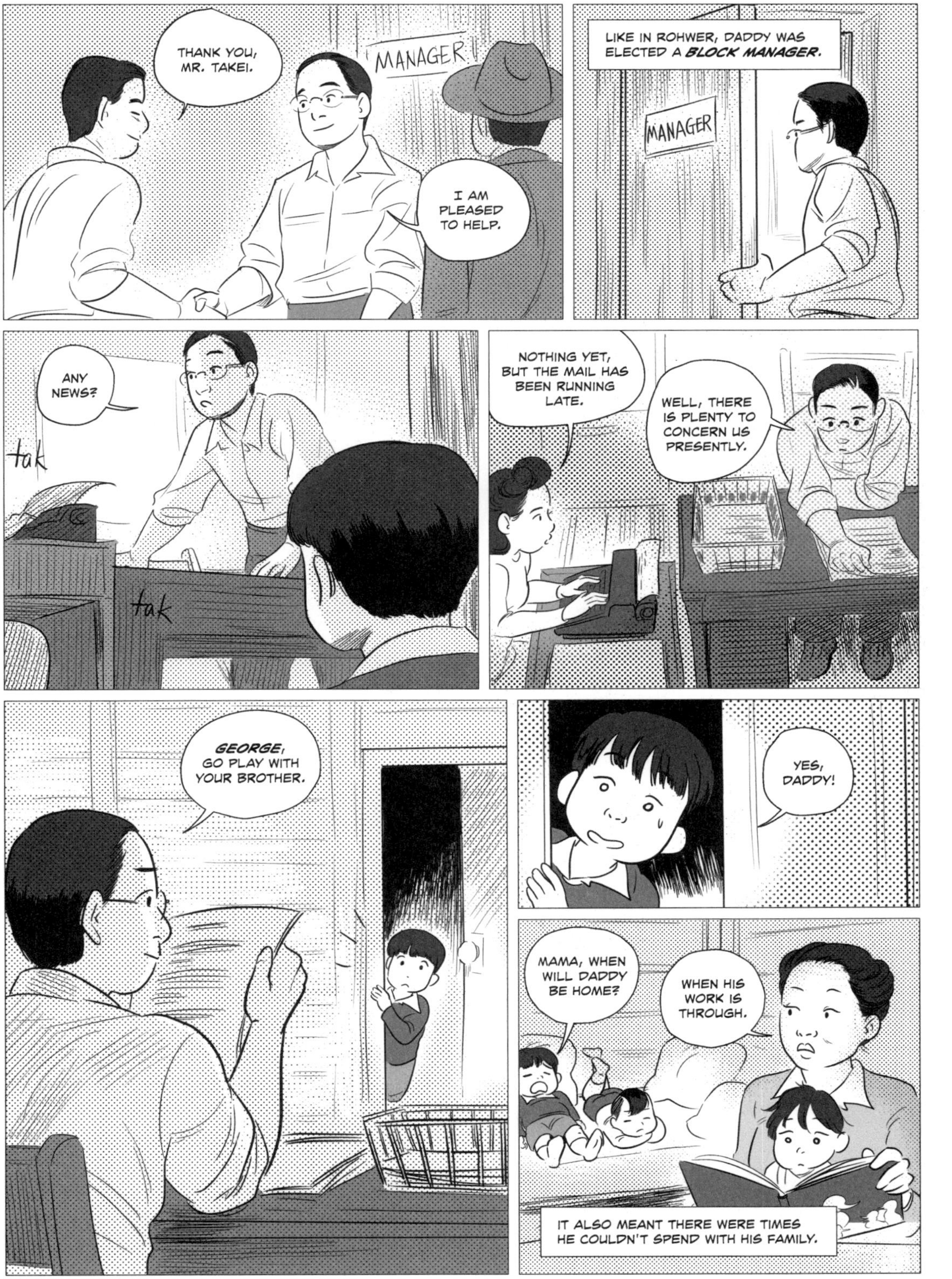
MANAGER
THANK YOU, MR. TAKEI.
I AM PLEASED TO HELP.
LIKE IN ROHWER, DADDY WAS ELECTED A BLOCK MANAGER.
MANAGER
ANY NEWS?
tak
tak
NOTHING YET, BUT THE MAIL HAS BEEN RUNNING LATE.
WELL, THERE IS PLENTY TO CONCERN US PRESENTLY.
GEORGE, GO PLAY WITH YOUR BROTHER.
YES, DADDY!
MAMA, WHEN WILL DADDY BE HOME?
WHEN HIS WORK IS THROUGH.
IT ALSO MEANT THERE WERE TIMES HE COULDN'T SPEND WITH HIS FAMILY.

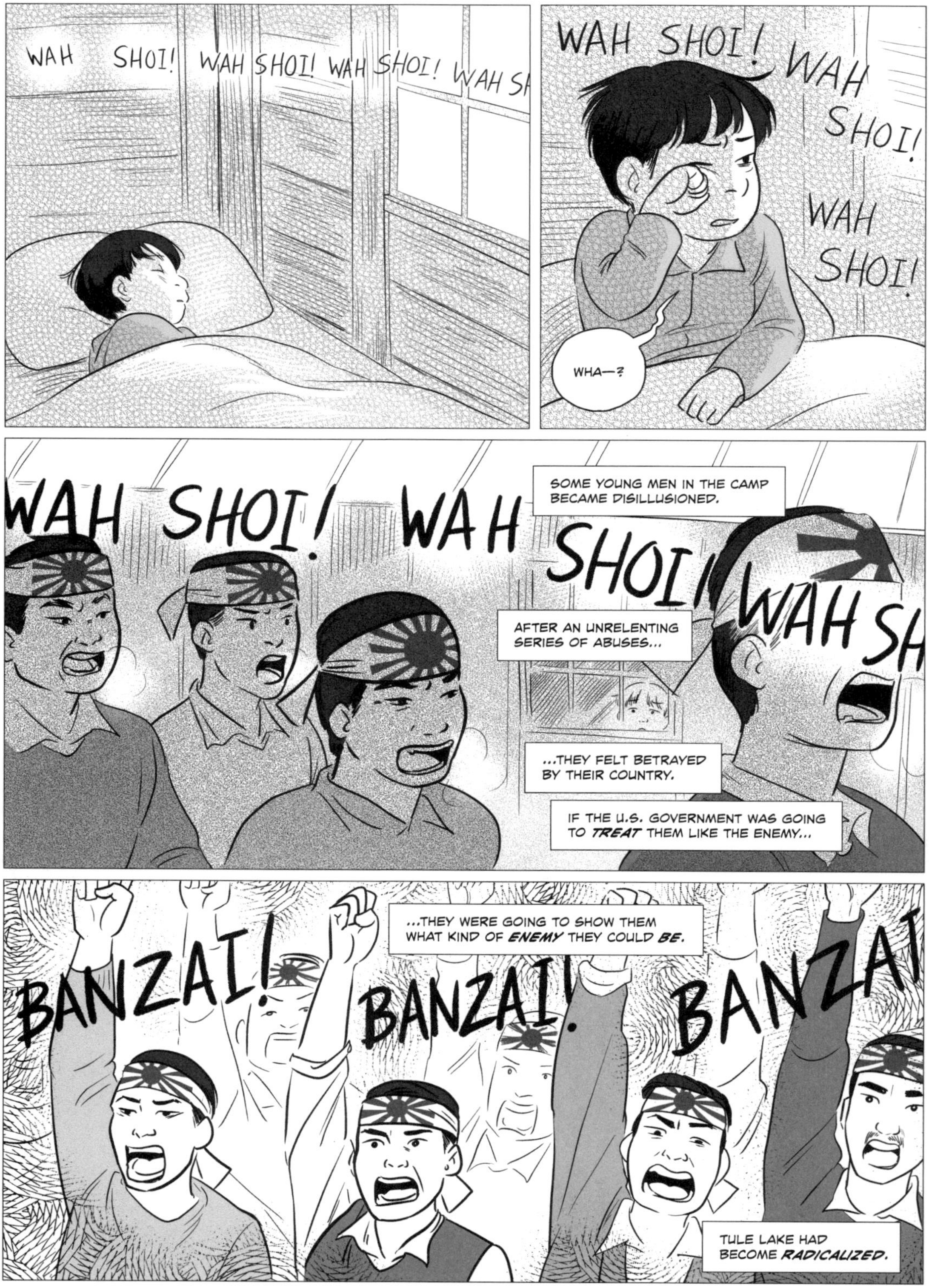
WAH SHOI! WAH SHOI! WAH SHOI! WAH SH
WAH SHOI! WAH SHOI! WAH SHOI!
WHA—?
WAH SHOI! WAH SHOI! WAH SH
SOME YOUNG MEN IN THE CAMP BECAME DISILLUSIONED.
AFTER AN UNRELENTING SERIES OF ABUSES...
...THEY FELT BETRAYED BY THEIR COUNTRY.
IF THE U.S. GOVERNMENT WAS GOING TO *TREAT* THEM LIKE THE ENEMY...
...THEY WERE GOING TO SHOW THEM WHAT KIND OF *ENEMY* THEY COULD *BE*.
BANZAI! BANZAI! BANZAI
TULE LAKE HAD BECOME *RADICALIZED*.

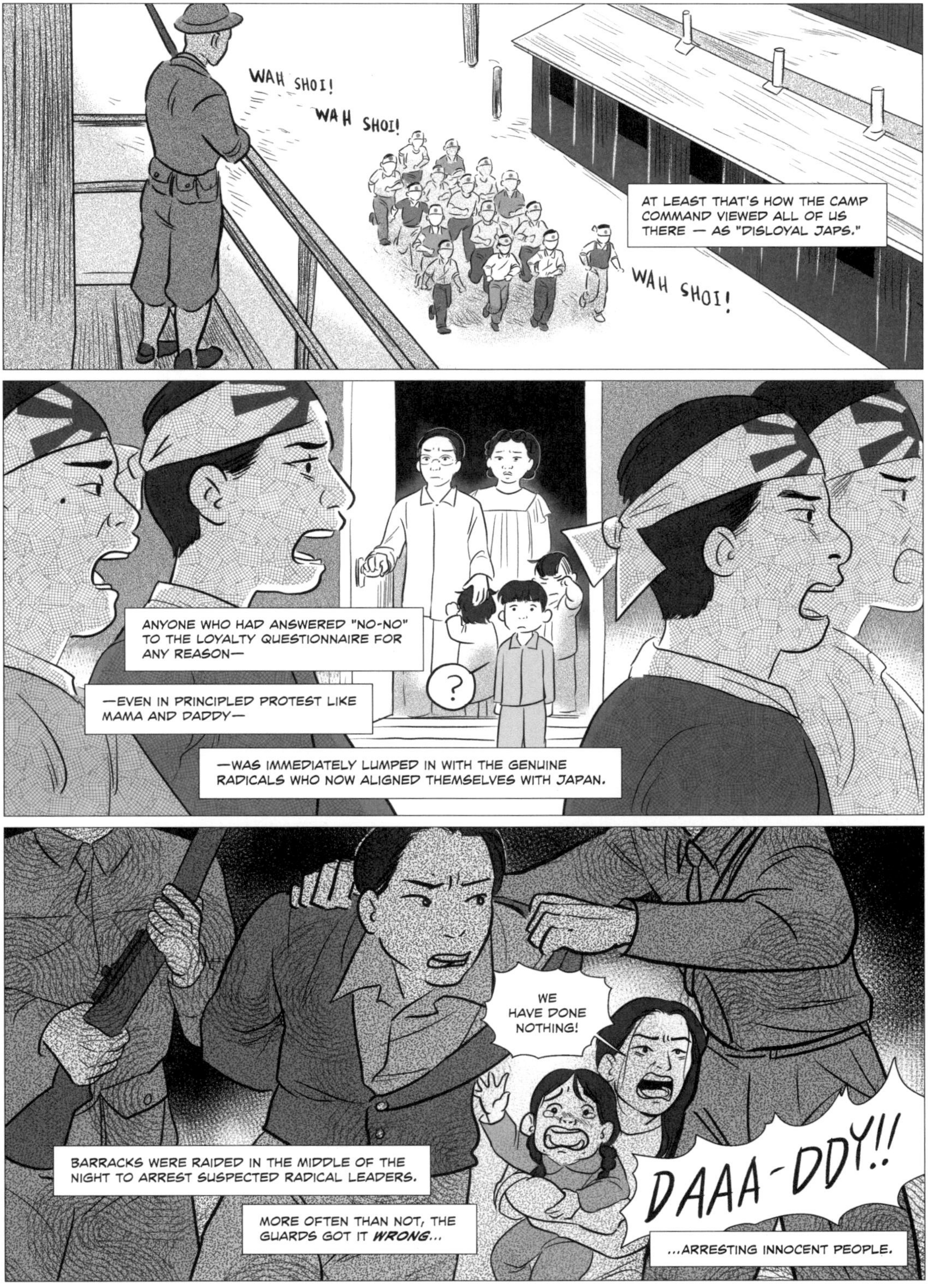
WAH SHOI!
WAH SHOI!
AT LEAST THAT'S HOW THE CAMP COMMAND VIEWED ALL OF US THERE — AS "DISLOYAL JAPS."
WAH SHOI!
ANYONE WHO HAD ANSWERED "NO-NO" TO THE LOYALTY QUESTIONNAIRE FOR ANY REASON—
?
—EVEN IN PRINCIPLED PROTEST LIKE MAMA AND DADDY—
—WAS IMMEDIATELY LUMPED IN WITH THE GENUINE RADICALS WHO NOW ALIGNED THEMSELVES WITH JAPAN.
WE HAVE DONE NOTHING!
BARRACKS WERE RAIDED IN THE MIDDLE OF THE NIGHT TO ARREST SUSPECTED RADICAL LEADERS.
DAAA-DDY!!
MORE OFTEN THAN NOT, THE GUARDS GOT IT ***WRONG***...
...ARRESTING INNOCENT PEOPLE.

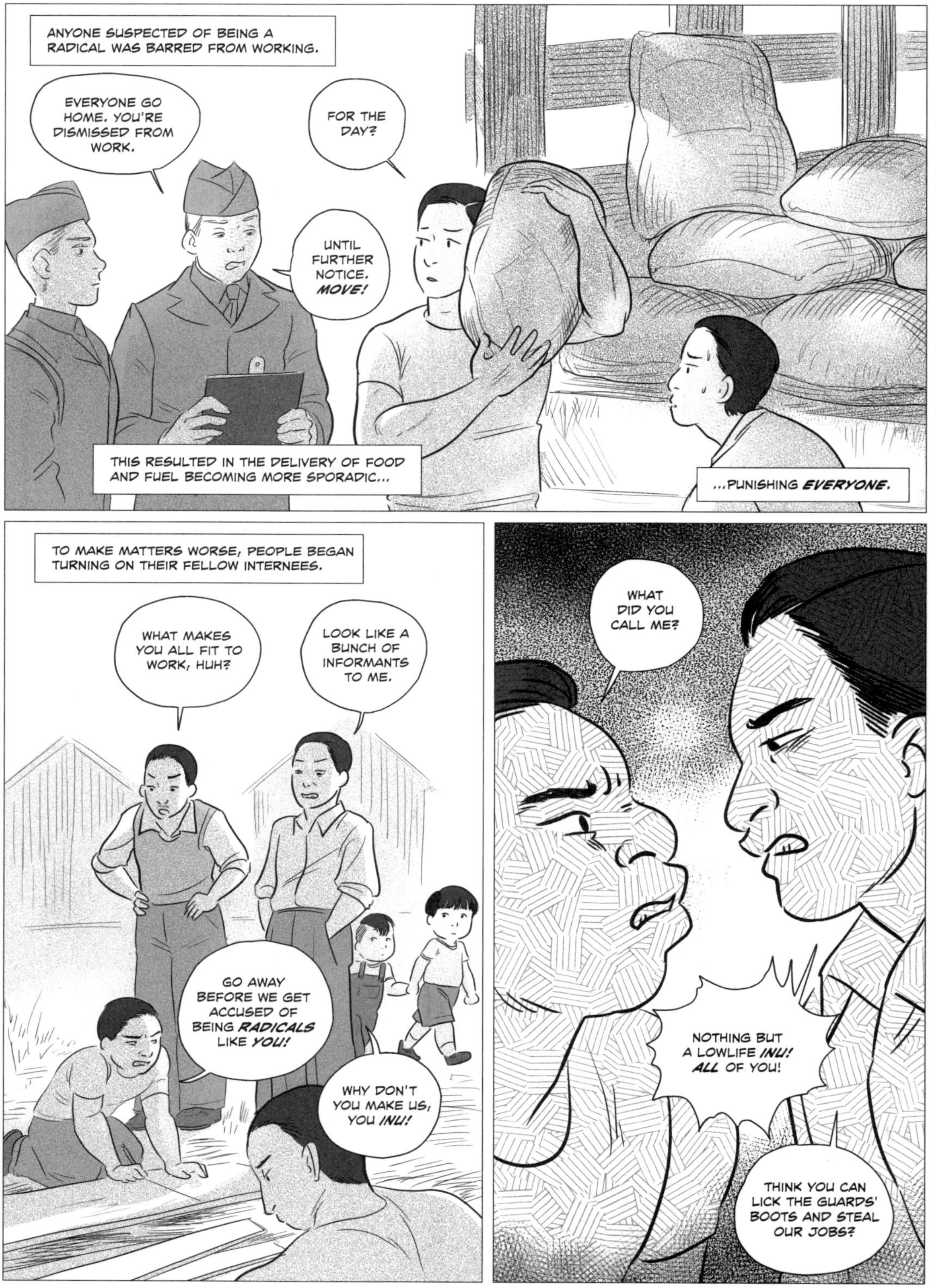

ANYONE SUSPECTED OF BEING A RADICAL WAS BARRED FROM WORKING.
EVERYONE GO HOME. YOU'RE DISMISSED FROM WORK.
FOR THE DAY?
UNTIL FURTHER NOTICE. *MOVE!*
THIS RESULTED IN THE DELIVERY OF FOOD AND FUEL BECOMING MORE SPORADIC...
...PUNISHING *EVERYONE.*
TO MAKE MATTERS WORSE, PEOPLE BEGAN TURNING ON THEIR FELLOW INTERNEES.
WHAT MAKES YOU ALL FIT TO WORK, HUH?
LOOK LIKE A BUNCH OF INFORMANTS TO ME.
GO AWAY BEFORE WE GET ACCUSED OF BEING *RADICALS* LIKE *YOU!*
WHY DON'T YOU MAKE US, YOU *INU!*
WHAT DID YOU CALL ME?
NOTHING BUT A LOWLIFE *INU! ALL* OF YOU!
THINK YOU CAN LICK THE GUARDS' BOOTS AND STEAL OUR JOBS?

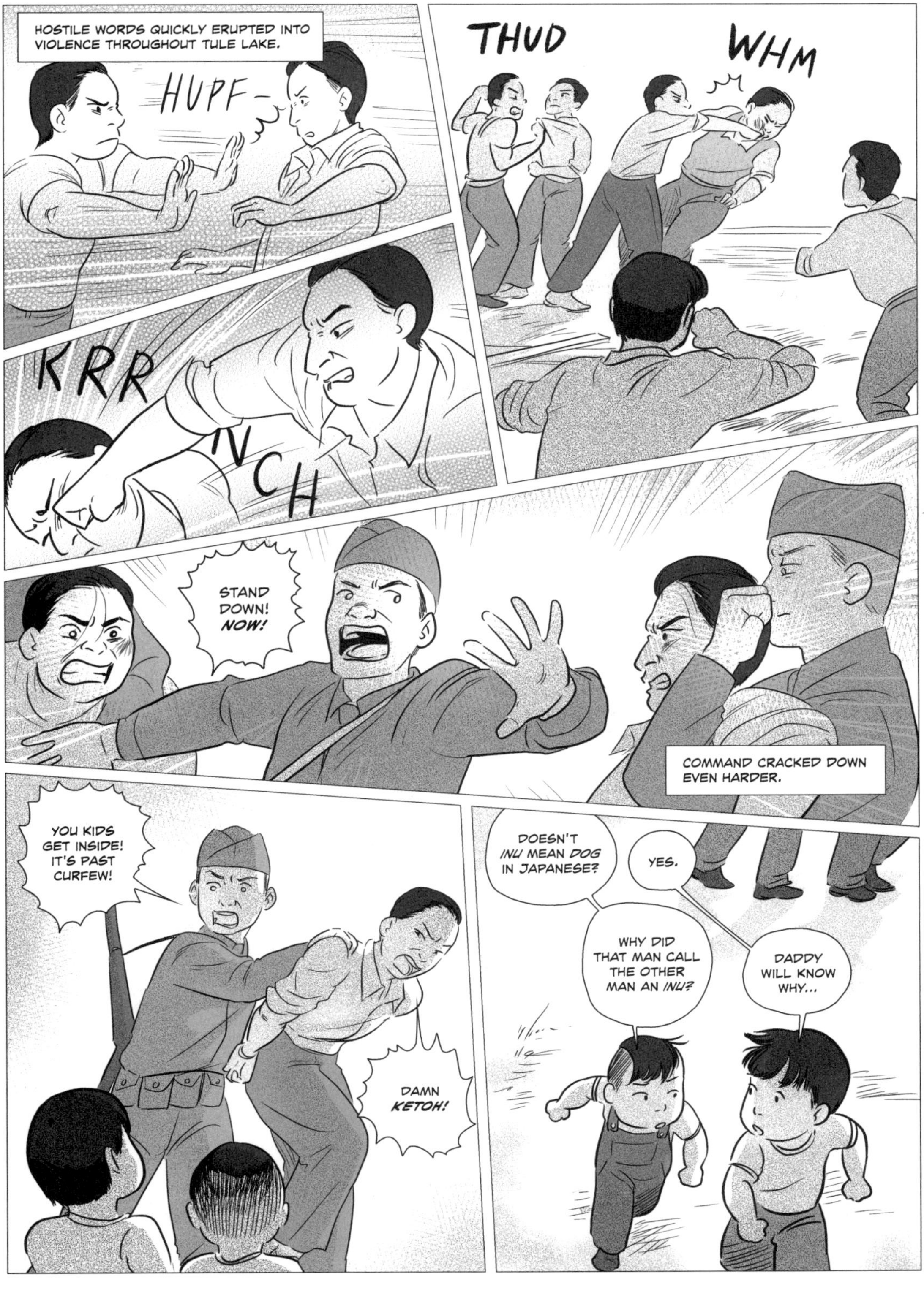
HOSTILE WORDS QUICKLY ERUPTED INTO VIOLENCE THROUGHOUT TULE LAKE.
HUPF
KRR
NCH
THUD
WHM
STAND DOWN! *NOW!*
COMMAND CRACKED DOWN EVEN HARDER.
YOU KIDS GET INSIDE! IT'S PAST CURFEW!
DAMN *KETOH!*
DOESN'T *INU* MEAN *DOG* IN JAPANESE?
YES.
WHY DID THAT MAN CALL THE OTHER MAN AN *INU?*
DADDY WILL KNOW WHY...

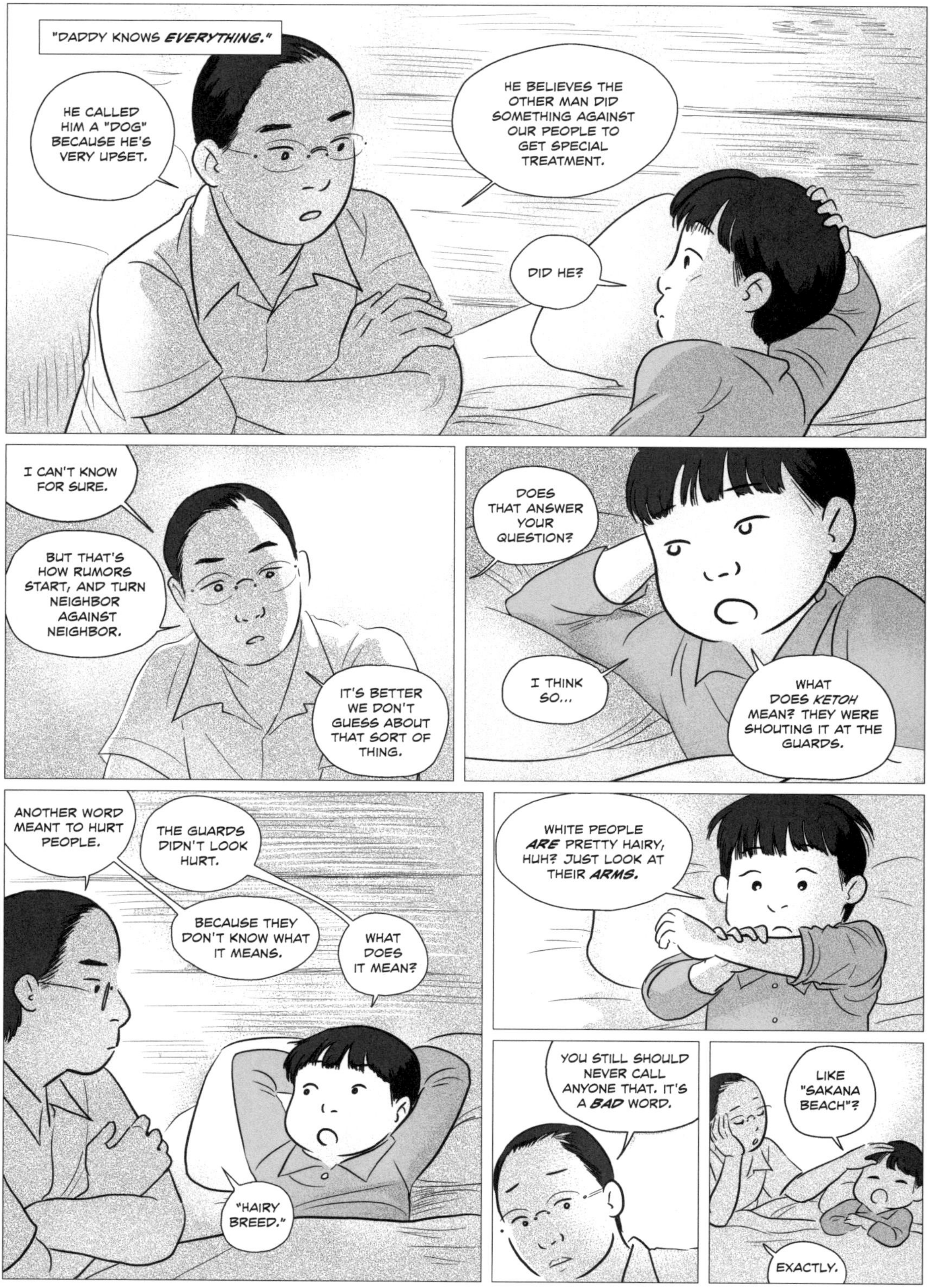
"DADDY KNOWS EVERYTHING."
HE CALLED HIM A "DOG" BECAUSE HE'S VERY UPSET.
HE BELIEVES THE OTHER MAN DID SOMETHING AGAINST OUR PEOPLE TO GET SPECIAL TREATMENT.
DID HE?
I CAN'T KNOW FOR SURE.
BUT THAT'S HOW RUMORS START, AND TURN NEIGHBOR AGAINST NEIGHBOR.
IT'S BETTER WE DON'T GUESS ABOUT THAT SORT OF THING.
DOES THAT ANSWER YOUR QUESTION?
I THINK SO...
WHAT DOES KETOH MEAN? THEY WERE SHOUTING IT AT THE GUARDS.
ANOTHER WORD MEANT TO HURT PEOPLE.
THE GUARDS DIDN'T LOOK HURT.
BECAUSE THEY DON'T KNOW WHAT IT MEANS.
WHAT DOES IT MEAN?
"HAIRY BREED."
WHITE PEOPLE ARE PRETTY HAIRY, HUH? JUST LOOK AT THEIR ARMS.
YOU STILL SHOULD NEVER CALL ANYONE THAT. IT'S A BAD WORD.
LIKE "SAKANA BEACH"?
EXACTLY.

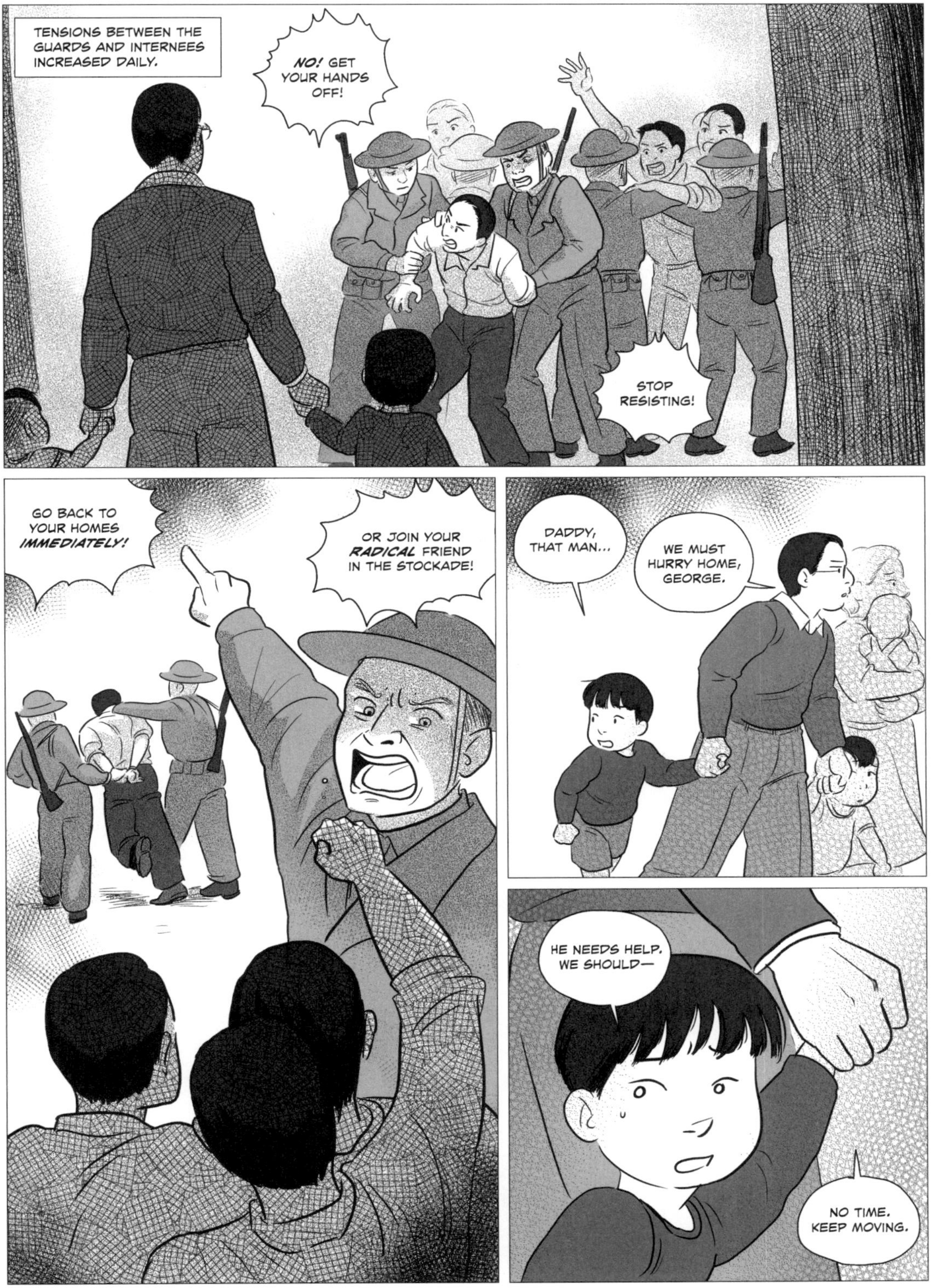
TENSIONS BETWEEN THE GUARDS AND INTERNEES INCREASED DAILY.
NO! GET YOUR HANDS OFF!
STOP RESISTING!
GO BACK TO YOUR HOMES *IMMEDIATELY!*
OR JOIN YOUR *RADICAL* FRIEND IN THE STOCKADE!
DADDY, THAT MAN...
WE MUST HURRY HOME, GEORGE.
HE NEEDS HELP. WE SHOULD—
NO TIME. KEEP MOVING.

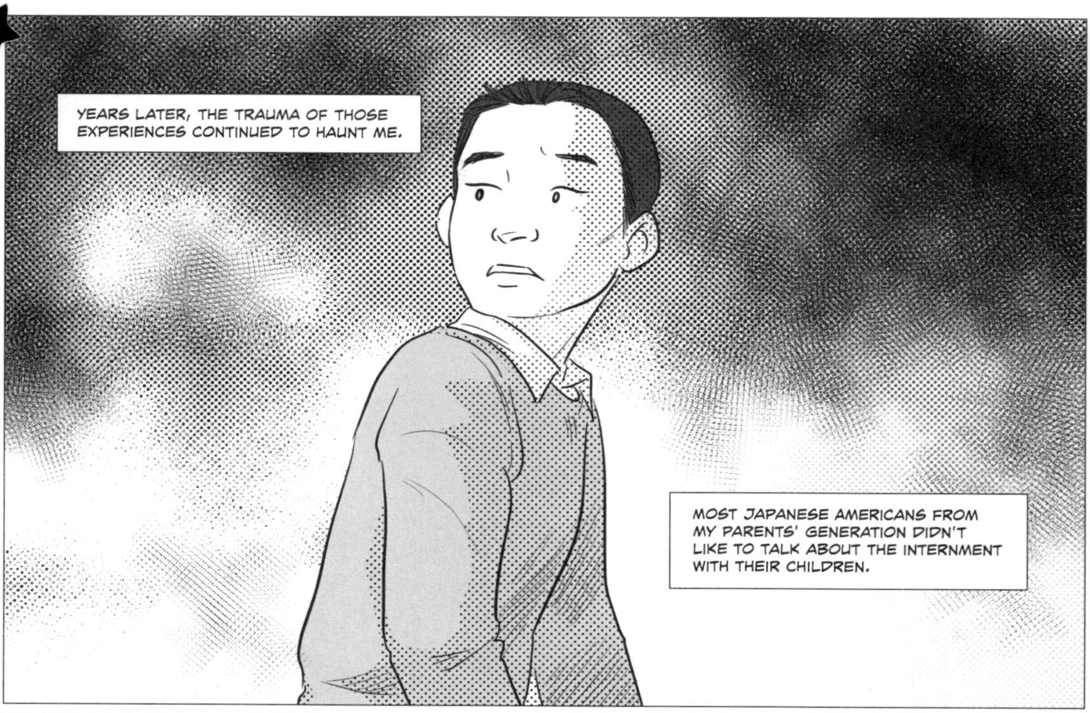
YEARS LATER, THE TRAUMA OF THOSE EXPERIENCES CONTINUED TO HAUNT ME.
MOST JAPANESE AMERICANS FROM MY PARENTS' GENERATION DIDN'T LIKE TO TALK ABOUT THE INTERNMENT WITH THEIR CHILDREN.

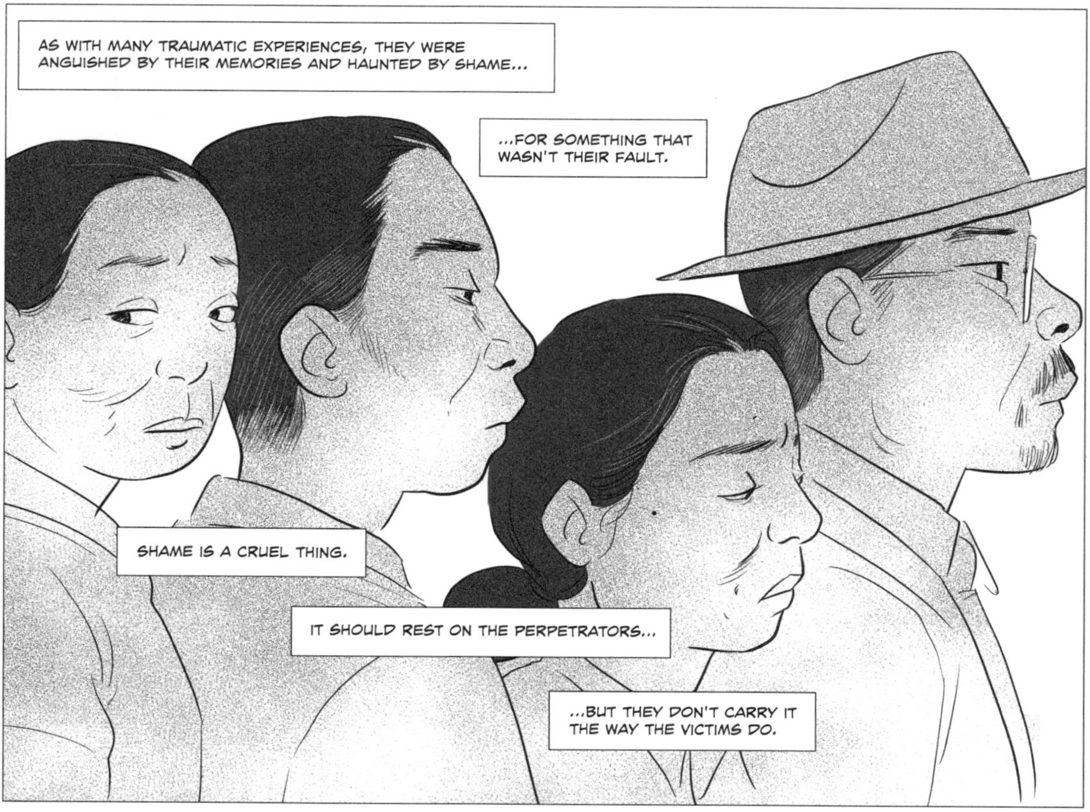
AS WITH MANY TRAUMATIC EXPERIENCES, THEY WERE ANGUISHED BY THEIR MEMORIES AND HAUNTED BY SHAME...
...FOR SOMETHING THAT WASN'T THEIR FAULT.
SHAME IS A CRUEL THING.
IT SHOULD REST ON THE PERPETRATORS...
...BUT THEY DON'T CARRY IT THE WAY THE VICTIMS DO.

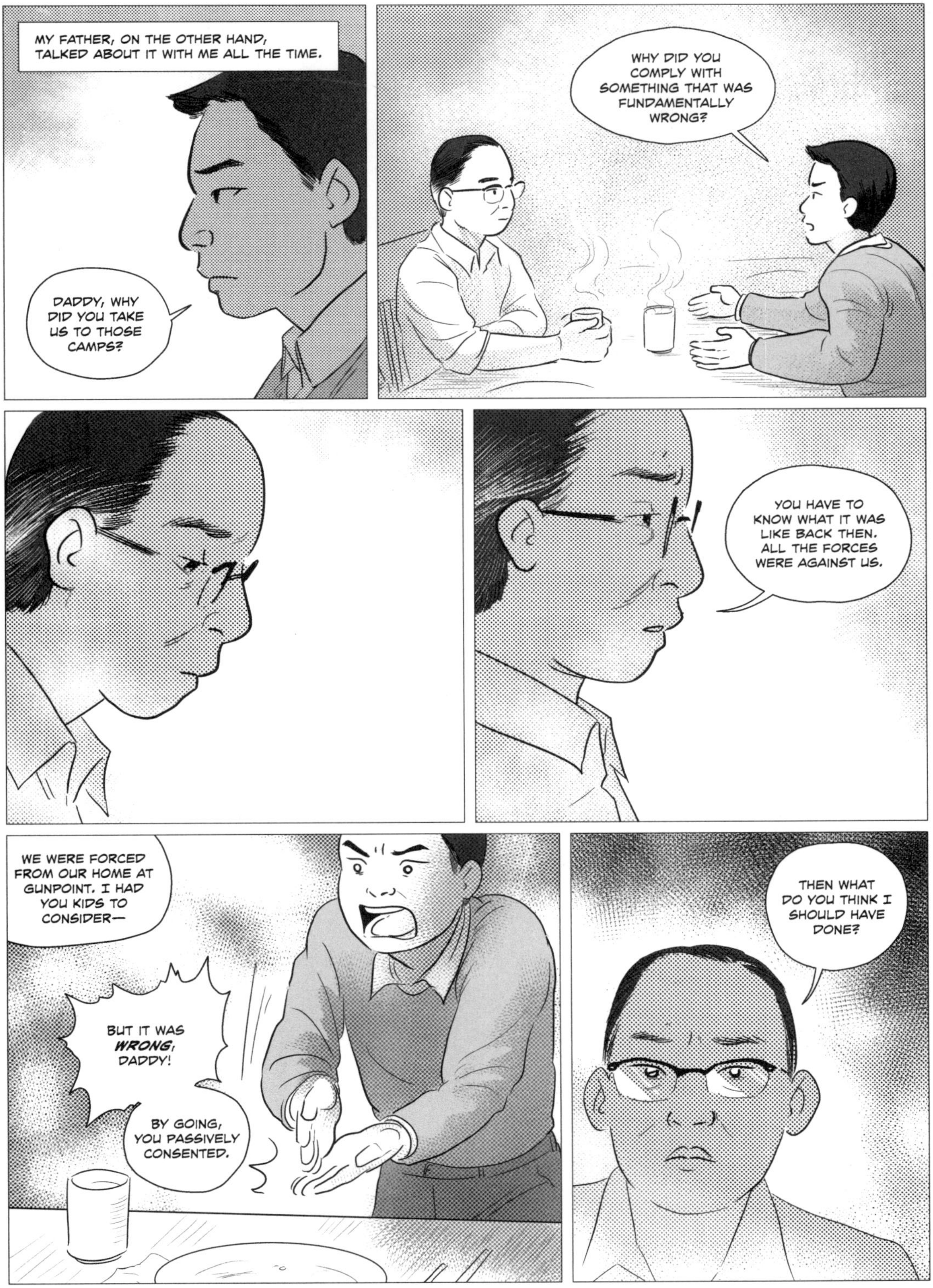
MY FATHER, ON THE OTHER HAND, TALKED ABOUT IT WITH ME ALL THE TIME.
DADDY, WHY DID YOU TAKE US TO THOSE CAMPS?
WHY DID YOU COMPLY WITH SOMETHING THAT WAS FUNDAMENTALLY WRONG?
YOU HAVE TO KNOW WHAT IT WAS LIKE BACK THEN. ALL THE FORCES WERE AGAINST US.
WE WERE FORCED FROM OUR HOME AT GUNPOINT. I HAD YOU KIDS TO CONSIDER—
BUT IT WAS ***WRONG***, DADDY!
BY GOING, YOU PASSIVELY CONSENTED.
THEN WHAT DO YOU THINK I SHOULD HAVE DONE?

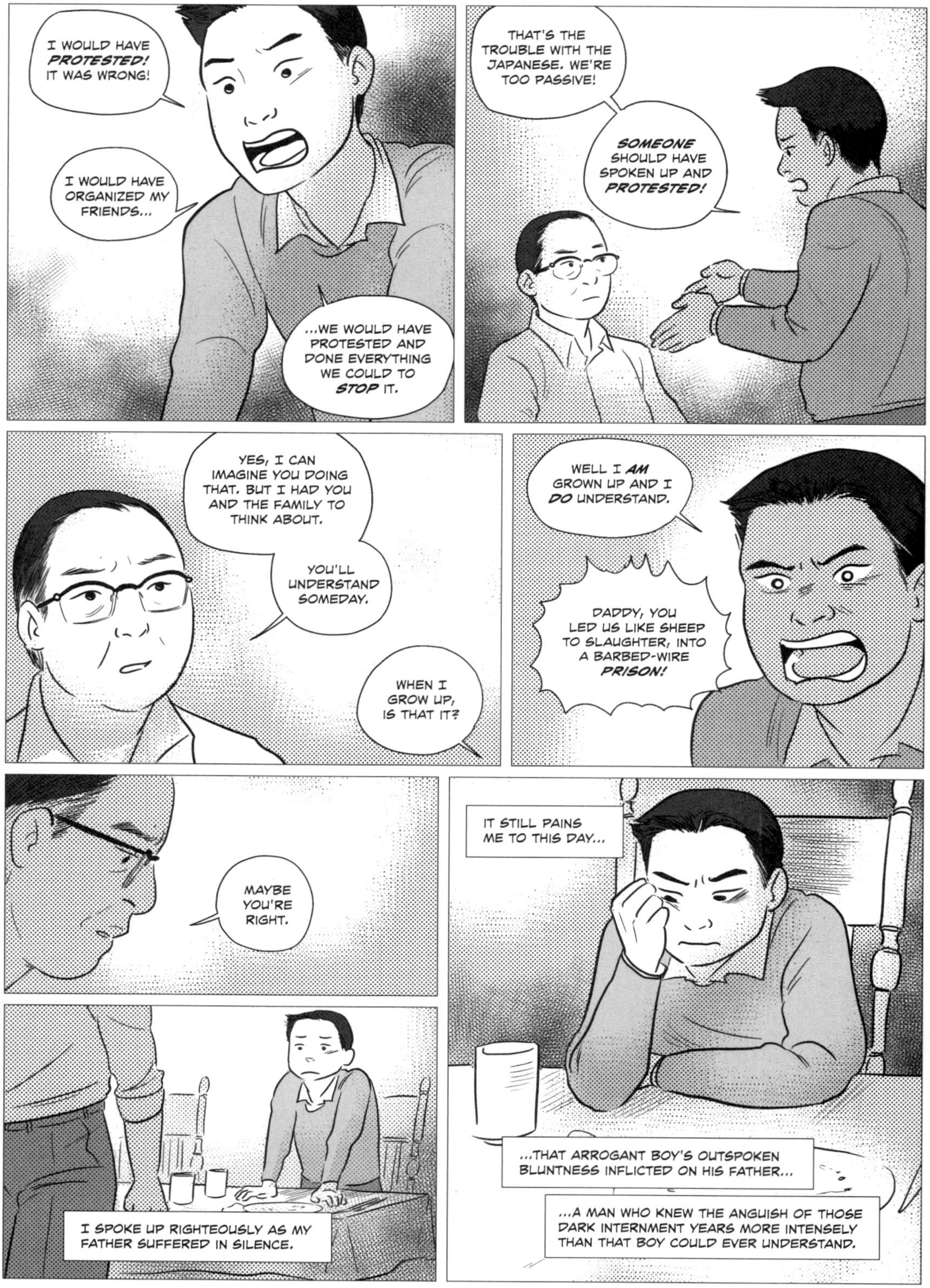
I WOULD HAVE *PROTESTED!* IT WAS WRONG!
I WOULD HAVE ORGANIZED MY FRIENDS...
...WE WOULD HAVE PROTESTED AND DONE EVERYTHING WE COULD TO *STOP* IT.
THAT'S THE TROUBLE WITH THE JAPANESE. WE'RE TOO PASSIVE!
SOMEONE SHOULD HAVE SPOKEN UP AND *PROTESTED!*
YES, I CAN IMAGINE YOU DOING THAT. BUT I HAD YOU AND THE FAMILY TO THINK ABOUT.
YOU'LL UNDERSTAND SOMEDAY.
WHEN I GROW UP, IS THAT IT?
WELL I *AM* GROWN UP AND I *DO* UNDERSTAND.
DADDY, YOU LED US LIKE SHEEP TO SLAUGHTER, INTO A BARBED-WIRE *PRISON!*
MAYBE YOU'RE RIGHT.
I SPOKE UP RIGHTEOUSLY AS MY FATHER SUFFERED IN SILENCE.
IT STILL PAINS ME TO THIS DAY...
...THAT ARROGANT BOY'S OUTSPOKEN BLUNTNESS INFLICTED ON HIS FATHER...
...A MAN WHO KNEW THE ANGUISH OF THOSE DARK INTERNMENT YEARS MORE INTENSELY THAN THAT BOY COULD EVER UNDERSTAND.

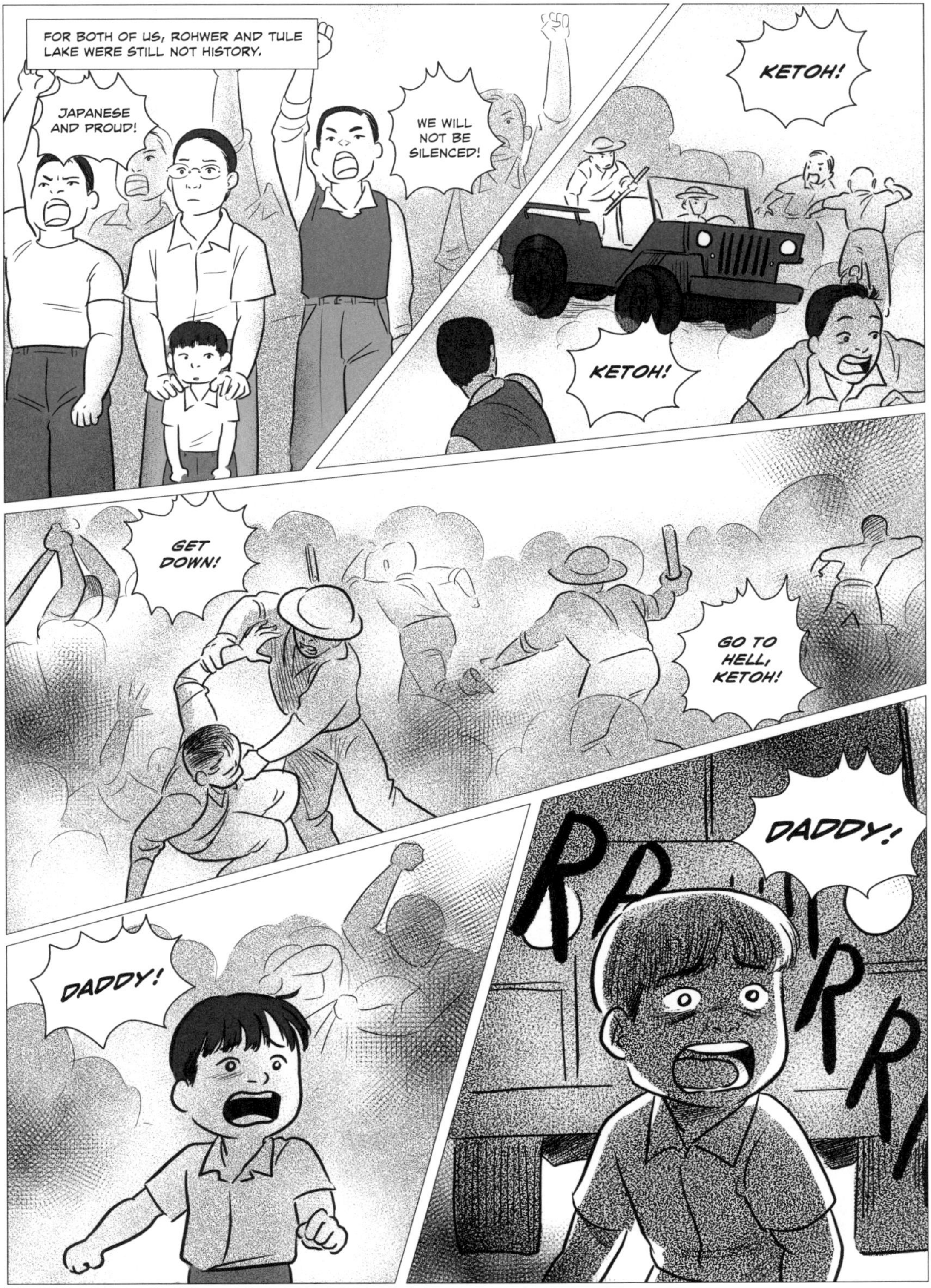
FOR BOTH OF US, ROHWER AND TULE LAKE WERE STILL NOT HISTORY.
JAPANESE AND PROUD!
WE WILL NOT BE SILENCED!
KETOH!
KETOH!
GET DOWN!
GO TO HELL, KETOH!
DADDY!
DADDY!
RRRRRR

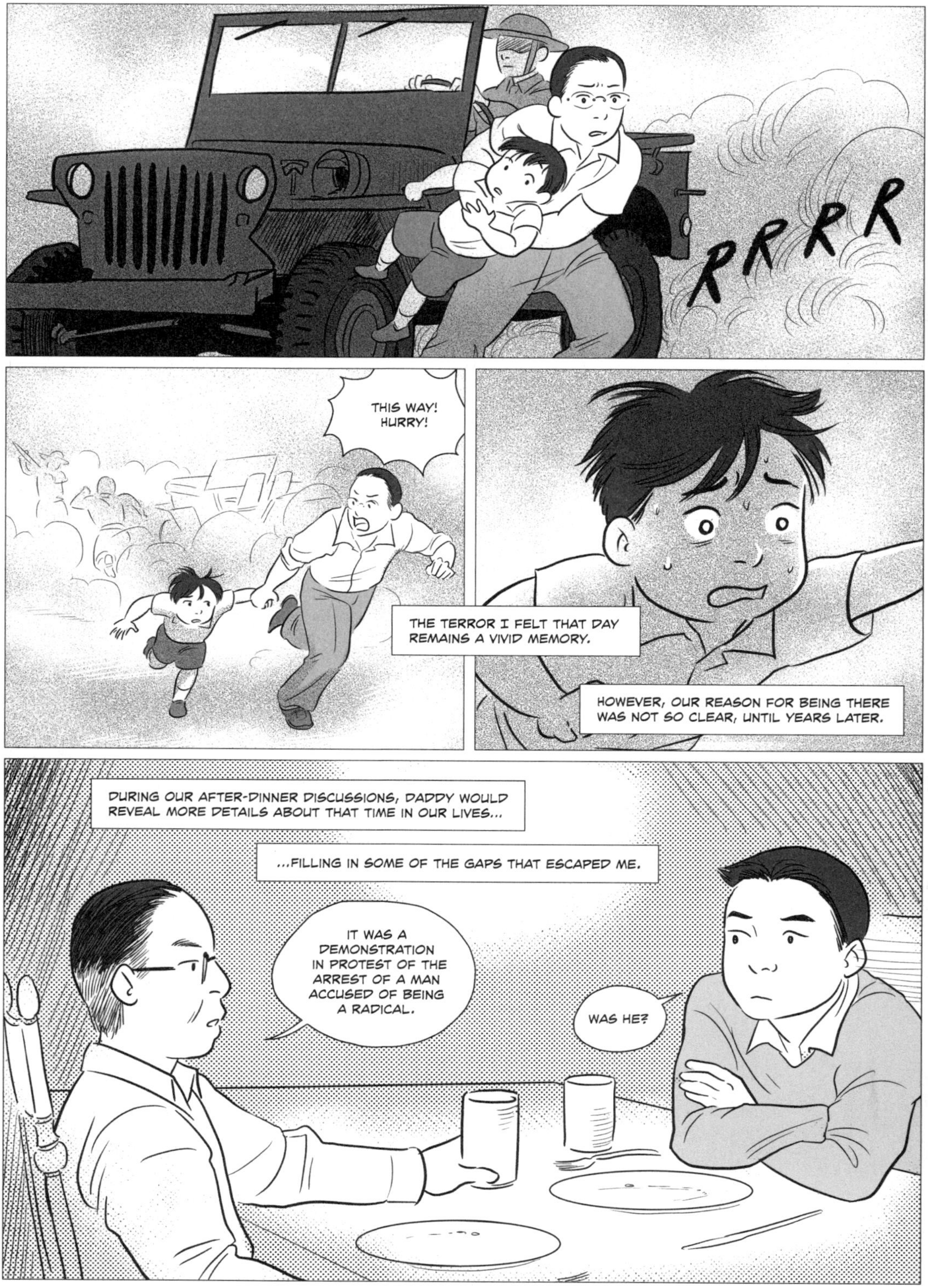
RRRR
THIS WAY! HURRY!
THE TERROR I FELT THAT DAY REMAINS A VIVID MEMORY.
HOWEVER, OUR REASON FOR BEING THERE WAS NOT SO CLEAR, UNTIL YEARS LATER.
DURING OUR AFTER-DINNER DISCUSSIONS, DADDY WOULD REVEAL MORE DETAILS ABOUT THAT TIME IN OUR LIVES...
...FILLING IN SOME OF THE GAPS THAT ESCAPED ME.
IT WAS A DEMONSTRATION IN PROTEST OF THE ARREST OF A MAN ACCUSED OF BEING A RADICAL.
WAS HE?

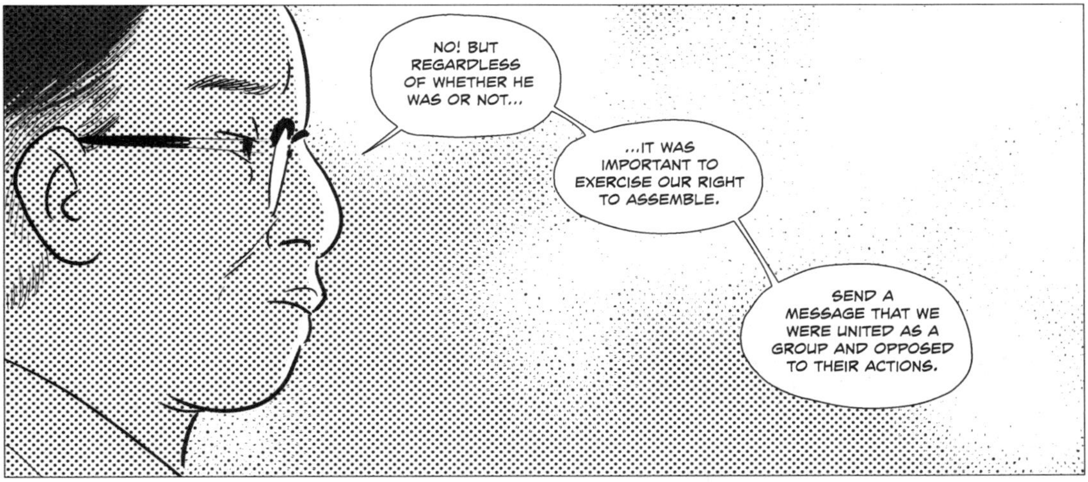
NO! BUT REGARDLESS OF WHETHER HE WAS OR NOT...
...IT WAS IMPORTANT TO EXERCISE OUR RIGHT TO ASSEMBLE.
SEND A MESSAGE THAT WE WERE UNITED AS A GROUP AND OPPOSED TO THEIR ACTIONS.

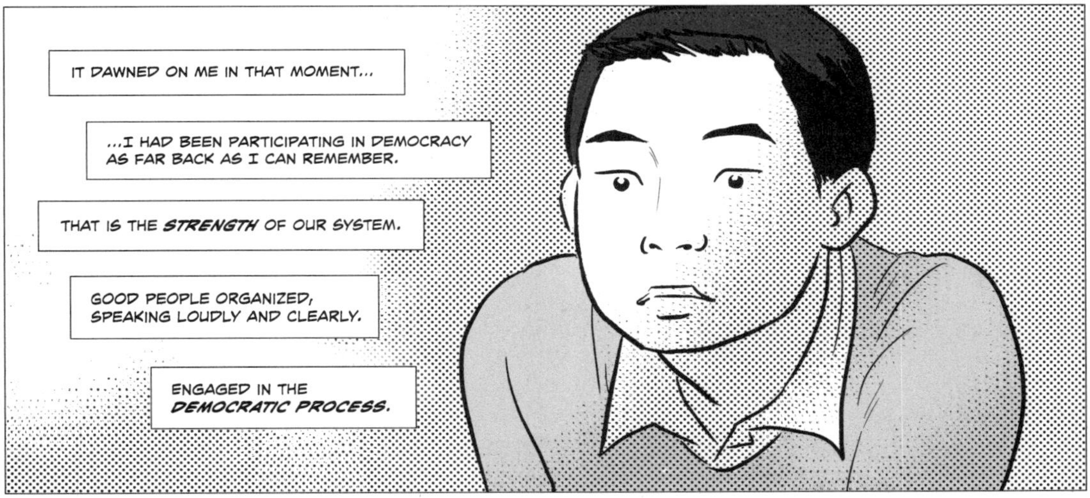
IT DAWNED ON ME IN THAT MOMENT...
...I HAD BEEN PARTICIPATING IN DEMOCRACY AS FAR BACK AS I CAN REMEMBER.
THAT IS THE *STRENGTH* OF OUR SYSTEM.
GOOD PEOPLE ORGANIZED, SPEAKING LOUDLY AND CLEARLY.
ENGAGED IN THE *DEMOCRATIC PROCESS.*

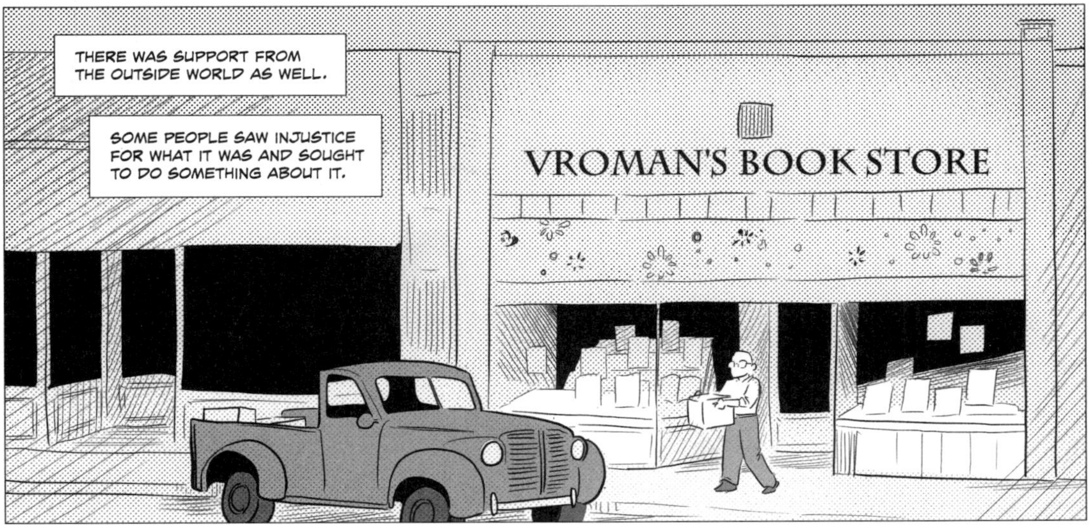
THERE WAS SUPPORT FROM THE OUTSIDE WORLD AS WELL.
SOME PEOPLE SAW INJUSTICE FOR WHAT IT WAS AND SOUGHT TO DO SOMETHING ABOUT IT.
VROMAN'S BOOK STORE

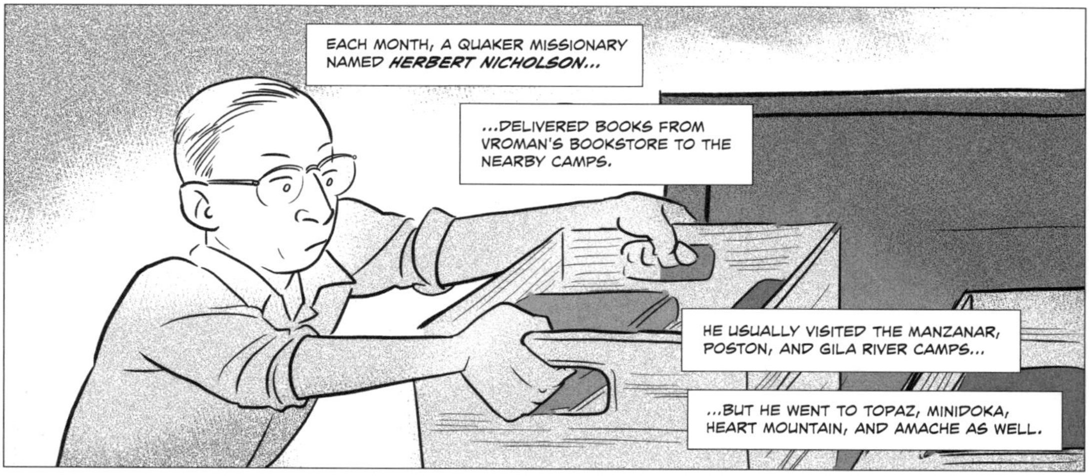
EACH MONTH, A QUAKER MISSIONARY NAMED ***HERBERT NICHOLSON***...
...DELIVERED BOOKS FROM VROMAN'S BOOKSTORE TO THE NEARBY CAMPS.
HE USUALLY VISITED THE MANZANAR, POSTON, AND GILA RIVER CAMPS...
...BUT HE WENT TO TOPAZ, MINIDOKA, HEART MOUNTAIN, AND AMACHE AS WELL.

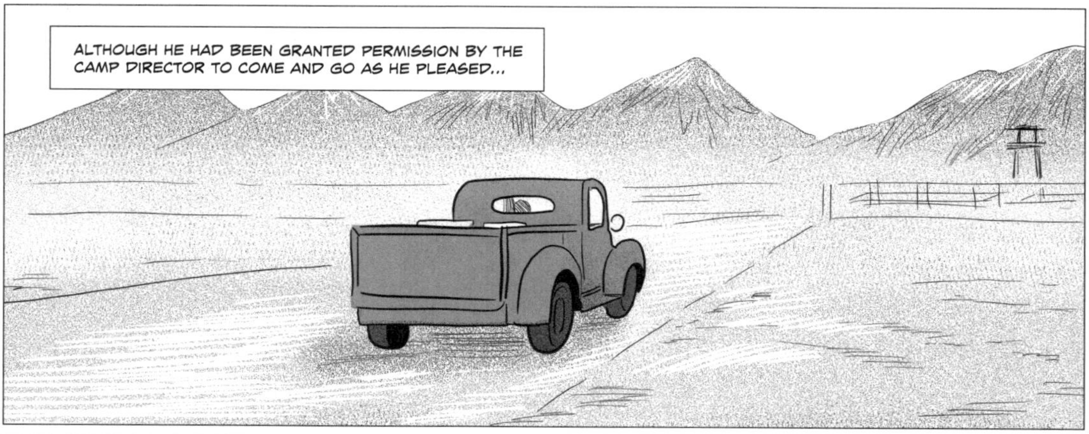
ALTHOUGH HE HAD BEEN GRANTED PERMISSION BY THE CAMP DIRECTOR TO COME AND GO AS HE PLEASED...

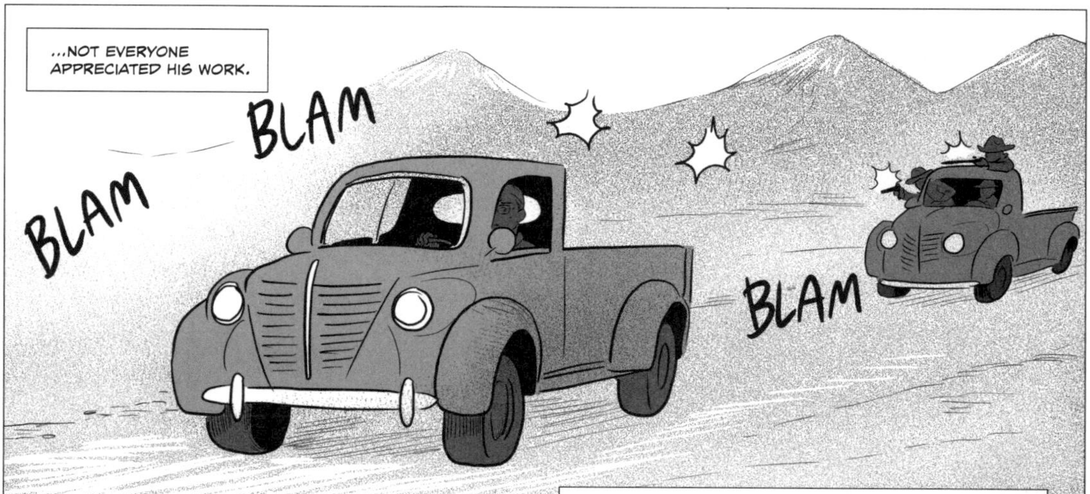
...NOT EVERYONE APPRECIATED HIS WORK.
BLAM
BLAM
BLAM
AFTER HE WAS ATTACKED, THE PEOPLE OF MANZANAR ASSUMED THEY'D SEEN THE LAST OF HERBERT...

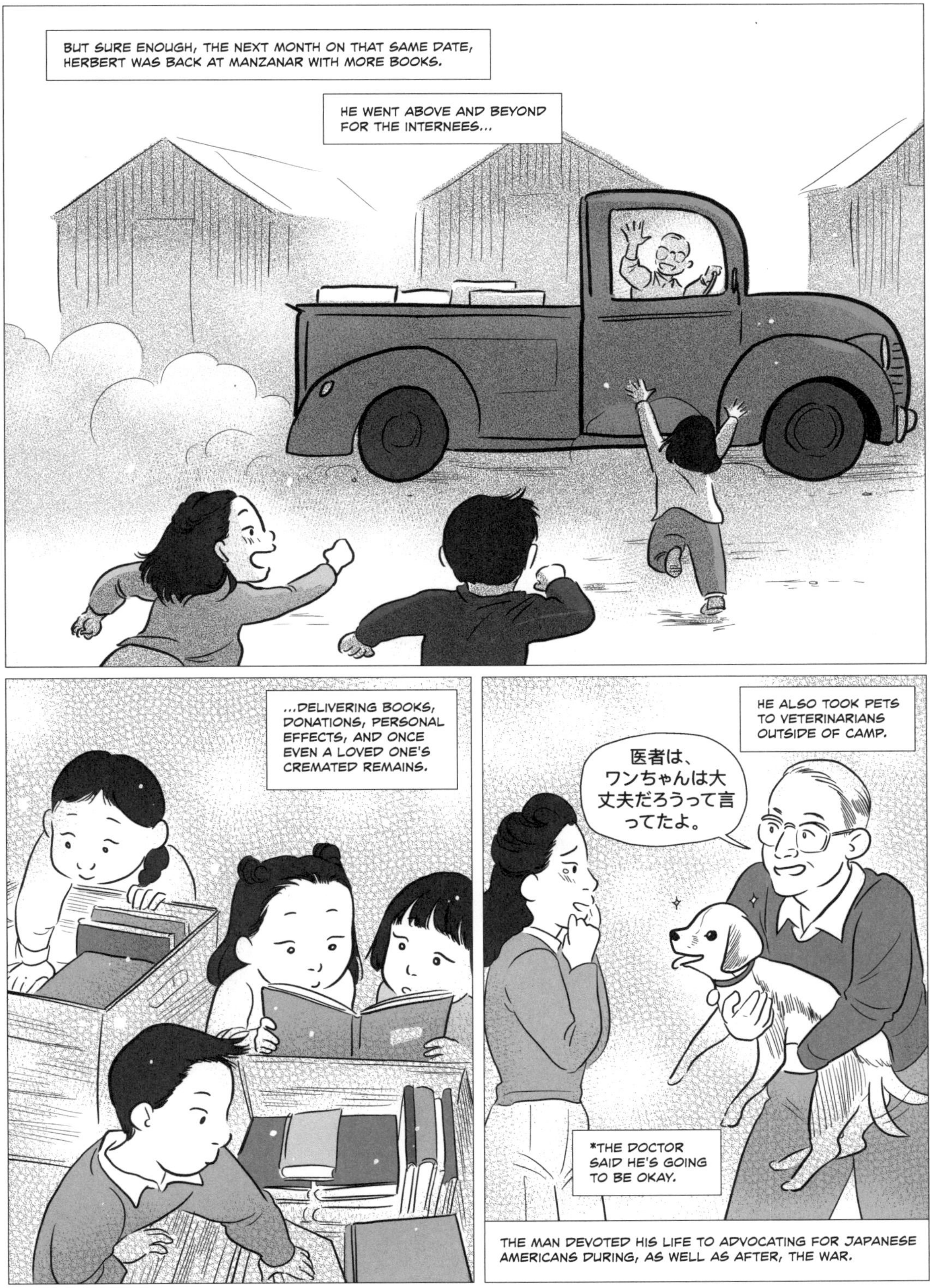
BUT SURE ENOUGH, THE NEXT MONTH ON THAT SAME DATE, HERBERT WAS BACK AT MANZANAR WITH MORE BOOKS.
HE WENT ABOVE AND BEYOND FOR THE INTERNEES...
...DELIVERING BOOKS, DONATIONS, PERSONAL EFFECTS, AND ONCE EVEN A LOVED ONE'S CREMATED REMAINS.
HE ALSO TOOK PETS TO VETERINARIANS OUTSIDE OF CAMP.
医者は、ワンちゃんは大丈夫だろうって言ってたよ。
*THE DOCTOR SAID HE'S GOING TO BE OKAY.
THE MAN DEVOTED HIS LIFE TO ADVOCATING FOR JAPANESE AMERICANS DURING, AS WELL AS AFTER, THE WAR.

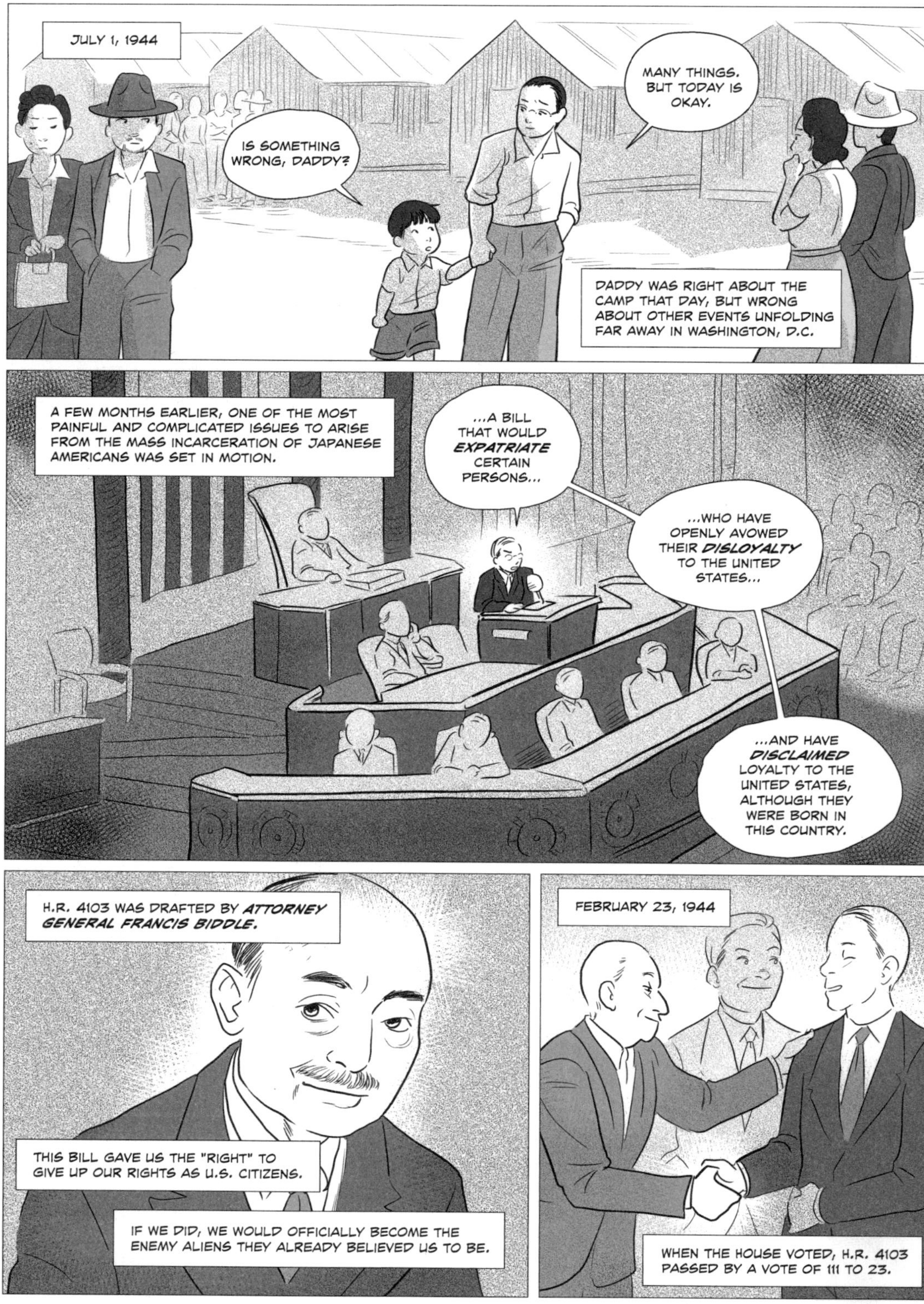
JULY 1, 1944
IS SOMETHING WRONG, DADDY?
MANY THINGS. BUT TODAY IS OKAY.
DADDY WAS RIGHT ABOUT THE CAMP THAT DAY, BUT WRONG ABOUT OTHER EVENTS UNFOLDING FAR AWAY IN WASHINGTON, D.C.
A FEW MONTHS EARLIER, ONE OF THE MOST PAINFUL AND COMPLICATED ISSUES TO ARISE FROM THE MASS INCARCERATION OF JAPANESE AMERICANS WAS SET IN MOTION.
...A BILL THAT WOULD *EXPATRIATE* CERTAIN PERSONS...
...WHO HAVE OPENLY AVOWED THEIR *DISLOYALTY* TO THE UNITED STATES...
...AND HAVE *DISCLAIMED* LOYALTY TO THE UNITED STATES, ALTHOUGH THEY WERE BORN IN THIS COUNTRY.
H.R. 4103 WAS DRAFTED BY *ATTORNEY GENERAL FRANCIS BIDDLE.*
THIS BILL GAVE US THE "RIGHT" TO GIVE UP OUR RIGHTS AS U.S. CITIZENS.
IF WE DID, WE WOULD OFFICIALLY BECOME THE ENEMY ALIENS THEY ALREADY BELIEVED US TO BE.
FEBRUARY 23, 1944
WHEN THE HOUSE VOTED, H.R. 4103 PASSED BY A VOTE OF 111 TO 23.

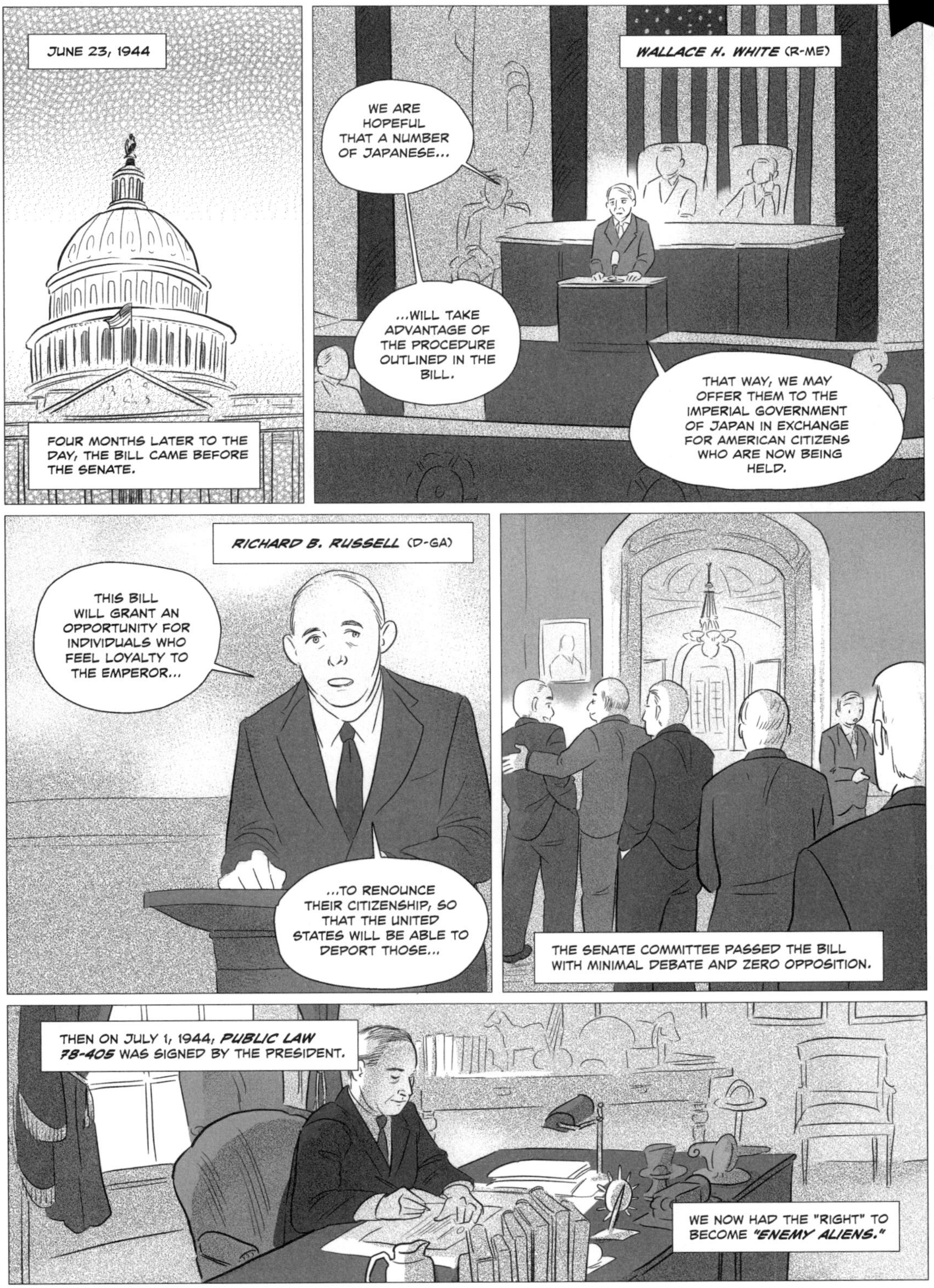
JUNE 23, 1944
FOUR MONTHS LATER TO THE DAY, THE BILL CAME BEFORE THE SENATE.
WALLACE H. WHITE (R-ME)
WE ARE HOPEFUL THAT A NUMBER OF JAPANESE...
...WILL TAKE ADVANTAGE OF THE PROCEDURE OUTLINED IN THE BILL.
THAT WAY, WE MAY OFFER THEM TO THE IMPERIAL GOVERNMENT OF JAPAN IN EXCHANGE FOR AMERICAN CITIZENS WHO ARE NOW BEING HELD.
RICHARD B. RUSSELL (D-GA)
THIS BILL WILL GRANT AN OPPORTUNITY FOR INDIVIDUALS WHO FEEL LOYALTY TO THE EMPEROR...
...TO RENOUNCE THEIR CITIZENSHIP, SO THAT THE UNITED STATES WILL BE ABLE TO DEPORT THOSE...
THE SENATE COMMITTEE PASSED THE BILL WITH MINIMAL DEBATE AND ZERO OPPOSITION.
THEN ON JULY 1, 1944, PUBLIC LAW 78-405 WAS SIGNED BY THE PRESIDENT.
WE NOW HAD THE "RIGHT" TO BECOME "ENEMY ALIENS."

WHILE CONGRESS WOULD NOT ADMIT TO TARGETING THE *NISEI* POPULATION...

...*NISEI* WOULD BE THE MOST AFFECTED BY THE NEW LAW.

OCTOBER 1944

AMERICA TREATS YOU LIKE *GARBAGE!*

WHY KEEP TAKING THEIR RACIST OUTRAGES?

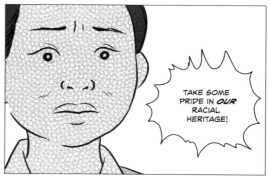

TAKE SOME PRIDE IN *OUR* RACIAL HERITAGE!

EVERYBODY WANT US TO LEAVE FOR JAPAN. WHAT DO WE DO?

AS ALWAYS, WE WILL CHOOSE WHAT IS BEST. TOGETHER.

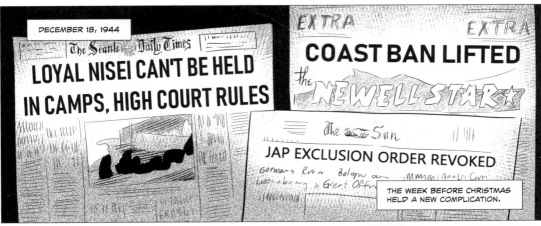

DECEMBER 18, 1944

The Seattle Daily Times

LOYAL NISEI CAN'T BE HELD IN CAMPS, HIGH COURT RULES

EXTRA   EXTRA

COAST BAN LIFTED

The NEWELL STAR ☆

The Sun

JAP EXCLUSION ORDER REVOKED

Germans Run Belgn a...
Luxembourg a Great Offen...

THE WEEK BEFORE CHRISTMAS HELD A NEW COMPLICATION.

THEY ARE CLOSING THE CAMP.

WHEN?

THIS SAYS SIX MONTHS TO A YEAR.

THEN WE HAVE TO *LEAVE* TULE LAKE.

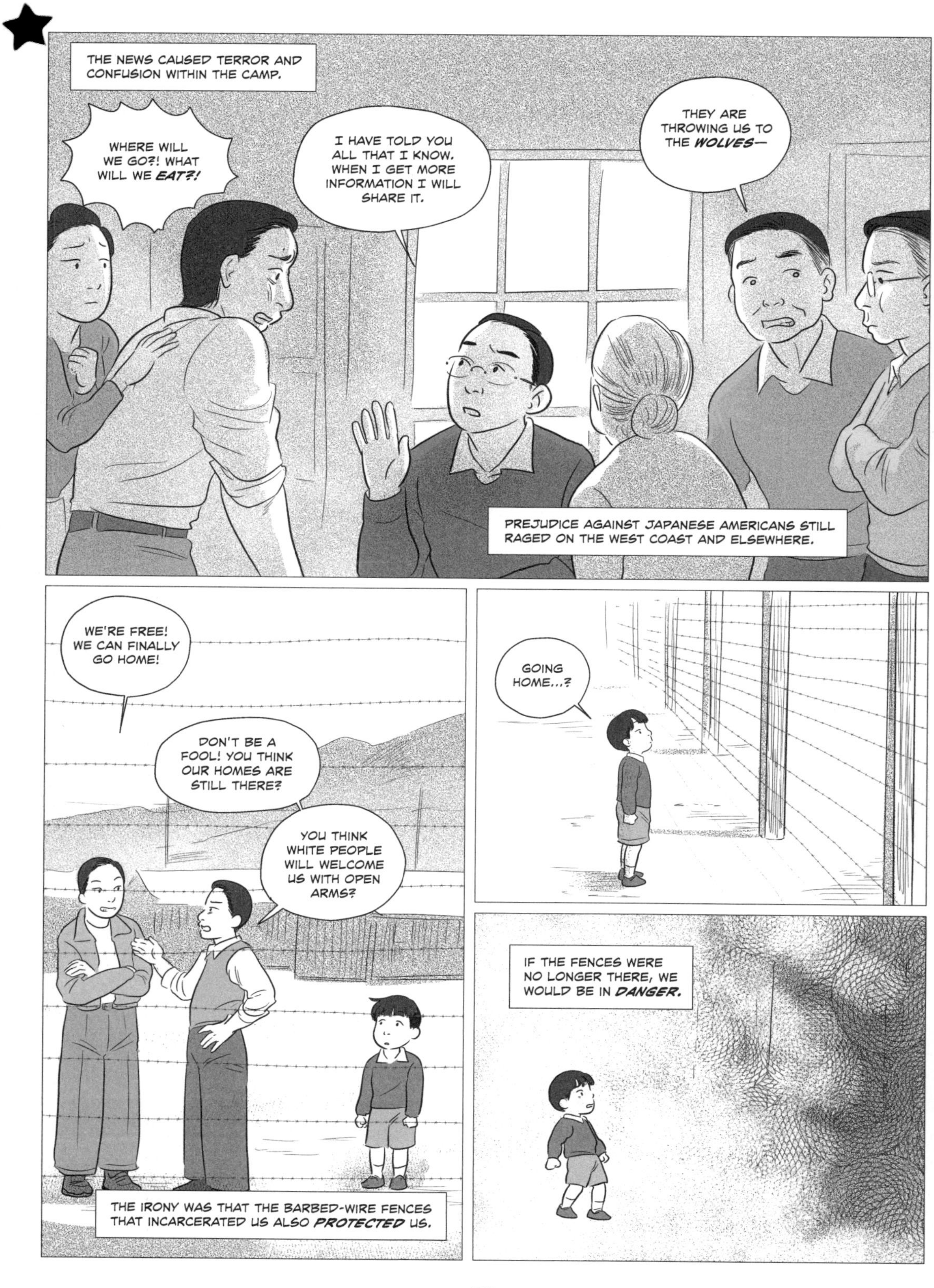
THE NEWS CAUSED TERROR AND CONFUSION WITHIN THE CAMP.
WHERE WILL WE GO?! WHAT WILL WE *EAT?!*
I HAVE TOLD YOU ALL THAT I KNOW. WHEN I GET MORE INFORMATION I WILL SHARE IT.
THEY ARE THROWING US TO THE *WOLVES*—
PREJUDICE AGAINST JAPANESE AMERICANS STILL RAGED ON THE WEST COAST AND ELSEWHERE.
WE'RE FREE! WE CAN FINALLY GO HOME!
DON'T BE A FOOL! YOU THINK OUR HOMES ARE STILL THERE?
YOU THINK WHITE PEOPLE WILL WELCOME US WITH OPEN ARMS?
THE IRONY WAS THAT THE BARBED-WIRE FENCES THAT INCARCERATED US ALSO *PROTECTED* US.
GOING HOME...?
IF THE FENCES WERE NO LONGER THERE, WE WOULD BE IN *DANGER*.

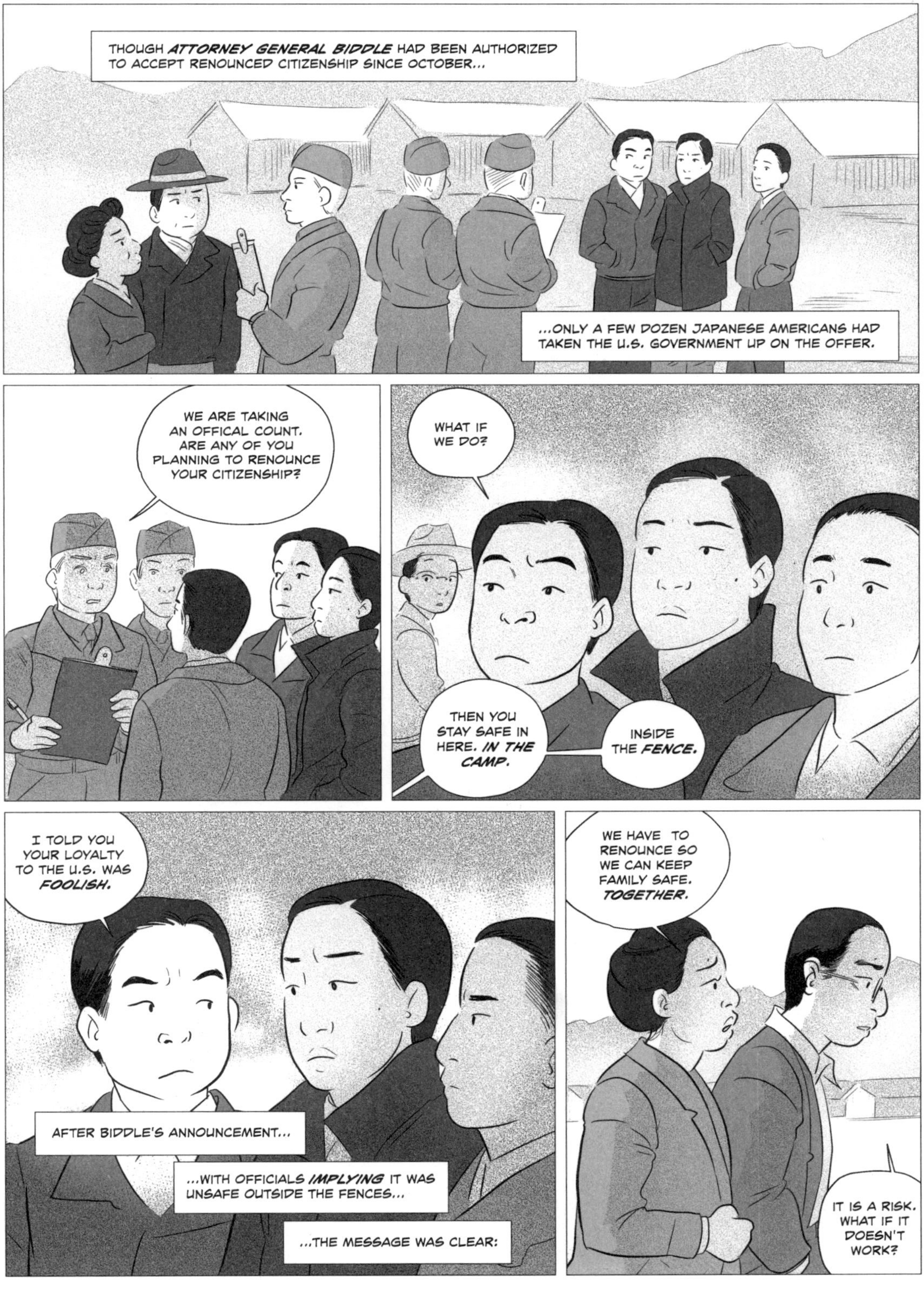

THOUGH ATTORNEY GENERAL BIDDLE HAD BEEN AUTHORIZED TO ACCEPT RENOUNCED CITIZENSHIP SINCE OCTOBER...
...ONLY A FEW DOZEN JAPANESE AMERICANS HAD TAKEN THE U.S. GOVERNMENT UP ON THE OFFER.
WE ARE TAKING AN OFFICAL COUNT. ARE ANY OF YOU PLANNING TO RENOUNCE YOUR CITIZENSHIP?
WHAT IF WE DO?
THEN YOU STAY SAFE IN HERE. IN THE CAMP.
INSIDE THE FENCE.
I TOLD YOU YOUR LOYALTY TO THE U.S. WAS FOOLISH.
AFTER BIDDLE'S ANNOUNCEMENT...
...WITH OFFICIALS IMPLYING IT WAS UNSAFE OUTSIDE THE FENCES...
...THE MESSAGE WAS CLEAR:
WE HAVE TO RENOUNCE SO WE CAN KEEP FAMILY SAFE. TOGETHER.
IT IS A RISK. WHAT IF IT DOESN'T WORK?

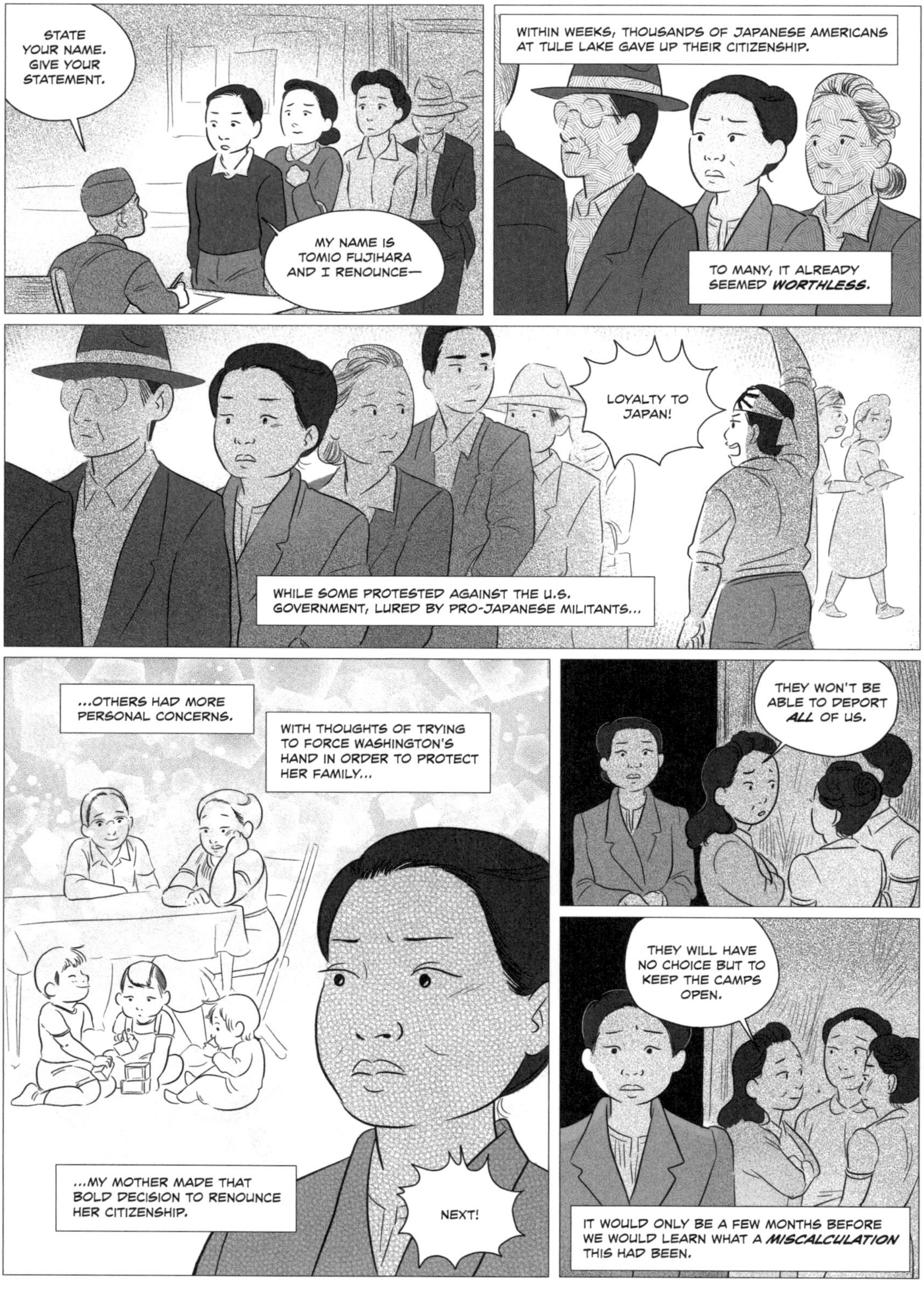
STATE YOUR NAME. GIVE YOUR STATEMENT.
MY NAME IS TOMIO FUJIHARA AND I RENOUNCE—
WITHIN WEEKS, THOUSANDS OF JAPANESE AMERICANS AT TULE LAKE GAVE UP THEIR CITIZENSHIP.
TO MANY, IT ALREADY SEEMED ***WORTHLESS.***
LOYALTY TO JAPAN!
WHILE SOME PROTESTED AGAINST THE U.S. GOVERNMENT, LURED BY PRO-JAPANESE MILITANTS...
...OTHERS HAD MORE PERSONAL CONCERNS.
WITH THOUGHTS OF TRYING TO FORCE WASHINGTON'S HAND IN ORDER TO PROTECT HER FAMILY...
...MY MOTHER MADE THAT BOLD DECISION TO RENOUNCE HER CITIZENSHIP.
NEXT!
THEY WON'T BE ABLE TO DEPORT ***ALL*** OF US.
THEY WILL HAVE NO CHOICE BUT TO KEEP THE CAMPS OPEN.
IT WOULD ONLY BE A FEW MONTHS BEFORE WE WOULD LEARN WHAT A ***MISCALCULATION*** THIS HAD BEEN.

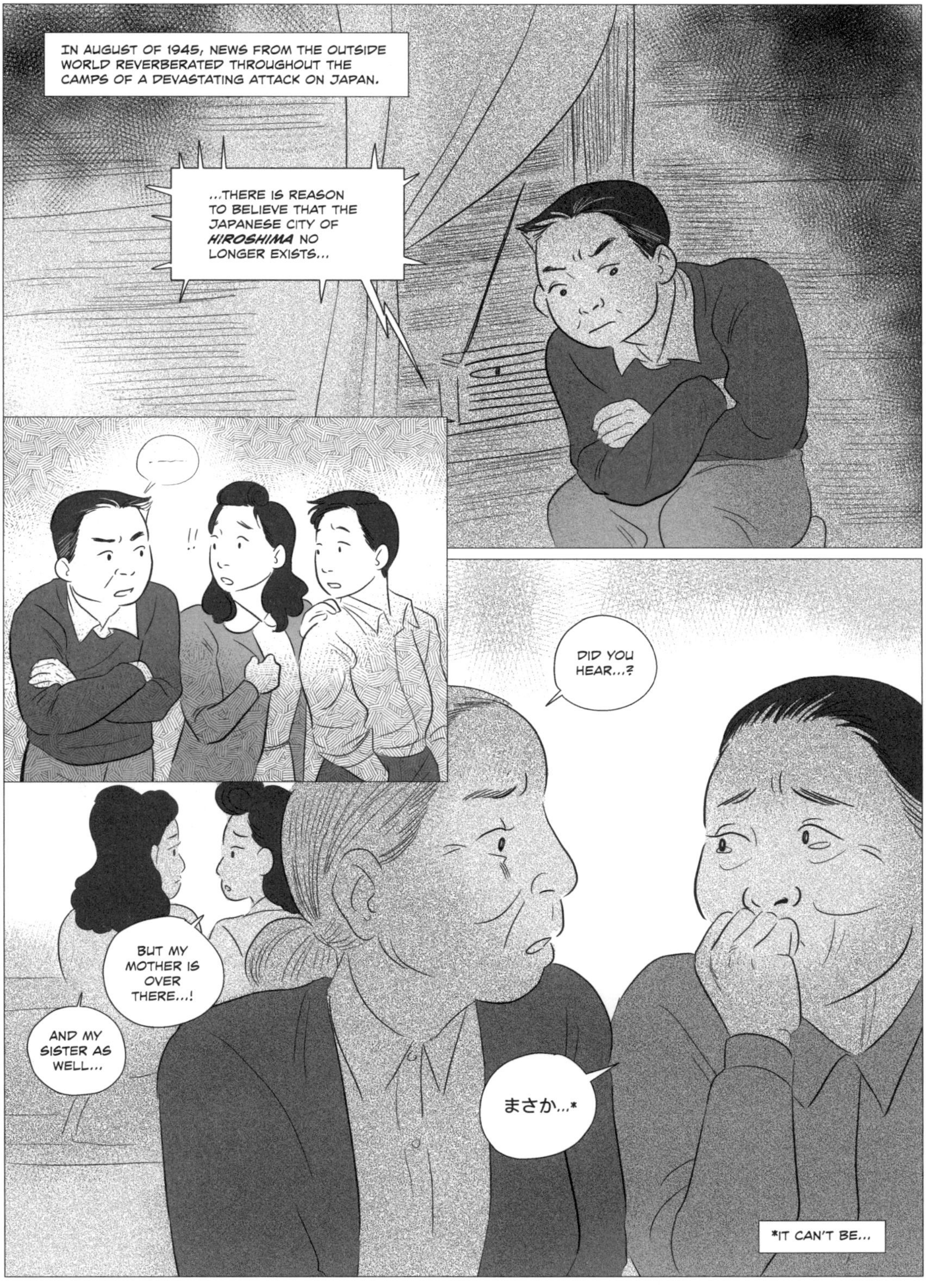
IN AUGUST OF 1945, NEWS FROM THE OUTSIDE WORLD REVERBERATED THROUGHOUT THE CAMPS OF A DEVASTATING ATTACK ON JAPAN.
...THERE IS REASON TO BELIEVE THAT THE JAPANESE CITY OF HIROSHIMA NO LONGER EXISTS...
!!
DID YOU HEAR...?
BUT MY MOTHER IS OVER THERE...!
AND MY SISTER AS WELL...
まさか...*
*IT CAN'T BE...

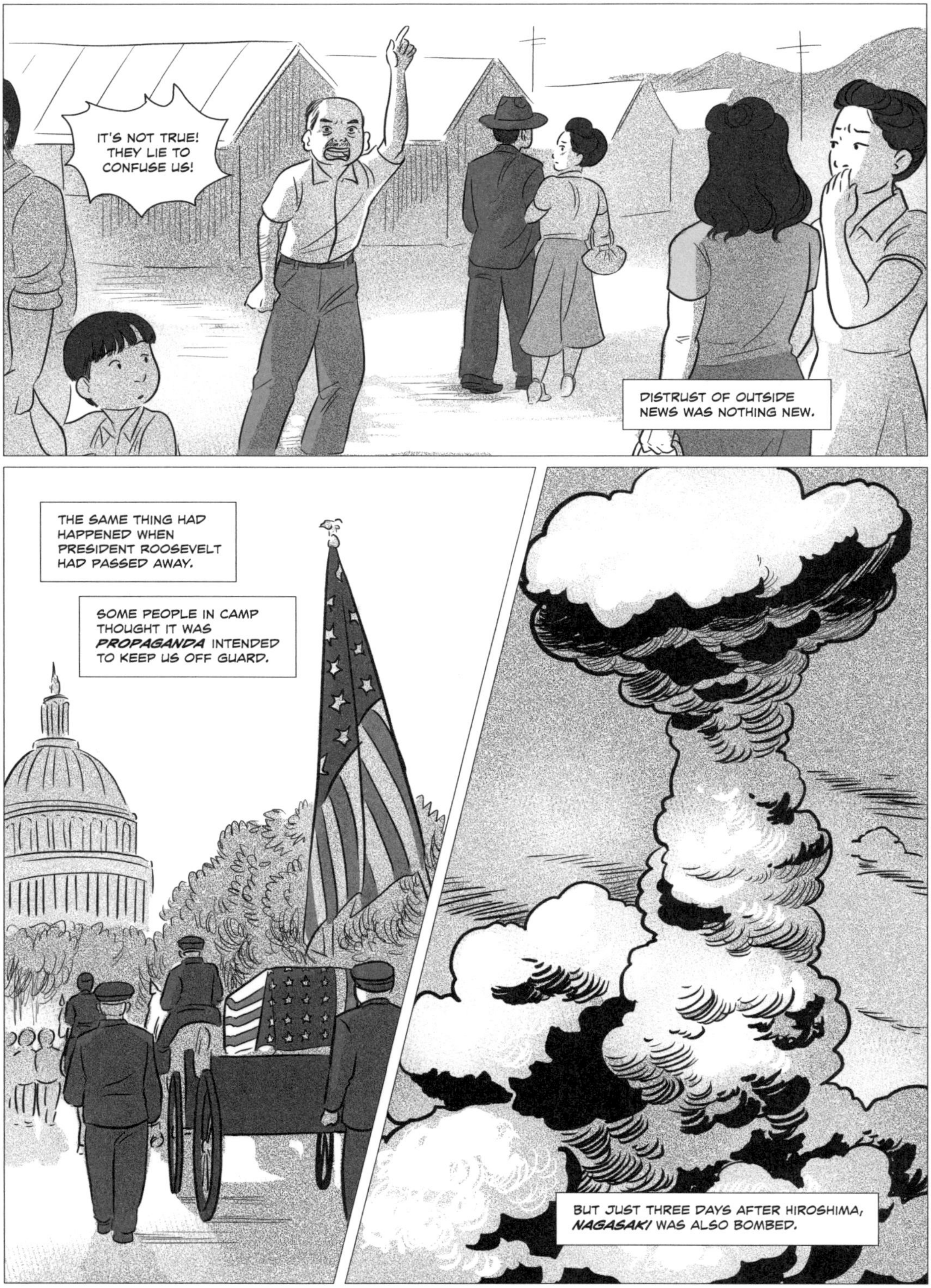
IT'S NOT TRUE! THEY LIE TO CONFUSE US!
DISTRUST OF OUTSIDE NEWS WAS NOTHING NEW.
THE SAME THING HAD HAPPENED WHEN PRESIDENT ROOSEVELT HAD PASSED AWAY.
SOME PEOPLE IN CAMP THOUGHT IT WAS *PROPAGANDA* INTENDED TO KEEP US OFF GUARD.
BUT JUST THREE DAYS AFTER HIROSHIMA, *NAGASAKI* WAS ALSO BOMBED.

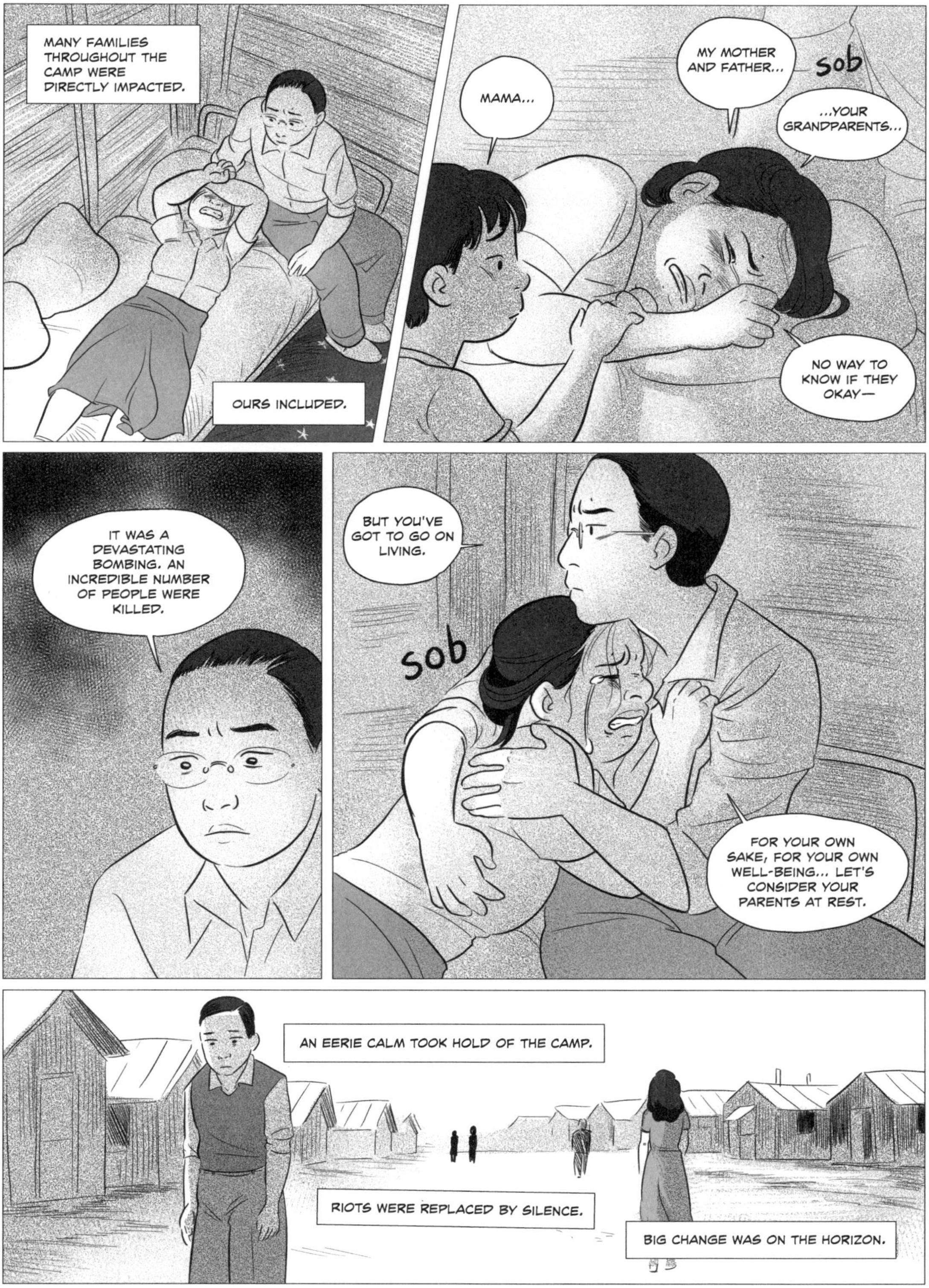
MANY FAMILIES THROUGHOUT THE CAMP WERE DIRECTLY IMPACTED.
OURS INCLUDED.
MAMA...
MY MOTHER AND FATHER...
sob
...YOUR GRANDPARENTS...
NO WAY TO KNOW IF THEY OKAY—
IT WAS A DEVASTATING BOMBING. AN INCREDIBLE NUMBER OF PEOPLE WERE KILLED.
BUT YOU'VE GOT TO GO ON LIVING.
sob
FOR YOUR OWN SAKE, FOR YOUR OWN WELL-BEING... LET'S CONSIDER YOUR PARENTS AT REST.
AN EERIE CALM TOOK HOLD OF THE CAMP.
RIOTS WERE REPLACED BY SILENCE.
BIG CHANGE WAS ON THE HORIZON.

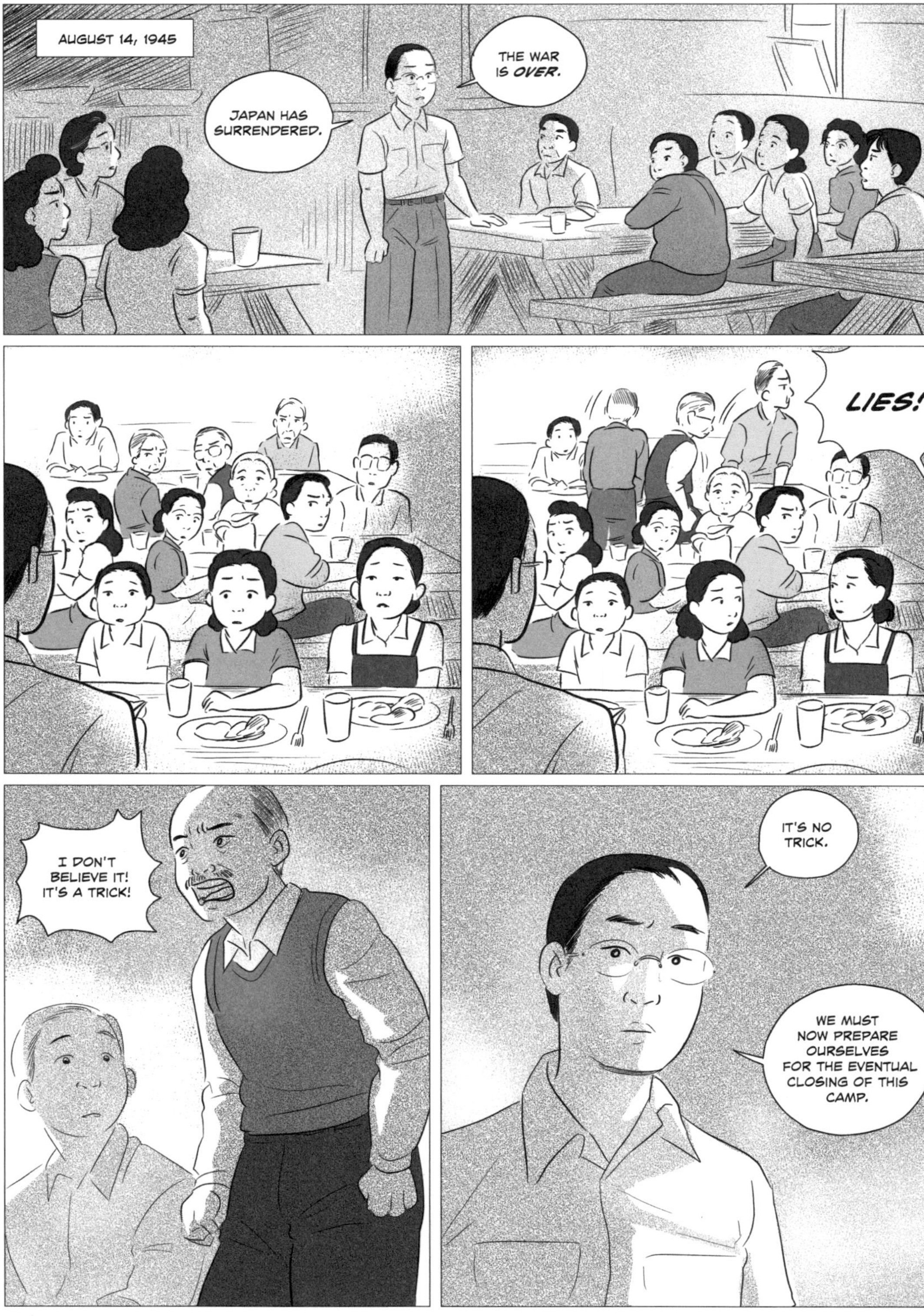
AUGUST 14, 1945
JAPAN HAS SURRENDERED.
THE WAR IS *OVER*.
LIES!
I DON'T BELIEVE IT! IT'S A TRICK!
IT'S NO TRICK.
WE MUST NOW PREPARE OURSELVES FOR THE EVENTUAL CLOSING OF THIS CAMP.

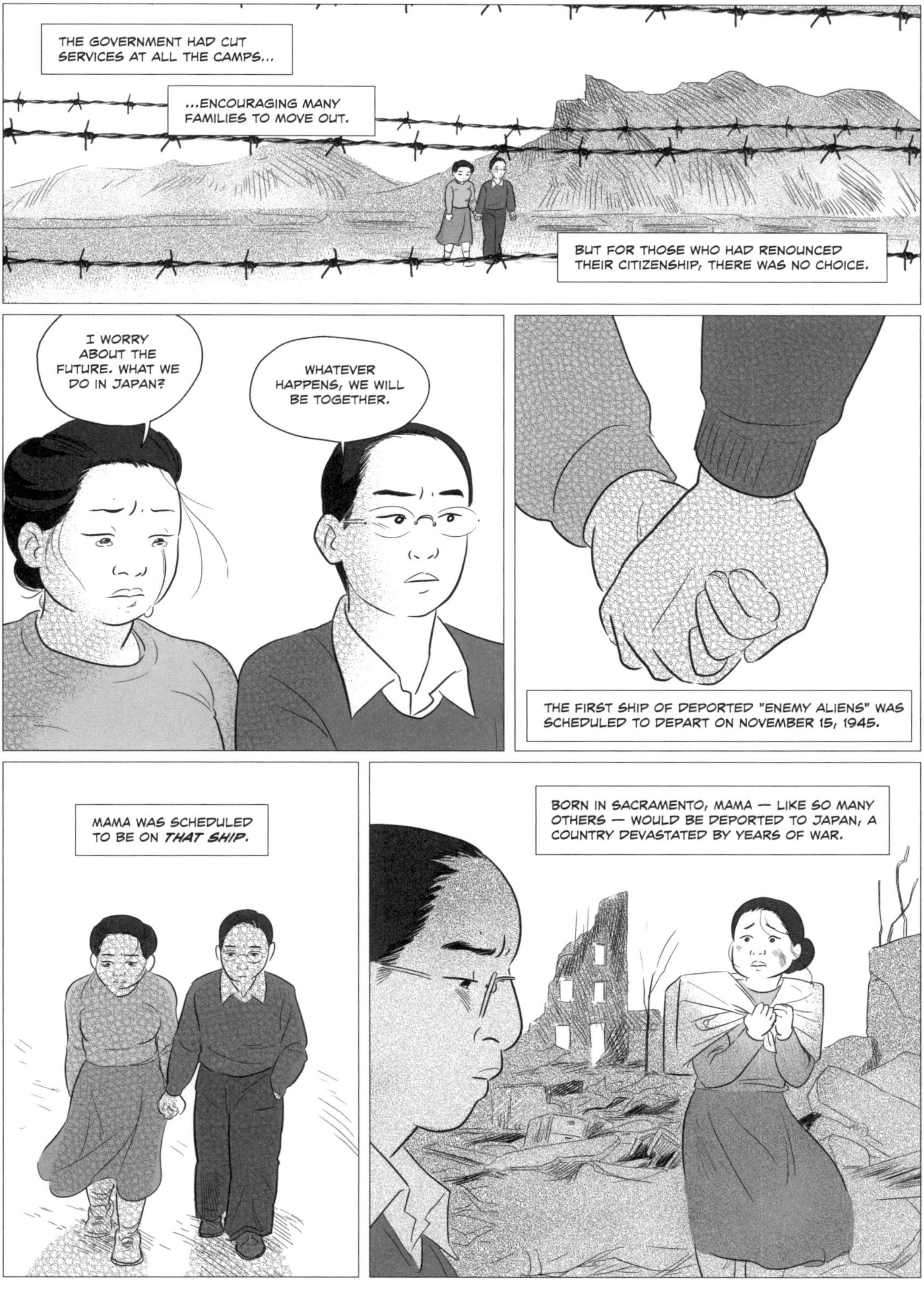
THE GOVERNMENT HAD CUT SERVICES AT ALL THE CAMPS...
...ENCOURAGING MANY FAMILIES TO MOVE OUT.
BUT FOR THOSE WHO HAD RENOUNCED THEIR CITIZENSHIP, THERE WAS NO CHOICE.
I WORRY ABOUT THE FUTURE. WHAT WE DO IN JAPAN?
WHATEVER HAPPENS, WE WILL BE TOGETHER.
THE FIRST SHIP OF DEPORTED "ENEMY ALIENS" WAS SCHEDULED TO DEPART ON NOVEMBER 15, 1945.
MAMA WAS SCHEDULED TO BE ON *THAT SHIP*.
BORN IN SACRAMENTO, MAMA — LIKE SO MANY OTHERS — WOULD BE DEPORTED TO JAPAN, A COUNTRY DEVASTATED BY YEARS OF WAR.

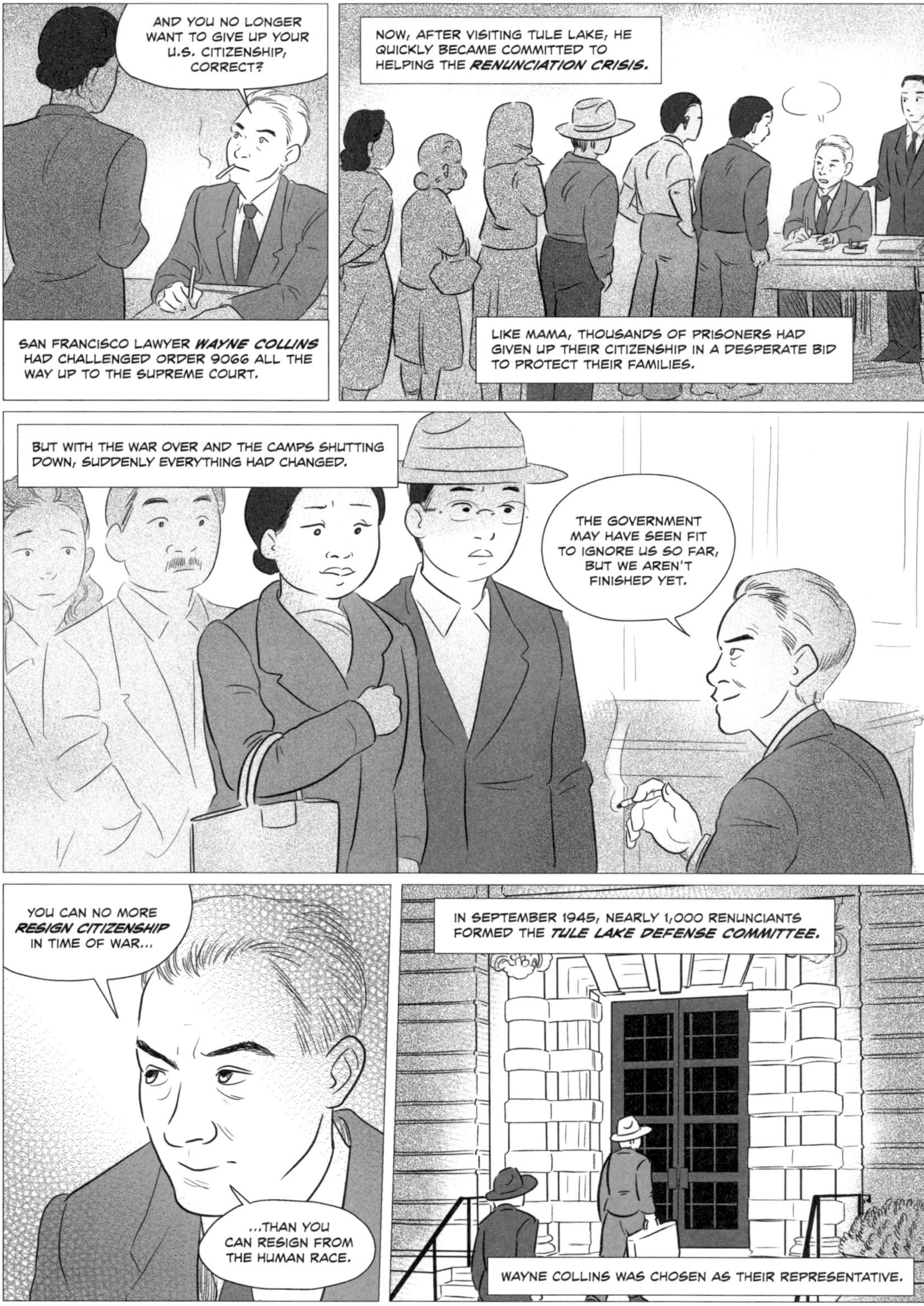
AND YOU NO LONGER WANT TO GIVE UP YOUR U.S. CITIZENSHIP, CORRECT?
SAN FRANCISCO LAWYER WAYNE COLLINS HAD CHALLENGED ORDER 9066 ALL THE WAY UP TO THE SUPREME COURT.
NOW, AFTER VISITING TULE LAKE, HE QUICKLY BECAME COMMITTED TO HELPING THE RENUNCIATION CRISIS.
LIKE MAMA, THOUSANDS OF PRISONERS HAD GIVEN UP THEIR CITIZENSHIP IN A DESPERATE BID TO PROTECT THEIR FAMILIES.
BUT WITH THE WAR OVER AND THE CAMPS SHUTTING DOWN, SUDDENLY EVERYTHING HAD CHANGED.
THE GOVERNMENT MAY HAVE SEEN FIT TO IGNORE US SO FAR, BUT WE AREN'T FINISHED YET.
YOU CAN NO MORE RESIGN CITIZENSHIP IN TIME OF WAR...
...THAN YOU CAN RESIGN FROM THE HUMAN RACE.
IN SEPTEMBER 1945, NEARLY 1,000 RENUNCIANTS FORMED THE TULE LAKE DEFENSE COMMITTEE.
WAYNE COLLINS WAS CHOSEN AS THEIR REPRESENTATIVE.

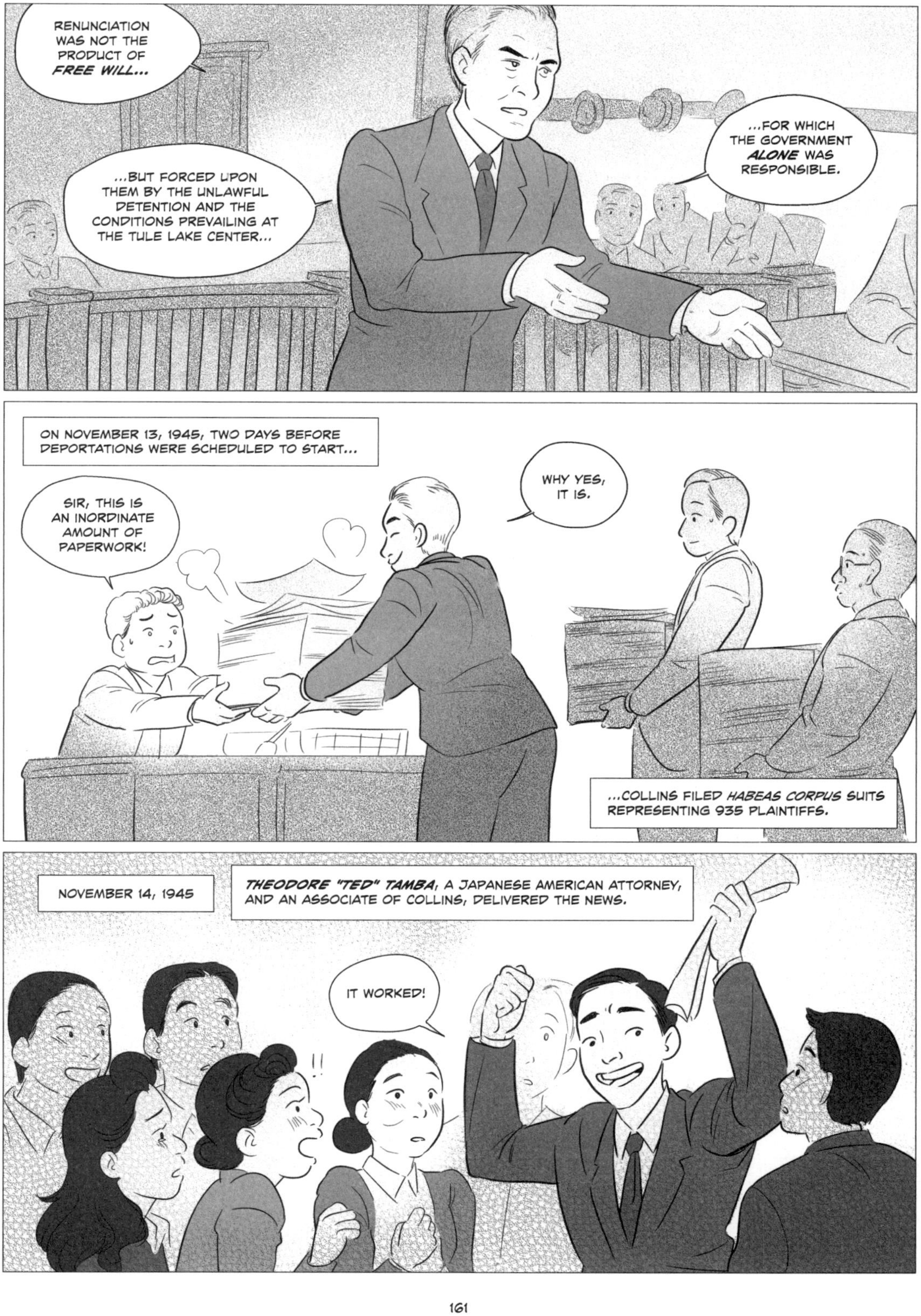
RENUNCIATION WAS NOT THE PRODUCT OF *FREE WILL...*
...BUT FORCED UPON THEM BY THE UNLAWFUL DETENTION AND THE CONDITIONS PREVAILING AT THE TULE LAKE CENTER...
...FOR WHICH THE GOVERNMENT *ALONE* WAS RESPONSIBLE.
ON NOVEMBER 13, 1945, TWO DAYS BEFORE DEPORTATIONS WERE SCHEDULED TO START...
SIR, THIS IS AN INORDINATE AMOUNT OF PAPERWORK!
WHY YES, IT IS.
...COLLINS FILED *HABEAS CORPUS* SUITS REPRESENTING 935 PLAINTIFFS.
NOVEMBER 14, 1945
THEODORE "TED" TAMBA, A JAPANESE AMERICAN ATTORNEY, AND AN ASSOCIATE OF COLLINS, DELIVERED THE NEWS.
IT WORKED!
!!

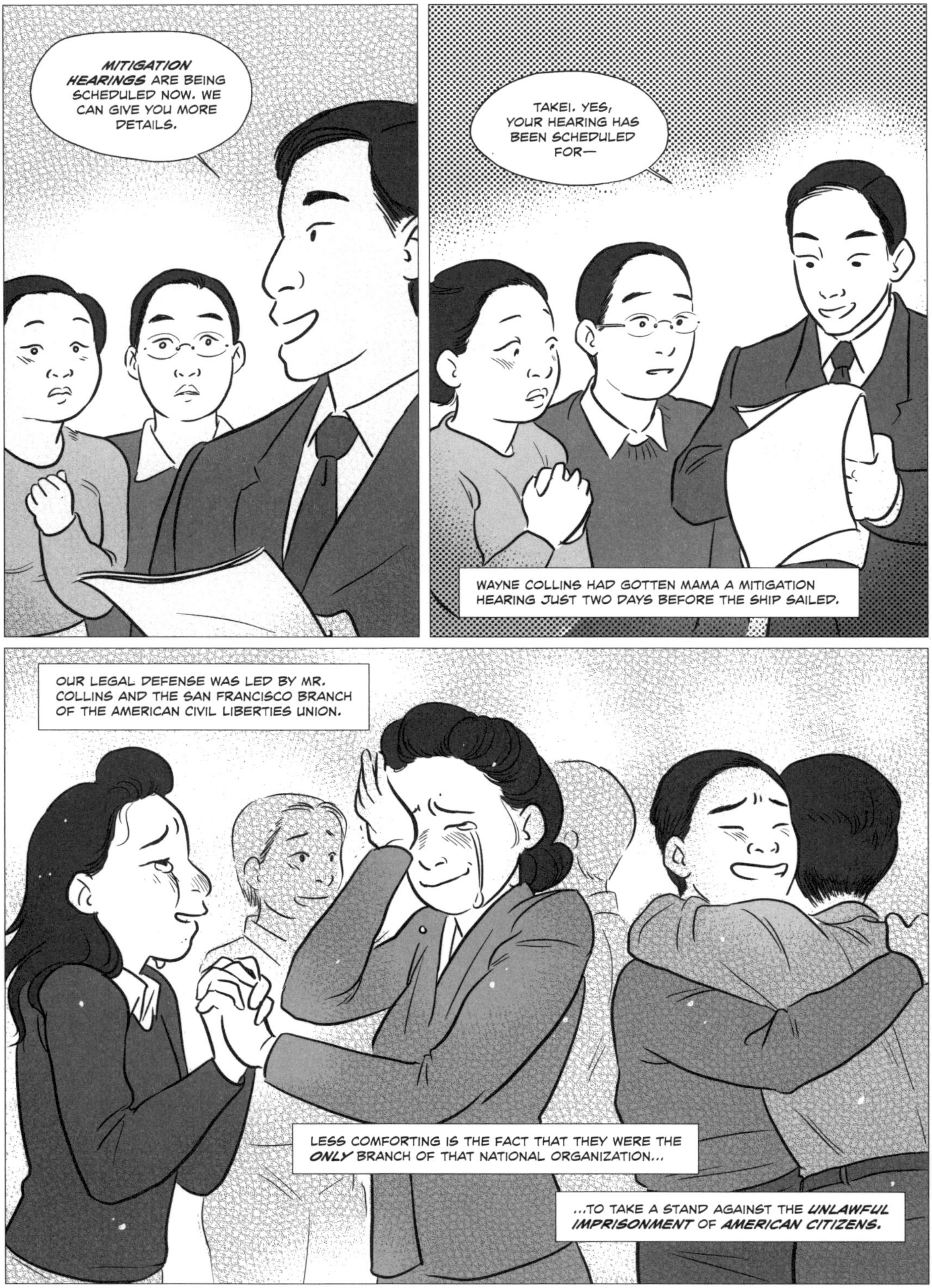
MITIGATION HEARINGS ARE BEING SCHEDULED NOW. WE CAN GIVE YOU MORE DETAILS.
TAKEI. YES, YOUR HEARING HAS BEEN SCHEDULED FOR—
WAYNE COLLINS HAD GOTTEN MAMA A MITIGATION HEARING JUST TWO DAYS BEFORE THE SHIP SAILED.
OUR LEGAL DEFENSE WAS LED BY MR. COLLINS AND THE SAN FRANCISCO BRANCH OF THE AMERICAN CIVIL LIBERTIES UNION.
LESS COMFORTING IS THE FACT THAT THEY WERE THE ONLY BRANCH OF THAT NATIONAL ORGANIZATION...
...TO TAKE A STAND AGAINST THE UNLAWFUL IMPRISONMENT OF AMERICAN CITIZENS.

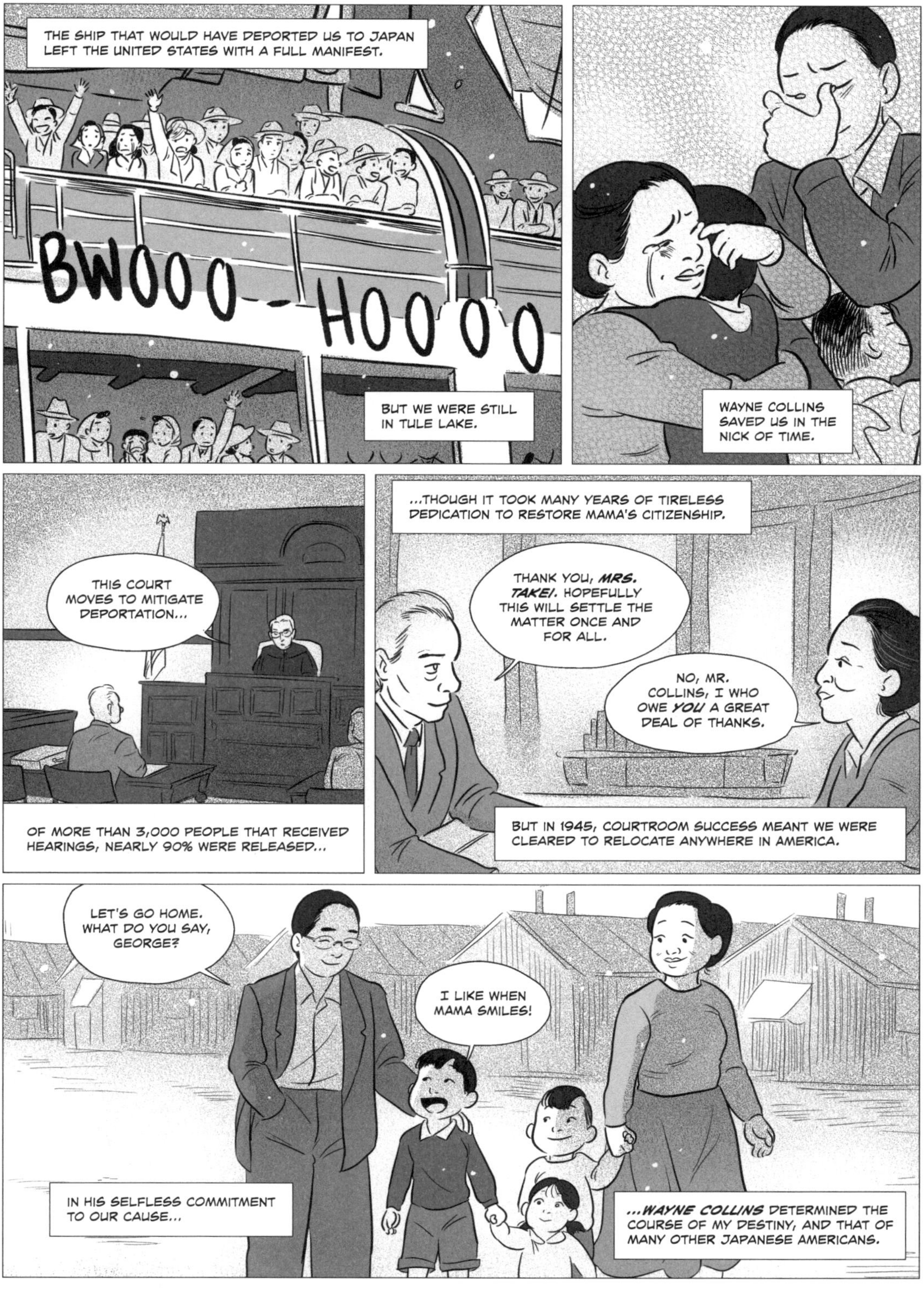
THE SHIP THAT WOULD HAVE DEPORTED US TO JAPAN LEFT THE UNITED STATES WITH A FULL MANIFEST.
BWOOO--HOOOO
BUT WE WERE STILL IN TULE LAKE.
WAYNE COLLINS SAVED US IN THE NICK OF TIME.
THIS COURT MOVES TO MITIGATE DEPORTATION...
OF MORE THAN 3,000 PEOPLE THAT RECEIVED HEARINGS, NEARLY 90% WERE RELEASED...
...THOUGH IT TOOK MANY YEARS OF TIRELESS DEDICATION TO RESTORE MAMA'S CITIZENSHIP.
THANK YOU, MRS. TAKEI. HOPEFULLY THIS WILL SETTLE THE MATTER ONCE AND FOR ALL.
NO, MR. COLLINS, I WHO OWE YOU A GREAT DEAL OF THANKS.
BUT IN 1945, COURTROOM SUCCESS MEANT WE WERE CLEARED TO RELOCATE ANYWHERE IN AMERICA.
LET'S GO HOME. WHAT DO YOU SAY, GEORGE?
I LIKE WHEN MAMA SMILES!
IN HIS SELFLESS COMMITMENT TO OUR CAUSE...
...WAYNE COLLINS DETERMINED THE COURSE OF MY DESTINY, AND THAT OF MANY OTHER JAPANESE AMERICANS.

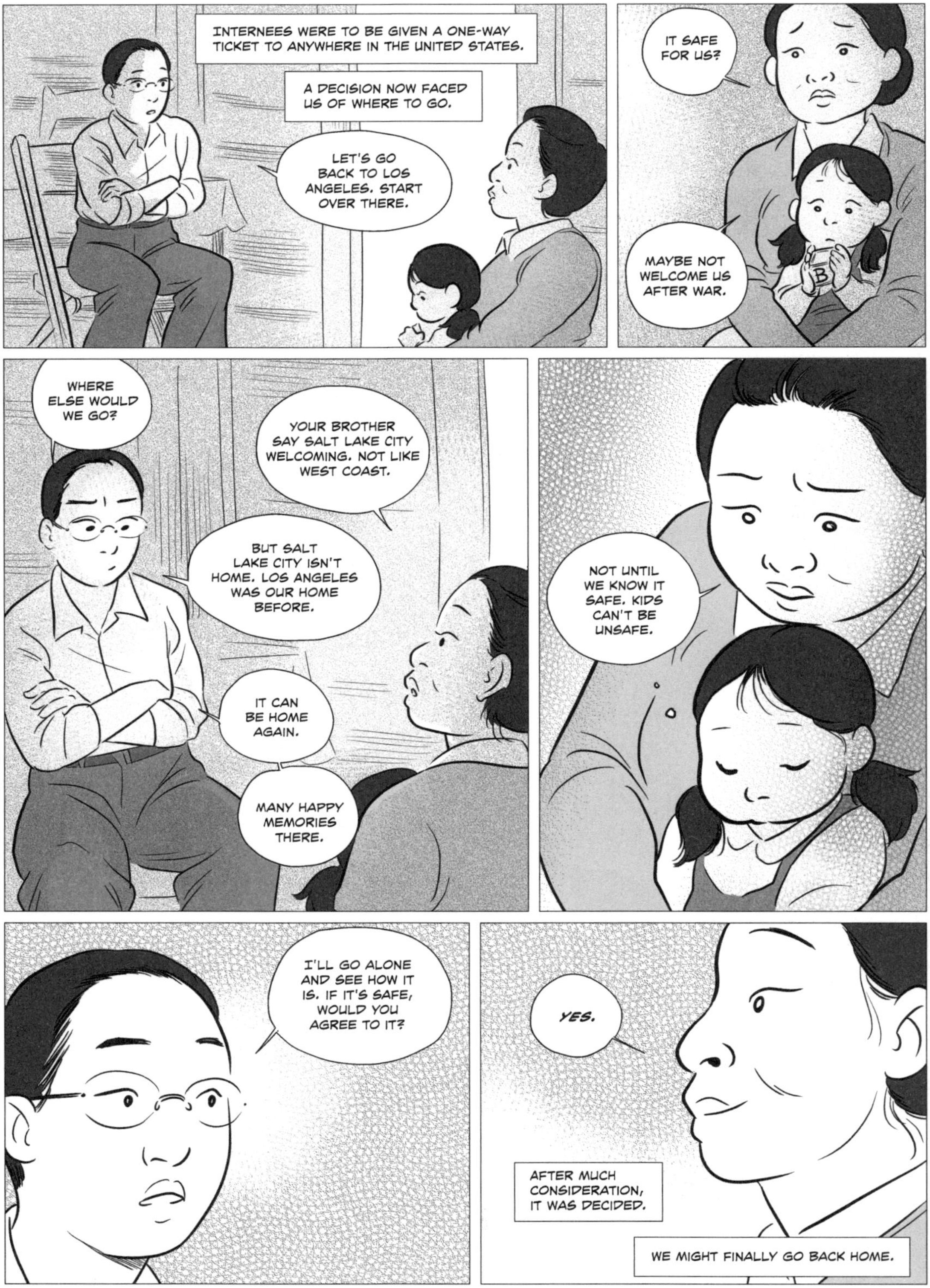
INTERNEES WERE TO BE GIVEN A ONE-WAY TICKET TO ANYWHERE IN THE UNITED STATES.
A DECISION NOW FACED US OF WHERE TO GO.
LET'S GO BACK TO LOS ANGELES. START OVER THERE.
IT SAFE FOR US?
MAYBE NOT WELCOME US AFTER WAR.
WHERE ELSE WOULD WE GO?
YOUR BROTHER SAY SALT LAKE CITY WELCOMING. NOT LIKE WEST COAST.
BUT SALT LAKE CITY ISN'T HOME. LOS ANGELES WAS OUR HOME BEFORE.
IT CAN BE HOME AGAIN.
MANY HAPPY MEMORIES THERE.
NOT UNTIL WE KNOW IT SAFE. KIDS CAN'T BE UNSAFE.
I'LL GO ALONE AND SEE HOW IT IS. IF IT'S SAFE, WOULD YOU AGREE TO IT?
YES.
AFTER MUCH CONSIDERATION, IT WAS DECIDED.
WE MIGHT FINALLY GO BACK HOME.

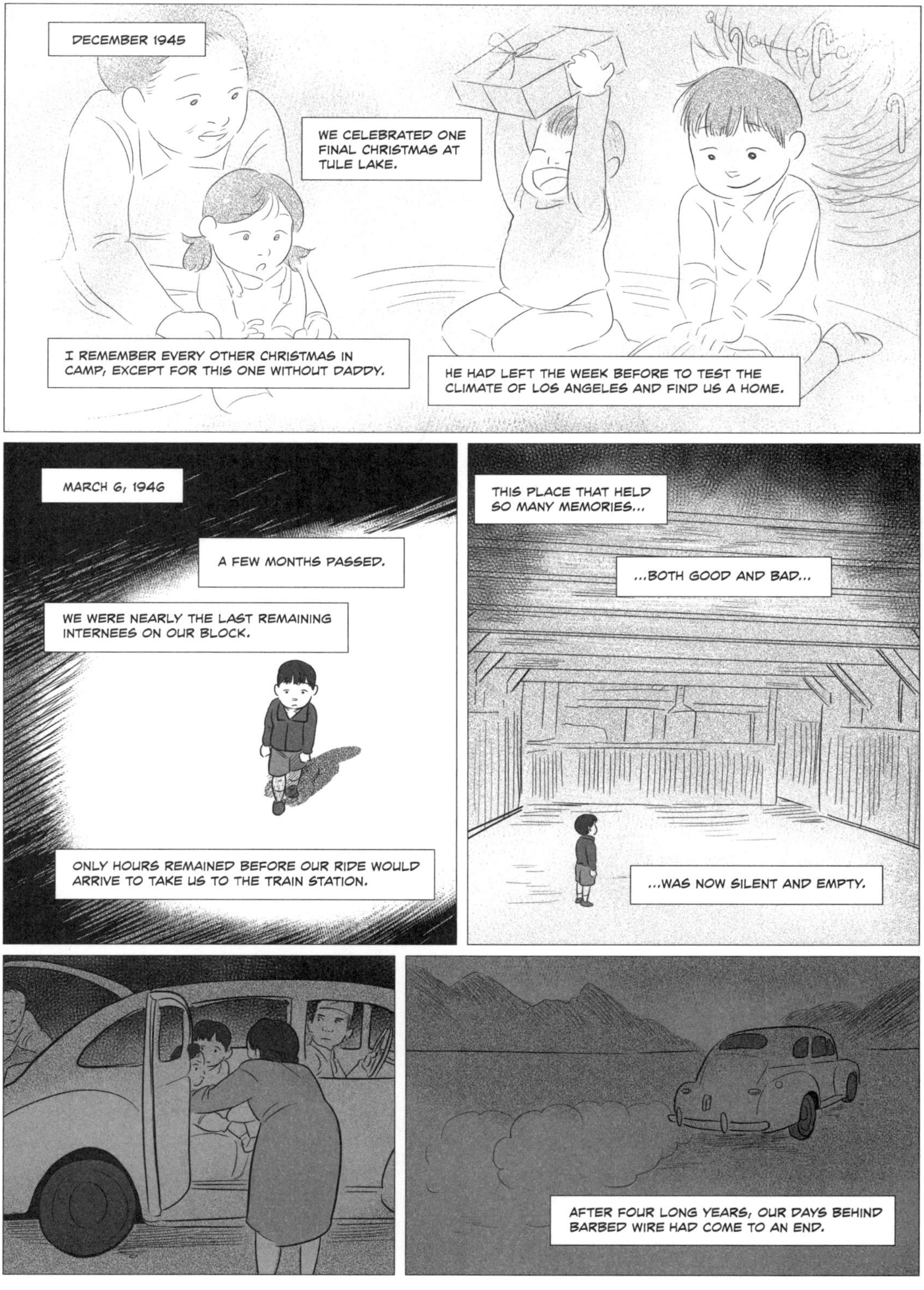
DECEMBER 1945
WE CELEBRATED ONE FINAL CHRISTMAS AT TULE LAKE.
I REMEMBER EVERY OTHER CHRISTMAS IN CAMP, EXCEPT FOR THIS ONE WITHOUT DADDY.
HE HAD LEFT THE WEEK BEFORE TO TEST THE CLIMATE OF LOS ANGELES AND FIND US A HOME.
MARCH 6, 1946
A FEW MONTHS PASSED.
WE WERE NEARLY THE LAST REMAINING INTERNEES ON OUR BLOCK.
ONLY HOURS REMAINED BEFORE OUR RIDE WOULD ARRIVE TO TAKE US TO THE TRAIN STATION.
THIS PLACE THAT HELD SO MANY MEMORIES...
...BOTH GOOD AND BAD...
...WAS NOW SILENT AND EMPTY.
AFTER FOUR LONG YEARS, OUR DAYS BEHIND BARBED WIRE HAD COME TO AN END.

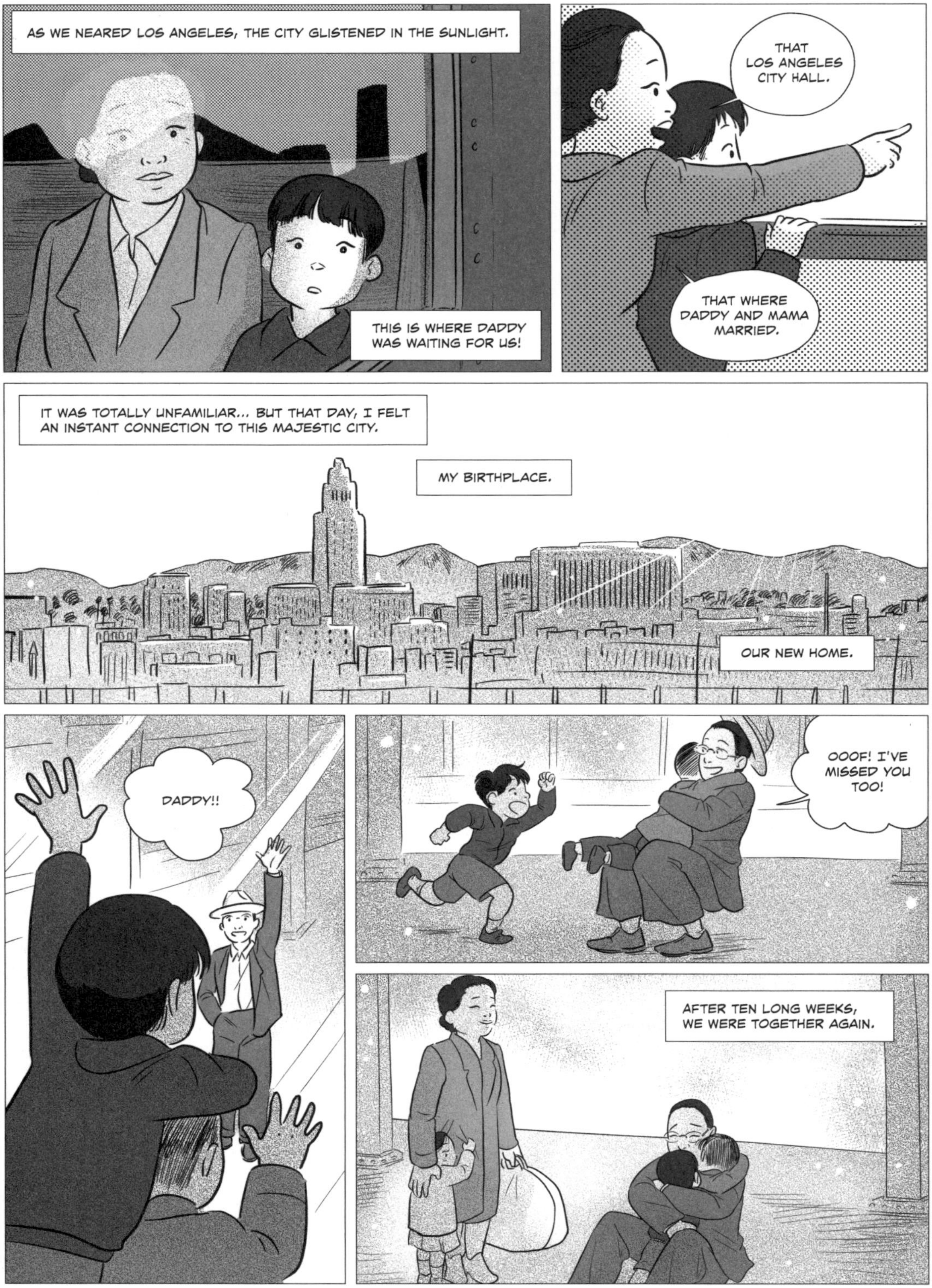
AS WE NEARED LOS ANGELES, THE CITY GLISTENED IN THE SUNLIGHT.
THIS IS WHERE DADDY WAS WAITING FOR US!
THAT LOS ANGELES CITY HALL.
THAT WHERE DADDY AND MAMA MARRIED.
IT WAS TOTALLY UNFAMILIAR... BUT THAT DAY, I FELT AN INSTANT CONNECTION TO THIS MAJESTIC CITY.
MY BIRTHPLACE.
OUR NEW HOME.
DADDY!!
OOOF! I'VE MISSED YOU TOO!
AFTER TEN LONG WEEKS, WE WERE TOGETHER AGAIN.

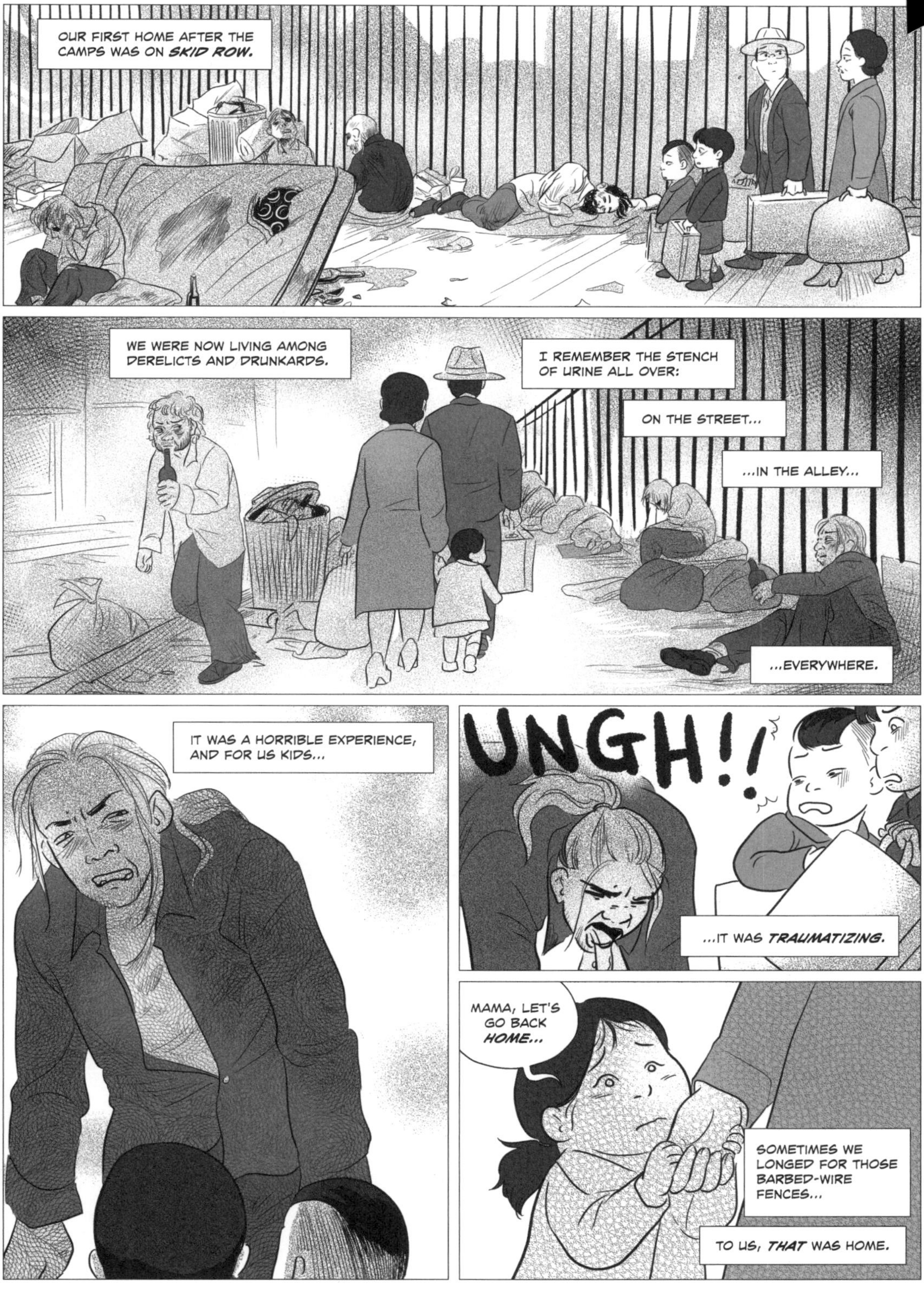
OUR FIRST HOME AFTER THE CAMPS WAS ON SKID ROW.
WE WERE NOW LIVING AMONG DERELICTS AND DRUNKARDS.
I REMEMBER THE STENCH OF URINE ALL OVER:
ON THE STREET...
...IN THE ALLEY...
...EVERYWHERE.
IT WAS A HORRIBLE EXPERIENCE, AND FOR US KIDS...
UNGH!!
...IT WAS TRAUMATIZING.
MAMA, LET'S GO BACK HOME...
SOMETIMES WE LONGED FOR THOSE BARBED-WIRE FENCES...
TO US, THAT WAS HOME.

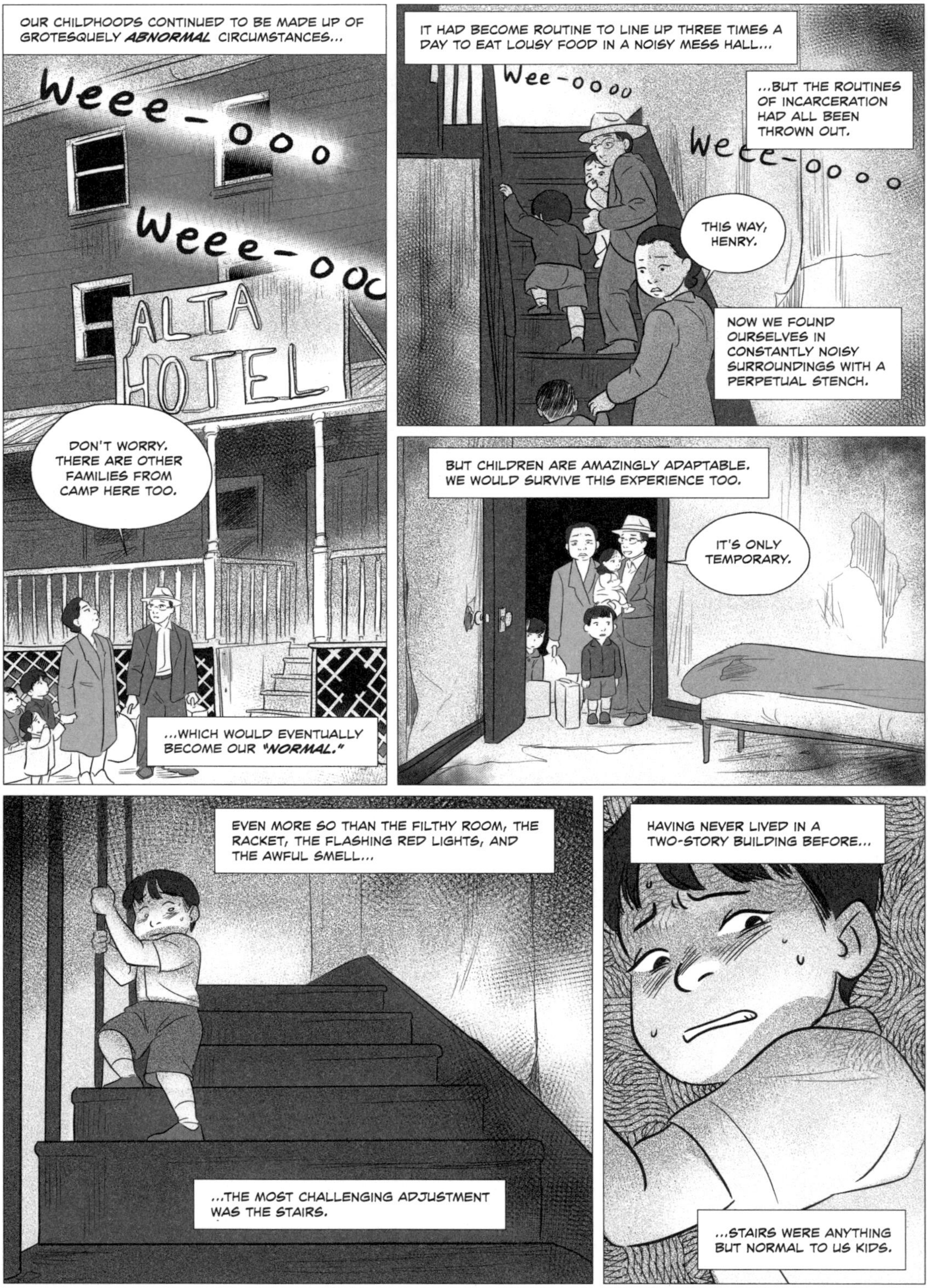
OUR CHILDHOODS CONTINUED TO BE MADE UP OF GROTESQUELY ABNORMAL CIRCUMSTANCES...
Weee-ooo
Weee-ooo
ALTA HOTEL
DON'T WORRY. THERE ARE OTHER FAMILIES FROM CAMP HERE TOO.
...WHICH WOULD EVENTUALLY BECOME OUR "NORMAL."
IT HAD BECOME ROUTINE TO LINE UP THREE TIMES A DAY TO EAT LOUSY FOOD IN A NOISY MESS HALL...
Wee-oooo
...BUT THE ROUTINES OF INCARCERATION HAD ALL BEEN THROWN OUT.
Weee-oooo
THIS WAY, HENRY.
NOW WE FOUND OURSELVES IN CONSTANTLY NOISY SURROUNDINGS WITH A PERPETUAL STENCH.
BUT CHILDREN ARE AMAZINGLY ADAPTABLE. WE WOULD SURVIVE THIS EXPERIENCE TOO.
IT'S ONLY TEMPORARY.
EVEN MORE SO THAN THE FILTHY ROOM, THE RACKET, THE FLASHING RED LIGHTS, AND THE AWFUL SMELL...
...THE MOST CHALLENGING ADJUSTMENT WAS THE STAIRS.
HAVING NEVER LIVED IN A TWO-STORY BUILDING BEFORE...
...STAIRS WERE ANYTHING BUT NORMAL TO US KIDS.

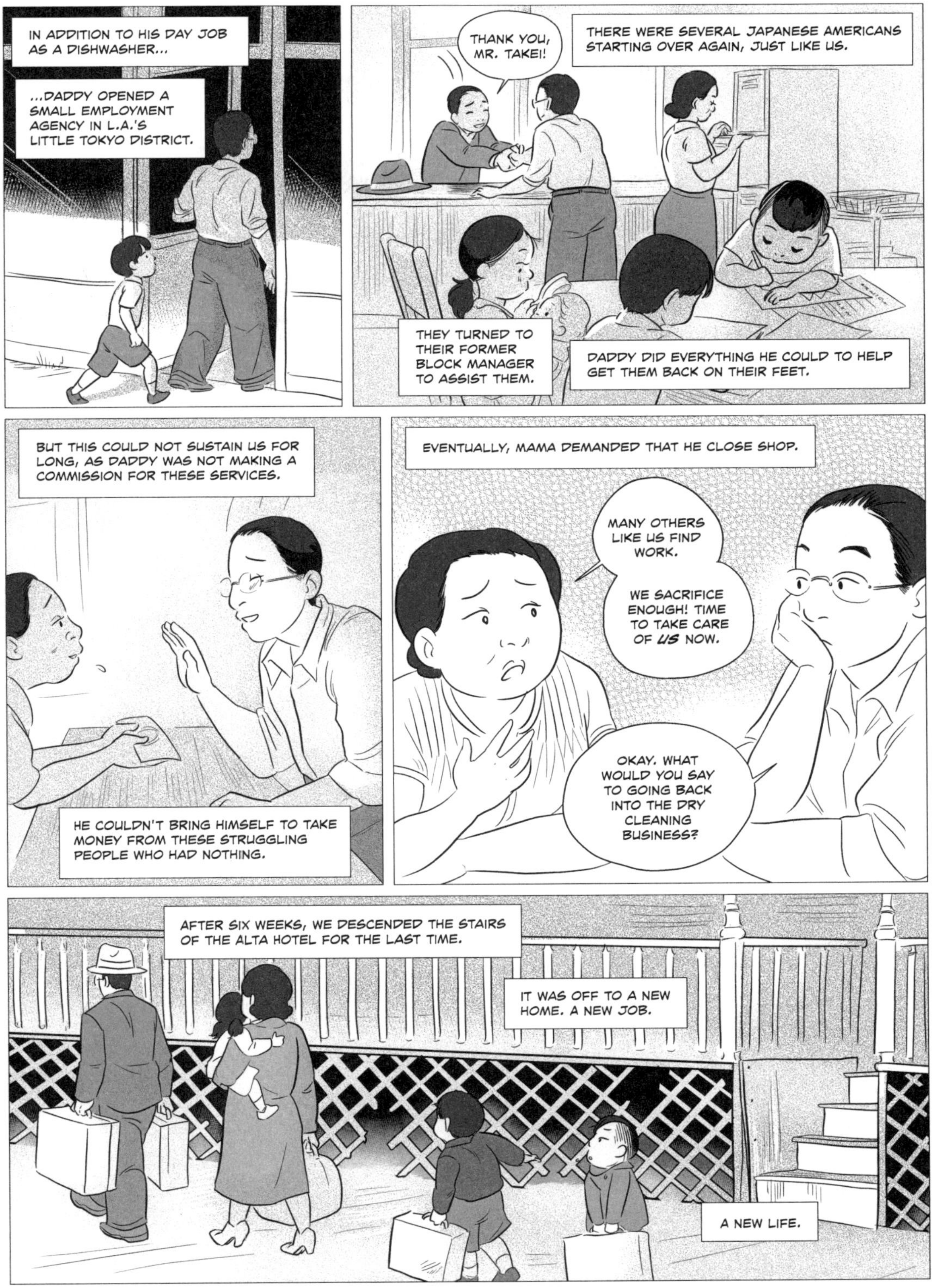

IN ADDITION TO HIS DAY JOB AS A DISHWASHER...
...DADDY OPENED A SMALL EMPLOYMENT AGENCY IN L.A.'S LITTLE TOKYO DISTRICT.
THANK YOU, MR. TAKEI!
THERE WERE SEVERAL JAPANESE AMERICANS STARTING OVER AGAIN, JUST LIKE US.
THEY TURNED TO THEIR FORMER BLOCK MANAGER TO ASSIST THEM.
DADDY DID EVERYTHING HE COULD TO HELP GET THEM BACK ON THEIR FEET.
BUT THIS COULD NOT SUSTAIN US FOR LONG, AS DADDY WAS NOT MAKING A COMMISSION FOR THESE SERVICES.
HE COULDN'T BRING HIMSELF TO TAKE MONEY FROM THESE STRUGGLING PEOPLE WHO HAD NOTHING.
EVENTUALLY, MAMA DEMANDED THAT HE CLOSE SHOP.
MANY OTHERS LIKE US FIND WORK.
WE SACRIFICE ENOUGH! TIME TO TAKE CARE OF *US* NOW.
OKAY. WHAT WOULD YOU SAY TO GOING BACK INTO THE DRY CLEANING BUSINESS?
AFTER SIX WEEKS, WE DESCENDED THE STAIRS OF THE ALTA HOTEL FOR THE LAST TIME.
IT WAS OFF TO A NEW HOME. A NEW JOB.
A NEW LIFE.

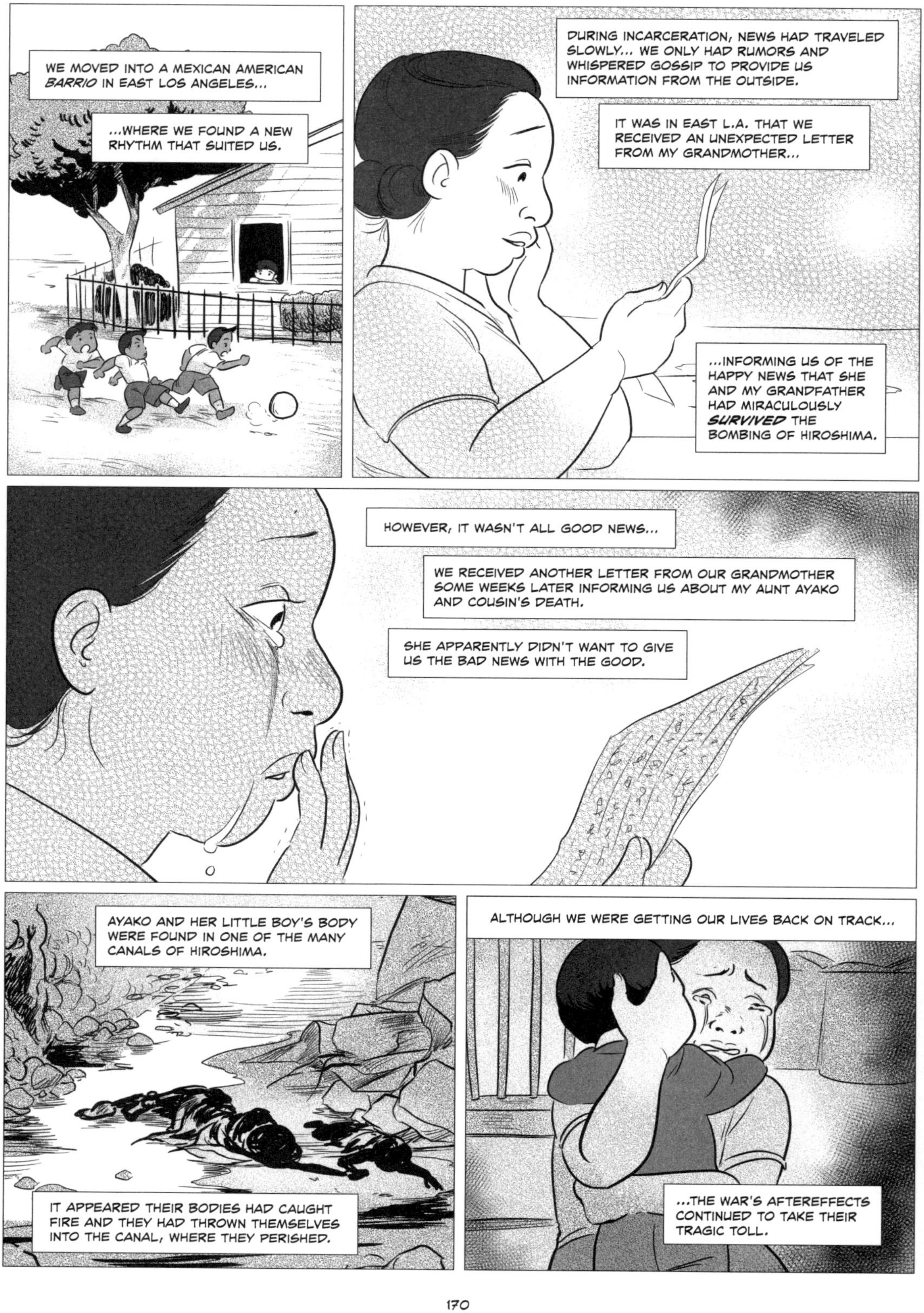
WE MOVED INTO A MEXICAN AMERICAN BARRIO IN EAST LOS ANGELES...
...WHERE WE FOUND A NEW RHYTHM THAT SUITED US.
DURING INCARCERATION, NEWS HAD TRAVELED SLOWLY... WE ONLY HAD RUMORS AND WHISPERED GOSSIP TO PROVIDE US INFORMATION FROM THE OUTSIDE.
IT WAS IN EAST L.A. THAT WE RECEIVED AN UNEXPECTED LETTER FROM MY GRANDMOTHER...
...INFORMING US OF THE HAPPY NEWS THAT SHE AND MY GRANDFATHER HAD MIRACULOUSLY SURVIVED THE BOMBING OF HIROSHIMA.
HOWEVER, IT WASN'T ALL GOOD NEWS...
WE RECEIVED ANOTHER LETTER FROM OUR GRANDMOTHER SOME WEEKS LATER INFORMING US ABOUT MY AUNT AYAKO AND COUSIN'S DEATH.
SHE APPARENTLY DIDN'T WANT TO GIVE US THE BAD NEWS WITH THE GOOD.
AYAKO AND HER LITTLE BOY'S BODY WERE FOUND IN ONE OF THE MANY CANALS OF HIROSHIMA.
IT APPEARED THEIR BODIES HAD CAUGHT FIRE AND THEY HAD THROWN THEMSELVES INTO THE CANAL, WHERE THEY PERISHED.
ALTHOUGH WE WERE GETTING OUR LIVES BACK ON TRACK...
...THE WAR'S AFTEREFFECTS CONTINUED TO TAKE THEIR TRAGIC TOLL.

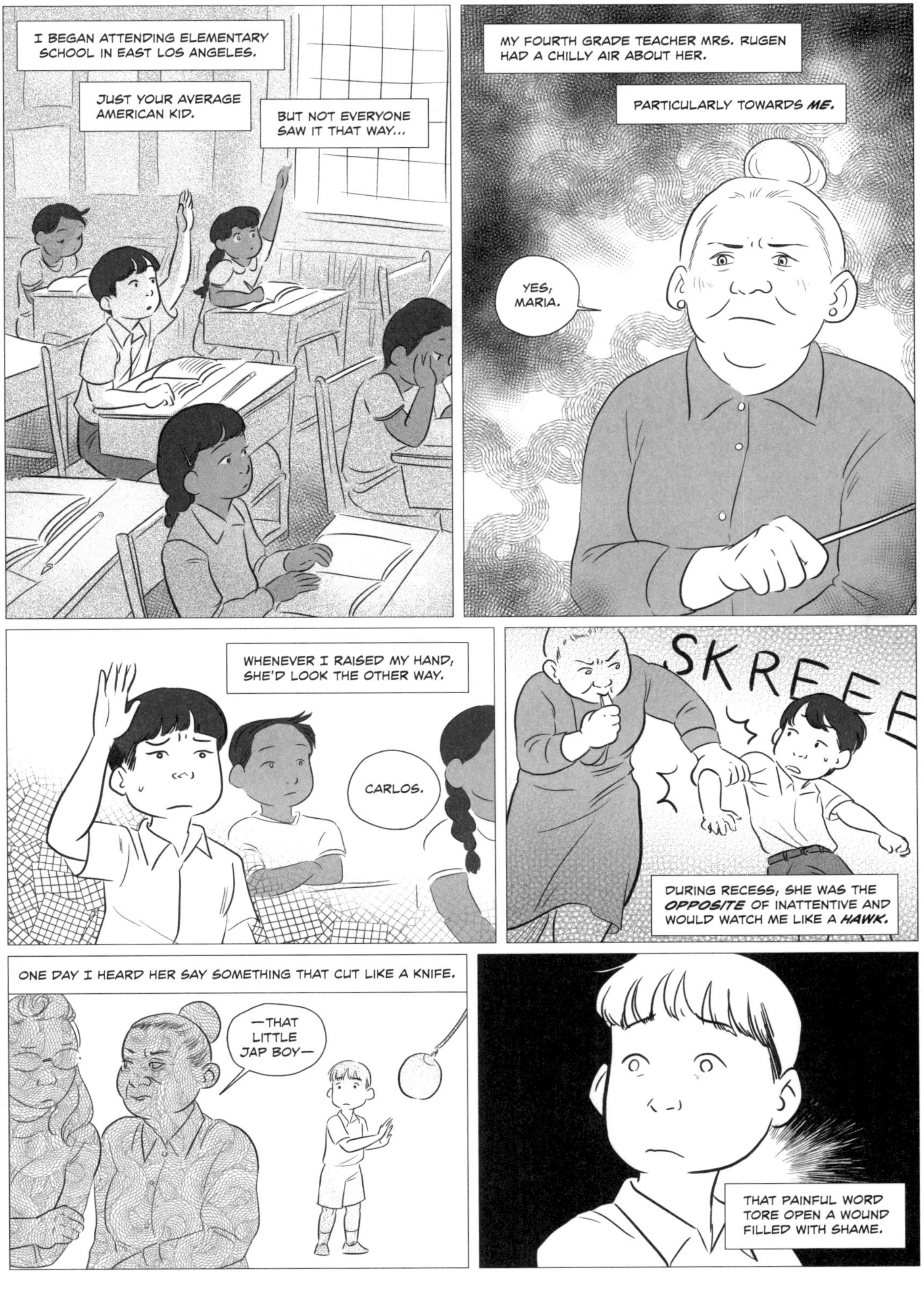
I BEGAN ATTENDING ELEMENTARY SCHOOL IN EAST LOS ANGELES.
JUST YOUR AVERAGE AMERICAN KID.
BUT NOT EVERYONE SAW IT THAT WAY...
MY FOURTH GRADE TEACHER MRS. RUGEN HAD A CHILLY AIR ABOUT HER.
PARTICULARLY TOWARDS ***ME.***
YES, MARIA.
WHENEVER I RAISED MY HAND, SHE'D LOOK THE OTHER WAY.
CARLOS.
SKREEE
DURING RECESS, SHE WAS THE ***OPPOSITE*** OF INATTENTIVE AND WOULD WATCH ME LIKE A ***HAWK.***
ONE DAY I HEARD HER SAY SOMETHING THAT CUT LIKE A KNIFE.
—THAT LITTLE JAP BOY—
THAT PAINFUL WORD TORE OPEN A WOUND FILLED WITH SHAME.

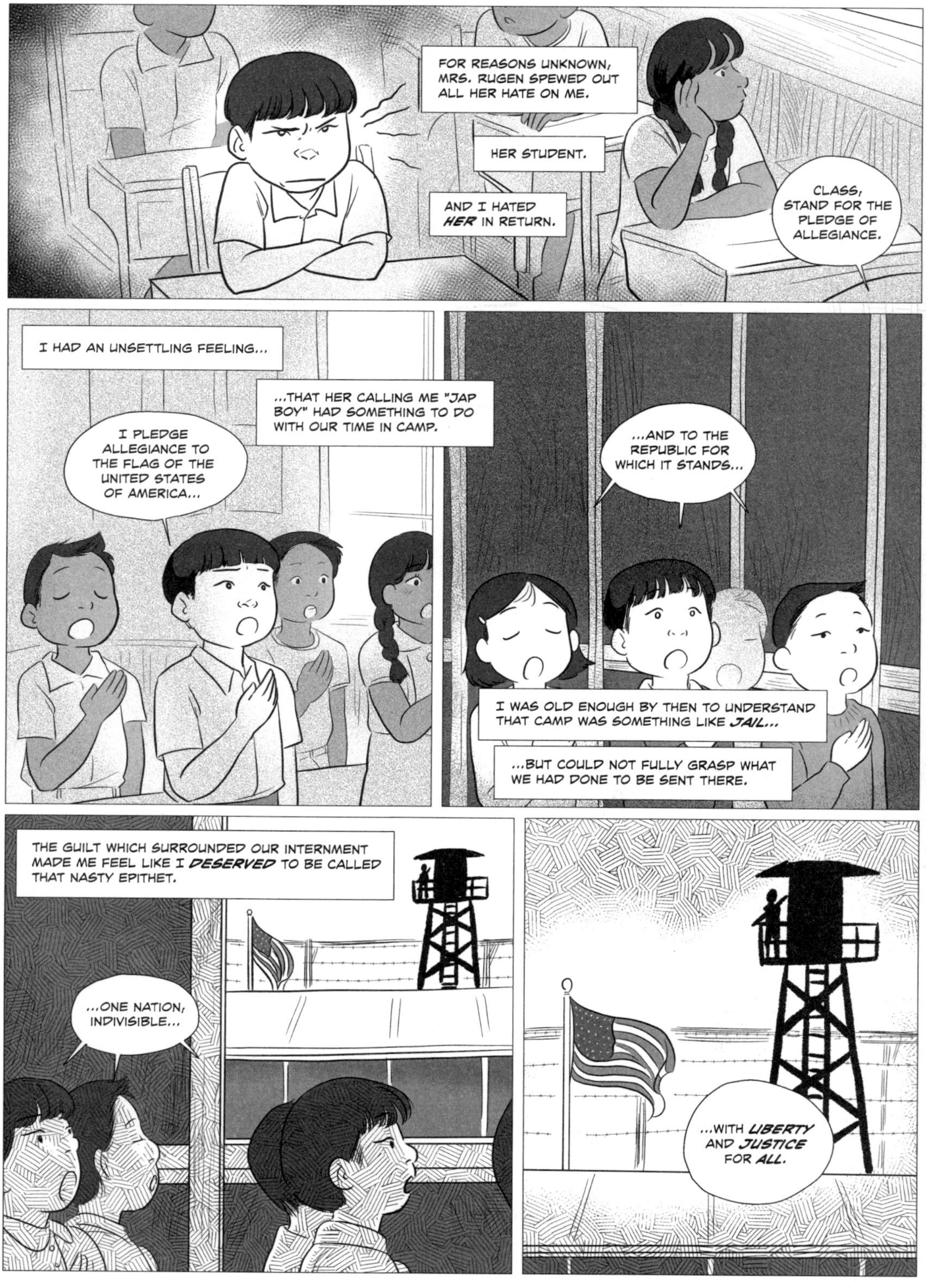
FOR REASONS UNKNOWN, MRS. RUGEN SPEWED OUT ALL HER HATE ON ME.
HER STUDENT.
AND I HATED *HER* IN RETURN.
CLASS, STAND FOR THE PLEDGE OF ALLEGIANCE.
I HAD AN UNSETTLING FEELING...
...THAT HER CALLING ME "JAP BOY" HAD SOMETHING TO DO WITH OUR TIME IN CAMP.
I PLEDGE ALLEGIANCE TO THE FLAG OF THE UNITED STATES OF AMERICA...
...AND TO THE REPUBLIC FOR WHICH IT STANDS...
I WAS OLD ENOUGH BY THEN TO UNDERSTAND THAT CAMP WAS SOMETHING LIKE *JAIL...*
...BUT COULD NOT FULLY GRASP WHAT WE HAD DONE TO BE SENT THERE.
THE GUILT WHICH SURROUNDED OUR INTERNMENT MADE ME FEEL LIKE I *DESERVED* TO BE CALLED THAT NASTY EPITHET.
...ONE NATION, INDIVISIBLE...
...WITH *LIBERTY* AND *JUSTICE* FOR *ALL.*

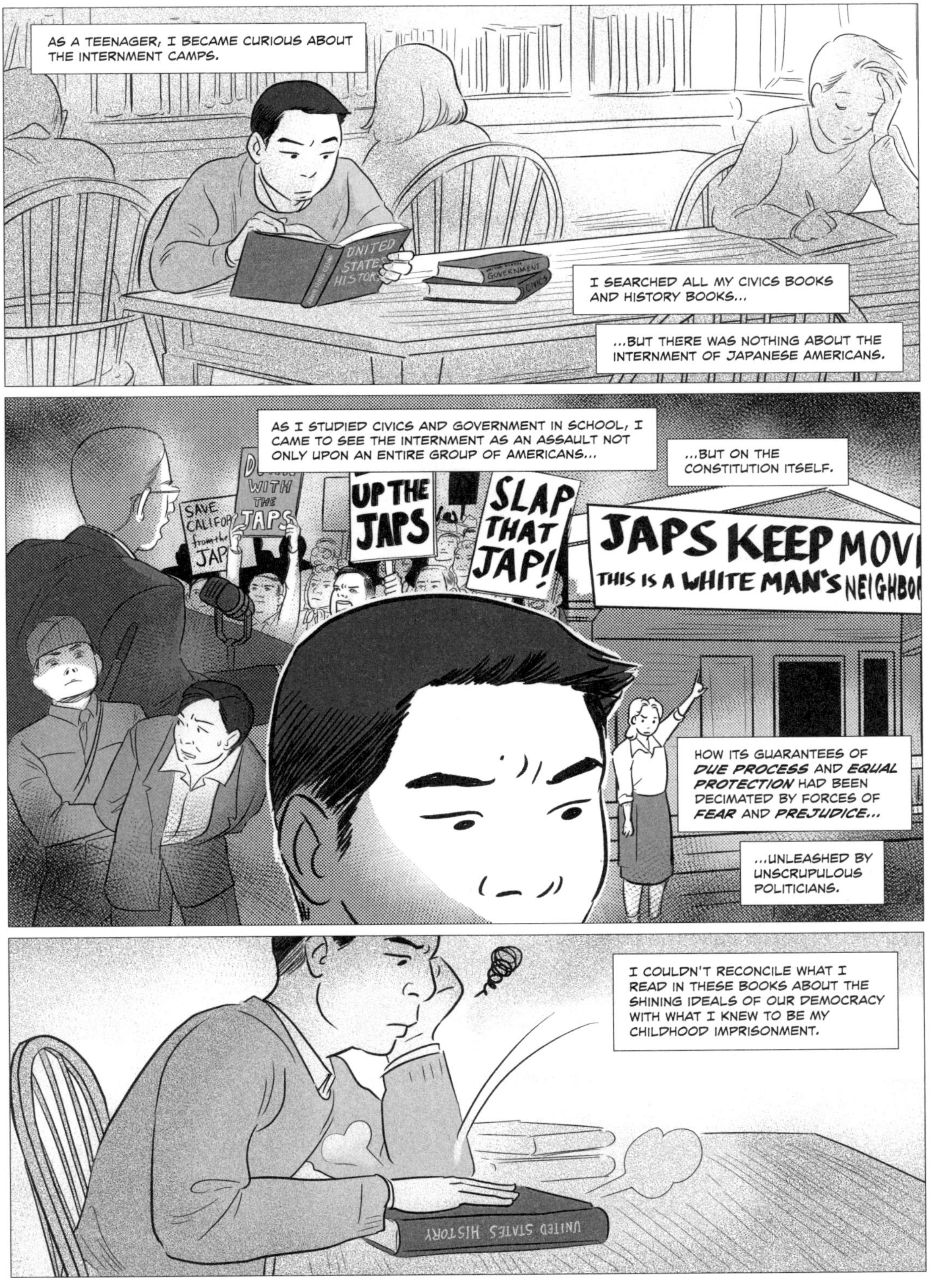
AS A TEENAGER, I BECAME CURIOUS ABOUT THE INTERNMENT CAMPS.
UNITED STATES HISTORY
GOVERNMENT
CIVICS
I SEARCHED ALL MY CIVICS BOOKS AND HISTORY BOOKS...
...BUT THERE WAS NOTHING ABOUT THE INTERNMENT OF JAPANESE AMERICANS.
AS I STUDIED CIVICS AND GOVERNMENT IN SCHOOL, I CAME TO SEE THE INTERNMENT AS AN ASSAULT NOT ONLY UPON AN ENTIRE GROUP OF AMERICANS...
...BUT ON THE CONSTITUTION ITSELF.
WITH THE JAPS
UP THE JAPS
SLAP THAT JAP!
JAPS KEEP
THIS IS A WHITE MAN'S
HOW ITS GUARANTEES OF ***DUE PROCESS*** AND ***EQUAL PROTECTION*** HAD BEEN DECIMATED BY FORCES OF ***FEAR*** AND ***PREJUDICE...***
...UNLEASHED BY UNSCRUPULOUS POLITICIANS.
I COULDN'T RECONCILE WHAT I READ IN THESE BOOKS ABOUT THE SHINING IDEALS OF OUR DEMOCRACY WITH WHAT I KNEW TO BE MY CHILDHOOD IMPRISONMENT.
UNITED STATES HISTORY

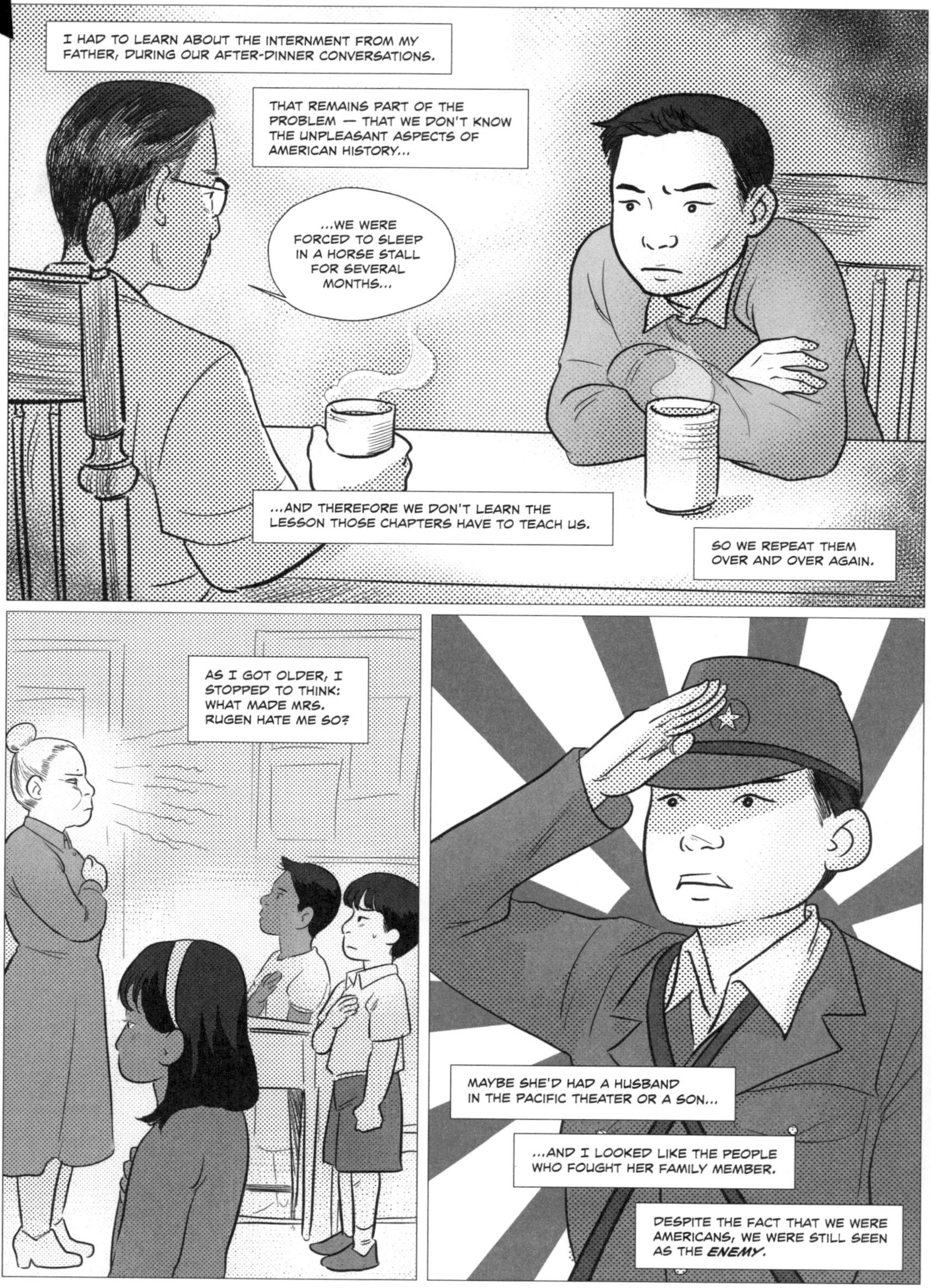
I HAD TO LEARN ABOUT THE INTERNMENT FROM MY FATHER, DURING OUR AFTER-DINNER CONVERSATIONS.
THAT REMAINS PART OF THE PROBLEM — THAT WE DON'T KNOW THE UNPLEASANT ASPECTS OF AMERICAN HISTORY...
...WE WERE FORCED TO SLEEP IN A HORSE STALL FOR SEVERAL MONTHS...
...AND THEREFORE WE DON'T LEARN THE LESSON THOSE CHAPTERS HAVE TO TEACH US.
SO WE REPEAT THEM OVER AND OVER AGAIN.
AS I GOT OLDER, I STOPPED TO THINK: WHAT MADE MRS. RUGEN HATE ME SO?
MAYBE SHE'D HAD A HUSBAND IN THE PACIFIC THEATER OR A SON...
...AND I LOOKED LIKE THE PEOPLE WHO FOUGHT HER FAMILY MEMBER.
DESPITE THE FACT THAT WE WERE AMERICANS, WE WERE STILL SEEN AS THE *ENEMY*.

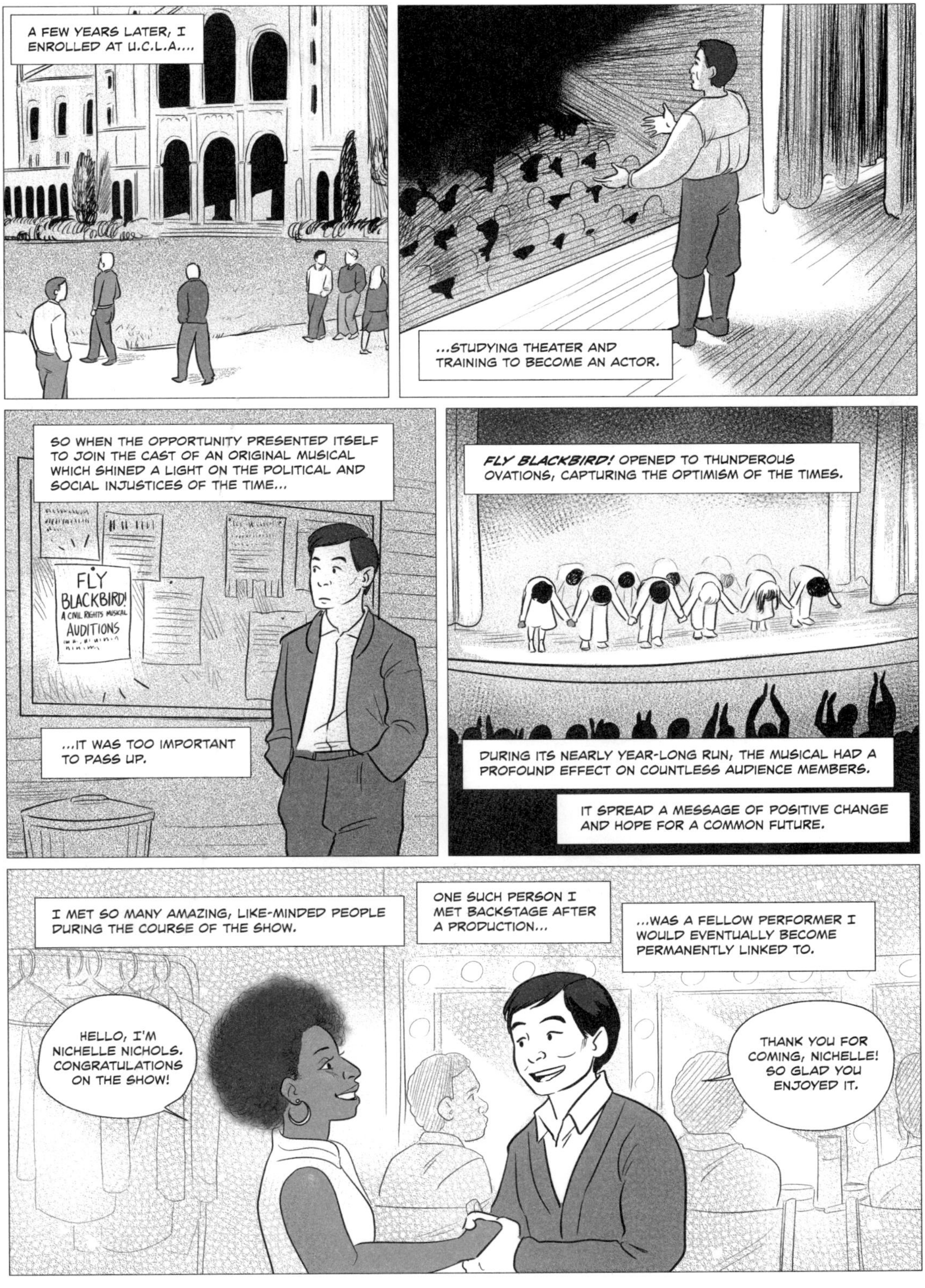
A FEW YEARS LATER, I ENROLLED AT U.C.L.A....
...STUDYING THEATER AND TRAINING TO BECOME AN ACTOR.
SO WHEN THE OPPORTUNITY PRESENTED ITSELF TO JOIN THE CAST OF AN ORIGINAL MUSICAL WHICH SHINED A LIGHT ON THE POLITICAL AND SOCIAL INJUSTICES OF THE TIME...
FLY BLACKBIRD! A CIVIL RIGHTS MUSICAL AUDITIONS
...IT WAS TOO IMPORTANT TO PASS UP.
FLY BLACKBIRD! OPENED TO THUNDEROUS OVATIONS, CAPTURING THE OPTIMISM OF THE TIMES.
DURING ITS NEARLY YEAR-LONG RUN, THE MUSICAL HAD A PROFOUND EFFECT ON COUNTLESS AUDIENCE MEMBERS.
IT SPREAD A MESSAGE OF POSITIVE CHANGE AND HOPE FOR A COMMON FUTURE.
I MET SO MANY AMAZING, LIKE-MINDED PEOPLE DURING THE COURSE OF THE SHOW.
ONE SUCH PERSON I MET BACKSTAGE AFTER A PRODUCTION...
...WAS A FELLOW PERFORMER I WOULD EVENTUALLY BECOME PERMANENTLY LINKED TO.
HELLO, I'M NICHELLE NICHOLS. CONGRATULATIONS ON THE SHOW!
THANK YOU FOR COMING, NICHELLE! SO GLAD YOU ENJOYED IT.

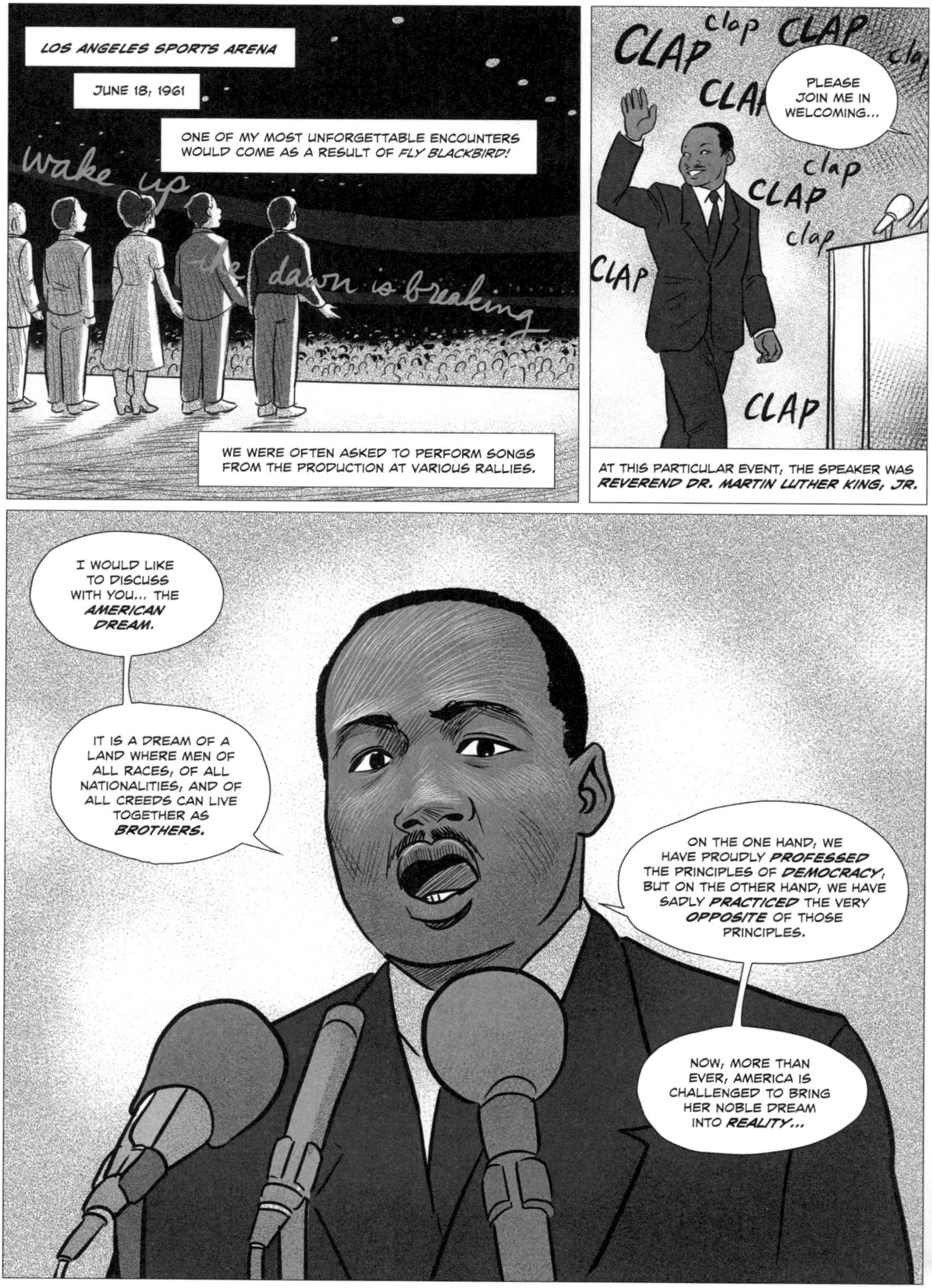
LOS ANGELES SPORTS ARENA
JUNE 18, 1961
ONE OF MY MOST UNFORGETTABLE ENCOUNTERS WOULD COME AS A RESULT OF *FLY BLACKBIRD!*
wake up
the dawn is breaking
WE WERE OFTEN ASKED TO PERFORM SONGS FROM THE PRODUCTION AT VARIOUS RALLIES.
CLAP clap CLAP clap
CLAP
PLEASE JOIN ME IN WELCOMING...
clap
CLAP
clap
CLAP
CLAP
AT THIS PARTICULAR EVENT, THE SPEAKER WAS ***REVEREND DR. MARTIN LUTHER KING, JR.***
I WOULD LIKE TO DISCUSS WITH YOU... THE ***AMERICAN DREAM.***
IT IS A DREAM OF A LAND WHERE MEN OF ALL RACES, OF ALL NATIONALITIES, AND OF ALL CREEDS CAN LIVE TOGETHER AS ***BROTHERS.***
ON THE ONE HAND, WE HAVE PROUDLY ***PROFESSED*** THE PRINCIPLES OF ***DEMOCRACY***, BUT ON THE OTHER HAND, WE HAVE SADLY ***PRACTICED*** THE VERY ***OPPOSITE*** OF THOSE PRINCIPLES.
NOW, MORE THAN EVER, AMERICA IS CHALLENGED TO BRING HER NOBLE DREAM INTO ***REALITY...***

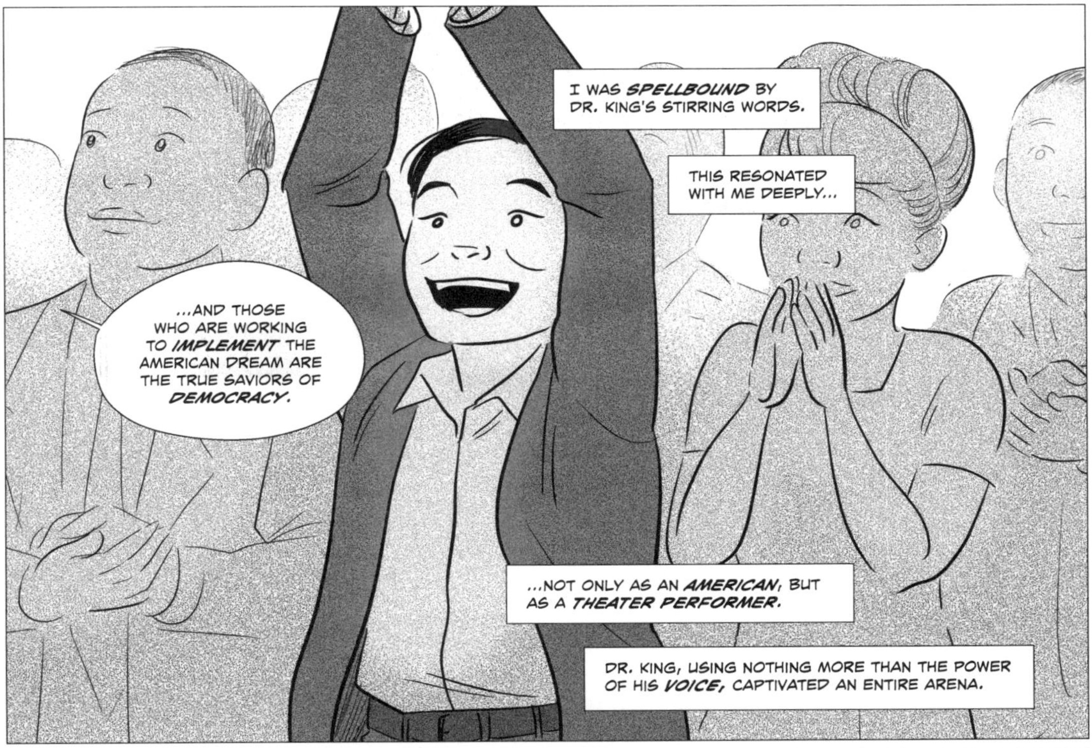
I WAS SPELLBOUND BY DR. KING'S STIRRING WORDS.
THIS RESONATED WITH ME DEEPLY...
...AND THOSE WHO ARE WORKING TO IMPLEMENT THE AMERICAN DREAM ARE THE TRUE SAVIORS OF DEMOCRACY.
...NOT ONLY AS AN AMERICAN, BUT AS A THEATER PERFORMER.
DR. KING, USING NOTHING MORE THAN THE POWER OF HIS VOICE, CAPTIVATED AN ENTIRE ARENA.

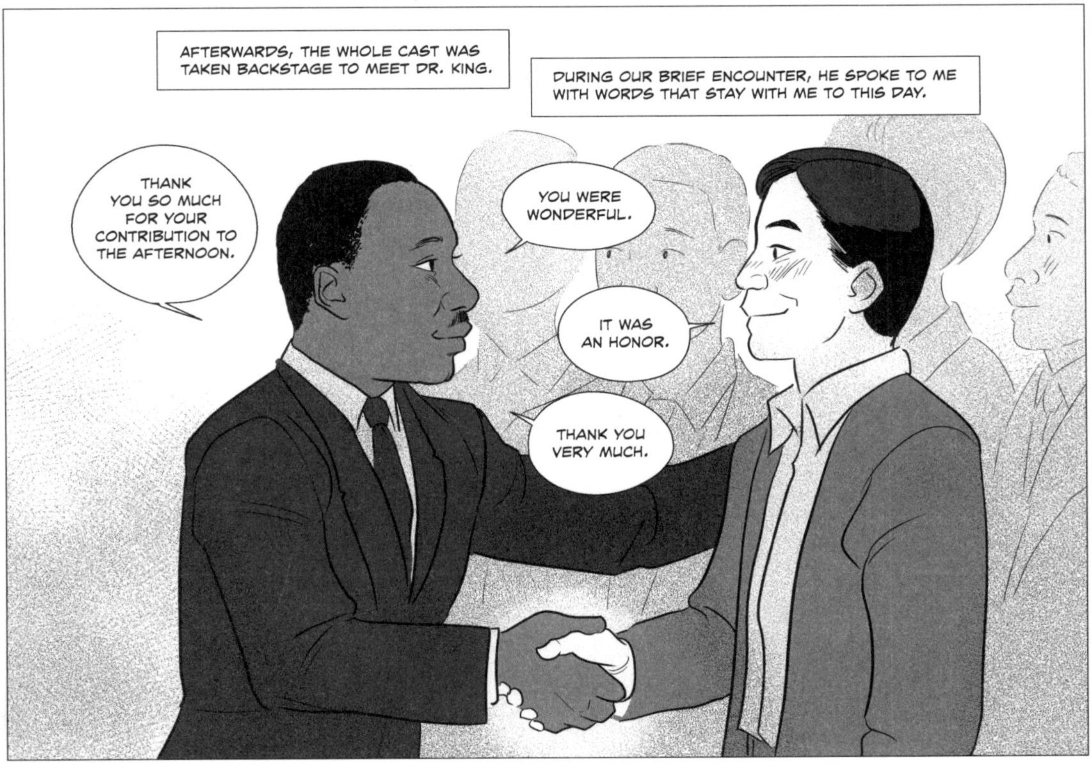
AFTERWARDS, THE WHOLE CAST WAS TAKEN BACKSTAGE TO MEET DR. KING.
DURING OUR BRIEF ENCOUNTER, HE SPOKE TO ME WITH WORDS THAT STAY WITH ME TO THIS DAY.
THANK YOU SO MUCH FOR YOUR CONTRIBUTION TO THE AFTERNOON.
YOU WERE WONDERFUL.
IT WAS AN HONOR.
THANK YOU VERY MUCH.

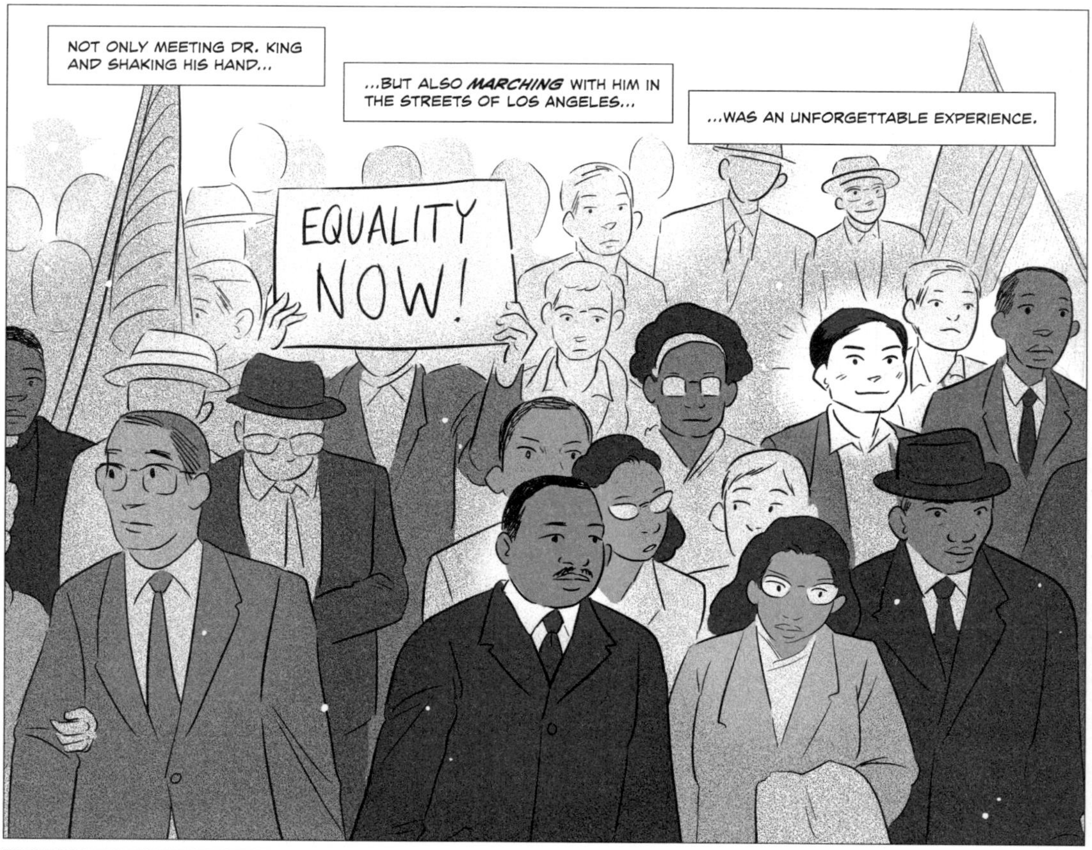
NOT ONLY MEETING DR. KING AND SHAKING HIS HAND...
...BUT ALSO MARCHING WITH HIM IN THE STREETS OF LOS ANGELES...
...WAS AN UNFORGETTABLE EXPERIENCE.
EQUALITY NOW!

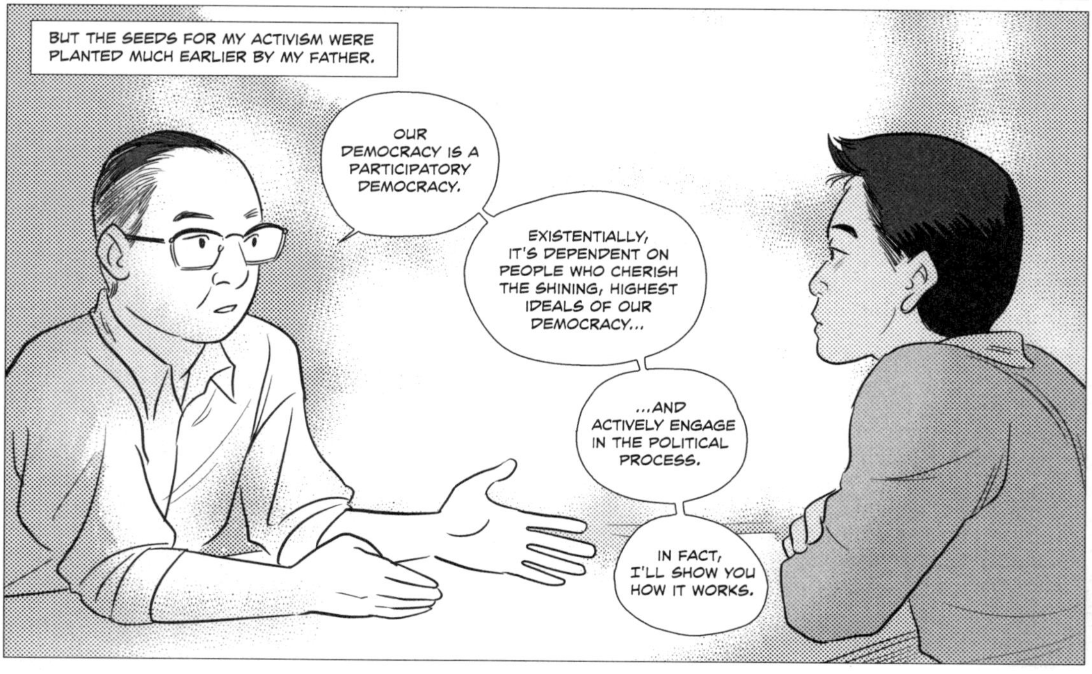
BUT THE SEEDS FOR MY ACTIVISM WERE PLANTED MUCH EARLIER BY MY FATHER.
OUR DEMOCRACY IS A PARTICIPATORY DEMOCRACY.
EXISTENTIALLY, IT'S DEPENDENT ON PEOPLE WHO CHERISH THE SHINING, HIGHEST IDEALS OF OUR DEMOCRACY...
...AND ACTIVELY ENGAGE IN THE POLITICAL PROCESS.
IN FACT, I'LL SHOW YOU HOW IT WORKS.

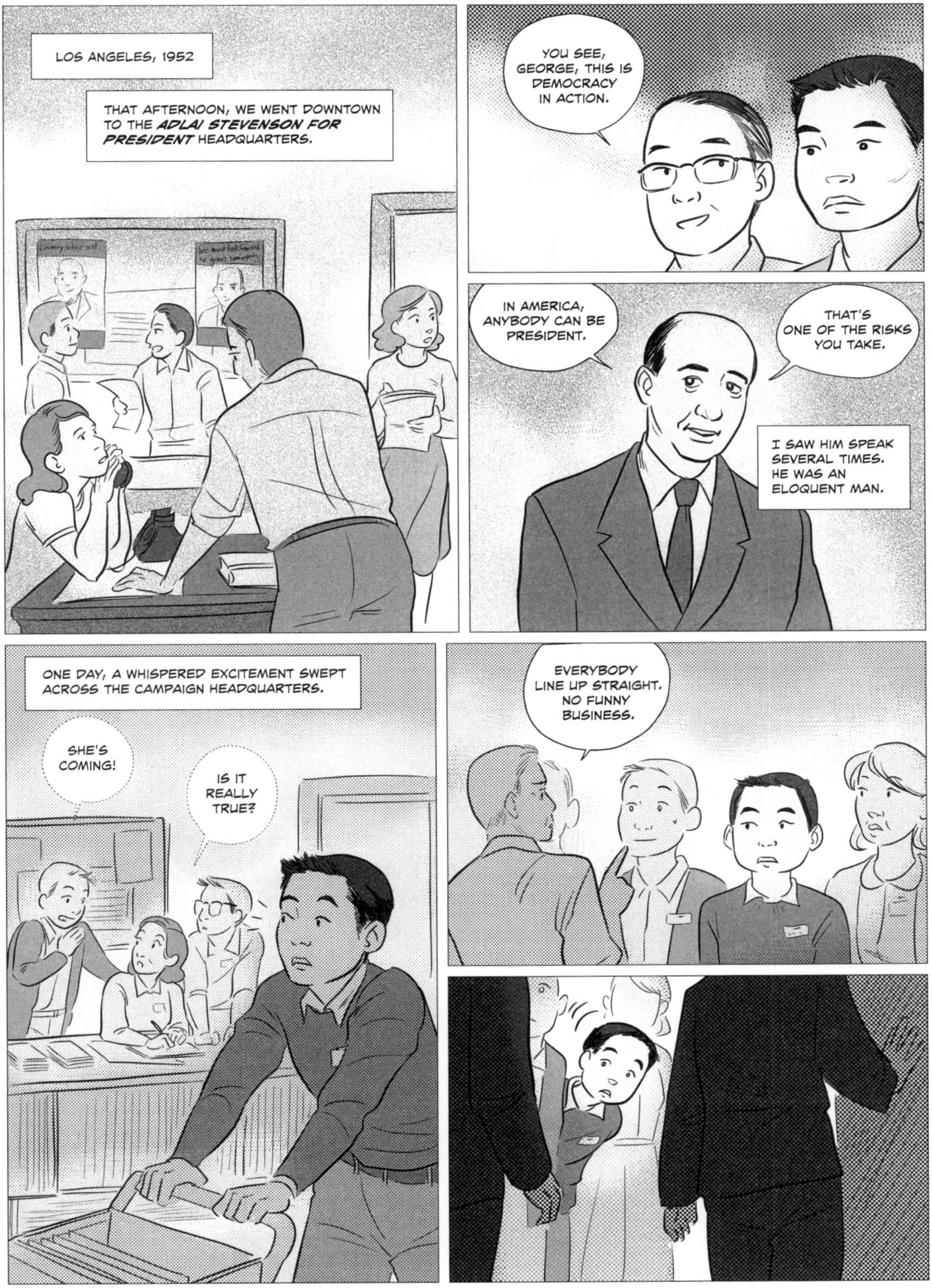
LOS ANGELES, 1952
THAT AFTERNOON, WE WENT DOWNTOWN TO THE ADLAI STEVENSON FOR PRESIDENT HEADQUARTERS.
YOU SEE, GEORGE, THIS IS DEMOCRACY IN ACTION.
IN AMERICA, ANYBODY CAN BE PRESIDENT.
THAT'S ONE OF THE RISKS YOU TAKE.
I SAW HIM SPEAK SEVERAL TIMES. HE WAS AN ELOQUENT MAN.
ONE DAY, A WHISPERED EXCITEMENT SWEPT ACROSS THE CAMPAIGN HEADQUARTERS.
SHE'S COMING!
IS IT REALLY TRUE?
EVERYBODY LINE UP STRAIGHT. NO FUNNY BUSINESS.

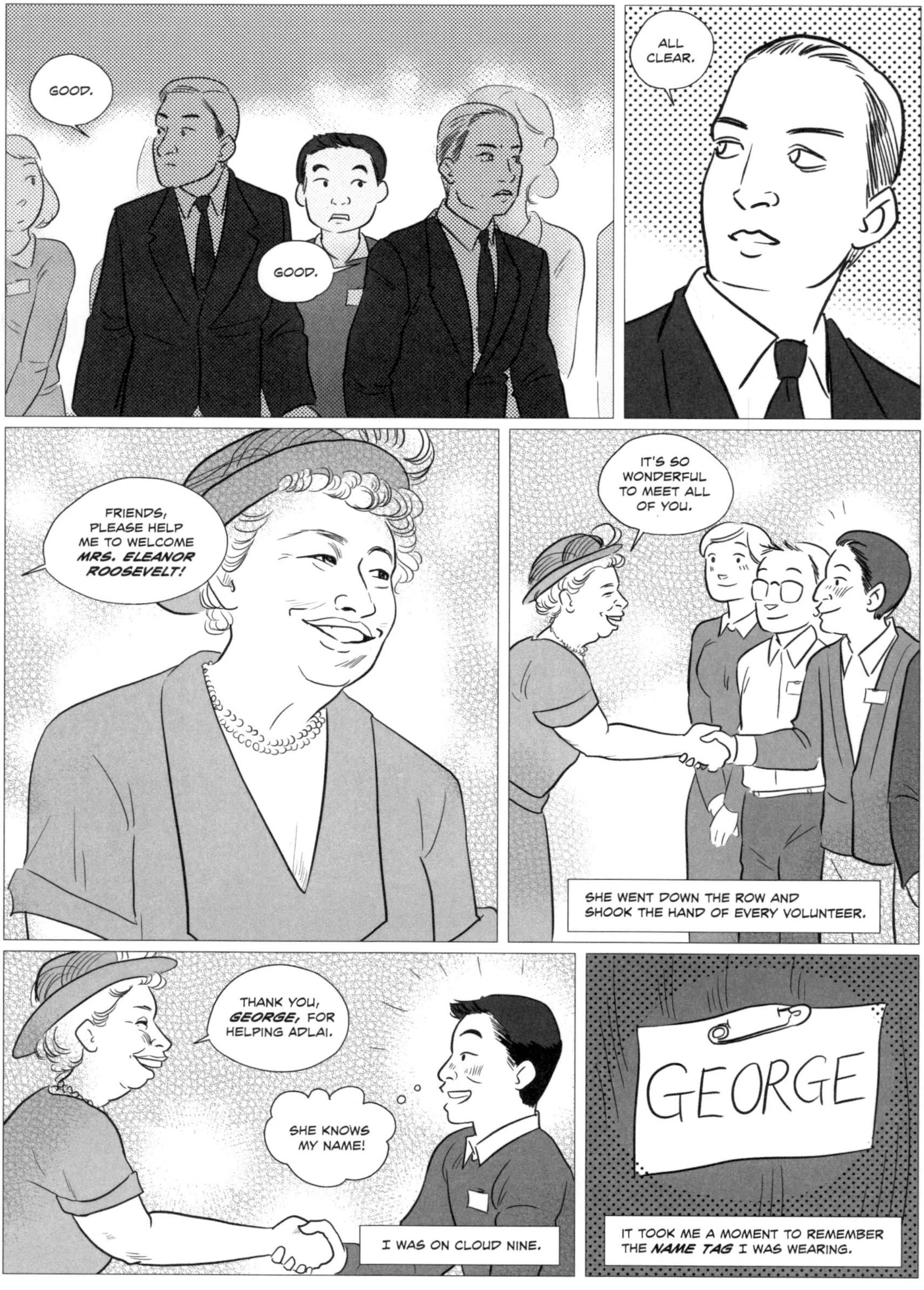
GOOD.
GOOD.
ALL CLEAR.
FRIENDS, PLEASE HELP ME TO WELCOME ***MRS. ELEANOR ROOSEVELT!***
IT'S SO WONDERFUL TO MEET ALL OF YOU.
SHE WENT DOWN THE ROW AND SHOOK THE HAND OF EVERY VOLUNTEER.
THANK YOU, ***GEORGE,*** FOR HELPING ADLAI.
SHE KNOWS MY NAME!
I WAS ON CLOUD NINE.
GEORGE
IT TOOK ME A MOMENT TO REMEMBER THE ***NAME TAG*** I WAS WEARING.

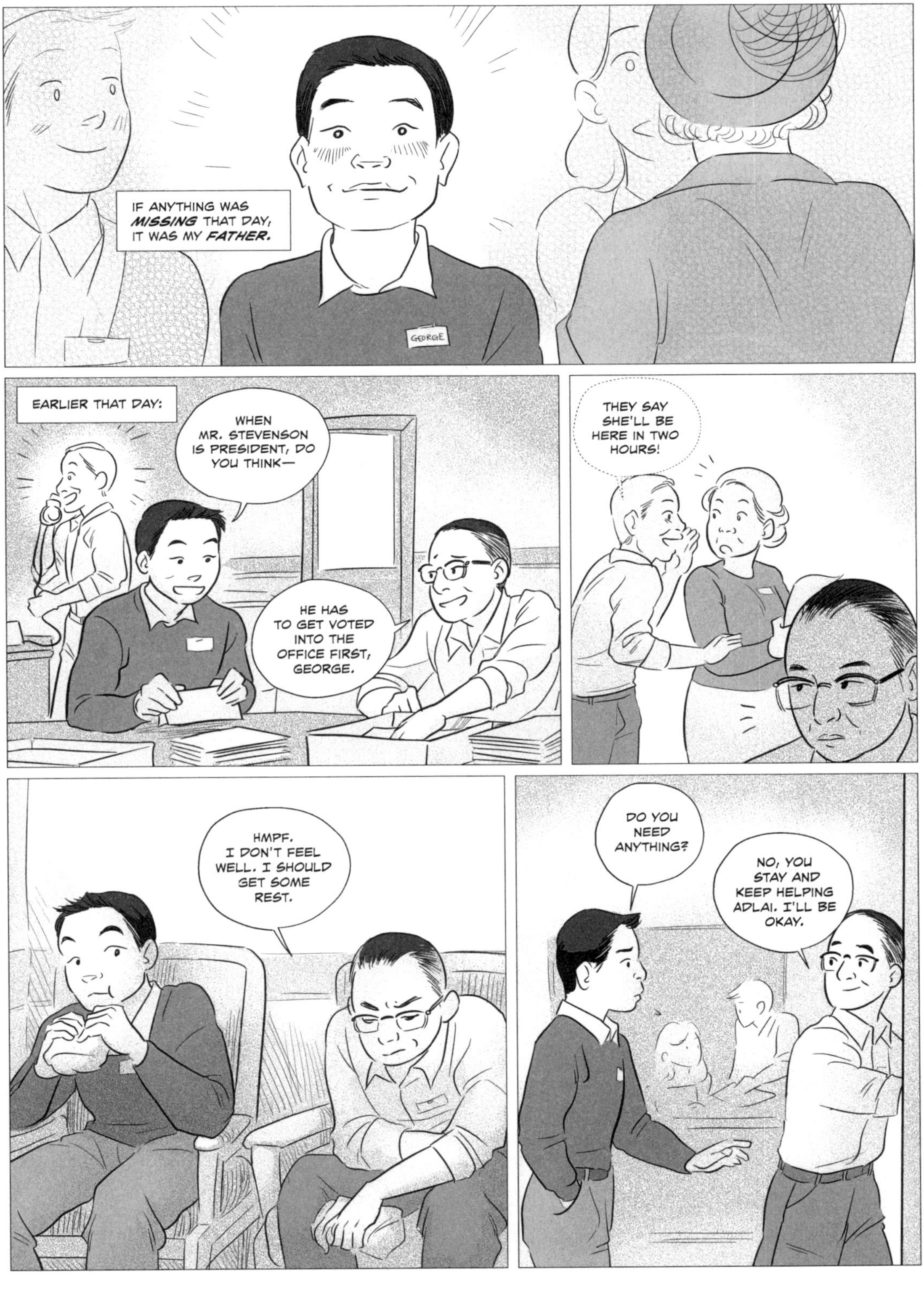
IF ANYTHING WAS *MISSING* THAT DAY, IT WAS MY *FATHER.*
GEORGE
EARLIER THAT DAY:
WHEN MR. STEVENSON IS PRESIDENT, DO YOU THINK—
HE HAS TO GET VOTED INTO THE OFFICE FIRST, GEORGE.
THEY SAY SHE'LL BE HERE IN TWO HOURS!
HMPF. I DON'T FEEL WELL. I SHOULD GET SOME REST.
DO YOU NEED ANYTHING?
NO, YOU STAY AND KEEP HELPING ADLAI. I'LL BE OKAY.

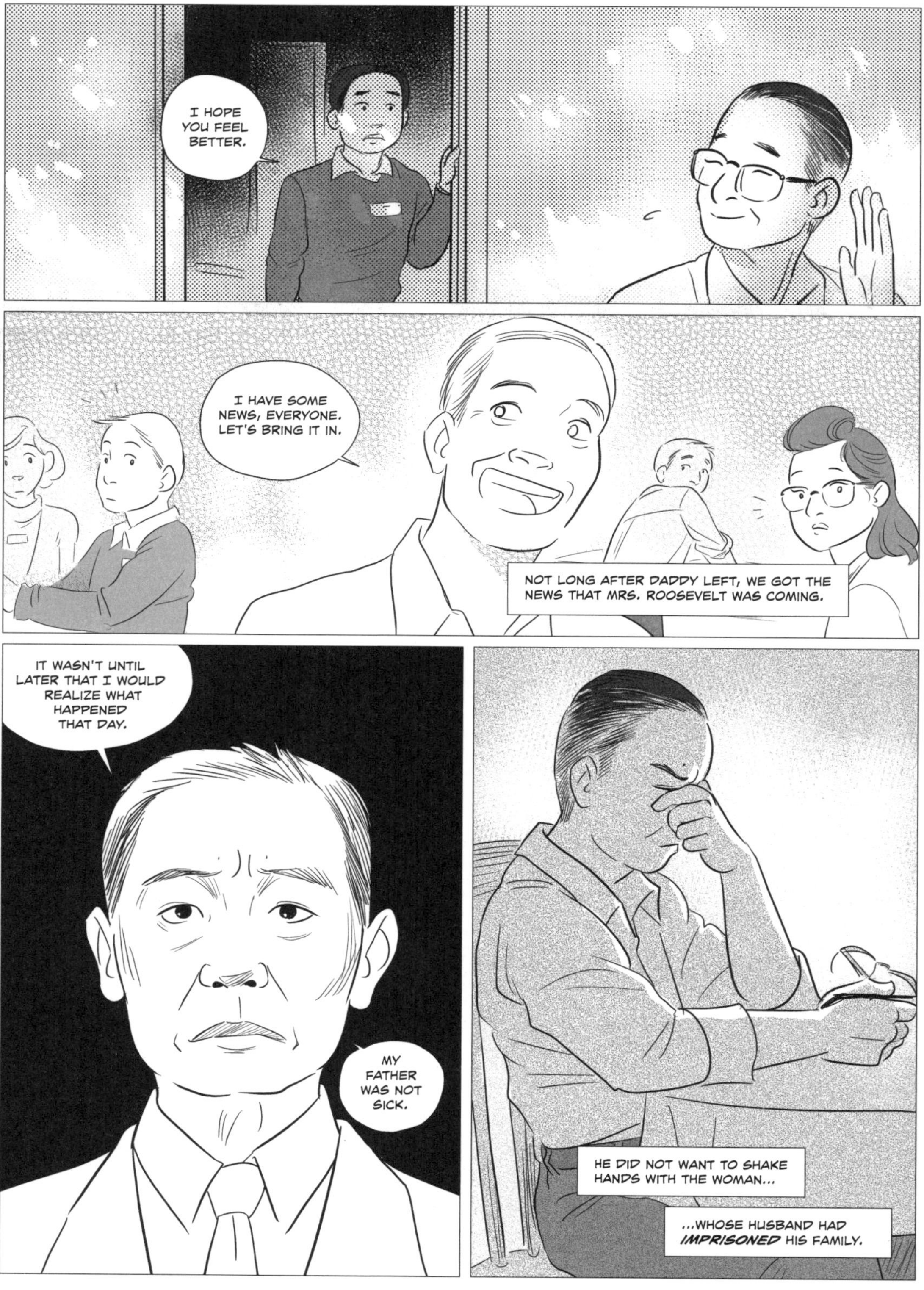
I HOPE YOU FEEL BETTER.
I HAVE SOME NEWS, EVERYONE. LET'S BRING IT IN.
NOT LONG AFTER DADDY LEFT, WE GOT THE NEWS THAT MRS. ROOSEVELT WAS COMING.
IT WASN'T UNTIL LATER THAT I WOULD REALIZE WHAT HAPPENED THAT DAY.
MY FATHER WAS NOT SICK.
HE DID NOT WANT TO SHAKE HANDS WITH THE WOMAN...
...WHOSE HUSBAND HAD *IMPRISONED* HIS FAMILY.

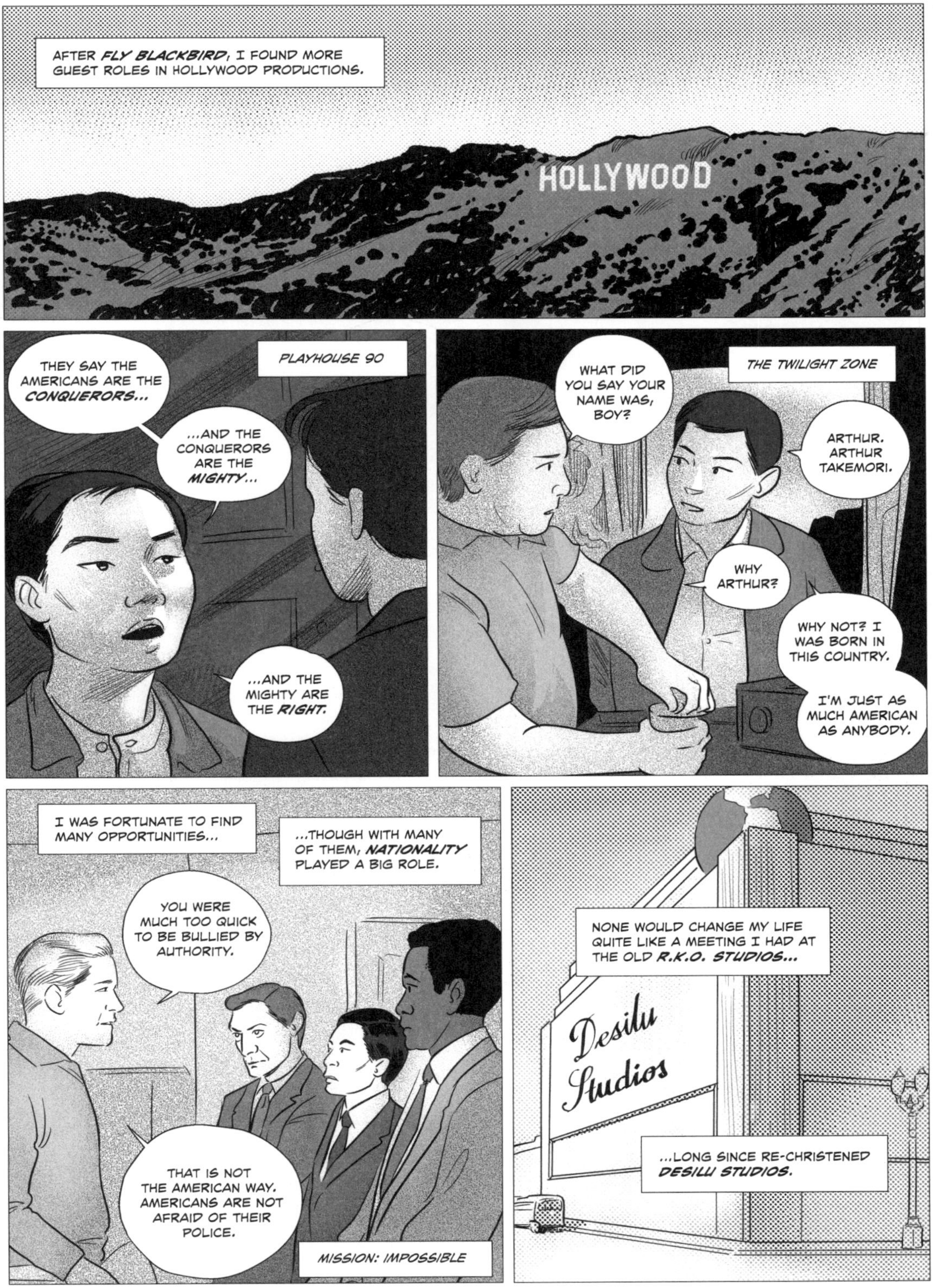
AFTER FLY BLACKBIRD, I FOUND MORE GUEST ROLES IN HOLLYWOOD PRODUCTIONS.
HOLLYWOOD
PLAYHOUSE 90
THEY SAY THE AMERICANS ARE THE CONQUERORS...
...AND THE CONQUERORS ARE THE MIGHTY...
...AND THE MIGHTY ARE THE RIGHT.
THE TWILIGHT ZONE
WHAT DID YOU SAY YOUR NAME WAS, BOY?
ARTHUR. ARTHUR TAKEMORI.
WHY ARTHUR?
WHY NOT? I WAS BORN IN THIS COUNTRY.
I'M JUST AS MUCH AMERICAN AS ANYBODY.
I WAS FORTUNATE TO FIND MANY OPPORTUNITIES...
...THOUGH WITH MANY OF THEM, NATIONALITY PLAYED A BIG ROLE.
YOU WERE MUCH TOO QUICK TO BE BULLIED BY AUTHORITY.
THAT IS NOT THE AMERICAN WAY. AMERICANS ARE NOT AFRAID OF THEIR POLICE.
MISSION: IMPOSSIBLE
NONE WOULD CHANGE MY LIFE QUITE LIKE A MEETING I HAD AT THE OLD R.K.O. STUDIOS...
Desilu Studios
...LONG SINCE RE-CHRISTENED DESILU STUDIOS.

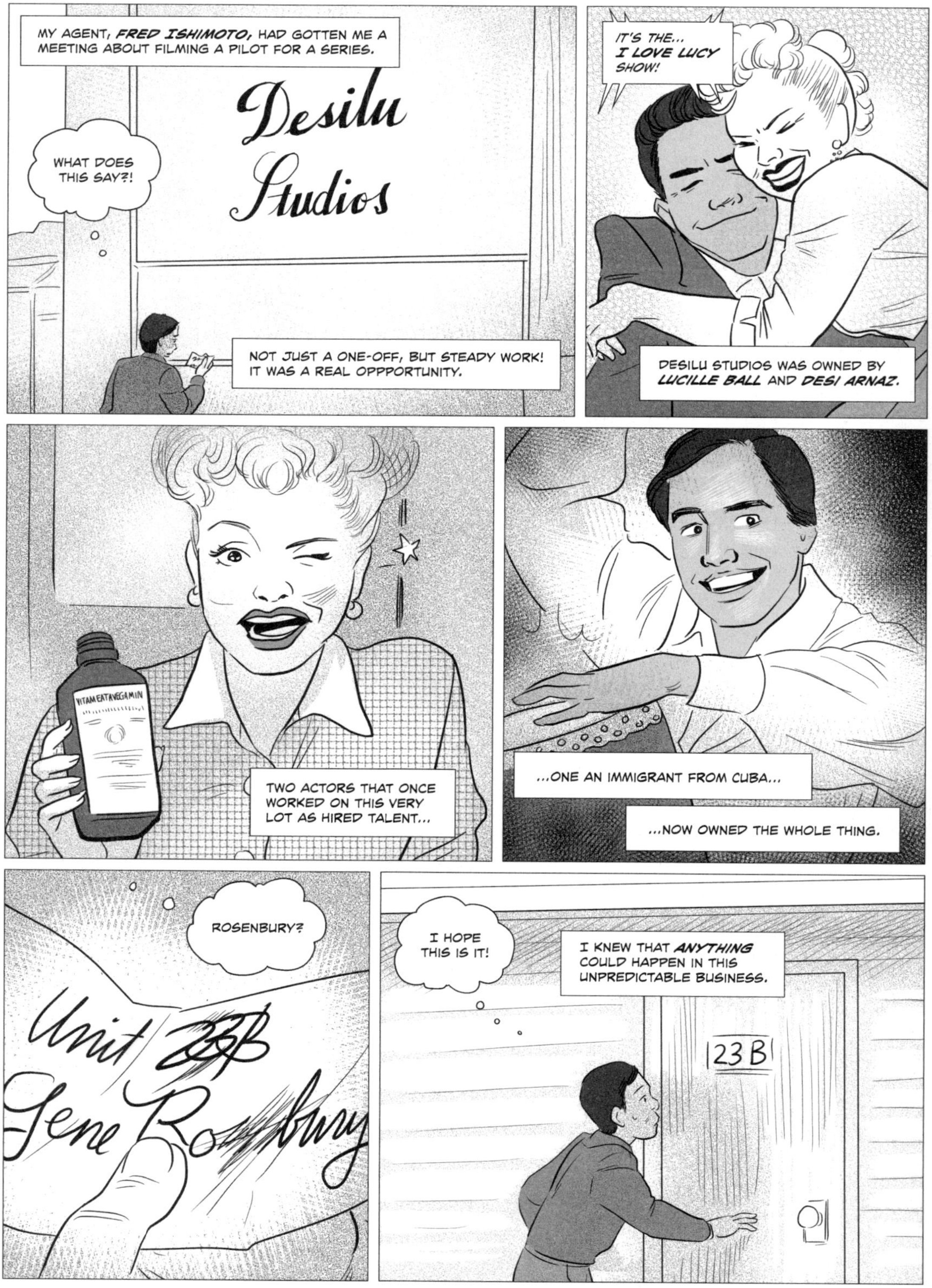

MY AGENT, FRED ISHIMOTO, HAD GOTTEN ME A MEETING ABOUT FILMING A PILOT FOR A SERIES.
Desilu Studios
WHAT DOES THIS SAY?!
NOT JUST A ONE-OFF, BUT STEADY WORK! IT WAS A REAL OPPPORTUNITY.
IT'S THE... I LOVE LUCY SHOW!
DESILU STUDIOS WAS OWNED BY LUCILLE BALL AND DESI ARNAZ.
VITAMEATAVEGAMIN
TWO ACTORS THAT ONCE WORKED ON THIS VERY LOT AS HIRED TALENT...
...ONE AN IMMIGRANT FROM CUBA...
...NOW OWNED THE WHOLE THING.
ROSENBURY?
I HOPE THIS IS IT!
I KNEW THAT ANYTHING COULD HAPPEN IN THIS UNPREDICTABLE BUSINESS.
23 B

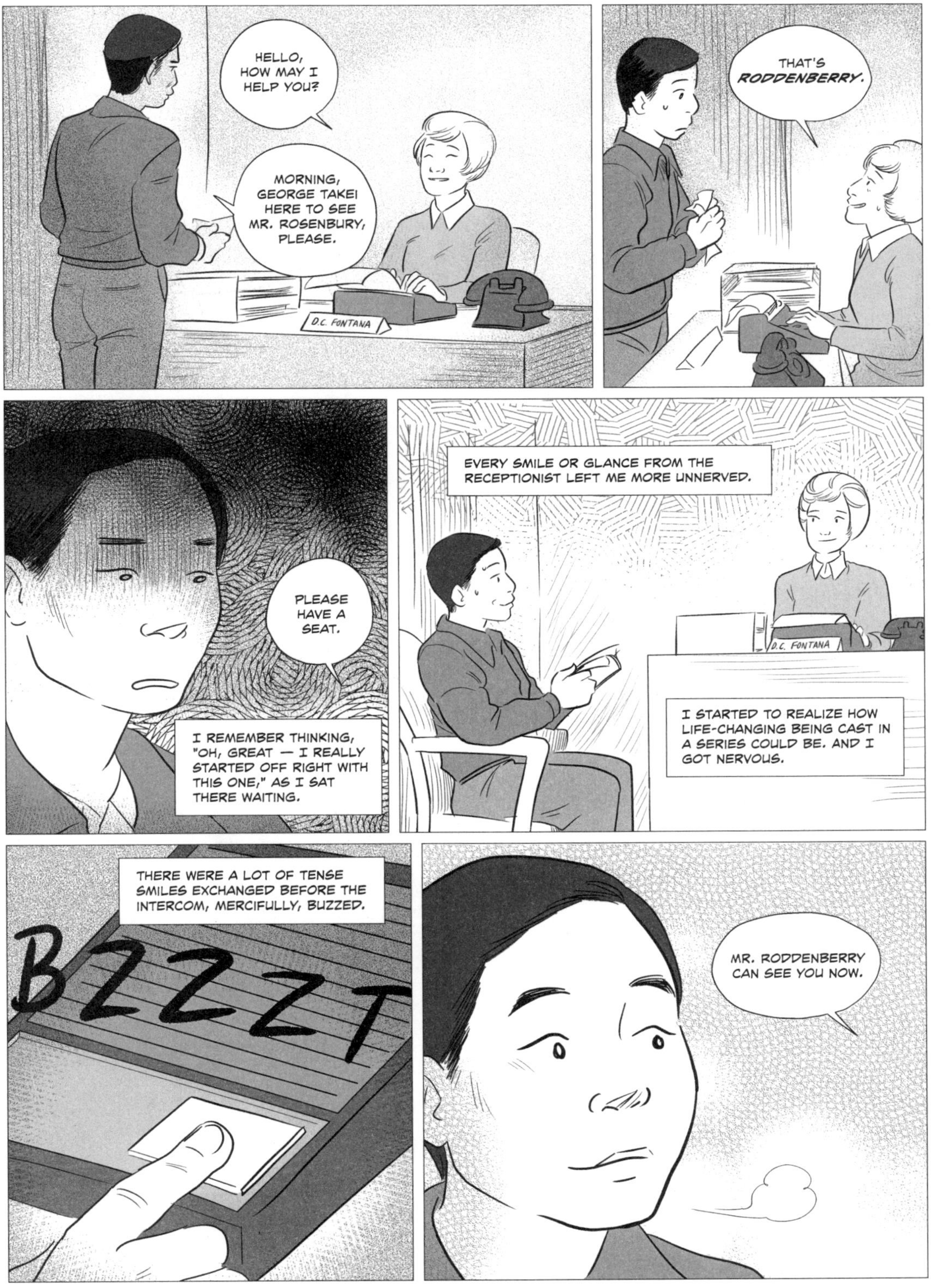
HELLO, HOW MAY I HELP YOU?
MORNING, GEORGE TAKEI HERE TO SEE MR. ROSENBURY, PLEASE.
D.C. FONTANA
THAT'S *RODDENBERRY.*
PLEASE HAVE A SEAT.
I REMEMBER THINKING, "OH, GREAT — I REALLY STARTED OFF RIGHT WITH THIS ONE," AS I SAT THERE WAITING.
EVERY SMILE OR GLANCE FROM THE RECEPTIONIST LEFT ME MORE UNNERVED.
D.C. FONTANA
I STARTED TO REALIZE HOW LIFE-CHANGING BEING CAST IN A SERIES COULD BE. AND I GOT NERVOUS.
THERE WERE A LOT OF TENSE SMILES EXCHANGED BEFORE THE INTERCOM, MERCIFULLY, BUZZED.
BZZZT
MR. RODDENBERRY CAN SEE YOU NOW.

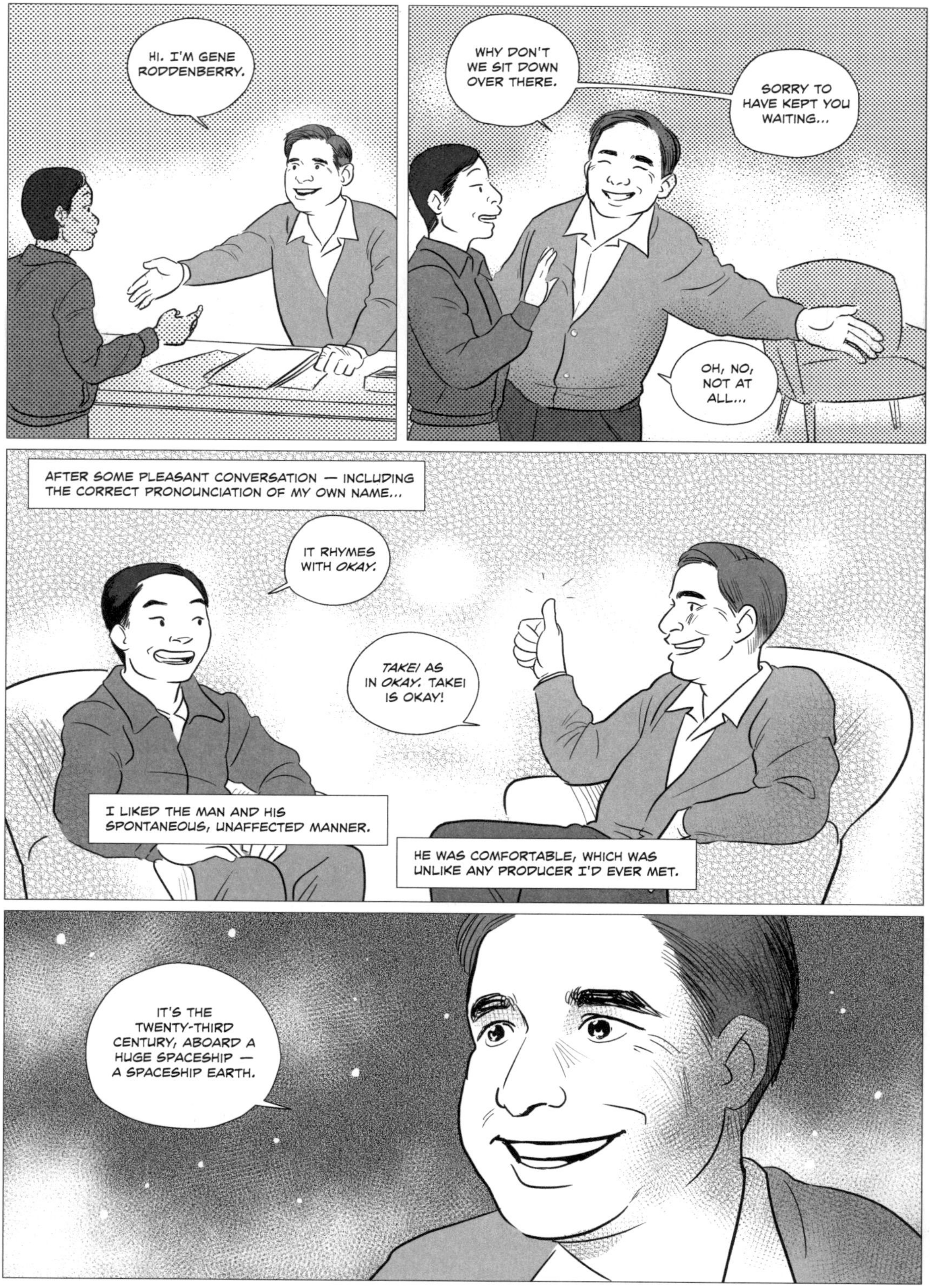
HI. I'M GENE RODDENBERRY.
WHY DON'T WE SIT DOWN OVER THERE.
SORRY TO HAVE KEPT YOU WAITING...
OH, NO, NOT AT ALL...
AFTER SOME PLEASANT CONVERSATION — INCLUDING THE CORRECT PRONOUNCIATION OF MY OWN NAME...
IT RHYMES WITH *OKAY.*
TAKEI AS IN *OKAY.* TAKEI IS OKAY!
I LIKED THE MAN AND HIS SPONTANEOUS, UNAFFECTED MANNER.
HE WAS COMFORTABLE, WHICH WAS UNLIKE ANY PRODUCER I'D EVER MET.
IT'S THE TWENTY-THIRD CENTURY, ABOARD A HUGE SPACESHIP — A SPACESHIP EARTH.

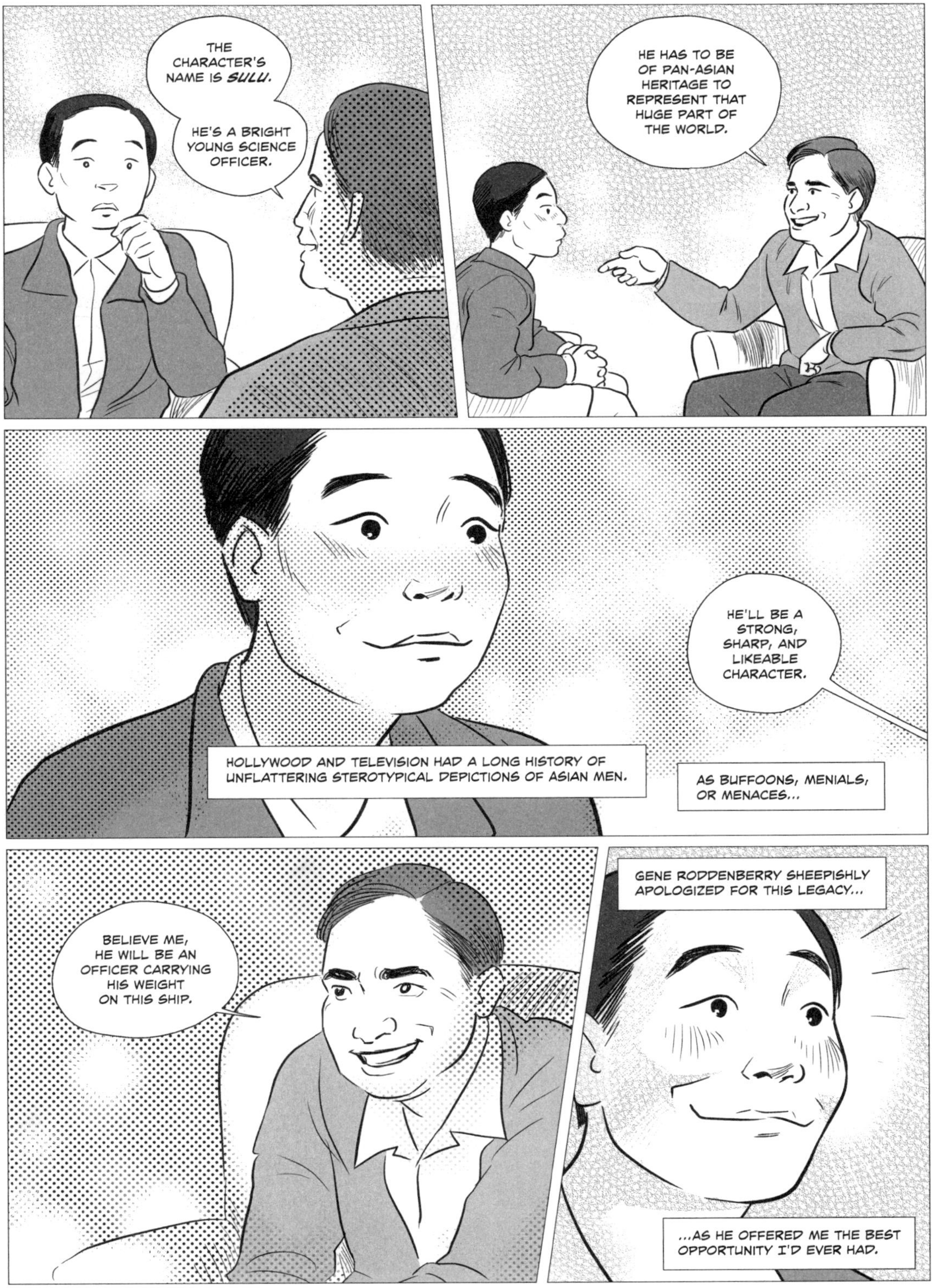

THE CHARACTER'S NAME IS SULU.
HE'S A BRIGHT YOUNG SCIENCE OFFICER.
HE HAS TO BE OF PAN-ASIAN HERITAGE TO REPRESENT THAT HUGE PART OF THE WORLD.
HE'LL BE A STRONG, SHARP, AND LIKEABLE CHARACTER.
HOLLYWOOD AND TELEVISION HAD A LONG HISTORY OF UNFLATTERING STEROTYPICAL DEPICTIONS OF ASIAN MEN.
AS BUFFOONS, MENIALS, OR MENACES...
BELIEVE ME, HE WILL BE AN OFFICER CARRYING HIS WEIGHT ON THIS SHIP.
GENE RODDENBERRY SHEEPISHLY APOLOGIZED FOR THIS LEGACY...
...AS HE OFFERED ME THE BEST OPPORTUNITY I'D EVER HAD.

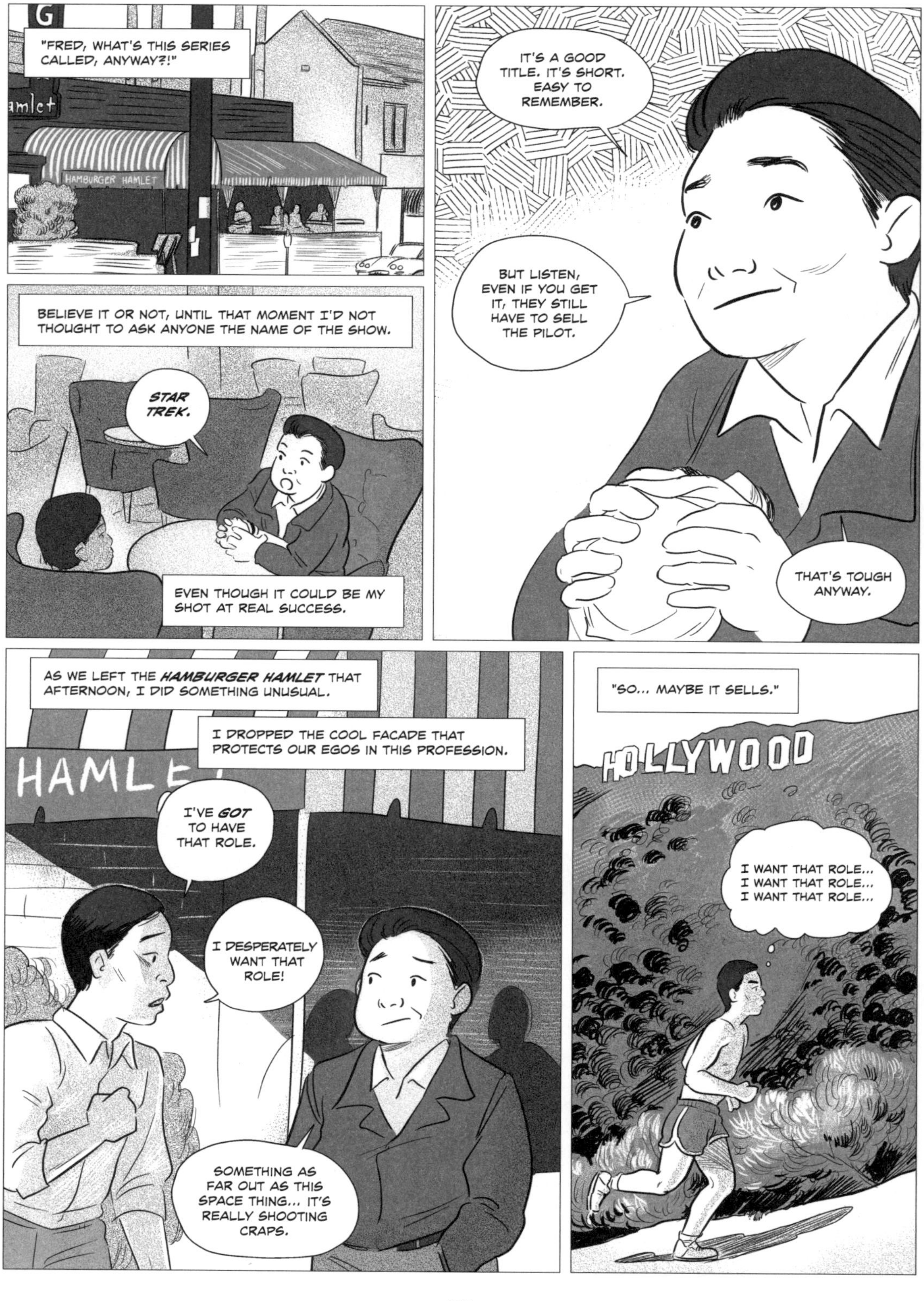
G
"FRED, WHAT'S THIS SERIES CALLED, ANYWAY?!"
amlet
HAMBURGER HAMLET
IT'S A GOOD TITLE. IT'S SHORT. EASY TO REMEMBER.
BUT LISTEN, EVEN IF YOU GET IT, THEY STILL HAVE TO SELL THE PILOT.
BELIEVE IT OR NOT, UNTIL THAT MOMENT I'D NOT THOUGHT TO ASK ANYONE THE NAME OF THE SHOW.
STAR TREK.
EVEN THOUGH IT COULD BE MY SHOT AT REAL SUCCESS.
THAT'S TOUGH ANYWAY.
AS WE LEFT THE HAMBURGER HAMLET THAT AFTERNOON, I DID SOMETHING UNUSUAL.
I DROPPED THE COOL FACADE THAT PROTECTS OUR EGOS IN THIS PROFESSION.
HAMLE
I'VE GOT TO HAVE THAT ROLE.
I DESPERATELY WANT THAT ROLE!
SOMETHING AS FAR OUT AS THIS SPACE THING... IT'S REALLY SHOOTING CRAPS.
"SO... MAYBE IT SELLS."
HOLLYWOOD
I WANT THAT ROLE... I WANT THAT ROLE... I WANT THAT ROLE...

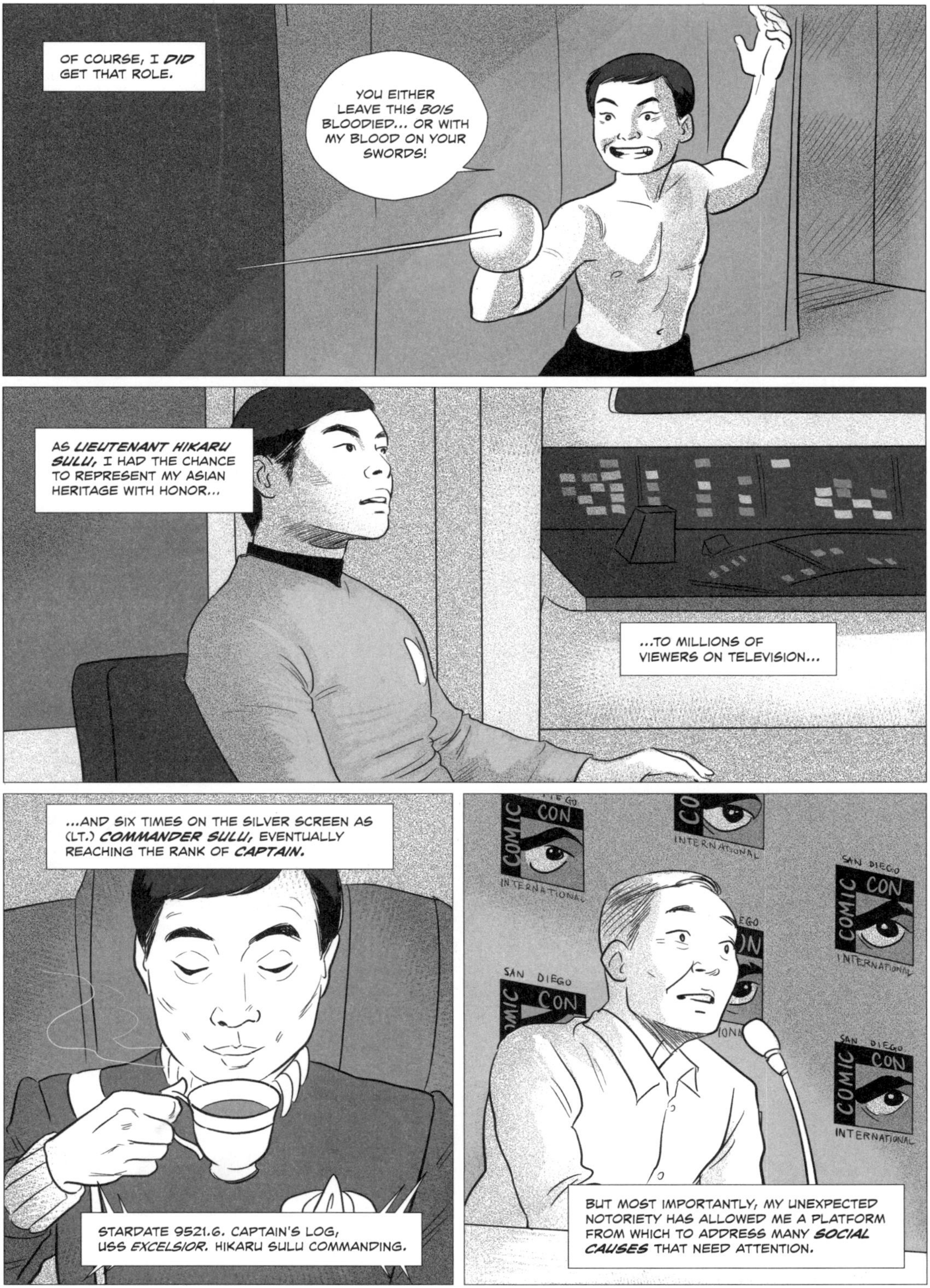
OF COURSE, I *DID* GET THAT ROLE.
YOU EITHER LEAVE THIS *BOIS* BLOODIED... OR WITH MY BLOOD ON YOUR SWORDS!
AS *LIEUTENANT HIKARU SULU,* I HAD THE CHANCE TO REPRESENT MY ASIAN HERITAGE WITH HONOR...
...TO MILLIONS OF VIEWERS ON TELEVISION...
...AND SIX TIMES ON THE SILVER SCREEN AS (LT.) ***COMMANDER SULU,*** EVENTUALLY REACHING THE RANK OF ***CAPTAIN.***
STARDATE 9521.6. CAPTAIN'S LOG, USS *EXCELSIOR.* HIKARU SULU COMMANDING.
SAN DIEGO COMIC CON INTERNATIONAL
BUT MOST IMPORTANTLY, MY UNEXPECTED NOTORIETY HAS ALLOWED ME A PLATFORM FROM WHICH TO ADDRESS MANY ***SOCIAL CAUSES*** THAT NEED ATTENTION.

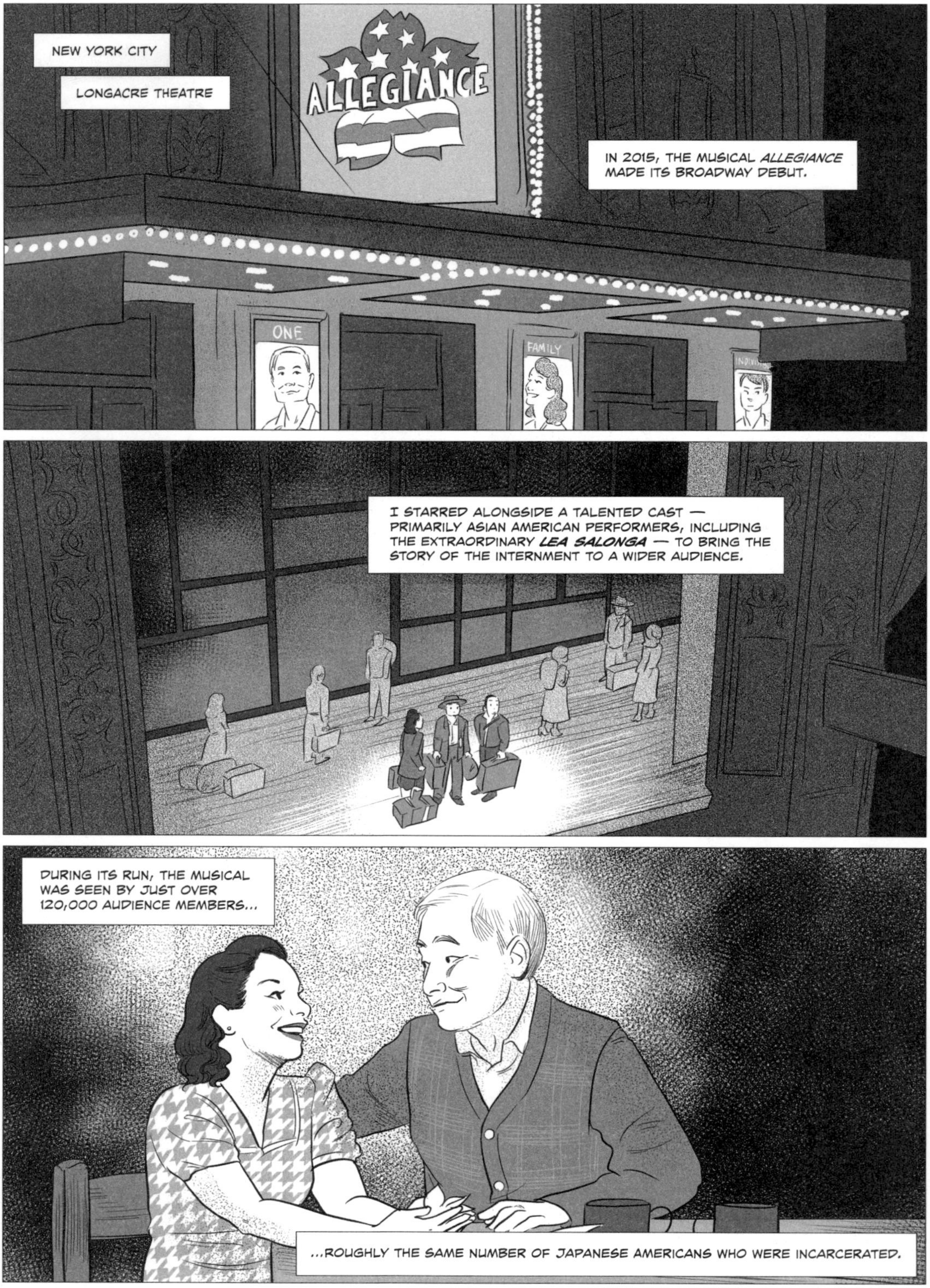
NEW YORK CITY
LONGACRE THEATRE
ALLEGIANCE
IN 2015, THE MUSICAL *ALLEGIANCE* MADE ITS BROADWAY DEBUT.
ONE
FAMILY
I STARRED ALONGSIDE A TALENTED CAST — PRIMARILY ASIAN AMERICAN PERFORMERS, INCLUDING THE EXTRAORDINARY ***LEA SALONGA*** — TO BRING THE STORY OF THE INTERNMENT TO A WIDER AUDIENCE.
DURING ITS RUN, THE MUSICAL WAS SEEN BY JUST OVER 120,000 AUDIENCE MEMBERS...
...ROUGHLY THE SAME NUMBER OF JAPANESE AMERICANS WHO WERE INCARCERATED.

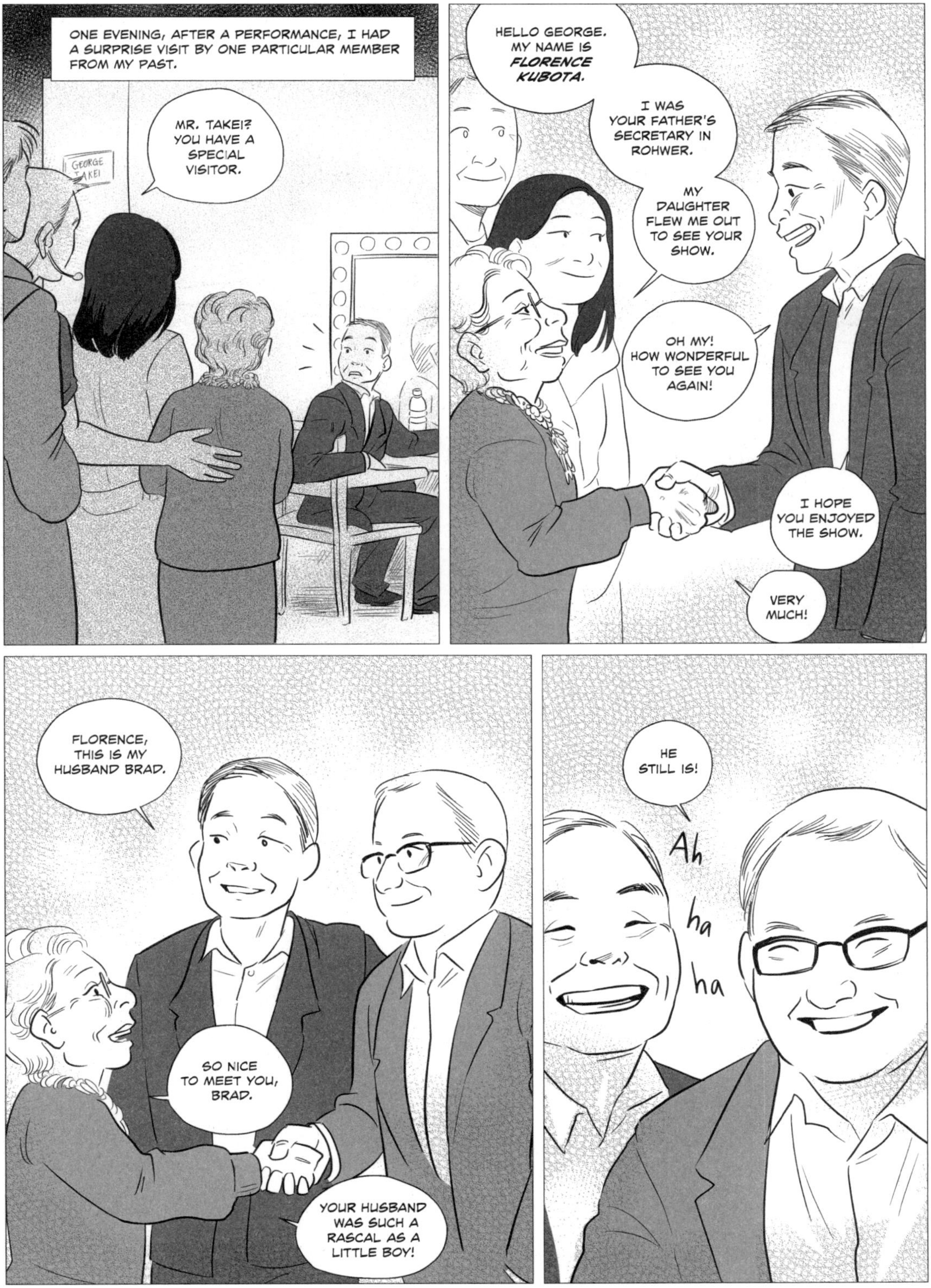
ONE EVENING, AFTER A PERFORMANCE, I HAD A SURPRISE VISIT BY ONE PARTICULAR MEMBER FROM MY PAST.
GEORGE TAKEI
MR. TAKEI? YOU HAVE A SPECIAL VISITOR.
HELLO GEORGE. MY NAME IS ***FLORENCE KUBOTA.***
I WAS YOUR FATHER'S SECRETARY IN ROHWER.
MY DAUGHTER FLEW ME OUT TO SEE YOUR SHOW.
OH MY! HOW WONDERFUL TO SEE YOU AGAIN!
I HOPE YOU ENJOYED THE SHOW.
VERY MUCH!
FLORENCE, THIS IS MY HUSBAND BRAD.
SO NICE TO MEET YOU, BRAD.
YOUR HUSBAND WAS SUCH A RASCAL AS A LITTLE BOY!
HE STILL IS!
Ah ha ha

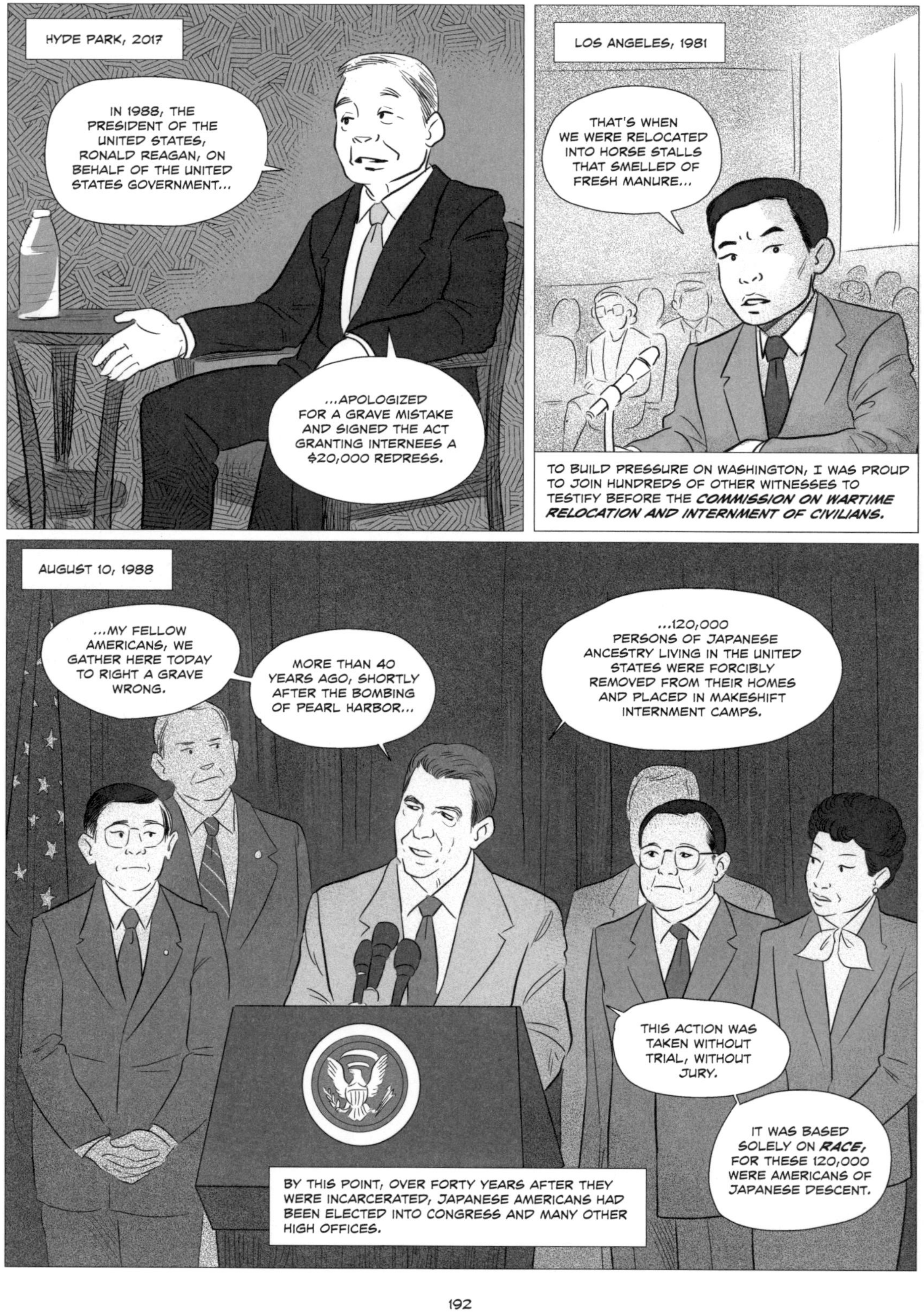
HYDE PARK, 2017
IN 1988, THE PRESIDENT OF THE UNITED STATES, RONALD REAGAN, ON BEHALF OF THE UNITED STATES GOVERNMENT...
...APOLOGIZED FOR A GRAVE MISTAKE AND SIGNED THE ACT GRANTING INTERNEES A $20,000 REDRESS.
LOS ANGELES, 1981
THAT'S WHEN WE WERE RELOCATED INTO HORSE STALLS THAT SMELLED OF FRESH MANURE...
TO BUILD PRESSURE ON WASHINGTON, I WAS PROUD TO JOIN HUNDREDS OF OTHER WITNESSES TO TESTIFY BEFORE THE ***COMMISSION ON WARTIME RELOCATION AND INTERNMENT OF CIVILIANS.***
AUGUST 10, 1988
...MY FELLOW AMERICANS, WE GATHER HERE TODAY TO RIGHT A GRAVE WRONG.
MORE THAN 40 YEARS AGO, SHORTLY AFTER THE BOMBING OF PEARL HARBOR...
...120,000 PERSONS OF JAPANESE ANCESTRY LIVING IN THE UNITED STATES WERE FORCIBLY REMOVED FROM THEIR HOMES AND PLACED IN MAKESHIFT INTERNMENT CAMPS.
THIS ACTION WAS TAKEN WITHOUT TRIAL, WITHOUT JURY.
IT WAS BASED SOLELY ON ***RACE,*** FOR THESE 120,000 WERE AMERICANS OF JAPANESE DESCENT.
BY THIS POINT, OVER FORTY YEARS AFTER THEY WERE INCARCERATED, JAPANESE AMERICANS HAD BEEN ELECTED INTO CONGRESS AND MANY OTHER HIGH OFFICES.

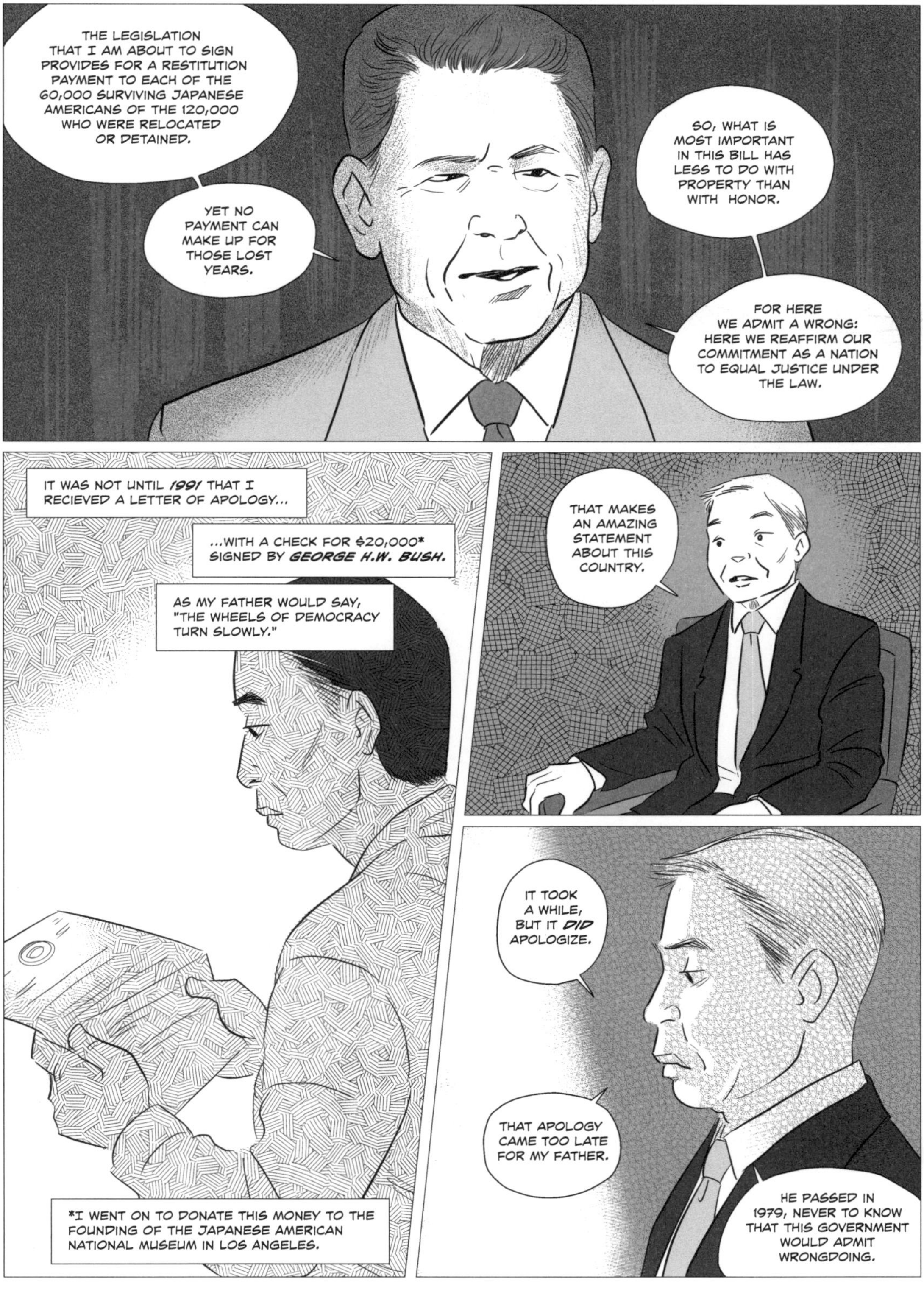
THE LEGISLATION THAT I AM ABOUT TO SIGN PROVIDES FOR A RESTITUTION PAYMENT TO EACH OF THE 60,000 SURVIVING JAPANESE AMERICANS OF THE 120,000 WHO WERE RELOCATED OR DETAINED.
YET NO PAYMENT CAN MAKE UP FOR THOSE LOST YEARS.
SO, WHAT IS MOST IMPORTANT IN THIS BILL HAS LESS TO DO WITH PROPERTY THAN WITH HONOR.
FOR HERE WE ADMIT A WRONG: HERE WE REAFFIRM OUR COMMITMENT AS A NATION TO EQUAL JUSTICE UNDER THE LAW.
IT WAS NOT UNTIL 1991 THAT I RECIEVED A LETTER OF APOLOGY...
...WITH A CHECK FOR $20,000* SIGNED BY GEORGE H.W. BUSH.
AS MY FATHER WOULD SAY, "THE WHEELS OF DEMOCRACY TURN SLOWLY."
*I WENT ON TO DONATE THIS MONEY TO THE FOUNDING OF THE JAPANESE AMERICAN NATIONAL MUSEUM IN LOS ANGELES.
THAT MAKES AN AMAZING STATEMENT ABOUT THIS COUNTRY.
IT TOOK A WHILE, BUT IT DID APOLOGIZE.
THAT APOLOGY CAME TOO LATE FOR MY FATHER.
HE PASSED IN 1979, NEVER TO KNOW THAT THIS GOVERNMENT WOULD ADMIT WRONGDOING.

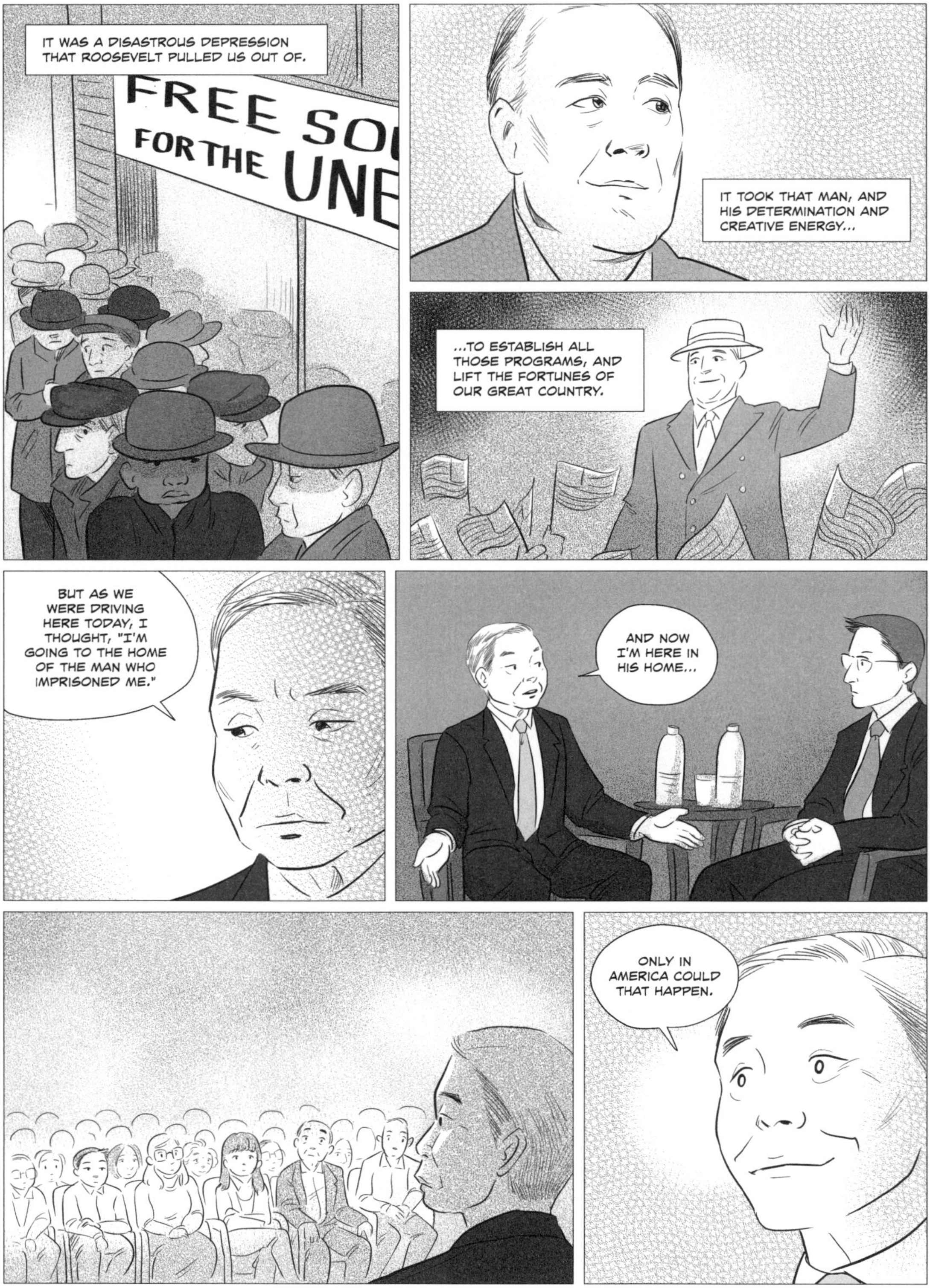
IT WAS A DISASTROUS DEPRESSION THAT ROOSEVELT PULLED US OUT OF.
FREE SOU
FOR THE UNE
IT TOOK THAT MAN, AND HIS DETERMINATION AND CREATIVE ENERGY...
...TO ESTABLISH ALL THOSE PROGRAMS, AND LIFT THE FORTUNES OF OUR GREAT COUNTRY.
BUT AS WE WERE DRIVING HERE TODAY, I THOUGHT, "I'M GOING TO THE HOME OF THE MAN WHO IMPRISONED ME."
AND NOW I'M HERE IN HIS HOME...
ONLY IN AMERICA COULD THAT HAPPEN.

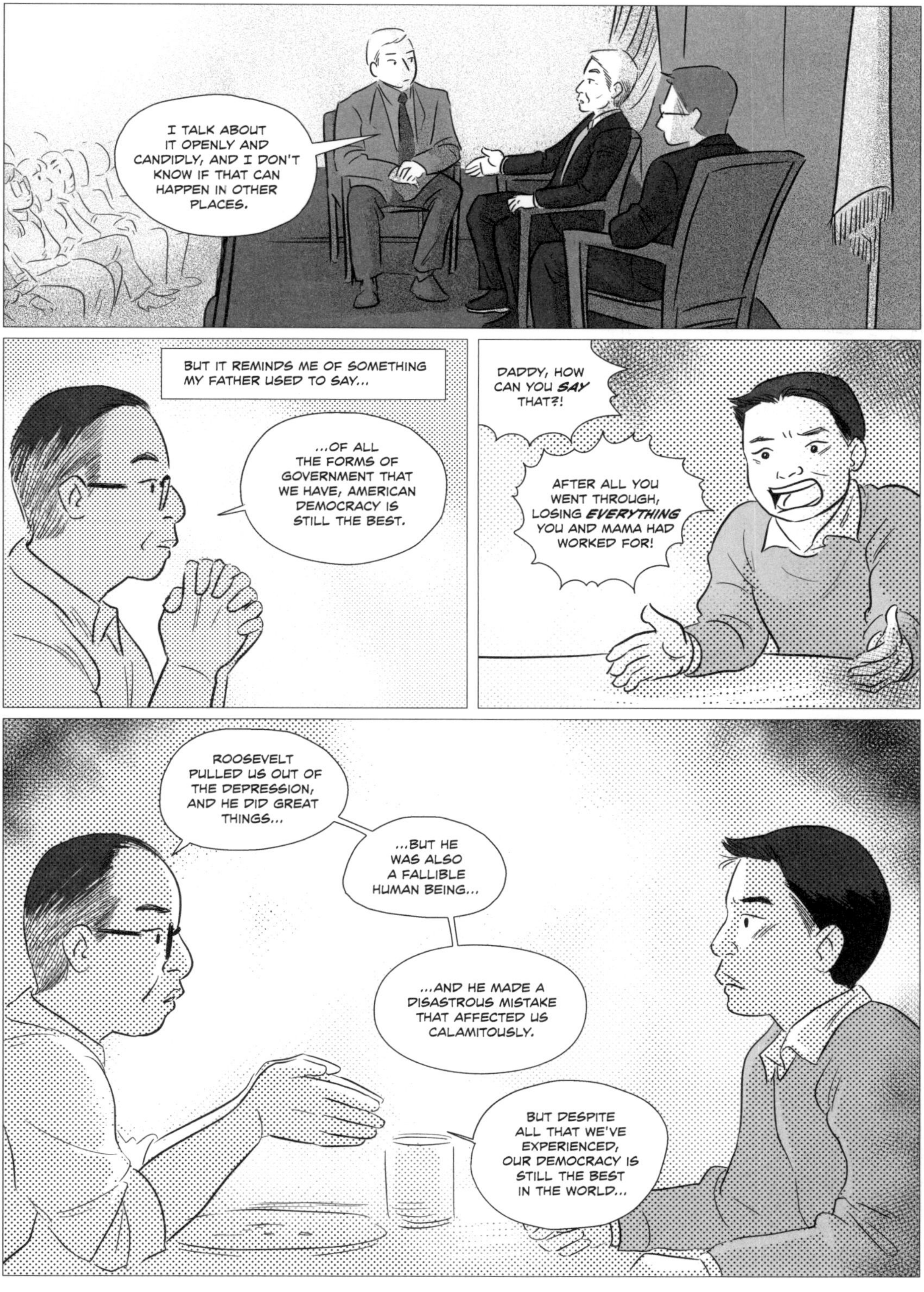
I TALK ABOUT IT OPENLY AND CANDIDLY, AND I DON'T KNOW IF THAT CAN HAPPEN IN OTHER PLACES.
BUT IT REMINDS ME OF SOMETHING MY FATHER USED TO SAY...
...OF ALL THE FORMS OF GOVERNMENT THAT WE HAVE, AMERICAN DEMOCRACY IS STILL THE BEST.
DADDY, HOW CAN YOU *SAY* THAT?!
AFTER ALL YOU WENT THROUGH, LOSING *EVERYTHING* YOU AND MAMA HAD WORKED FOR!
ROOSEVELT PULLED US OUT OF THE DEPRESSION, AND HE DID GREAT THINGS...
...BUT HE WAS ALSO A FALLIBLE HUMAN BEING...
...AND HE MADE A DISASTROUS MISTAKE THAT AFFECTED US CALAMITOUSLY.
BUT DESPITE ALL THAT WE'VE EXPERIENCED, OUR DEMOCRACY IS STILL THE BEST IN THE WORLD...

...BECAUSE IT'S A *PEOPLE'S* DEMOCRACY...

we shall overco~oommee

...AND THE PEOPLE CAN DO GREAT THINGS.

THINKING ABOUT IT NOW...

GEORGE TAKEI — CITY COUNCIL DISTRICT

...IT WAS THOSE AFTER-DINNER TALKS WITH MY FATHER THAT INFORMED SO MUCH OF MY WORLDVIEW...

TOGETHER WE CAN INITIATE *CHANGE* IN LOS ANGELES.

GEORGE

GEORGE TAKEI — CITY COUNCIL, 10th DISTRICT

...AND INSTILLED IN ME A DESIRE TO SHARE OUR STORY WITH AS MANY PEOPLE AS POSSIBLE.

YOU'RE AFFILIATED WITH THE JAPANESE AMERICAN NATIONAL MUSEUM.

YOU AND YOUR FAMILY WERE, IN FACT, IN ONE OF THE INTERNMENT CAMPS DURING THE SECOND WORLD WAR.

SCOTT SIMON, NPR'S *WEEKEND EDITION*

AS A MATTER OF FACT, *TWO* OF THEM.

AND I WENT TO SCHOOL IN A BLACK TARPAPER BARRACK AND BEGAN THE DAY SEEING THE BARBED-WIRE FENCE.

AND THANK GOD THOSE BARBED-WIRE FENCES ARE NOW LONG GONE FOR JAPANESE AMERICANS.

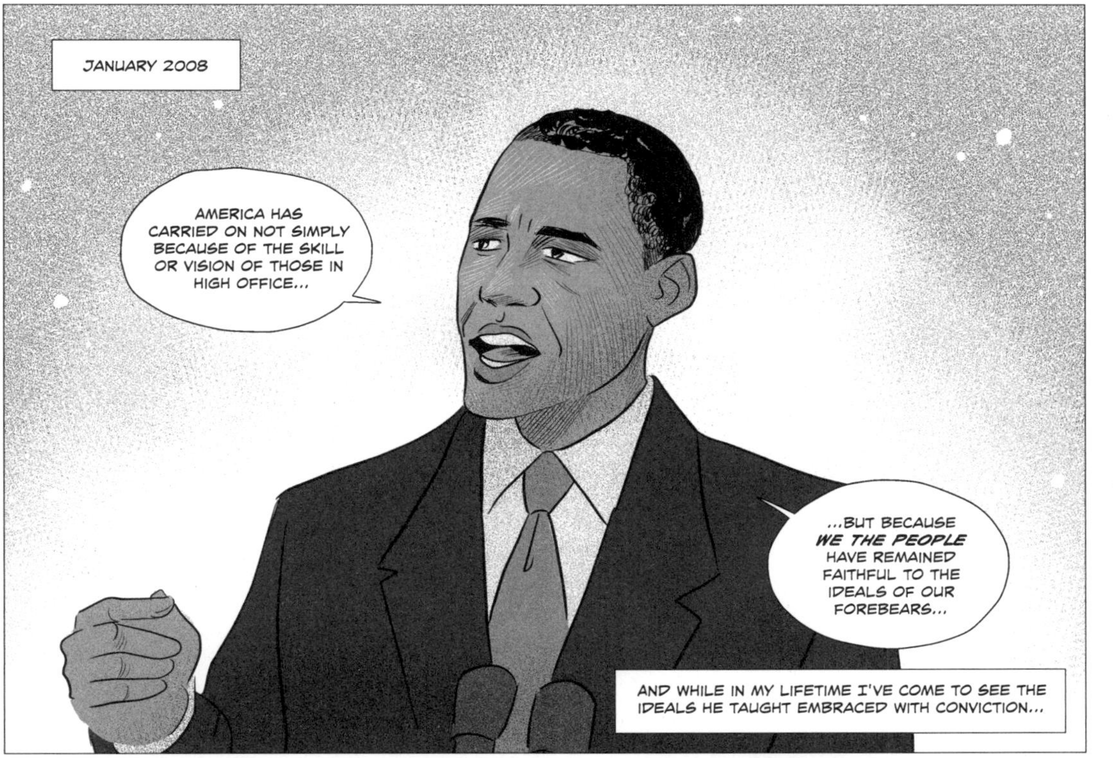
JANUARY 2008
AMERICA HAS CARRIED ON NOT SIMPLY BECAUSE OF THE SKILL OR VISION OF THOSE IN HIGH OFFICE...
...BUT BECAUSE *WE THE PEOPLE* HAVE REMAINED FAITHFUL TO THE IDEALS OF OUR FOREBEARS...
AND WHILE IN MY LIFETIME I'VE COME TO SEE THE IDEALS HE TAUGHT EMBRACED WITH CONVICTION...

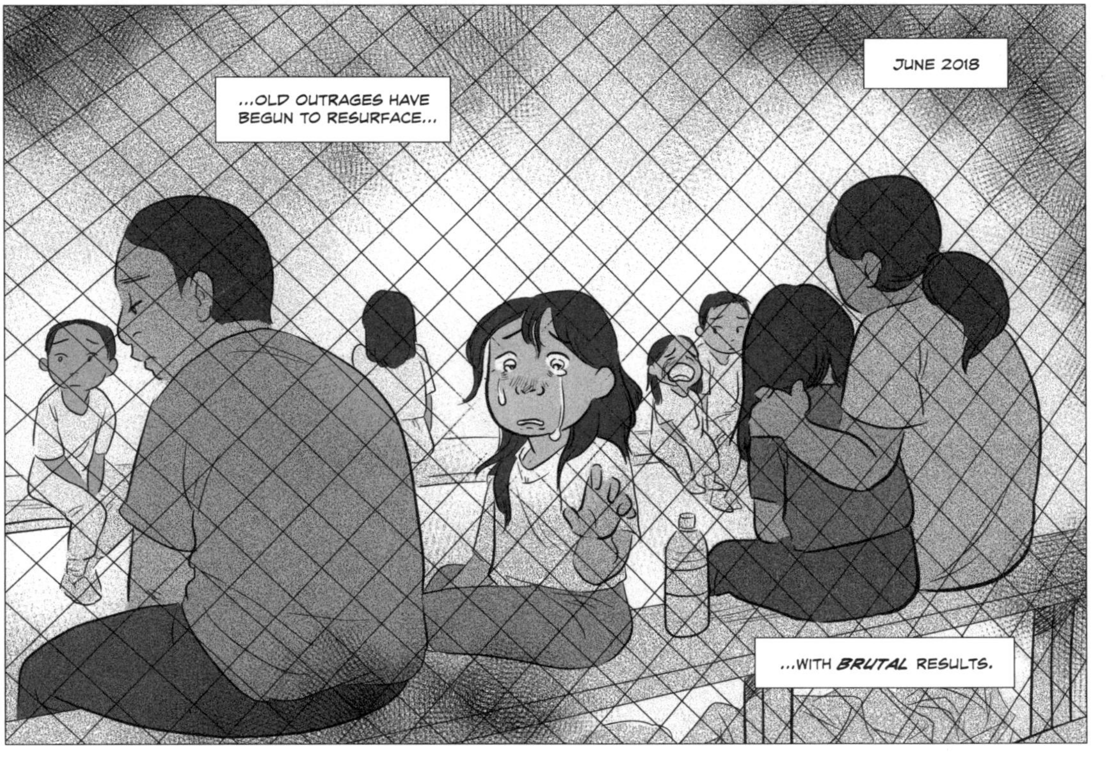
JUNE 2018
...OLD OUTRAGES HAVE BEGUN TO RESURFACE...
...WITH *BRUTAL* RESULTS.

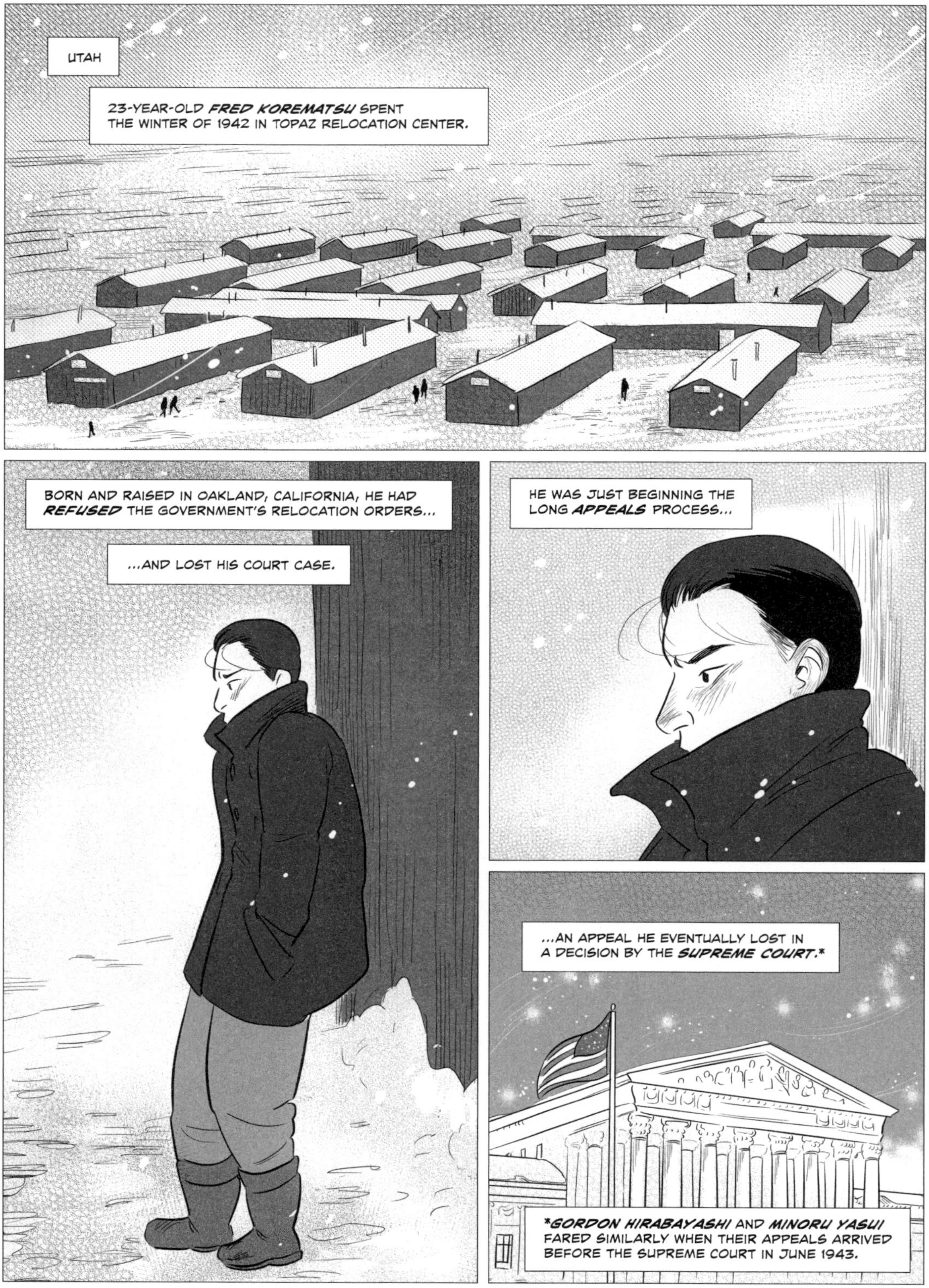
UTAH
23-YEAR-OLD FRED KOREMATSU SPENT THE WINTER OF 1942 IN TOPAZ RELOCATION CENTER.
BORN AND RAISED IN OAKLAND, CALIFORNIA, HE HAD REFUSED THE GOVERNMENT'S RELOCATION ORDERS...
...AND LOST HIS COURT CASE.
HE WAS JUST BEGINNING THE LONG APPEALS PROCESS...
...AN APPEAL HE EVENTUALLY LOST IN A DECISION BY THE SUPREME COURT.*
*GORDON HIRABAYASHI AND MINORU YASUI FARED SIMILARLY WHEN THEIR APPEALS ARRIVED BEFORE THE SUPREME COURT IN JUNE 1943.

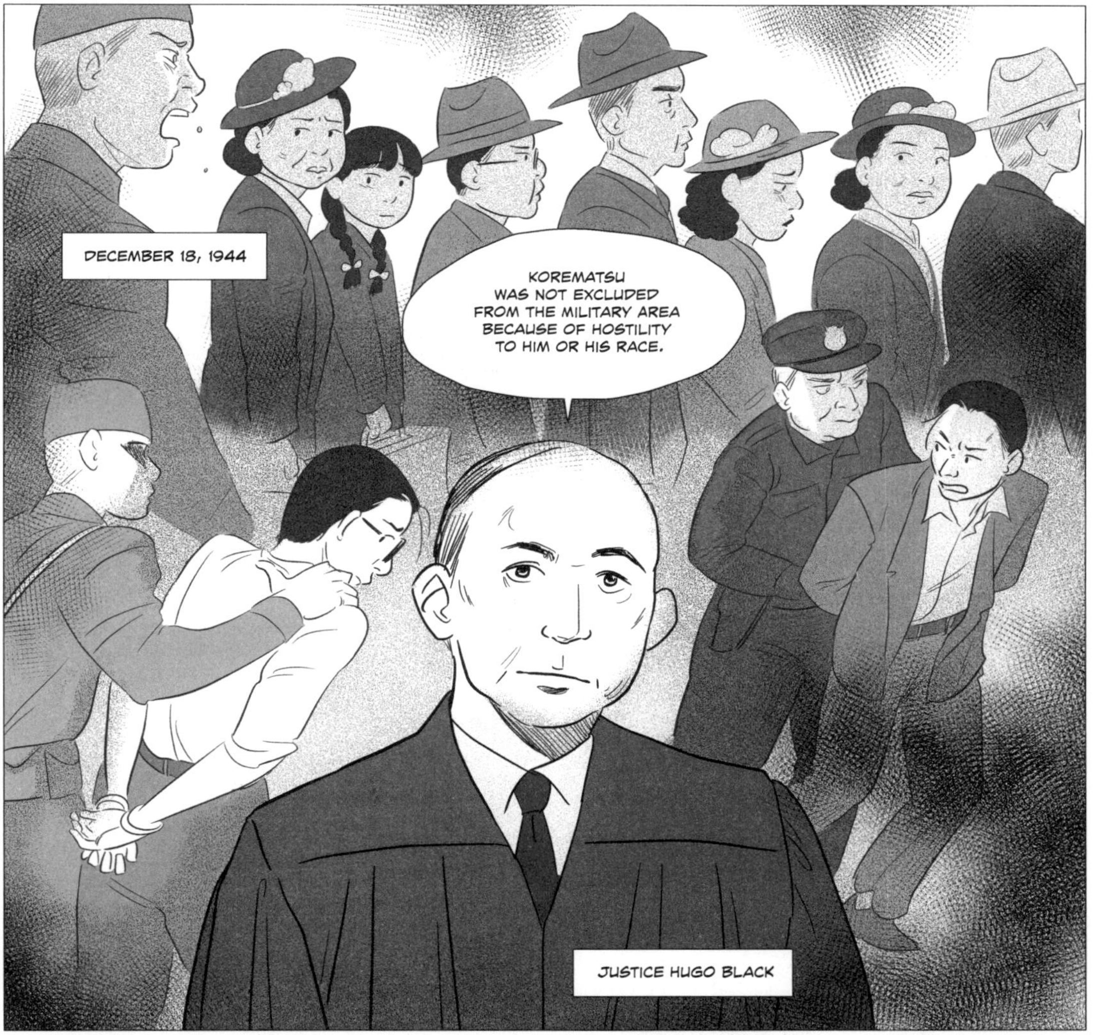
DECEMBER 18, 1944
KOREMATSU WAS NOT EXCLUDED FROM THE MILITARY AREA BECAUSE OF HOSTILITY TO HIM OR HIS RACE.
JUSTICE HUGO BLACK

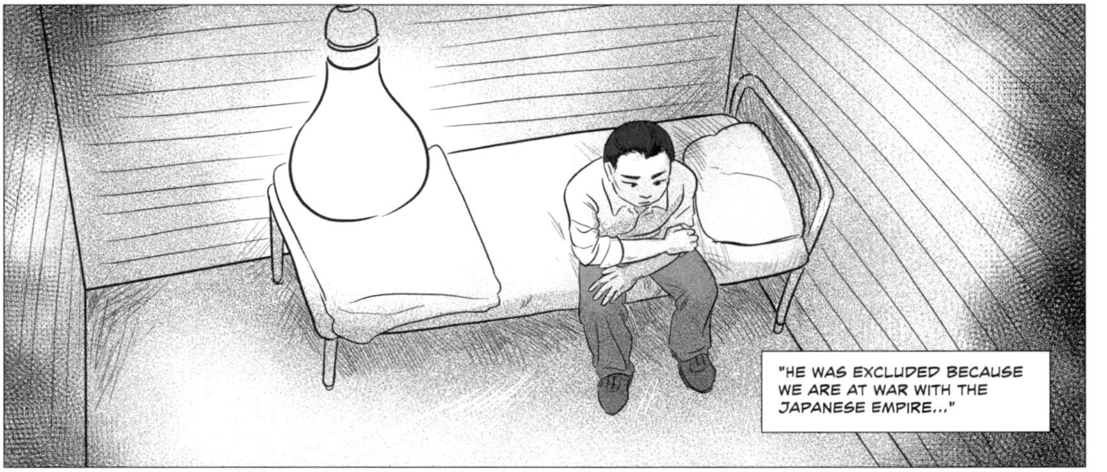
"HE WAS EXCLUDED BECAUSE WE ARE AT WAR WITH THE JAPANESE EMPIRE..."

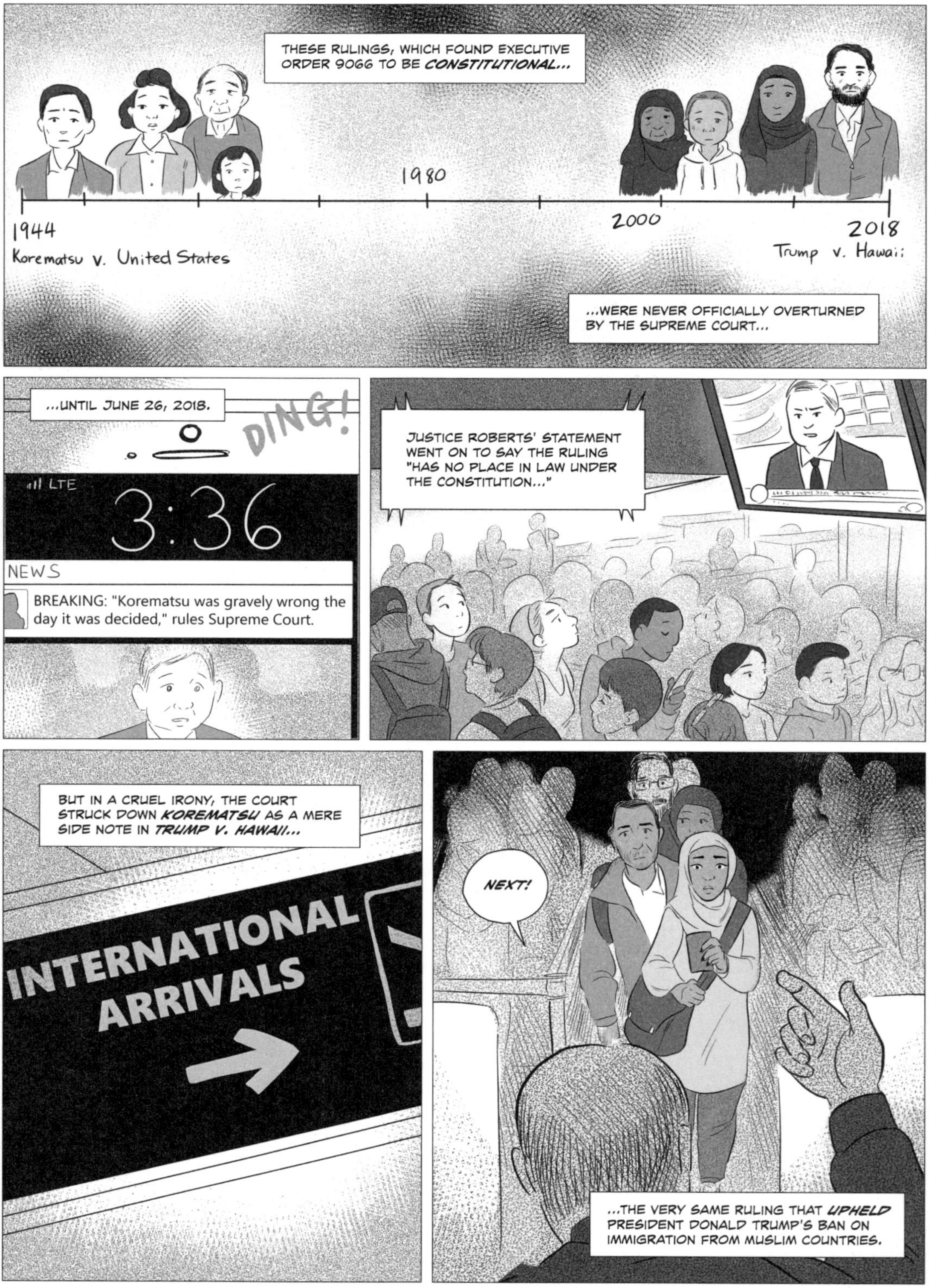
THESE RULINGS, WHICH FOUND EXECUTIVE ORDER 9066 TO BE *CONSTITUTIONAL*...
1944
Korematsu v. United States
1980
2000
2018
Trump v. Hawaii
...WERE NEVER OFFICIALLY OVERTURNED BY THE SUPREME COURT...
...UNTIL JUNE 26, 2018.
DING!
LTE
3:36
NEWS
BREAKING: "Korematsu was gravely wrong the day it was decided," rules Supreme Court.
JUSTICE ROBERTS' STATEMENT WENT ON TO SAY THE RULING "HAS NO PLACE IN LAW UNDER THE CONSTITUTION..."
BUT IN A CRUEL IRONY, THE COURT STRUCK DOWN *KOREMATSU* AS A MERE SIDE NOTE IN *TRUMP V. HAWAII*...
INTERNATIONAL ARRIVALS
NEXT!
...THE VERY SAME RULING THAT *UPHELD* PRESIDENT DONALD TRUMP'S BAN ON IMMIGRATION FROM MUSLIM COUNTRIES.

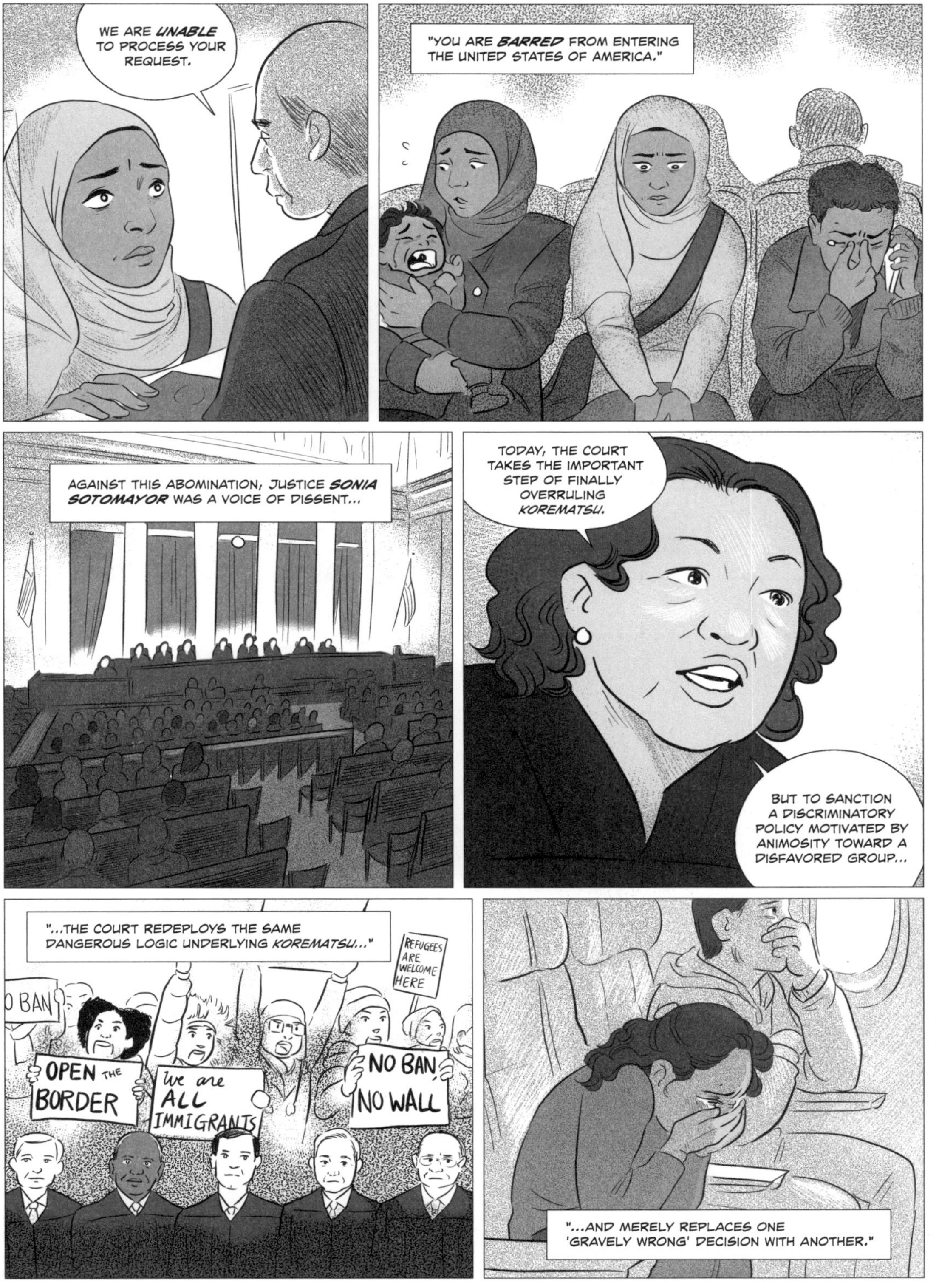
WE ARE *UNABLE* TO PROCESS YOUR REQUEST.
"YOU ARE *BARRED* FROM ENTERING THE UNITED STATES OF AMERICA."
AGAINST THIS ABOMINATION, JUSTICE *SONIA SOTOMAYOR* WAS A VOICE OF DISSENT...
TODAY, THE COURT TAKES THE IMPORTANT STEP OF FINALLY OVERRULING *KOREMATSU*.
BUT TO SANCTION A DISCRIMINATORY POLICY MOTIVATED BY ANIMOSITY TOWARD A DISFAVORED GROUP...
"...THE COURT REDEPLOYS THE SAME DANGEROUS LOGIC UNDERLYING *KOREMATSU*..."
REFUGEES ARE WELCOME HERE
O BAN
OPEN THE BORDER
We are ALL IMMIGRANTS
NO BAN, NO WALL
"...AND MERELY REPLACES ONE 'GRAVELY WRONG' DECISION WITH ANOTHER."

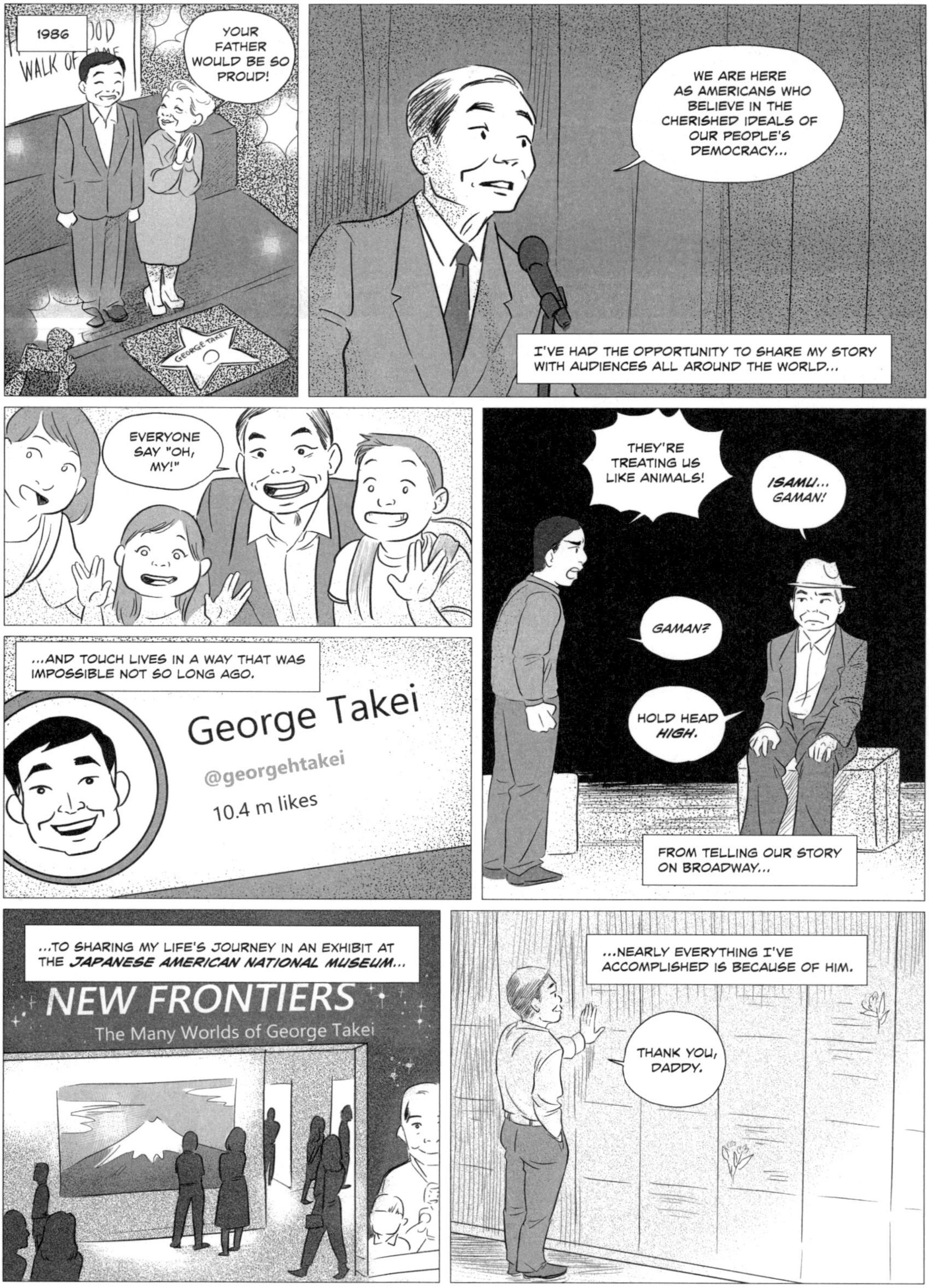
1986
WALK OF
YOUR FATHER WOULD BE SO PROUD!
GEORGE TAKEI
WE ARE HERE AS AMERICANS WHO BELIEVE IN THE CHERISHED IDEALS OF OUR PEOPLE'S DEMOCRACY...
I'VE HAD THE OPPORTUNITY TO SHARE MY STORY WITH AUDIENCES ALL AROUND THE WORLD...
EVERYONE SAY "OH, MY!"
...AND TOUCH LIVES IN A WAY THAT WAS IMPOSSIBLE NOT SO LONG AGO.
George Takei
@georgehtakei
10.4 m likes
THEY'RE TREATING US LIKE ANIMALS!
ISAMU... GAMAN!
GAMAN?
HOLD HEAD HIGH.
FROM TELLING OUR STORY ON BROADWAY...
...TO SHARING MY LIFE'S JOURNEY IN AN EXHIBIT AT THE JAPANESE AMERICAN NATIONAL MUSEUM...
NEW FRONTIERS
The Many Worlds of George Takei
...NEARLY EVERYTHING I'VE ACCOMPLISHED IS BECAUSE OF HIM.
THANK YOU, DADDY.

EPILOGUE

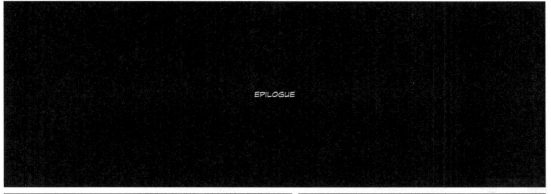

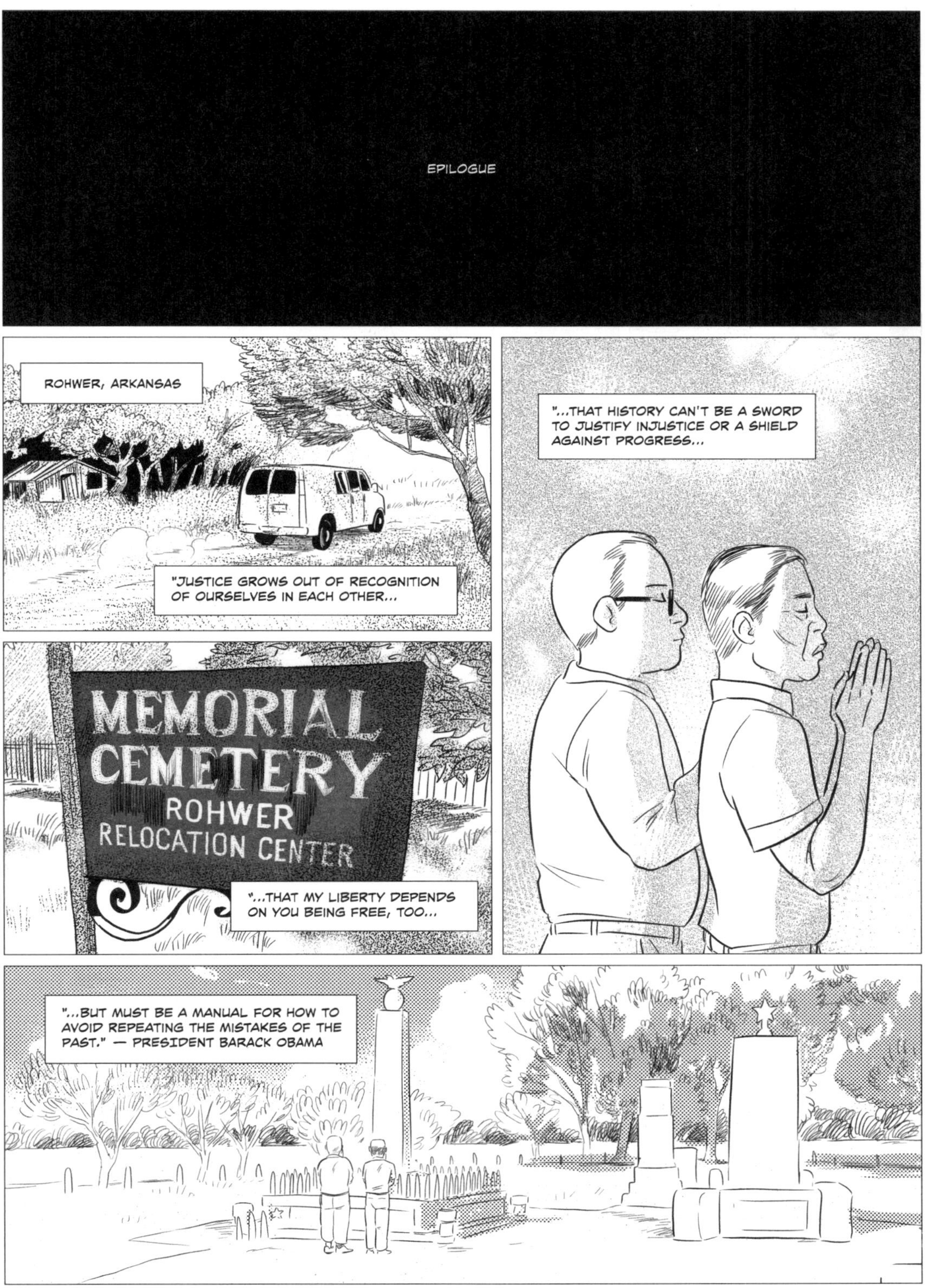
ROHWER, ARKANSAS
"JUSTICE GROWS OUT OF RECOGNITION OF OURSELVES IN EACH OTHER...
MEMORIAL CEMETERY ROHWER RELOCATION CENTER
"...THAT MY LIBERTY DEPENDS ON YOU BEING FREE, TOO...
"...THAT HISTORY CAN'T BE A SWORD TO JUSTIFY INJUSTICE OR A SHIELD AGAINST PROGRESS...
"...BUT MUST BE A MANUAL FOR HOW TO AVOID REPEATING THE MISTAKES OF THE PAST." — PRESIDENT BARACK OBAMA

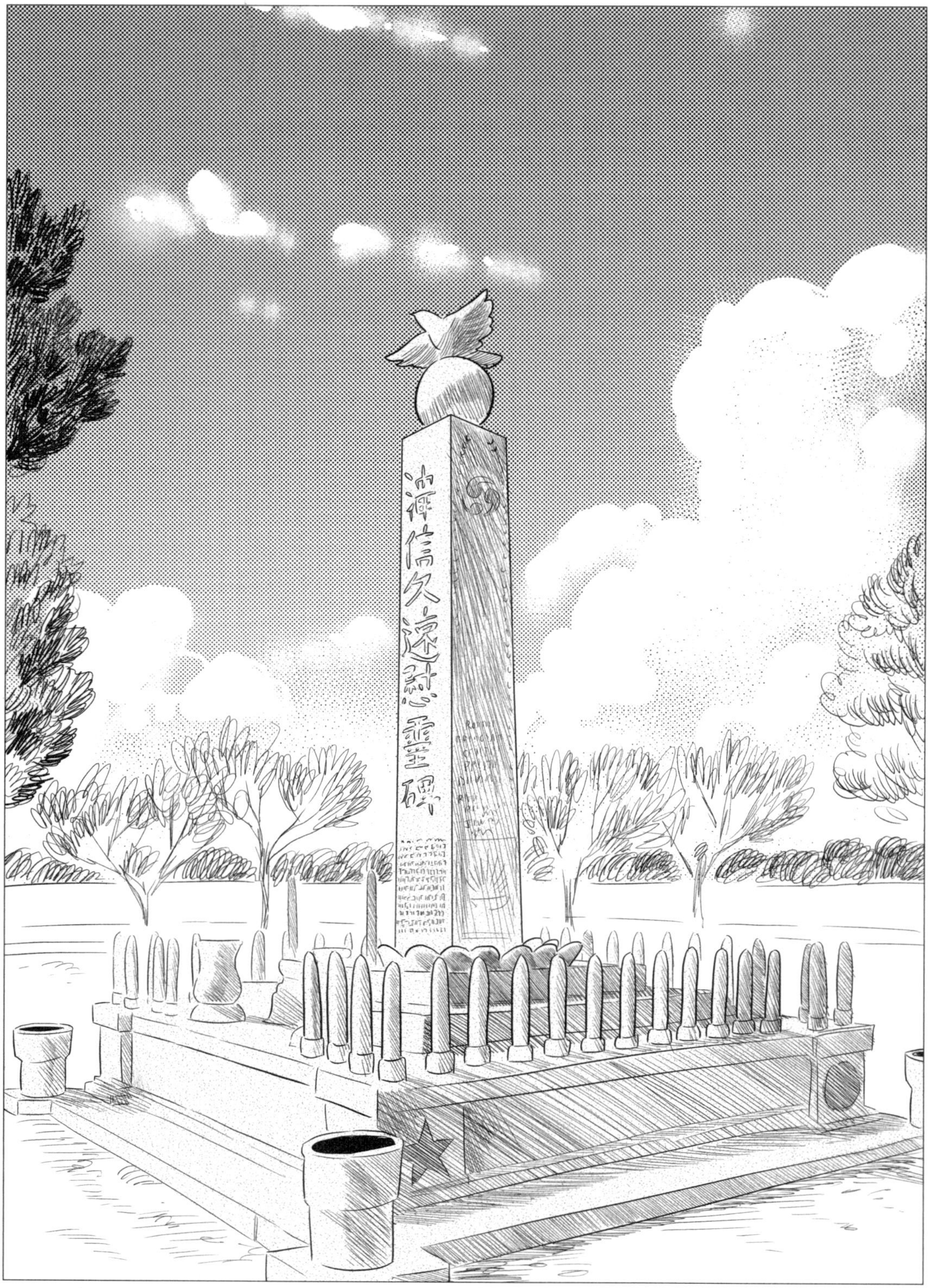

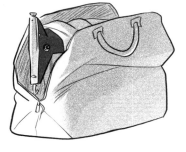

ABOUT THE CREATORS

With an acting career spanning six decades, **George Takei** is known around the world for his founding role in the acclaimed television series *Star Trek*, in which he played Hikaru Sulu, helmsman of the starship *Enterprise*. But Takei's story goes where few stories have gone before. From a childhood spent with his family wrongfully imprisoned in Japanese American internment camps during World War II, to becoming one of the country's leading figures in the fight for social justice, LGBTQ rights, and marriage equality, Takei remains a powerful voice on issues ranging from politics to pop culture. *Mashable.com* named Takei the #1 most-influential person on Facebook, with 10.4 million likes and 2.8 million followers on Twitter.

Takei has been a passionate advocate for social justice, outspoken supporter of human right issues and a community activist. He has served as the spokesperson for the Human Rights Campaign "Coming Out Project," and was Cultural Affairs Chairman of the Japanese American Citizens League. He is also chairman emeritus and a trustee of the Japanese American National Museum in Los Angeles. He was appointed to the Japan-US Friendship Commission by former President Clinton and the government of Japan awarded Takei the Order of the Rising Sun, Gold Rays with Rosette, for his contribution to US-Japanese relations. The decoration was conferred by His Majesty, Emperor Akihito, at the Imperial Palace in Tokyo.

Justin Eisinger is Editorial Director, Graphic Novels & Collections for IDW Publishing, where he has spent more than twelve years immersed in graphic storytelling. Following a fateful encounter with *March* author and Civil Rights pioneer Congressman John Lewis, Eisinger turned his experience adapting television episodes and film for properties such as *My Little Pony*, *Transformers*, and *Teenage Mutant Ninja Turtles* towards bringing engaging non-fiction stories to readers. Born in Akron, Ohio, Eisinger lives in San Diego, California, with his wife and two dogs, and in his spare time publishes North America's only inline skating magazine.

Since publishing his debut comic book in 2010, **Steven Scott** has worked regularly in comics, most notably as a publicist. His writing has appeared in publications by Archie Comics, Arcana Studios, and *Heavy Metal* magazine. As a blogger/columnist he has written for the pop culture sites *Forces of Geek*, *Great Scott Comics*, and *PopMatters*.

Harmony Becker is an artist and illustrator. She is the creator of the comics *Himawari Share*, *Love Potion*, and *Anemone and Catharus*. She is a member of a multicultural family and has spent time living in South Korea and Japan. Her work often deals with the theme of the language barrier and how it shapes people and their relationships. She currently lives in Columbus, Ohio.

Photo by Jon Ortiz

(L-R) Justin Eisinger, George Takei, Harmony Becker, Steven Scott

ACKNOWLEDGMENTS

I am deeply grateful for the loving and stern organizational support of my hubby Brad, the amazing artistry of Harmony Becker and the dedication and expert guidance of Justin Eisinger, Steven Scott and Leigh Walton.

— George Takei

Thanks to George Takei for entrusting us to tell his life story as a graphic novel. Deepest love to my wife, Jenn, for the trust and support she provides. To Steven, Harmony, Leigh, and Brad, I'm so proud of what we've created. And finally, sincere appreciation to everyone that joined us on this endeavor to educate for a better tomorrow.

— Justin Eisinger

To my family for their love and support throughout the years, I am forever grateful. My thanks to George for his encouragement and inspiring words that propelled us forward, to Justin for having my back from day one, to Harmony for taking this project to greater heights, to Brad for making it all possible, and to Leigh for everything else imaginable.

— Steven Scott

For always picking up the phone and listening when there was nothing else that could be done, I want to thank Gracie and Kaori. I am so grateful to George Takei and the team at Top Shelf for taking a chance on me and entrusting me with this story.

— Harmony Becker